IMMIGRATION ISSUES

Recent Titles in
Major Issues in American History

America and the World
Jolyon P. Girard

IMMIGRATION ISSUES

Henry Bischoff

Major Issues in American History
Randall M. Miller, Series Editor

GREENWOOD PRESS
Westport, Connecticut • London

Library of Congress Cataloging-in-Publication Data

Bischoff, Henry.
Immigration issues / Henry Bischoff.
p. cm.—(Major issues in American history, ISSN 1535–3192)
Includes bibliographical references and index.
ISBN 0–313–31177–3 (alk. paper)
1. United States—Emigration and immigration—Government policy. 2. United States—Emigration and immigration—History. I. Title. II. Series.
JV6483.B57 2002
325.73—dc21 2001031241

British Library Cataloguing in Publication Data is available.

Library of Congress Catalog Card Number: 2001031241
ISBN: 0–313–31177–3
ISSN: 1535–3192

First published in 2002

Greenwood Press, 88 Post Road West, Westport, CT 06881
An imprint of Greenwood Publishing Group, Inc.
www.greenwood.com

Printed in the United States of America

The paper used in this book complies with the Permanent Paper Standard issued by the National Information Standards Organization (Z39.48–1984).

10 9 8 7 6 5 4 3 2 1

Copyright Acknowledgments

Every reasonable effort has been made to trace the owners of copyright materials in this book, but in some instances this has proven impossible. The editor and publisher will be glad to receive information leading to more complete acknowledgments in subsequent printings of the book and in the meantime extend their apologies for any omission.

Pages 56–63, 66, 148–53 from *American Immigration Policy: A Reappraisal* by William S. Bernard and Carolyn Zeleny et al. Copyright 1950 by Harper & Brothers. Reprinted by permission of HarperCollins Publishers, Inc.

Extract from Wayne Lutton, "Welfare Costs for Immigrants," *The Social Contract* (Fall 1992): 1–3. Reprinted by permission of the Social Contract Press.

"Skilled Immigrants and Silicon Valley," *Immigrant Policy Reports*, American Immigration Law Foundation, July 1999, 1–3 (www.AILF.org). Copyright © 2000 American Immigration Law Foundation.

"Newcomers Help Massachusetts Economy," *Immigrant Policy Reports*, Immigration Law Foundation, January 2000, 1–3 (www.AILF.org). Copyright © 2000 American Immigration Law Foundation.

Extract from Andrew E. Schacknove, "American Duties to Refugees: Their Scope and Limits," in Mark Gibney, ed., *Open Borders? Closed Societies? The Ethical and Political Issues* (Westport, CT: Greenwood Press, 1988), 131–32, 136–38.

Extract from Lindsay Grant, "How Many Americans?" in David Simcox, ed., *U.S. Immigration in the 1980s: Reappraisal and Reform* (Boulder, CO: Westview Press, 1988), 82–84, 279–80.

Pages 77–83 from *A Nation of Immigrants* by John F. Kennedy. Copyright © 1964 by Anti-Defamation League of B'nai B'rith. Reprinted by permission of HarperCollins Publishers, Inc.

Paul Craig Roberts, "The Ethnic Cleansing of European-Americans," *Washington Times National Weekly*, June 21–27, 1999, 1. www.usbc.org. By permission of Paul Craig Roberts and Creators Syndicate Inc.

Extract from Philip Martin, "Religion and Immigration," *Migration News, North America* 3, no. 12 (December 1996), 1–3.

Extract from Scipio Garling, "Why Environmentalists Support Immigration Reform," *Issue Brief*, FAIR (November 1999), 1–3.

Extract from "Immigration: The Demographic and Economic Facts, Effects on Natural Resources and the Environment," The Cato Institute and the National Immigration Forum, November 17, 2000, 1–3, (www.cato.org),

Pages 76–78, 99–100, 112, 121, 123–24 from *The Immigration Time Bomb* by Richard D. Lamm and Gary Imhoff, copyright © 1985 by Richard D. Lamm and Gary Imhoff. Used by permission of Dutton, a division of Penguin Putnam Inc. and JCA Literary Agency.

Excerpts from Peggy Noonan, "Why the World Comes Here," *Readers Digest* 139, July 1991, 39–42. Reprinted by permission of Peggy Noonan.

From Arturo Madrid, "Official English: A False Policy Issue," *Annals of the American Academy of Political & Social Science* (March 1990): 62–65. Reprinted by permission of Sage Publications.

Extract from Rosalie Pedalino Porter, "The Case against Bilingual Education," *Atlantic Monthly* 281, no. 5 (May 1998): 28–39 at www.theatlantic.com. Copyright by Rosalie Porter.

Excerpts from Mark Krikorian, "Will Americanization Work in America?" *Freedom Review* (Fall 1997), 8 pp.

Extract from Douglas Massey, "Dimensions of the New Immigration to the United States and the Prospects for Assimilation," *Annual Review of Sociology* 7 (1981): 70–72.

Scipio Garling, "Criminal Aliens," Federation for American Immigration Reform, December 1998, 1–3.

Extract from Paul Taylor, "The Future of Mexican Immigration," in Arthur Corwin, ed., *Immigrants and Immigrants: Perspectives on Mexican Labor Migration to the United States* (Westport, CT: Greenwood Press, 1978), 348–52.

"The Truth Behind the Face: Castro Has Not Changed in 41 Years," an advertisement (Miami, FL: Cuban Patriotic Forum, October 2000).

Extract from Lawrence Fuchs, "The Search for a Sound Immigration Policy: A Personal View," in Nathan Glazer, ed., *Clamor at the Gates: The New American Immigration* (San Francisco: ICS Press, 1985), 26–30.

"Illegal Immigrants: The U.S. May Gain More Than It Loses." Reprinted from May 14, 1984 *Business Week* by special permission, copyright © 1984 by The McGraw-Hill Companies, Inc.

Extract from Thomas Muller and Thomas Espenshade, *The Fourth Wave: California's Newest Immigrants* (Washington, DC: Urban Institute, 1985), 172–73.

Pete Wilson, "Don't Give Me Your Tired, Your Poor . . . ," *San Diego Union-Tribune*, January 9, 1994. By permission of Governor Pete Wilson.

Extract from Gene McNary, "Curbing Illegal Immigration: Employers Must Help," *USA Today Magazine* September 1992, 22–23.

Maria Jiménez, "Enforcement: A Tool to Control the Flow of Labor at the U.S.-Mexico Border," *Fact Sheets*, National Network for Immigration and Refuge Rights, Spring 1997, 1–3.

Extract from "Support Fair Detention Policies," *In Congress*, American Civil Liberties Union, August 18, 1999, 1–4.

Peter Schuck, "The Transformation of Immigration Law," *Columbia Law Review* 84, no. 1 (January 1984): 54–58. This article originally appeared at 84 *Colum. L. Rev.* 1 (1984). Reprinted by permission.

Pages 218–21 from *Ethnic Americans: A History of Immigration*, by Leonard Dinnerstein and David M. Reimers. © 1999 Columbia University Press. Reprinted by permission of the publisher.

Rudolph Giuliani, "Keep America's Doors Open," *Wall Street Journal*, January 9, 1997, A12. Reprinted by permission of Mayor Rudolph Giuliani and *Wall Street Journal*.

ADVISORY BOARD

Contents

Series Foreword

This series of books presents major issues in American history as they have developed since the republic's inception to their present incarnation. The issues range across the spectrum of American experience and encompass political, economic, social, and cultural concerns. By focusing on the "major issues" in American history, the series emphasizes the importance of an issues-centered approach to teaching and thinking about America's past. *Major Issues in American History* thus reframes historical inquiry in terms of themes and problems rather than as mere chronology. In so doing, the series addresses the current, pressing need among educators and policymakers for case studies charting the development of major issues over time, so as to make it possible to approach such issues intelligently in our time.

The series is premised on the belief that understanding America demands grasping the contentious nature of its past and applying that understanding to current issues in politics, law, government, society, and culture. If "America" was born, and remains, as an idea and an experiment, as so many thinkers and observers have argued, issues inevitably have shaped whatever that America was and is. In 1801, in his presidential inaugural, Thomas Jefferson reminded Americans that the great strength of the new nation resided in the broad consensus citizens shared as to the rightness and necessity of republican government and the Constitution. That consensus, Jefferson continued, made dissent possible and tolerable, and, we might add, encouraged dissent and debate about critical issues thereafter. Every generation of Americans has wrestled with such issues as defining and defending freedom(s), determining America's place in the world, waging war and making peace, receiving and assimilating new peoples, balancing church and state, forming a "more perfect union," and pursuing "happiness." American identity(ies) and interest(s) are not fixed. A nation of many peoples on the move across space and up and down the socioeconomic ladder cannot have it so. A nation charged with ensuring that, in Lincoln's words, "government of the people, by the people, and for the people shall not perish from the earth" cannot have it so. A nation whose heroes are not only soldiers and statesmen but also ex-slaves, women reformers, inventors, thinkers, and cowboys and Indians cannot have it so. Americans have never rested content locked into set molds in thinking and doing—not so long as dissent and difference are built into the character of a people that dates its birth to an American Revolution and annually celebrates that lineage. As such, Americans have been, and are, by heritage and habit an issues-oriented people.

We are also a political people. Issues as varied as race relations, labor organizing, women's place in the work force, the practice of religious beliefs, immigration, westward movement, and environmental protection have been, and remain, matters of public concern and debate and readily intrude into politics. A people committed to "rights" invariably argues for them, low voter turnout in recent elections notwithstanding. All the major issues in American history have involved political controversies as to their meaning and application. But the extent to which issues assume a political cast varies.

As the public interest spread to virtually every aspect of life during the twentieth century—into boardrooms, ballparks, and even bedrooms—the political compass enlarged with it. In time, every economic, social, and cultural issue of consequence in the United States has entered the public realm of debate and political engagement. Questions of rights—for example, to free speech, to freedom of religion, to equality before the law—and authority are political by nature. So, too, are questions about war and society, foreign policy, law and order, the delivery of public services, the control of the nation's borders, and access to and the uses of public land and resources. The books in *Major Issues in American History* take up just those issues. Thus, all the books in this series build political and public policy concerns into their basic framework.

The format for the series speaks directly to the issues-oriented character of the American people and the democratic polity and to the teaching of issues-centered history. The issues-centered approach to history views the past thematically. Such a history respects chronology but does not attempt to recite a single narrative or simple historical chronology of "facts." Rather, issues-centered history is problem-solving history. It organizes historical inquiry around a series of questions central to understanding the character and functions of American life, culture, ideas, politics, and institutions. Such questions invariably derive from current concerns that demand historical perspective. Whether determining the role of women and minorities and shaping public policy, or considering the "proper" relationship between church and state, or thinking about U.S. military obligations in the global context, to name several persistent issues, the teacher and student—indeed, responsible citizens everywhere—must ask such questions as "how and why did the present circumstance and interests come to be as they are" and "what other choices as to policy and practice have there been" so as to measure the dimensions and point the direction of the issue. History matters in that regard.

Each book in the series focuses on a particular issue, with an eye to encouraging readers and users to consider how Americans at different times engaged the issue based on the particular values, interests, and political and social structures of the day. As such, each book is also necessarily events-based in that the key event that triggered public concern and debate about a major issue at a particular moment serves as the case study for the issue as it was understood and presented during that historical period. Each book offers a historical narrative overview of a major issue as it evolved; the narrative provides both the context for understanding the issue's place in the larger American experience and the touchstone for considering the ways Americans encountered and engaged the issue at different times. A timeline further establishes the chronology and place of the issue in American history. The core of each book is the series of between ten to fifteen case studies of watershed events that defined the issue, arranged chronologically to make it possible to track the development of the issue closely over time. Each case study stands as a separate chapter. Each case study opens with a historical overview of the event and a discussion of the significant contemporary opposing views of the issue as occasioned by the event. A selection of four to nine critical primary documents (printed whole or in excerpts and introduced with brief headnotes) from the period under review presents differing points of view on the issue. In some volumes, each chapter also includes an annotated research guide of print and nonprint sources to guide further research and reflection on the event and the issue. Each volume in the series concludes with a general bibliography that provides ready reference to the key works on the subject at issue.

Such an arrangement ensures that readers and users—students and teachers alike—will approach the major issues within a problem-solving framework. Indeed, the design of the series and each book in it demands that students and teachers understand that the crucial issues of American history have histories and that the significance of those issues might best be discovered and recovered by understanding how Americans at different times addressed them, shaped them, and bequeathed them to the next generation. Such a dialectic for each issue encourages a comparative perspective not only in seeing America's past but also, and perhaps even more so, in thinking about its present. Individually and collectively, the books in the *Major Issues in American History* thereby demonstrate anew William Faulkner's dictum that the past is never past.

Randall M. Miller
Series Editor

Preface

Immigration has been a central, ongoing factor in the history of the American people. Indeed, as historian Oscar Handlin once observed, immigration is *the story* of the American people. But it has been a contested story and history. From the earliest time in this history a continuous influx of people has come to America. America, that "distant magnet," has drawn people from all over the globe, with every prospect that this process will continue into the future. Immigration has brought challenges, problems, and benefits for the newcomers and for established citizens. Immigration issues range from deep personal and group attachments, prejudices, and hopes, to questions of national identity, culture, language, diversity, acculturation, economics, humanitarianism, the environment, security, foreign relations, law enforcement, and constitutional and human rights. Hardly any aspect of American culture and public life has not had, and does not have, a question of immigration or ethnicity associated with it. Controversy has marked immigration issues from the early national period to the present.

This book offers students and teachers of immigration an examination of the most salient, and often persistent, issues related to immigration. The book begins with an introductory historical overview of immigration, which locates the origins and ongoing nature of these various issues and puts them in a historical context. A timeline listing major immigration events provides a chronology useful in tracking public policy and thinking on the subject. Each chapter discusses an immigration issue, examines differing points of view in successive historical periods down to the present, reproduces excerpts from important documents that illustrate the various interests in and opinions about the issues, provides a number of annotated references for further research and lists Web sites primarily of advocacy groups with varying positions on mostly current immigration concerns.

Chapters 1 through 4 present issues that focus on arguments for and against a more open American immigration policy based on economic, humanitarian, diversity, and environmental considerations. Chapter 1 describes briefly the economic opportunities in the United States which collectively have been a major factor in attracting immigrants to this country, and it presents the controversy over whether immigrants help the American economy and what impact immigration has on already resident workers. Chapter 2 examines the role and degree of humanitarian concerns in determining America's immigration policy. Disagreements have touched on which immigrants and refugees the United States should help, how many should be helped, the type of help the country is willing to offer, and which prospective immigrants or refugees the United States decides not to help. Chapter 3 is concerned with the issue of diversity. Sharp differences of opinion have been expressed over the decades, particularly during periods of large-scale immigration, about the impact of diverse new people on America. Some observers have looked upon diversity as divisive and as undermining American culture; others have maintained that it enriches the nation with new vitality and creativity. Chapter 4 examines the effect of immigration on the environment. In earlier years critics of immigration warned that crowding, particularly in American cities, strained health resources and added to the polluted environment of urban life. Since World War II environmentalists have been concerned about the negative impact of immigration on population growth, while others have argued that with the low American birthrate immigrants are needed to sustain economic progress.

Chapter 5 through 7 present issues concerning the relation of immigration to national identity as expressed in a democratic polity, linguistic cohesiveness, and cultural unity. Chapter 5 looks at the relationship between immigration and America's national identity as rooted in a civic culture. From the Revolutionary years forward this evolving culture has centered on the ideal of liberty and has included participatory republican government and open economic opportunity. Throughout the nation's history, Americans have argued about whether only certain people could properly carry forward the national ideals—first the Anglo-Saxons, then the descendants of Northern and Western Europeans, and then more widely Euro-Americans—or whether the national identity was best sustained by diverse people from all over the world united by embracing liberty, democracy, and economic opportunity. Chapter 6 considers a number of controversies related to immigrants and the English language as a means of communication and as a component of American unity and identity. Some critics of immigration have held that immigrants should know English or at least be literate to be admitted to the United States, but advocates of open immigration have maintained that immigrants, particularly the poor, should be admitted and then they themselves or their children be given the opportunity to learn English here. A post–World War II dispute has arisen over bilingual education as an opportunity for immigrant children to learn content subjects while they learn English or as an opportunity to learn the language and culture of their ethnicity at the same time they learn English. Chapter 7 presents differences of opinion among longer resident Americans about the potential for acculturation of newcomers from different countries and cultures in each of the major waves of immigration. At different times, opponents of immigration have asserted that immigrants whose culture was markedly different from mainstream Americans were inferior and so set in their ways that they could not be acculturated into the life of the nation. Other Americans have argued that education and experience with the American ideals of political participation and economic opportunity could bring people from any country or race successfully into the American civic culture. Additionally, Americans have disagreed over optimal acculturation in the United States, with opinions ranging from assimilation, to a melting pot, to cultural pluralism.

Chapters 8 through 11 present issues on the relation of immigration to certain aspects of the public order in the United States, including national security, foreign relations, the inflow of undocumented immigrants, and efforts to enforce immigration laws. Chapter 8 compares different opinions on the effect of immigration on national security. Fear of at least some immigrants has extended from the 1790s Federalist alarm about the presence of French Revolutionary emigrés through the nineteenth-century fears about subversion by Catholic and Asian immigrants to World War II alarm about Japanese residents and to more recent apprehensions about Communist and terrorist immigrants. Friends of immigration have countered such arguments by pointing to immigrant contributions to American security through extensive participation in the growing American economy and through loyal service and sacrifice in a succession of American wars. Chapter 9 examines the relationship of immigration and foreign policy. America's admission of immigrants at various times has had positive effects on relations with some countries, while other admissions hurt relations with certain countries. The exclusion of certain immigrants has had varying impacts on America's foreign relations. The restrictive immigration policy of the United States in the mid-twentieth century, for example, damaged America's claim to stand for "freedom" during the Cold War and this, in turn, forced changes in immigration legislation. Additionally, immigrant groups have worked to influence certain aspects of American foreign policy. The treatment of immigrants in the United States also has had foreign policy consequences. Chapter 10 treats the issue of undocumented immigration. A relatively recent phenomenon, it began as a national concern only when the federal government started to pass restrictive immigration legislation in the second half of the nineteenth century. The presence of undocumented immigrants has become a larger issue in the years since World War II. Critics of this presence in the United States hold that, in addition to questions of illegality, the undocumented aliens depress wages and working conditions in the American labor market, contribute to crowding, and raise the cost of public services. Supporters of the undocumented, including many agricultural and other employers, as well as members of humanitarian, religious, and ethnic groups in the United States, argue for a more open border. Chapter 11 recognizes that concurrent with the debate about the value of undocumented immigrants is the controversy about the proper enforcement of America's immigration laws. A major continuing point of contention from the post–Civil War decades to today has been between the effectiveness and the costs of enforcement. In the decades since World War II, differences of opinion have erupted over such issues as methods for border control, issuance of visas, types of detention, employer sanctions, identification documents, and the Immigration and Naturalization Service's budget, manpower, and priorities.

Chapter 12 considers the constitutional and universal human rights of immigrants who have entered the United States in relation to the sovereign right of the United States to regulate immigration. Particular attention is given to the right of the United States, as a nation, to deport immigrants and to designate the recipients of public services and benefits, and to the rights of immigrants to due process and equal protection under the law.

Although this book is designed to assist students and teachers interested in issues or "problems" related to immigration, there is in its structure a recognition that many teachers focus on chronological history. Thus, in Appendix 2, all the documents included in this work are listed in chronological order and grouped by major immigration eras. Appendix 1 lists the number of immigrants to the United States by country for the decades from 1820 to 1995. The general annotated bibliography and an index provide ready reference to the significant sources on the issues and a guide to their treatment in this book.

Acknowledgments

Randall Miller, the series editor, provided major support, direction, and assistance throughout the development and writing of this book. Barbara Rader, of Greenwood Press, gave prompt editorial help. I want to thank my Ramapo College colleagues for years of stimulating discussions on a wide range of social and historical issues. I learned much about immigration from Sydney Weinberg, Yolanda Prieto, and Kathryn Koop; from fellow faculty members across the state of New Jersey in the Garden State Immigration History Consortium; from my participation as a member of the Academic Advisory Council of the Balch Institute for Ethnic Studies in Philadelphia; and from my experience as an Ellis Island Fellow at Rutgers University with Virginia Yans-McLaughlin. I particularly want to express my deep appreciation to my wife, Pam, for her challenges to my thinking, her support, and her love.

Chronology of Events

1783	George Washington states America will welcome oppressed of all nations.
1789	Constitution gives Congress right to adopt naturalization laws that will grant citizenship to immigrants. Foreign-born citizens are given the right to hold any government office except the presidency.
1790	Congress enacts naturalization law that limits citizenship to immigrants who are white. Approximately one million immigrants enter the United States in the next fifty years, from 1790 to 1840.
1798	Alien and Sedition laws are passed by Congress. The president is given the right to deport aliens.
1807	Congress outlaws African slave trade (involuntary black immigration) effective January 1, 1808.
1819	Federal government requires ship captains to supply a list of passengers, with their age, sex, occupation, and country of origin, and indicate the number who died on the voyage.
1825	English laws against emigration are repealed.
1840s	Crop failures in Ireland and Germany result in large-scale emigration to America. The first major wave of

	immigration brings some 10 million immigrants to the United States over the next forty years, from 1840 to 1880.
1845	Anti-immigrant Native American Party holds first national convention.
1848	Failed revolutions on the European continent send political refugees to America.
1849	U.S. Supreme Court rules that only the federal government, not the states, can tax incoming immigrants. Discovery of gold attracts Chinese and other immigrants to California.
1854–1855	Anti-immigrant Know Nothing Party at height of power.
1855	New York State establishes the Castle Garden immigrant receiving station in Manhattan.
1868	In the Burlingame Treaty, the United States agrees to unrestricted immigration from China.
1875	Congress passes a law prohibiting the admission of immigrants who are prostitutes or convicts.
1880s	The second major wave of immigration into the United States begins. A large portion of the newcomers originate in Eastern and Southern Europe; some come from Japan, the West Indies, and the Middle East. Approximately 23 million immigrants enter the United States in the next forty years, from 1880 to 1920.
1882	Excluded immigrants list is extended to lunatics, idiots, convicts (except those convicted of political offenses), and people likely to become public charges. The Treasury Department is charged with making rules under this law, but enforcement was contracted out to a number of states. A head tax of 50 cents is charged to incoming immigrants. The Chinese Exclusion Act prohibits admission of Chinese laborers.
1885	Congress passes Foran Act which prohibits the importing of contract laborers.
1887	The anti-immigrant and anti-Catholic American Protective Association is organized.

1891 Congress directs the federal government to take charge of the enforcement of national immigration laws. A Bureau of Immigration with a superintendent of immigration is established. The excluded list is extended to include polygamists and those with loathsome or dangerously contagious diseases.

1892 A federal immigration station is opened at Ellis Island in New York harbor. Other stations are established in key port cities.

1893 Detailed rules for the administration of the immigration stations and for the questioning, detention, deportation of, and appeals by immigrants are promulgated by the Bureau of Immigration.

1894 The Immigration Restriction League is organized and led by Senator Henry Cabot Lodge of Massachusetts.

1897 Congress passes a law requiring a literacy test for incoming immigrants. It is vetoed by President Grover Cleveland.

1903 Anarchists and those advocating the overthrow of the United States government are added to the excluded list.

1907 Excluded list is expanded to include imbeciles, the feebleminded, persons with physical defects that might affect their ability to make a living, those with tuberculosis, and children under the age of sixteen without their parents. The head tax is increased to $4.00.

A Gentlemen's Agreement is negotiated between the United States and Japan in which Japan agrees not to issue passports to laborers wanting to go the United States.

1911 The Dillingham Commission recommends further restrictions on immigrants, including a literacy test.

1913 Federal immigration is put under the new Department of Labor.

The literacy test requirement is passed by Congress but is vetoed by President Howard Taft.

1917 Congress passes, over President Woodrow Wilson's veto, a law requiring immigrants over sixteen years of

	age to be able to read some language in order to be admitted to the United States.
1917–1918	The United States engages in World War I.
1919	The "Red Scare" results in deportation of alien radicals.
1921	Congress sets maximum Eastern Hemisphere immigration at 358,000 a year. Quotas for immigrants from any one country are set at the percentage of foreign-born of that nationality living in the United States in 1910.
1924	National Origins Law (Johnson-Reed Act) sets Eastern Hemisphere immigration at 153,714 a year. Quotas set at 2 percent of nationality in United States in 1890. Oriental Exclusion Act, which prohibits immigration from Asia, abrogates the Gentlemen's Agreement with Japan.
1927	National origins quotas set according to 1920 census.
1930s	The Great Depression occurs, and the 1930s is the only decade in which more people leave or are forced out of the United States than enter it.
1939	Bill to admit 20,000 children over the quota from Nazi Germany is defeated in Congress.
1941–1945	The United States engages in World War II.
1942	The Bracero program, providing contracted labor for the United States from Mexico, Jamaica, Barbados, and British Honduras, is initiated. The U.S. government forces the evacuation of Japanese Americans from the West Coast to isolated detention camps.
1943	An annual immigration quota of 101 is given to China. Chinese immigrants become eligible for citizenship.
1945	The War Brides Act is passed to permit admission of foreign-born wives, husbands, and children of American servicemen and servicewomen.
1946	An annual immigration quota of 101 is given to India and to the newly independent Philippines.
1948 and 1950	The Displaced Persons Act permits 400,000 refugees primarily from Eastern and Central Europe to be admitted to the United States beyond the quota.

1950	McCarthy anti-Communist hysteria erupts in the United States. The Internal Security Act increases grounds for exclusion and deportation of alleged subversive aliens.
1952	The McCarran-Walter Immigration and Naturalization Act continues the national origin system, but gives every nation, including Korea and Japan, at least a token quota; establishes preferences, among quota immigrants, for skilled workers and relatives of citizens; and tightens security and screening procedures for incoming immigrants.
1953	The Refugee Relief Act admits refugees beyond the quotas.
1954	Ellis Island is closed.
1957	The Refugee-Escape Act defines a refugee-escapee as any alien who has fled from a Communist country or from the Middle East because of persecution or the fear of persecution on account of race, religion, or politics.
1960	The Cuban refugee program is established. A third major wave of immigration brings over 25 million foreign-born persons to the United States in the next 35 years, 1960–1995.
1962	The Migration and Refugee Assistance Act gives support to incoming refugees
1964	The Bracero program is terminated.
1965	The Immigration Act of 1965 eliminates the national origins quota system; sets an annual ceiling of 170,000 for the Eastern Hemisphere with a 20,000 per-country limit and an annual ceiling of 120,000 for the Western Hemisphere without a per-country limit; and establishes preferences for family reunification, persons with desirable work skills, resident aliens, and refugees.
1975	The Indochinese Refugee Resettlement program is initiated.
1976	The Western Hemisphere annual limit is extended to 170,000, with a 20,000 per-country limit.
1978	Congress enacts a single annual global ceiling of 290,000 immigrants with a uniform preference system.

	Congress establishes the Select Commission on Immigration and Refugee Policy.
1980	The Refugee Act of 1980 sets annual immigration at 270,000; increases annual refugees from 17,400 to 50,000; admits refugees from any country; and provides for a Coordinator for Refugee Affairs. The president is allowed to admit additional refugees in an emergency.
1981	The Commission on Immigration and Refugee Policy issues its report, "United States Immigration Policy and the National Interest."
1982	The Supreme Court rules in *Plyler v. Doe* that a state cannot deny children of undocumented immigrants admission to public schools.
1986	The Immigration and Control Act grants amnesty, with the opportunity to become citizens, to undocumented immigrants who have been resident in the United States since before 1982; establishes employer sanctions that involve penalties for businesses knowingly employing undocumented immigrants; and establishes a legal admission policy for temporary foreign farm workers.
1990	The Immigration Act of 1990 increases the annual immigration and refugee total to 700,000 and extends the number of employment visas from 54,000 to 140,000.
1994	The voters of California approve Proposition 187, which denies public services to undocumented immigrants, but a federal judge enjoins it from being put into law.
1996	The Illegal Immigration Reform and Immigrant Responsibility Act increases restrictions on undocumented immigrants and asylum seekers and increases resources to tighten border control. The Anti-Terrorism Act increases the number of immigrants held in detention.

Introduction

In 1607 the British planted their first permanent colonial settlement in North America at a place they called Jamestown in Virginia. In the following decades English and other Europeans founded additional settlements along the Atlantic Coast of this "new world." Here they traded and mingled with the native Americans and decimated their numbers by disease and armed conflict. The early settlers were followed by a continuing flow of new people, first from Europe and Africa, and then from every continent of the world. The large majority of these newcomers, those who chose to take up permanent residence in this new world, have been known as immigrants. The immigrants and their descendants make up the great majority of the contemporary American people.

The early settlers in the northern portion of British North America, New England, strongly motivated by a desire for religious homogeneity, tried to limit their provinces primarily to selected English people and were largely successful, at least through the seventeenth century. The southern provinces also drew colonists heavily from England, although some settlers did come from Scotland, Ireland, and France. When indentured servants did not prove fully satisfactory in meeting a growing need for commercial agricultural labor, landowners bought an increasing number of African slaves.

The middle colonies, with commercial port cities and landowners who looked to make profits through the sale of property, attracted a much more diverse population. Most of the early Dutch and Swedish settlers remained after their colonies were taken over by England, many new settlers came from England, and then there followed growing numbers from Scotland, Ireland, Germany, Scandinavia, France, and slaves from the West Indies and Africa, but fewer than in the South. Early on in New York City, a visitor claimed to hear eighteen different languages spoken in a relatively small population. It was this region, in particular, that a French immigrant, J. Hector St. John de Crèvecoeur, in 1782, spoke of as a melting pot, a melting of people primarily from different parts of Northern and Western Europe.

While the English settlers in the middle provinces, in control of the government and in many places a majority, endeavored to adapt a British way of life to the new world environment, the people from varied other places in Europe and from multiple places in Africa brought their own differing cultures to this region. To the Anglicans, Congregationalists, and Quakers from England were added Lutherans, Moravians, Huguenots, Catholics, and Jews from continental Europe as well as Africans with varying religious practices. Such a religious swirl brought both friction and growing tolerance. German and Dutch customs began to be intermingled with English ways, and German and Dutch words entered into the American English way of speaking. Although many English strove to retain their Anglo-Saxon traditions and values, there developed in the middle colonies a powerful impetus that would lead America, not without strife and difficulty, into a future open to a fusion of many different peoples. In 1782 the observant de Crevecouer reported that here, in this middle Atlantic region, there had evolved a new man, the American.

Self-reliant, cooperative to a degree across ethnic and religious lines, and ambitious, these Americans contributed significantly to a growing restiveness with the colonial restrictions that, by the mid-1770s, led to a striking out for independence from England. In the crucible of the American Revolution and in the early national period, the people of the United States fashioned, from British roots and colonial experience, a republican form of government and a civic culture based on liberty and involving a widening concept of political participation and responsibility together with expanding economic opportunities. While these ideals were widely held among the new nation's leaders, some among them thought that there was a particular convergence between the ideals and an Anglo-Saxon ancestry and culture. Such a viewpoint influenced a wary outlook on immigrants from beyond the British Isles, even while they recognized the value of these other newcomers for the economic development of the westwardly expanding nation.

George Washington, for one, in 1783 proclaimed that the United States should welcome immigrants who were in need and who sought freedom. However, in 1790, the first naturalization law, which he signed, declared that only white immigrants could become citizens. In the nation's first half century, the number of new immigrants in the United States was relatively small—a little over a million, or an average of between 20,000 and 25,000 a year. Some fled the revolutions in France and Ireland, mechanics were recruited from England, and a small stream of Germans and Scotch-Irish and a growing number of Catholic Irish came to America. As early as the 1790s, the place of immigrants in American society and its polity raised questions as to the wisdom of an open-door policy regarding immigrants. As political parties developed in that decade, the tendency of the Irish to join with the more open Democratic Republicans caused the Federalists to want to increase the length of the citizenship process. The arrival in New York, Philadelphia, and Charleston of French-speaking slaveholders fleeing the slave rebellions in Haiti in the 1790s worried Americans, who feared that the influx of emigrés might destabilize local politics. Slaveholders worried that the emigrés and their slaves might bring the Haitian revolution with them. Toward the end of the decade, a negative reaction to immigrants from Revolutionary France led a Federalist-dominated Congress to pass a short-lived, restrictive Alien and Sedition law.

Despite Americans' boastfulness about the vigor of the republican experiment and the ability of free people to absorb and adapt ideas and people from abroad, revolutions elsewhere were causing Americans to consider which ideas and people might strengthen their own republic and which ones ought to be kept at arm's length. When the wars of the French Revolution abated and after the United States acquired the Louisiana Purchase and, Americans thought, removed a foreign menace from the continent, American, self-confidence in the regenerative powers of America soared. The relatively small, if steady, stream of immigrants each year posed no dangers. In fact, the United States welcomed immigrants who brought capital, technical skills, and willing hands to build the new nation. While Great Britain was trying to hold skilled workers in, various states in the United States offered bounties to such people to settle in America.

In the first four decades of the nineteenth century, Germans and Irish increasingly acculturated into America's civic culture. To be sure, complaints were heard about immigrant crowding and pauperism in growing cities, and about the increase in the number of Roman Catholics in the country, but overall the United States seemed to be handling immigration with little problem. Indeed, immigration policy was not on the public agenda. The only major law regarding immigration was the requirement that ships carrying immigrants to the United States provide manifests listing the immigrants by name, port of debarkation, and status.

In the 1840s the United States experienced its first major wave of immigration. Some 10 million persons entered the country from abroad in the forty years between 1840 and 1880. Mostly Irish and German, but also some English as well as other Europeans, came to America, and Chinese, Mexicans, and others settled in the West after the discovery of gold there in 1849. The Irish emigrated in especially large numbers after a potato blight ravaged Ireland and caused famine from the mid-1840s through the 1850s. The "famine Irish" literally fled Ireland, taking any ship from any port to anywhere to escape starvation and misery and begin a new life, or at least get enough work to send remittances home to help relieve the suffering of those left behind. This "scattering" of the Irish brought them to many places in America where previously they had not settled in large numbers. The famine Irish were mostly poor, generally unskilled, and Catholic. Their numbers, social and cultural condition, and desperation made them seem especially alien to the native-born Protestant Americans, already suspicious of the Irish Catholics from their reading of English history and literature. The Germans, on the average, came with somewhat more resources and skills than the Irish. They included Protestants, Catholics, and Jews. Although no single German culture emerged from the many different German people, those Germans who settled in cities became identified in the public mind as "Germans" by their attachment to their language and customs, including public, recreational beer drinking, particularly on Sunday, their only day off from work.

These new immigrants were regarded as an asset by those who advocated a more rapid development of the nation and by those who wanted labor for the increasing number of factories, the growing cities, and the expanding canals and railroads. Many native workers, however, objected to the competition for jobs from cheap immigrant labor, and others complained about urban congestion and the development of ethnic neighborhoods. Protestants considered the influx of so many Catholics a threat to their religious dominance, and many citizens argued that immigrants from countries with authoritarian governments endangered American democratic institutions. Such concerns gave rise to the nativist Know Nothing political party, which enjoyed considerable success in electing state and federal legislators, particularly in the mid-1850s. But organized nativism never commanded a national majority, and nativists failed in their efforts to get Congress, or even state legislatures, to enact restrictive immigration laws. The nativist movement was subverted by the growing North/South tension over slavery, which led to the Civil War. In fact, during the Civil War, the Union, suffering from a worker shortage, enacted a contract labor law in order to bring added immigrant workers to America, and offered citizenship to Irish and German immigrants who would come to America and join the Union Army. The contribution of the immigrants to the war effort and to the economy lessened, for a time, anti-immigrant sentiment, except against the Chinese.

After the annexation of California by the United States from Mexico, and then the discovery of gold in 1849, many immigrants from around the world, including China, went to make their fortunes there. As the number of Chinese increased through the 1850s into the 1870s, opposition to them grew, especially from Irish workers and organized labor who claimed the Chinese undermined wages and competed unfairly for work. Harassment, discriminatory state laws, and even violence followed, leading to the first federal exclusion legislation, against Chinese laborers, in 1882.

While the federal government's only immigration legislation prior to the 1870s was the required listing of newcomers by ship captains, some states with major ports, like New York, Louisiana, Massachusetts, and Pennsylvania, concerned with the health of their citizens, established inspection stations for arriving immigrants and also quarantines for those judged to be ill. In the 1870s, with continued immigration, Congress began to pass restrictive federal immigration laws intended to bar persons with criminal records, prostitutes, contract laborers, and persons with physical and mental impairments. After first contracting enforcement to states and then recognizing their lack of tight control, the federal government took charge in 1891 by establishing a Bureau of Immigration (a forerunner of the Immigration and Naturalization Service) and building immigration stations at New York's Ellis Island and in a number of other large port cities.

These stations were inaugurated just as the second major wave of immigration was gaining momentum. Facilitating movement was the increased use of steamships in ocean crossings and of the railroad which enabled newcomers to spread throughout the United States. Approximately 27 million immigrants came to this country in the fifty years between 1880 and 1930. While immigrants continued to come from Germany and Ireland, and there was an upswing of persons from the Netherlands and Scandinavia, the largest numbers now came from Southern and Eastern Europe. Many came from Italy, particularly southern Italy and Sicily; also Catholics, Orthodox Christians, and Jews came from Poland, Russia, Austria Hungary, the Baltic and Balkan regions, and Greece. Others, in smaller numbers, arrived from Armenia, from Lebanon and Syria, from Spain and Portugal, from the Caribbean and the West Indies, and from Japan. A few came from India and Korea. Most of these people came for economic reasons, some to earn money and return to their homeland, but the majority to find better life opportunities in the United States. Some, primarily the Jews, but also some others like the Armenians, came because religious and ethnic persecution drove them from their countries of origin. Such immigrants knew they would never return to the old country, and they responded differently to American conditions than the "sojourners" who looked upon America as a place to earn money for a time.

At least some of these new immigrants could be found almost everywhere in the United States in the early twentieth century. They tended, though, to concentrate where there were greatest opportunities for work. Many, particularly those with limited resources, crowded into port cities close to where they landed by ship. Here they formed colonies in Italian, Jewish, Hungarian, Polish, Russian, French Canadian, Armenian, Lithuanian, and Greek neighborhoods. Work could be found in growing numbers of factories, refineries, and sweatshops; in infrastructure and urban building (e.g., putting in water, sewer, and gas lines and laying track for streetcars); on the docks and in transportation; and as domestics in the homes of the affluent. Many immigrants, though, did have some resources that enabled them to move inland, to cities, particularly in the Midwest with their concentration of heavy industry, to mining and lumbering sites, and to agricultural work and farm ownership. A considerable number of immigrants became entrepreneurs, most often owners of small businesses—food and other retail stores, restaurants, saloons, places of recreation, and producers of clothing, metal, wood, tobacco, and a wide variety of other products. Peddlers were numerous. Additionally, among the new immigrants were craftsmen and other skilled laborers, a limited number of white-collar workers, a small percentage of professionals, and a few who were inventors and who were able to rise in the business world.

As the numbers of immigrants increased, and particularly as so many of them settled in relatively self-contained ethnic enclaves removed in part from Americanizing influences, nativistic-fears and consequent opposition grew toward this large wave of newcomers. Immigrants from countries, cultures, and religions that seemed so different made many turn-of-the-century Americans uncomfortable and brought friction and conflict. Poverty, disease, and crime added to anti-immigrant sentiment. In a seeming backlash against both the newly freed African Americans and the flood of different immigrants, racism and ethnic prejudice became more overt. The majority Northern and Western European population, fearful of what was seen as a dilution of the dominant culture and power structure, increasingly made race determinative in their thinking about the new immigrants, with the result that advocacy for a major, new, restrictive American immigration policy gained increasing political and public attention.

Additionally, antagonism to the new immigrants was fueled by religious fears and opposition. Many Americans, particularly Protestants, continued to be alarmed by the growth of the Catholic Church. The American Protective Society, sometimes called the Anti Papal Society, regarded Catholicism's hierarchical church structure and adherence to papal authority as antithetical to Americanism as they understood it. They also reacted adversely when Catholic Church leaders vigorously defended their mission, called for active faithful cohesion among its members, and aggressively expanded parochial schools and other church facilities. Not only Protestants, but also some Catholics, recoiled at the increasing influx of Jews and the strangeness of the Eastern Orthodox, and they considered Asians heathens. Additionally, many established Irish and German Catholics felt uncomfortable with the poverty and unfamiliar practices of Southern and Eastern European Catholics, and many established German Jews were disturbed by the poverty and orthodox religious practices of the new Eastern European Jews.

American workers and struggling labor unions were in a particularly difficult position. While many of the longer resident workers, particularly in the cities, were themselves immigrants or children of immigrants and thus sympathetic to the problems of newcomers, they realized that the new foreign-born increased the supply of labor and thus tended to keep wages lower and unemployment higher than it would otherwise have been and in the process weakened the bargaining position of unions. Immigrants, often desperate for work, were at times used as strikebreakers. These issues were most prevalent in businesses that hired large numbers of unskilled or semiskilled workers—in the coalfields and in other mining operations, in ironworks and steelworks, and in food-processing plants.

Members of the New England elite, who had developed an ethnocentric, mythical sense of an American Anglo-Saxon past and of its importance for the country, feared that their America was threatened by the flood of what they judged to be very inferior new immigrants. They formed the Immigration Restriction League, spearheaded by Senator Henry Cabot Lodge of Massachusetts, and called on the federal government to limit the flow of immigration. As science was then gaining wide respect in intellectual circles, the League spokespersons and others turned to those scientists who supported their contentions about the physical and mental superiority of the Northern and Western Europeans over other Europeans and those from other continents.

Many rural and small-town Americans feared losing political, economic, and cultural power to the rapidly growing cities filled with the culturally and religiously different foreign-born, dominated in most places by Democratic Party boss rule, and often anchored in neighborhood saloons. A national temperance crusade was one expression of rural and small-town antagonism and a challenge to the urban immigrant. Additionally, some middle-class Progressive political reformers, including some academics, who advocated a more rational, patronage-free democracy, joined in attacking city political bosses and the immigrants who supported them. These reformers argued that the new immigrants were incapable of participating intelligently and constructively in America's civic culture, and they lobbied for greater restrictions on immigration. Others, though, insisted that immigrants might be "saved" from the urban political bosses by reforming the ballot, closing the saloons, and otherwise cleaning up both the social conditions and the political arrangement that fostered boss rule. They also sought to change the immigrants' behavior through schooling, from adult language classes to kindergartens to "catch the little" Russians, Italians, Greeks, and others, as one Progressive said, while they were still malleable.

Still the immigrants kept coming. Shipping companies and railroads advertised for immigrants; many businesses thrived on cheap, overworked, or, in some cases, specially skilled labor from abroad; and the lifestyle of the rich depended on foreign-born servants. Many Catholic and Jewish religious leaders, a growing number of ethnic organizations and newspapers, and immigrant-oriented political clubs gave much support to immigration. Young college-educated settlement workers, humanitarians, and urban Progressives, while critical of some of the ways of the foreign-born and intent on Americanizing them, often spoke on behalf of the immigrants and their contributions to the United States.

As the number of newcomers grew, particularly after the turn of the twentieth century, the critics of the foreign-born succeeded in pressuring Congress into passing an increasing number of legal restrictions on immigration. Admittance to America was denied to anarchists, epileptics, the feebleminded, those with tuberculosis, and children under the age of sixteen without parents. Anti-Japanese activism became strong on the West Coast, and, in order not to insult the increasingly powerful Japanese nation, President Theodore Roosevelt negotiated with that country a Gentlemen's Agreement in 1907, in which Japan agreed to withhold passports from Japanese workers who wanted to come to America, and the United States government agreed not to enact humiliating legislation specifically designating the Japanese for exclusion from this country.

Meanwhile, opponents of the growing number of Southern and Eastern European immigrants sought to restrict their number through the enactment of a literacy requirement for immigrants seeking to enter the United States. It passed Congress in 1897, 1911, and 1915 and was vetoed respectively, by presidents Cleveland, Taft, and Wilson, as being contrary to American traditions and practices in regard to immigrants. Finally, in 1917, Congress overrode a veto by Wilson to pass a law requiring that, to be admitted into the United States, an immigrant had to be able to read in at least one language.

As the United States prepared to enter World War I, increased criticism was directed toward immigrants who wanted to preserve some of their Old World ways—persons who came to be labeled hyphenated Americans. In particular, all things German became suspect and were vilified, and Irish Americans were castigated for supporting a rebellion in Ireland for freedom from England, while that country was engaged in the conflict with Germany. Immigrants became the target of increased Americanization campaigns. Spearheaded by the National Americanization Committee, it reached into the schools and into businesses. The Ford Motor Company and other firms increased pressure on workers to learn and use English. Attacks were launched against many local socialist groups. In 1917 almost all Asian immigrants were officially barred from entering the United States.

Still, large numbers of immigrants gave America strong support once the country entered the war. Immigrants and their children served in the armed forces, and many gave their lives for their adopted country. Such patriotism cooled nativism for the moment, but the fear of division and subversion in a hyphenated America worried the public mind. The forced unity of the war effort and the "Hate the Hun" campaigns actually heightened concerns about immigrants' loyalties. During the war, arguments for prohibition on alcohol traded on anti-German and anti-Irish feeling as much as they emphasized the moral and physical health of staying off the bottle. Progressives, too, made the war a test of support for middle-class American values. They stepped up their Americanization efforts or enlisted in government campaigns established for that purpose.

In 1919, in reaction to the Bolshevik success in Russia and the seeming spread of communism in Europe, a "Red Scare" gripped the United States. Labor strikes, violence, and talk of bringing socialism to America provided the pretext for nativists to clamp down on immigrants after World War I. The federal government, with the active encouragement of Attorney General A. Mitchell Palmer, deported several thousand foreign-born members of the Communist Party and other radical organizations. These "Palmer Raids" were a prelude to the 1920s, a decade that saw a revival of the Ku Klux Klan and other organizations critical of and opposed to immigrants. Starting in the South and spreading to the Midwest and much of rural America, the Klan, feeding on a reaction to the internationalism of World War I and on an assertion of white, Anglo-Saxon, Nordic supremacy, waged an aggressive anti-black, anti-Semitic, anti-Catholic, and anti-immigrant campaign. They, together with other nativists, including some eugenicists, psychologists, and social scientists, succeeded in persuading Congress to pass some of the most restrictive immigration laws in the nation's history.

After initial legislation in 1921, Congress, in 1924, limited annual Eastern Hemisphere immigration to 153,714 and, in a National Origins Act, set immigration quotas at 2 percent of each nationality resident in the United States in 1890. This designation, even when demarked by the 1920 census, in 1927 legislation, strongly favored immigrants from Northern and Western Europe and greatly limited those from Southern and Eastern Europe. An Oriental Exclusion Act, in 1924, which prohibited immigration from Asia, including Japan, was a unilateral abrogation of the Gentlemen's Agreement. The Japanese reacted very negatively, marking the American action with humiliation days. Thus, a totally unnecessary piece of legislation, outlawing what already had been agreed upon by negotiation, impaired friendly relations between Japan and the United States and would have dire foreign relations consequences in the future.

The Great Depression of the 1930s further reduced immigration in the United States. While a few newcomers came, more foreign-born left the country or were forced out. In all, during the 1930s, more people left America than entered it, the only decade in the history of the country in which this was a reality. Principal among those forced out were approximately 400,000 Mexican immigrants, including some Mexican American citizens. These people had been used for labor in mines, on the railroads, and in agriculture during times when it was economically beneficial for U.S. employers, but in hard times were seen by "Anglos" as competition for scarce jobs and for relief payments. In order to avoid paying unemployment relief during the Depression, localities, primarily in the Southwest, sought and obtained government deportation action. With the growing persecution of Jews in Germany in the 1930s, some, particularly a number of outstanding scientists and artists, did find asylum in America, but, in general, the United States provided little aid for most of the victims of the growing Nazi anti-Jewish campaign. This included a reluctance to issue visas by the American consulates in Germany and a refusal by Congress to pass legislation to admit 20,000 refugee children over the German quota. Some were turned back at American port cities.

Japan's attack on Pearl Harbor brought the United States into World War II in 1941. Shortly thereafter, fear and long-festering racism resulted in the removal of some 110,000 Japanese Americans, long resident aliens and citizens, from their West Coast homes to distant, isolated, mountain and desert relocation camps. There were no formal accusations, trials, or due process. In fact, no evidence was produced to indicate any disloyalty on the part of these Japanese Americans, and, indeed, many of them served in the U.S. armed forces in intelligence work in the Pacific and in combat units in Europe. Yet most of the relocated persons lost homes, farms, businesses, and personal property. Only years after the war did the U.S. government apologize for its gross abrogation of the constitutional and civil rights of Japanese Americans and offer them a small remuneration for their losses and suffering.

The World War II years, nevertheless, did mark some basic changes in American policy which gradually moved the country toward more fairness and more open immigration. During the war, a labor shortage made immigration necessary. As hundreds of thousands of persons went into the American armed forces at a time when there also was a great demand for increased production for the war effort, jobs for women, blacks, and others previously excluded from many forms of industrial work opened up. The national government also developed a Bracero program, which contracted for workers, particularly from Mexico, but also from a number of Caribbean countries, to supply laborers, primarily for American farms. Aspects of this program lasted until 1964. In the process, it created patterns of migration and employment which continued long after the official end of the program.

World War II also forced the United States to distinguish its immigration policy and race relations in the United States from the overt racism of Germany and to some extent Japan. During the war, Congress attempted to counter Japanese propaganda in China about the American exclusion of Asians in its immigration policy. Thus, in 1943, legislation was enacted to extend an immigration quota to a U.S. ally, China, but only for 101 persons annually. This action, though, did mean that, for the first time since the passage of the 1790 Naturalization Act, Chinese immigrants living in the United States, or who would come under the quota, could become citizens. At the end of the war, a like quota was extended to India and the newly independent Philippines. Another immigration bill, the War Brides Act, allowed overseas spouses of American service personnel to gain citizenship outside of the quotas.

Toward the end of the war and during its aftermath, the advance of the Soviet Union into most of Eastern Europe resulted in several million refugees fleeing into Germany, Austria, and neighboring countries. Through the lobbying of Congress, by American Catholic, Lutheran, Jewish, and a variety of humanitarian groups, a Displaced Persons Act was passed in 1948 and extended in 1950. This law allowed some 400,000 displaced persons to settle in the United States. This, in effect, was the beginning of a refugee policy which would continue in multiple forms and would be debated in the 1950s and beyond.

Despite pressure from such organizations as the National Committee on Immigration Policy and such leaders as President Harry Truman to eliminate the immigration quota system, the 1952 immigration law retained it, but, within its parameters, preferences were set for persons who had members of their family in America and for those with job skills designated as needed in the United States. Korea and Japan were given quotas of 100 persons annually. The 1952 law also reflected the impact of the developing Cold War on American immigration and refugee policies. The spreading power of the Soviet Union and the fear of Communists in the United States motivated congressmen to include in this law a provision to exclude prospective immigrants who had ever had any affiliation with Communists abroad.

The Cold War also affected American refugee policy in that special treatment through the 1950s and beyond was given to refugees fleeing from Communist countries. In 1956 persons who fled from Hungary after a failed effort to oppose a Soviet-imposed government gained American refugee status and some federal government resettlement assistance, and then from 1959 forward the United States welcomed persons who left Cuba after Fidel Castro brought communism to power there. Many in the first wave of those leaving Cuba were persons from the upper strata of society, although afterward middle- and working-class Cubans also came to the United States. These refugees received some financial and other help from the American government. While efforts were made to settle them throughout the country, major concentrations developed in the greater Miami area, the American city closest to Cuba, and in New Jersey, close to the economically important New York City. A growing and strongly anti-Communist Cuban population in the United States would exert continuing pressure on the American government to maintain unswerving opposition to the Castro regime and an open door to those fleeing Communist-dominated countries.

Another aspect of the Cold War was the negative impact of America's immigration quota system on the nation's foreign policy. As the United States vied with the Soviet Union for influence among Third World countries, particularly in the Eastern Hemisphere, America was put on the defensive by the minute quotas given to those countries compared to those of the nations in Northern and Western Europe. In the United States, the civil rights movement, which was gaining ground in the 1960s, attacked prejudices arising out of America's predominantly Eurocentric worldview and contributed to a greater appreciation and wider acceptance of culturally and racially diverse peoples.

Additionally, Americans of Southern and Eastern European backgrounds, most, by then, second-and third-generation Americans, had, despite earlier predictions of some to the contrary, gained upward economic and social mobility, had acculturated to a large degree, and had contributed significantly and loyally to the nation during World War II. In the postwar years, these "ethnic" Americans had increased their standing and political power in the nation through their participation in the electorate and as members of their communities, and some had risen to be mayors of important cities, state legislators and governors, and members of Congress. This evidence of immigrant acculturation for Americans, together with increased cosmopolitanism through education, global military and economic contacts, and international travel, also helped mute to a very considerable extent fear of cultural differences in general and of immigration in particular.

In 1960 the nation elected John F. Kennedy as president. He wrote and gave speeches on the benefits of immigrants to the country and against the quota system as being unfair and harmful to American foreign policy. He called for its repeal but was assassinated before that could be accomplished. His successor, President Lyndon Johnson, amid important civil rights and many social legislative initiatives, led Congress to the passage of the 1965 Immigration Law, one of the most significant immigration laws in the history of the country. It markedly changed the direction of immigration in the United States in multiple ways.

The 1965 law ended the prejudicial quota system, set an annual ceiling of 170,000 immigrant admissions for the Eastern Hemisphere with an equal upper limit for every country of 20,000, and set a ceiling of 120,000 for the Western Hemisphere without a per-country limit. A per-country limit was added for the Western Hemisphere in 1976. Within these parameters, preferences, already begun to some extent in the 1952 immigration law, were assigned for family reunification, persons with work skills designated as needed in the United States, resident aliens, and refugees. The 1965 law, in the face of changing world conditions and the civil rights movement at home, altered American immigration priorities from persons originating in a small number of selected European countries to one that favored persons regardless of country who from an economic viewpoint had higher job skills and education and from a humanitarian perspective were refugees or had family already in the United States.

While it was thought, particularly by congressmen descended from the turn-of-the-century immigrants, that the 1965 law would help increase immigration from Southern and Eastern Europe, it actually increased the numbers from Latin America and Asia. Over the next three decades, some immigrants did come from Europe, especially Poland, Ireland, Germany, Italy, Portugal, Russia, and Greece, but the markedly improved economic conditions in Europe made emigrating less attractive. On the other hand, the earning potential for professional and other educated persons from Asia and Latin America was so much greater in the United States than in their homelands that moving to the United States became very attractive. In some cases, professional health workers, engineers, professors, students, and others came because they were recruited by American firms and institutions.

Thus, the 1965 law markedly changed the countries of origin of the immigrants who came to the United States in the last decades of the twentieth century. Prior to this law, some 90 percent of America's immigrants had come from Europe. From 1970 to the end of the century, only about 10 percent came from that continent, while about 40 percent came from Asia and another 40 percent came from Latin America. In the beginning of this new third major wave of immigration in the history of the United States, a very considerable number of persons admitted had professional and technological job skills and thus came with a college education or more or attained those in this country often on student visas. These people, in turn, were then able to bring relatives under the family reunification immigration category.

Additionally, the number of refugees accepted into the United States increased. In the 1980 Refugee Act, Congress moved from a policy that had been primarily based on the refugee needs of specific, designated populations, like Hungarians, Cubans, Vietnamese, to one in which a set limit, 50,000, could be accepted annually, although provisions allowed the president to accept larger numbers in emergencies. The majority of the refugees who did come, again, were largely from Latin America and Asia—Cubans continued to come, as well as persons from Central America, many from Southeast Asia who had been allied with the United States in the Vietnam War, some Jews from the Soviet Union, and Poles and others from Communist-dominated Eastern Europe. After much protest about the primarily anti-Communist focus of America's refugee policy, Congress, in the 1980 Refugee Act, declared that the United States should be open to the persecuted from any country regardless of the ideology of the regime in power. Nevertheless, President Ronald Reagan's Republican administration, in the 1980s, continued to favor refugees from Communist or Communist-leaning regimes in Cuba, Nicaragua, Afghanistan, and Yugoslavia over right-wing repressive governments in El Salvador, Haiti, and Guatemala with whom the United States was on friendly terms. The Cold War continued to shape immigration policy through the 1980s.

An additional dimension of the post-1965 increase in immigration has been the marked growth in the number of undocumented immigrants settling in the United States. Improved transportation, pervasive American media abroad advertising the prosperity of the United States, and the availability of jobs in the United States, together with poverty, unsettled political conditions, and warfare globally have drawn illegal immigrants to this country. Many Mexicans and other Hispanics have come across the southern border; Caribbean peoples have come by boats to Florida; Chinese and others have been smuggled in by ship; and a very considerable number, including many Irish and students, fly into the United States legally and then overstay their visas. Some have come to stay and others to work with plans to return to their home country. In multiple ways, and particularly in socioeconomic terms, many of the undocumented are more like the majority of those who came in the earlier waves of immigration than many of the more affluent, legal post-1965 newcomers.

Some 24 million immigrants legally settled in the United States between 1950 and 1995, of which more than 18 million came after 1970. The 1990 immigration law lifted the number of immigrants and refugees that the United States would legally accept annually to 700,000. The Census Bureau in the year 2000 estimated that, through the decade of the 1990s, the Asian population had increased by 43 percent and the Hispanic by 28 percent. In addition, it is estimated that several hundred thousand new undocumented immigrants settle in this country each year. This means that the United States has been receiving more than a million new immigrants in some years in this new major wave of immigration.

The new immigrants have settled throughout the country in all fifty states, but most heavily in America's coastal regions, along the southern border, and in major inland metropolitan centers. California has received the most immigrants, but sizeable numbers have taken up residence in New York, Florida, Texas, New Jersey, and Illinois. Many newcomers have found homes in the traditional inner cities, but many more than in the past have been able to settle in suburban locations. A considerable number work and live in rural America. While crowding, job competition, and cultural differences have caused some degree of friction with established residents and among the immigrants themselves, particularly in poorer urban and rural areas, there seems to be more tolerance of immigrants, especially when the newcomers are middle class, than in the earlier waves of immigration.

Employment for the new immigrants has been enormously varied, in part reflecting wide cultural, educational, and class differences. Job preferences in the 1965 immigration law have brought engineers, scientists, doctors, nurses, professors, corporate personnel, financial analysts, artists, technicians, and other highly skilled workers to America. Hospitals, universities, and high-technology firms have hired many foreign-born persons. As in earlier immigration, a considerable number of newcomers have become entrepreneurs, mostly in small businesses, but some have established firms of considerable size. Some groups have developed business niches—Asian Indians in motels and gas stations, Greeks in diners, Koreans as greengrocers, and Chinese and other Asians in high-tech firms. Almost all groups have ethnic food stores and restaurants. There also are teachers, craftsmen, and mechanics in the latest immigrant stream. Many, particularly among the undocumented, are factory workers, food processors, service workers, domestics, agricultural workers, and day laborers.

The new immigrants, now from every country, have brought the world to America and have been helping to globalize the nation. A greater range of foods, languages, customs, and religions than ever before in the history of the United States have become available to the nation's people. Islamic mosques, Buddhist temples, and Hindu cultural centers have become American religious and social meeting places. While there have been continuing efforts among the new immigrant groups to preserve valued aspects of their native cultures, they all have been influenced, to some extent, by Americanizing forces, through the media, social interactions, businesses, schools, and recreation.

As with the previous waves of immigration, the late twentieth-century newcomers have been both valued and criticized by established residents of the United States. Some of the issues have a long history—the economic value of immigrants to the United States, humanitarian concerns, ethnic and cultural differences, degree of acculturation, political participation, language, and security. Some of the issues are newer or at least have a new emphasis, such as the concern about the environmental impact of immigration, immigration and foreign policy, universal human rights, and the containment of the influx of undocumented immigrants.

America's public sector has given particular attention to the illegal entrance and settlement of many newcomers in the United States and the variety of efforts to enforce immigration laws. While the numbers of the undocumented in the country have been large, an estimated three to five million, these persons constitute only a small percentage of the total American population, probably less than 2 percent. Opposition to them has come primarily from persons in the states where the undocumented have been more numerous—California, the Southwest, Texas, and Florida—on the basis of labor competition, added costs of public services, racial and ethnic prejudices, a concern about the environment, and a support for "law and order." Congress has been pressured into legislating more protection along the nation's borders, mandating penalties on employers who knowingly hire the undocumented, and increasing the budget for the Immigration and Naturalization Service (INS). Enforcement efforts have expanded, but not sufficiently, given the very extensive American borders and territory; undocumented immigrants have continued to enter and settle in the United States. The key factor has been the many American agricultural and other employers who find it profitable to hire those illegally present in the country. The undocumented also have support from numerous civil rights, religious, humanitarian, and ethnic groups. The efforts of these supporters, plus taxpayer resistance to added government expenditures, have kept the INS budget, despite increases, inadequate for its very complex and extensive enforcement tasks. In fact, the INS has concentrated its efforts on criminal aliens and has actually done very little to apprehend the otherwise law-abiding undocumented immigrants and very little to enforce employer sanctions, particularly in the strong economy of the latter 1990s.

Environmentalists argue that immigrants, legal as well as undocumented, increase the population, and thus consumption, and in the process use up natural resources. They call for a restriction on immigration. Others, however, point to the fact that reproduction among the existing American citizens has not been at a replacement level and that immigration is necessary for economic growth and national security. There also have been economic disputes about the costs of services used by immigrants in relation to the amount of taxes paid by them, and on whether newcomers depress wages and job opportunities, particularly for already resident minorities, or by helping to increase overall production, they actually create more jobs and better wages.

As in the past, some Americans have objected to the different languages, cultures, ethnicities, races, and religions brought into the country by immigrants. Such people regard immigrants as inferior and as the cause of friction among groups thus eroding American standards and identity by creating added divisions in the nation. Others hold that these differences enrich the country with new vitality, creativity, and ability. They argue that immigrants help make the United States better prepared for an increasingly globalized economy.

Anti-immigrant forces contend that many of the new immigrants, particularly those from Third World countries, are unprepared and unfit for participation in democratic political activity, and that they will not assimilate well into the American civic culture and society. Supporters of immigration counter by pointing out that in earlier immigration waves groups thought not to be able to meld successfully into American life have done so with great benefit to the nation. They further have noted that immigrants who have come since 1965, persons voluntarily choosing American freedom, have already begun the process of Americanization, are participating politically, and are contributing to the country's cultural richness and its economic productivity.

The question of rights for immigrants, legal and undocumented, has involved multiple contentious issues. On the one hand, the federal government, through legislation and the courts, has maintained that decisions on the admission of aliens to the nation, on the deportation of aliens, and on the availability of public benefits for aliens all are rights of the sovereign United States. On the other hand, immigrants, their advocates, and American federal courts have held that aliens, by the fact of residence in the United States, are protected by certain Constitutional rights, including the prohibition of the deprivation of life, liberty, and property without due process and equal protection of the law. It also has been claimed that aliens, as persons, are due civil and human rights—the right of education and employment and the right to health and welfare benefits when in need. Controversies over these issues have reached into the 1990s and beyond. The 1996 Anti-Terrorism Act brought to the fore the contending rights of the U.S. government to protect national security as against the due process rights of accused immigrants to know classified evidence against them. This act also has raised rights issues related to mandatory detention and indefinite detention of immigrants. Additional cases have involved the right to apprehend prospective Haitian and other immigrants on the high seas and proposed negotiations over the rights of free mutual border entry for Mexicans and Americans. Such controversies are ongoing.

America's continuing flow of newcomers throughout its history has given rise to many immigration issues. Immigrants have built and peopled America. They are us. While the number and diversity of the newcomers have created an ever-expanding American identity, the struggle to accept and meld the immigrants into the American civic and social culture has revealed much about the character of the American people. The contentiousness caused by the influx of immigrants, particularly when their numbers were large and the people were different, has exposed limitations and failings in the national character, but also its power to adapt, heal, and move to new possibilities. Immigration issues thus reveal much about who we have been, who we are, and perhaps who we may become.

I

Should the United States Have an Open Immigration Policy?

1

Have Immigrants Been an Economic Asset or an Economic Liability for the United States?

The major factor in motivating most immigrants to come to British North America in colonial times, and then to the United States after the American Revolution, has been the opportunity for economic advancement. The settlers who came in the colonial period were attracted primarily by the abundance of land with woods and meadows for farming, raising livestock, and building homes. Persons with some wealth or with connections were able to obtain large sections of land. Some of these large landholders, particularly in the mainland colonies in the South, turned to commercial agriculture. They needed laborers. Landowners in Virginia and Maryland sought indentured servants (persons bound to work for another for a period of time, often seven years, usually in return for payment of their passage to America), primarily from England, to work their tobacco plantations. After Bacon's Rebellion in 1676, when farmworkers, indentured servants, and others without property threatened to overthrow the planters' rule, the large landholders increasingly turned to enslaved Africans for needed labor. In South Carolina the use of Africans in the growing of rice foreclosed the need for indentured servants. Approximately one half of all the migrants to colonial mainland British North America came as slaves or indentured servants.

The situation in the middle Atlantic provinces was quite different. In Pennsylvania, proprietor William Penn waged a vigorous campaign to attract settlers from the British Isles and the European continent with the promise of religious freedom and fertile land. Such appeals drew thousands of immigrants, including many German redemptioners who sold their labor for passage to "Penn's Woods" and made the province the fastest growing, most diverse colony by the mid-eighteenth century. The availability of land drew a varied immigrant population also to New Jersey.

While more than 90 percent of colonial Americans engaged in some kind of farming, immigrants from numerous European countries also found work, in multiple activities, in the small but growing Atlantic Coast cities. Here populations with considerable ethnic, cultural, and religious diversity marked urban life. Cities included merchants, a growing variety of craftsmen, day laborers, lawyers, ministers, midwives, doctors, and teachers among their many occupations.

In the half century following the American Revolution and independence, the flow of immigrants was relatively small due to disruptions in the Atlantic world caused by the French Revolution and the Napoleonic wars, and the uncertain politics and unsettled economy of the fledgling American republic. Some immigrants, among whom were Scotch-Irish, moved to the trans-Appalachian western frontier. In a number of New England and other Eastern locations, the early beginnings of industrial activity brought a demand for mechanics and other skilled workers, particularly from England and Scotland. Irish and other immigrants found work in construction in cities and in building roads and canals.

The first major economic impact of immigration in the United States came in the decades after 1840. More than two million new persons per decade entered the country. The largest numbers were from Ireland and Germany, but there also was a considerable influx from France, Switzerland, Scandinavia, and China. Some of those who settled in American towns and cities, like a portion of the Germans, came with mechanical and trade skills, but many, like a large percentage of the Irish, were unskilled or semiskilled. Land remained as the distant magnet that drew many Europeans to the United States. Newcomers bought farms or became farmworkers in the Midwest, and even moved across the Mississippi and into Oregon. Natural resources, including gold, lured immigrants, not only from Europe but also from Mexico and other parts of Latin America and from China, to newly acquired California and into other Western territories. Immigration supplied engineers and mechanics and Irish, Chinese, and Mexican laborers for building roads and the new railroads, which were spreading across the countryside and stitching together the basic structure of a "national market" connecting urban and rural America and the Atlantic and Pacific coasts.

The largest percentage of those who came in this first mass wave of immigration settled in such cities as Philadelphia, New York, Lowell, Newark, and Boston. Here they added to the supply of mechanics, craftsmen, and weavers working as individuals, in small workshops, or in developing factories. Less skilled immigrants found work in tanneries, on urban construction, as factory hands, and in a host of other activities. Although there was a marked overall growth in the economy of the nation, there also were economic dislocations. The development of factories and the growing supply of immigrant labor gave some native and immigrant craftsmen and others entrepreneurial opportunities, but it also put some of them out of work. The displacement of some native workers contributed to the anti-immigrant sentiment that led to nativist demands for restrictions on immigrants and in some cases, for example, in Newark and Philadelphia, violence against immigrant workers.

Typical of such nativist criticism was one writer who opined in 1854 that the "unlimited and unrestricted admission of foreign emigrants is a serious injury to the native laboring population, socially, morally, religiously, and politically, by overstocking the labor market and thus keeping wages down." He also reported the use of immigrants as strikebreakers in the iron industry in Pittsburgh.[1]

The most vicious attack on immigrants came against the Chinese workers in the West where they were subjected to special taxes, prohibition against participating in many lines of work, segregation, violence, and, in 1882, exclusion from further immigration. The main economic complaint from both native and Irish immigrant laborers was that the Chinese worked too efficiently and for too little money and thereby drove down wages for everyone. Additionally, critics objected to the rise in municipal costs caused by the growing number of poor immigrants, some of whom sought shelter in poorhouses, utilized public infirmaries, and increased the population in prisons.

On the other hand, there were those who regarded immigrants as a great economic benefit to the United States. They included many businessmen, some who sought mechanics, artisans, and other skilled workers and others who looked for cheap unskilled or semiskilled factory hands, construction workers, and day laborers. In 1864, at a time of labor shortage owing primarily to the Civil War, a U.S. Congressional committee reported: "The advantages which have accrued heretofore from immigration can scarcely be computed. The labor of immigrants has contributed vastly to the value of our cities, towns, and villages, our railroads, our farms, our manufactures, and our productions."[2]

In the latter half of the nineteenth century, lands continued to be opened up in the West, drawing both American citizens and immigrants into new farming, ranching, mining, and forestry endeavors. Improved transportation within Europe, as well as within the United States, expanded the pull of America across Europe. Steamship advertisements for passengers and railroad advertisements for sale of land helped to draw immigrants westward. Large numbers of Swedes settled in Minnesota,

Finns in northern Michigan, and Germans and Eastern Europeans in many locations across Texas and the Great Plains. Many Irish, Polish, Hungarian, Slovakian, and Mexican immigrants worked in mines from Pennsylvania to Arizona to Montana.

Even larger numbers of newcomers, in the second mass wave of immigration after 1880, settled in the rapidly growing American cities and provided much of the labor for expanding industrial, transportation, and urban development. People from many different countries worked in the factories that made the United States the leading industrial nation in the world by the end of the nineteenth century. The growing variety of work and the expanding need for laborers made it possible for large numbers of immigrants in each national and cultural group to choose lines of work particularly suited to their skills, interests, and habits. Italians did much of the hard labor in building and transportation construction, Jews made significant contributions to the garment industry, English were skilled workers in silk mills and the pottery industry, Polish workers labored in the new oil refineries, and Germans operated breweries, chemical works, and worsted mills. Many immigrants opened small businesses, and some from each group started food stores and restaurants that catered to the food preferences of people of similar cultural backgrounds.

Many of the jobs taken by immigrants involved considerable danger from accidents and disease. Hours of work were often long, and pay was low. A considerable number of the newcomers made progress by attaining new skills, and some gained bargaining power by joining or forming labor unions. A small percentage spoke and acted on behalf of socialist and radical principles.

The large number of immigrants, even in the expanding American economy, and particularly during economic downturns, provided significant competition for native workers. Organized labor, struggling to represent and protect the interests of workers in the face of capital, was ambivalent about immigration. Although not uniformly anti-immigrant—in some trades, they actively recruited the foreign-born—organized labor generally feared that the influx of large numbers of new people increased the supply of workers, which made it difficult for unions to win concessions from management on wages, hours, and working conditions. A particular dread of the unions and of workers, generally, was the ability of owners to contract with laborers abroad for low wages or to hire them as strikebreakers. American labor did succeed in getting Congress to pass legislation in the 1885 outlawing contract labor, but the government did not aggressively enforce the law.

Labor and capital were spoiling for a fight in the days of the unregulated marketplace and workplace. With immigrants crowding into the

United States, capital held the trump card. Edward Devine, a New York social worker, in 1911 wrote,

> Employers of the exploiting type . . . demand cheap immigrant labor. . . . Lower wages, longer hours, crowded living quarters, fewer claimants in case of death or injury from accidents, less trade-union "nonsense," . . . less sympathy from the disinterested public for the laborer's side when there is a dispute, less public concern generally as to what is happening in the mill when the laborers are foreigners.[3]

Henry Fairchild, a professor of sociology, observed that "the American workman is continually underbid in the labor market by vast numbers of alien laborers."[4] Under such circumstances organized labor increasingly added its voice to calls for restricting immigration.

The abundance of new labor at the turn of the century, however, did enable many American workers to move up the employment ladder. By the beginning of the twentieth century, a large number of second- and third-generation Irish and German laborers had progressed from the unskilled and semiskilled work of the immigrant generation into skilled labor, service work, and even into white-collar and supervisory positions. Those from families who were in the United States even earlier moved in even greater numbers into white-collar and management jobs. In addition, the availability of a large, new immigrant workforce in general together with technological innovations and mass production generated a growth in economic activity that enabled some Americans to become very wealthy, including even a few immigrants like Andrew Carnegie. These factors also provided Americans with an increasing abundance of consumer goods and, in general, declining prices.

In the 1920s, when Congress placed an annual limit on incoming immigrants, many businesses sought to replace workers with technology, and some began to look to African Americans who were migrating to the Northern and the Midwestern industrial cities from the South in substantial numbers. Then, during the very severe 1930s depression, more people left the country than entered it. In general, throughout the nation's history, economic downturns have resulted in decreased immigration, but, in addition, in the 1930s, in an effort to reduce the nation's labor surplus and to lessen welfare rolls, several hundred thousand Mexican immigrants in the Southwest were forced to return to their country of origin.

Just a few years later, with the outbreak of World War II and a consequent labor shortage, the U.S. government instituted a Bracero program to bring by contract a large number of mostly Mexican and some Caribbean workers to engage in agricultural labor, primarily harvesting fruits and vegetables. Under this program the number of Mexicans offered contracts to work in the United States grew from some 50,000 in 1943 to nearly 450,000 in 1956 before ending in 1964. The Bracero program developed an interrelated dependence between American employers and Mexican workers that has continued into the twenty-first century. The Mexicans have come to depend on this work to support families, and employers have come to depend on this cheap and hard-working labor source. Additionally, and particularly in the 1990s, as an increasing number of younger Americans have been abandoning farming for other occupations, immigrants have been replacing them in running small farms.

Since World War II, the immigrant occupational profile has changed. This change has been due in part to the 1952 and 1965 American immigration laws which gave an admission preference to persons with job skills the federal government deemed desirable for the nation's economy and security. Most striking has been the numbers of scientists, engineers, technicians, computer specialists, health professionals, and educators in the immigrant stream. Approximately a quarter of the post-1965 immigrants have been highly educated. Many have received their schooling abroad before coming to the United States, or they have come as students and, after obtaining degrees, have remained to work here, or they have come as immigrants and after arrival have pursued more education. More than half of some immigrant groups, such as Asian Indians, and a high percentage of still others, such as Koreans and Russians, have a college degree or more. The flow of well-educated people from Third World countries to the United States has been a brain drain on the sender nations and a boon to the United States. The harmful effects of this brain drain on poorer countries and to the establishment of an international balance of talent and wealth has been a source of growing international tension since the 1970s.

Well-educated immigrants are attracted to the United States by high pay, opportunities to work with advanced equipment and grow in their professions, and stable economic and political conditions. In addition, businesses, hospitals and other health organizations, educational institutions, and other American establishments have actively recruited abroad for employees and students. The shift to an "information economy" in the computer age has accelerated and intensified such recruitment efforts. These skilled newcomers benefit the American economy by bringing knowledge resources and new productive processes and, additionally, by the fact that the cost of all or much of their education was borne by another country. Edwin Reubens, writing in *The Public Interest*, stated in 1978, "In recent years, foreign medical graduates constituted about 30 percent of the resident medical staff in all hospitals in the United States, and over half in New York City's municipal hospitals. . . .

Many big-city hospitals declare they cannot carry on without their (mostly legal) alien doctors and nurses."[5]

As in the past, among the new immigrants are a considerable number who have become entrepreneurs. Most often they become owners of small businesses, such as Asian Indians who operate motels and gas stations, Koreans who are greengrocers, and Chinese and some from most other groups who run ethnic food stores and restaurants. The variety of "ethnic" establishments has increased the food, entertainment, and service choices open to an ever-larger number of American consumers. Some immigrants have started businesses that have grown to a considerable size, most notably in a variety of technological fields. Scott Thurm wrote in the *Wall Street Journal* in 1999,

> Ethnic Chinese and Indian immigrants run nearly 25% of the high-tech companies started in the (Silicon) Valley since 1980. . . . The 2,775 immigrant-run companies had total sales of $16.8 billion and more than 58,000 employees. . . . Immigrant entrepreneurs also strengthen Silicon Valley's bonds with the rest of the world. . . . States such as California and New York tend to export more goods to countries from which large numbers of immigrants come.[6]

Most immigrants are craftsmen or semiskilled or unskilled laborers. They work in factories, construction, service industries, or various day labor jobs. In large cities and elsewhere immigrants form a major component of the workforce in restaurants; garment, leather, food-processing, and other manufacturing concerns; laundries; landscaping and cleaning firms; and custodial and domestic service. Additionally, immigrants constitute a large portion of the nation's agricultural laborers.

The current post–World War II wave of immigration has generated an ongoing controversy on how economically beneficial overall the immigration has been, if at all. Critics point out that immigrants, with their cultural differences, have difficulty adjusting to American workplaces and cause friction among workers. Others see advantages to the country from immigrants who bring new ideas and new methods as well as added vitality to businesses and other organizations.

Then there are those who hold that, as in the past, immigrants hurt American workers because they increase the labor supply and lower wages by their willingness to work for less. They maintain that American minorities are hurt the most, both because some get replaced by immigrants and also because the added supply of alien workers decreases the incentive for employers to provide openings and needed training for these citizens.

Other critics of post-1965 federal policies point to the preference given to immigrants for family reunification. Even some of the highly educated and professional immigrants have brought relatives to the United States who are less educated and less skilled, and they have brought older parents and relatives who do not enter the workforce. Other critics complain that immigrants, especially illegal immigrants, add to the cost of government by using public services and by the number of those on welfare. Wayne Lutton, editor of *The Social Contract* and an advocate for more restrictions on immigration, stated that "immigrant welfare dependency rates have been rising steadily since the onset of the 1965 immigration revisions" and that "unskilled immigrants are particularly prone to enter the welfare system."[7]

Proponents of more open immigration argue that, with the exception of some older immigrants and some refugees, the percentage of newcomers on welfare has been small. They maintain that most immigrants have been in the workforce, add to American productivity and creativity, and pay more in taxes than the cost of services they use. Julian Simon, professor of business administration at the University of Maryland, a fellow at the pro-immigration Cato Institute, and one of the most influential, most often quoted proponents of more open immigration, asserts that immigrants have given the United States "a sharply increased rate of technological advance, spurred by the addition of top scientific talent from all over the world." Simon argues that "the best way for the U.S. to . . . raise its standard of living, is simply to take in more immigrants."[8]

Immigrants have made large contributions to the development of the American economy since the inception of the nation. The contributions of individuals or of groups of immigrants have varied with the degree of skills they brought with them and the particular needs of the country at any given time. Then too immigration has involved costs in terms of the utilization of public services and benefits. Such costs have been a concern particularly in the decades since World War II. Additionally, immigrants have had an impact on already settled American workers in terms of competition resulting for some in a loss of jobs, decreased wages, and poorer working conditions and for others an opening to new and improved economic opportunities.

NOTES

1. A Foreigner, *Emigration, Emigrants, and Know Nothings* (Philadelphia, 1854), 30–36.
2. U.S. Senate, *Report from the Committee on Agriculture . . . on the Enactment of Suitable Laws for the Encouragement and Protection of Foreign Immigrants Arriving within Jurisdiction of the United States*, 38th Cong. 1st sess. February 18, 1864, S. Rept. 15.
3. Edward T. Devine, "The Selection of Immigrants," *Survey*, February 4, 1911.

4. Henry Fairchild, *Immigration* (New York: Macmillan, 1913).
5. Edwin Reubens, "Aliens, Jobs and Immigration Policy," *Public Interest* 51 (Spring 1978): 117–18.
6. Scott Thurm, "Asian Immigrants Are Reshaping Silicon Valley," *Wall Street Journal*, June 24, 1999, B6.
7. Wayne Lutton, "Welfare Cost for Immigrants," *Social Contract* (Fall 1992): 1. (www.thesocialcontract.com).
8. Julian Simon, "The Case for Greatly Increased Immigration," *Public Interest* 102 (Winter 1991): 90, 103.

DOCUMENTS

1.1. Immigrants in the 1850s Harm America and Native-Born Workers

The author, an immigrant from England, who had been in the United States for thirteen years and a citizen for seven years, adopted the anti-immigration viewpoints of the nativist movement which reacted negatively to the large influx of the Irish and Germans after 1840. Writing in 1854 at the height of that movement, he expressed the concern of the nativists about the adverse impact of the many newcomers on the wages of American-born workers. He regarded this flow of immigrants as the work of European governments attempting to rid themselves of poor and needy people and of American business owners seeking cheap labor. The author also feared rising costs for the government due to a growing number of the foreign-born in poorhouses and prisons. In making his case for less open immigration the author, like most nativists, focused only on the negative aspects of immigration

And what have I learned in the course of my travels and observations concerning the unlimited and unguarded admittance of foreigners into the country? What conclusion have I come to? That it is a glaring and grievous evil; an evil to the United States, and an evil to many of the emigrants themselves. Why? Because anybody, or everybody, may come without let or hindrance. The rogues and vagabonds from London, Paris, Amsterdam, Vienna, Naples, Hamburg, Berlin, Rome, Genoa, Leghorn, Geneva, &c., may come and do come. The outpouring of alms and work houses, and prisons and penitentiaries, may come and do come. Monarchies, oligarchies, and aristocracies may and do reduce the millions of the people to poverty and beggary, and compel the most valueless to seek for a shelter and a home in the United States of America, and they do so. And what are the consequences? The consequences are that about 400,000 souls, from Europe, chiefly Germans, Irish, and Dutch are annually arriving in this country and making it their permanent abode. That a vast number of these emigrants come without money, occupation, friends, or business; many, very many, have not the means of buying land, getting to it, stocking it, and waiting for first crops, and many others would not settle upon land if they could. That, go where you will in the United States, you find nearly all the dens of iniquity, taverns, grog-shops, beer houses, gambling places, and houses of ill fame and worse deeds, are kept by foreigners. That, at the various ports, the alms-houses and hospitals are in the main, occupied by foreigners; and that numerous objects of poverty and destitution are to be seen crawling along the streets in every direction. That not a few become criminals, filling our prisons and putting the country to great expense.

This is a fearful catalogue of consequences, but they are by no means all. This unlimited and unrestricted admission of foreign emigrants is a serious injury to the native laboring population, socially, morally, religiously, and politically; socially, by overstocking the labor market and thus keeping wages down; morally and religiously, by unavoidable contact and intercourse; and politically, by consequence of want of employment and low wages, making them needy and dependent, whereby they become the easy prey or willing tools of designing and unprincipled politicians. And in this way the native population is deteriorated and made poor, needy, and subservient: and these realities produce want of self-respect, hopelessness, laxity in morals, recklessness, delinquencies, and crimes.

But there is another consequence which is deserving of notice, and it is this: Our manufacturers, ironmakers, machinists, miners, agriculturists, railway, canal, and other contractors, private families, hotel-keepers, and many others, have got into the way of expecting and seeking for cheap labor, through the supply of operatives, workmen, laborers, house-help, and various kinds of workers, kept up by the indiscriminate and unrestrained admission of emigrants. Indeed it is no secret that emigrants, or rather foreign workers, have become an article of importation; professedly for the purpose of providing for the deficiency of supply in the labor market, but in reality with the intention of obtaining efficient workers at lower wages.

I remember well in the early part of 1846, when our manufacturers and ironmakers, far and near, were struggling hard for the retention of the high protective tariff then in existence, and the profits on cotton spinning and manufacturing ranged from thirty to one hundred per cent, that hundreds of operatives were imported from England for the purpose of obtaining practised hands and to keep wages from rising. And I remember also that some years ago when there was an attempt to reduce the wages of ironmakers and machinists at Pittsburgh and elsewhere, and the men resisted, that importation was resorted to with considerable success; and that those importations, and others both before and since, were obtained in a great measure by partial, fallacious, and incorrect representations.

This last mentioned consequence has had, and probably will continue to have, a very unfair and deplorable effect upon the native laboring population; for it needs no proof to sustain the assertion, that but for these specific and large importations of cotton and woolen manufacturing operatives, machinists and ironworkers, the wages of the then located population must have risen, and the natives been made better off.

Source: A Foreigner, *Emigration, Emigrants, and Know Nothings* (Philadelphia, 1854), 30–36.

1.2. Congressional Committee Reports on the Value of Immigrants to the American Economy

The Civil War in the United States, which lasted from 1861 to 1865, caused severe labor shortages. In 1864 a congressional committee seeking a solution to this problem recommended an increase in immigration. The committee prefaced this recommendation with a glowing report on the economic contributions that immigrants had already made to the nation. Eager to promote immigration, the committee reported only on the positive aspects of new workers coming to America.

The advantages which have accrued heretofore from immigration can scarcely be computed. The labor of immigrants has contributed vastly to the value of our cities, towns, and villages, our railroads, our farms, our manufactures, and our productions. Comparatively few of the race now predominant on this continent can trace their American ancestry more than a century back. Though a seeming paradox, it nevertheless approaches historical truth, that we are all immigrants. In 1790 the population of the United States was less than four millions; in 1860 it was little less than thirty-one millions and a half, showing an increase of twenty-seven millions and a half in seventy years. . . .

The advantages of foreign immigration, as between the United States and the people of European countries, are mutual and reciprocal. If our prairies and mineral lands offer inducements to the immigrant and promise him requital for the pangs of severed family ties and separation from the scenes of his early childhood, he, in his turn, contributes to the development of the resources of our country and adds to our material wealth. Such is the labor performed by the thrifty immigrant that he cannot enrich himself without contributing his full quota to the increase of the intrinsic greatness of the United States. This is equally true whether he work at mining, farming, or as a day laborer on one of our railroads.

The special wants for labor in this country at the present time are very great. The war has depleted our workshops, and materially lessened our supply of labor in every department of industry and mechanism. In their noble response to the call of their country, our workmen in every branch of the useful arts have left vacancies which must be filled, or the material interest of the country must suffer. The immense amount of native labor occupied by the war calls for a large increase of foreign immigration to make up the deficiency at home. The demand for labor never was greater than at present, and the fields of usefulness were never so varied and promising.

Source: U.S. Senate, *Report from the Committee on Agriculture . . . on the Enactment of Suitable Laws for the Encouragement and Protection of Foreign Immigrants Arriving within Jurisdiction of the United States*, 38th Cong., 1st sess., February 18, 1864, S. Rept. 15.

1.3. Early Twentieth-Century Immigrants Endanger Standards of Labor in the United States

The second major wave of immigration, from the 1880s into the 1920s, brought controversy about the economic impact of large numbers of newcomers in the United States. A federal Immigration Commission was appointed by Congress in 1907 to study the new immigration. After four years of work, its forty-seven volume report recommended some reduction in the admittance of unskilled labor from abroad. Edward T. Devine, editor of Survey *and the well-known director of the New York School of Philanthropy (later known as a school of social work), was among a number of Progressive reformers who agreed with the commission. These reformers, together with labor unions, were working to improve conditions for workers in the United States, and they regarded large numbers of immigrants as contributing to a lowering of wages and working standards and making more possible the exploitation of labor. Devine expressed his opinion in a 1911 issue of* Survey, *one of the most important magazines that concerned social issues in the early twentieth century.*

The Immigration Commission has spoken clearly and its recommendation should become law. There must be effective restriction and selection for the purpose of maintaining American standards of living. . . .

It is precisely because of a passionate attachment to the true interests of humanity that social workers may look with profound distrust upon the demand for cheap immigrant labor. Genuine humane sentiment is not inconsistent with the maintenance of community and national standards.

Employers of the exploiting type make no mistake, from their own point of view, when they demand cheap immigrant labor. They can figure it out with great precision. They know that as a rule this labor is less skillful, less intelligent, less efficient, less inherently desirable, than the native labor or the earlier immigrant labor from more closely related peoples. But there are great compensations. It is the very best labor in one particular. It can be exploited. That is the whole disagreeable truth in a nutshell. Lower wages, longer hours, crowded living quarters, fewer claimants in case of death or injury from accidents, less trade-union "nonsense," fewer trade disputes, less sympathy from the disinterested public for the laborer's side when there is a dispute, less public concern generally as to what is happening in the mill when the laborers are foreigners. Such are some of the considerations which turn the balance in favor of immigrant labor. The wages demanded are enough lower to give an ample margin for more effective supervision. The general tendency of improved machinery is to decrease relatively the demand for skilled labor, thus permitting the profitable employment of fresh supplies of entirely unskilled, but physically strong, immigrants. Out on the railways of the Northwest the first object for which immigrants will strike is for the privilege of working twelve hours instead of ten, and the next is for the privilege of working on Sunday. In this instance employers, paying by the hour and not having expensive mills in operation, resist the demand, for the labor of the eleventh and twelfth hours is relatively unproductive. The men are already exhausted. To laborers of a higher standard the leisure for physical recuperation would be worth more than the small addition to their wages. To these men the money is more important. Here we have a simple, but perfect, illustration of that conflict of standards to which the nation as a whole cannot afford to be indifferent.

It is then in the ultimate and in the very immediate interests of the oppressed and struggling everywhere that America should maintain her standards. She may give generously from her surplus. She may enlighten by her example. She may throw her influence and if necessary exert her might against oppression. But one thing she may not do: extinguish the light with which she is to enlighten the world. To lower our own standards is the only treason. To reduce the position of our workingmen to that of the communities from which our immigration is coming is to destroy, perhaps forever, the very power to serve. . . . Under the conditions of actual life we shall have to deal in partial solutions, among which, as we have intimated, the recommendation of the Immigrant Commission as to restriction deserves prompt and favorable consideration.

Source: The Editor, "The Selection of Immigrants," *Survey*, February 4, 1911, 711–16.

1.4. Turn-of-the-Century Immigrants Depress the Wages of American-Born Workers

Henry Pratt Fairchild, a prominent sociologist, was a critic of immigration in the early twentieth century. Writing in 1913, he joined those who believed that the "new" immigrants, mainly from Southern and Eastern Europe, were decreasing the opportunities for longer-resident American laborers to raise their wages and work standards. Fairchild and his fellow critics helped build public and political support for restrictive immigration legislation which culminated in the 1920s when Congress enacted an annual limit on the number of immigrants who would be allowed to enter the United States and, within that limit, a quota system particularly unfavorable to Southern and Eastern Europeans.

Into this favored section of the earth's surface have been introduced ever increasing numbers of the lower classes of foreign nations. What has been their effect upon the prevailing standard of living? As a major premise, it will be granted that the standard of living of the working classes of the United States has been and still is superior to that of the nations which have furnished the bulk of the immigrants. Common observation and general testimony establish this beyond the need of proof. Particularly at the present time, if this were not so, very few of our immigrants would come, for, as we have seen, this is the great incentive which draws them. It is significant, however, that the bulk of immigration has been recruited from more and more backward races of Europe as the decades have succeeded each other. There is not now the relative advantage for the peasant of England, Germany, or Scandinavia that there was during the first two thirds of the nineteenth century. As regards the new immigrants—those who have come during the last thirty years—the one great reason for their coming is that they believe that on the wage which they can receive in America they can establish a higher standard than the one to which they have been accustomed. And this wage for which they are willing to sell their labor is in general appreciably below that which the native American workman requires to support his standard. What does this mean? It means in the first place that the American workman is continually underbid in the labor market by vast numbers of alien laborers who can do his work approximately as well as he. But it means more than this. It means that he is denied the opportunity of profiting by those exceptionally advantageous periods which as we have seen recur from time to time, and provide the possibility of an improved standard. From his point of view these periods include any circumstances which occasion a sudden increase in the demand for labor—such as the establishment of a great new industry or the opening up of new territory by the completion of a railroad or recurring "good times" after a period of depression. If this new demand must perforce be met by the labor already in the country, there would be an opportunity for an increase in wages to the working man. But the condition which actually confronts the American workman at such a time is this—not only is the amount of wages which can be successfully demanded by labor profoundly influenced by the number and grade of foreign workers already in the country, but there comes at once, in response to improved conditions, a sudden and enormous increase in the volume of immigration. Thus the potential advantage which might accrue to the laborers already in the country is wholly neutralized. The fluctuating nature of the immigration current is of vital importance to the American workman. It means that for him the problem is not that of taking the fullest advantage of a possibility of an improved standard, but of maintaining intact the standard which he has.

Source: Henry Fairchild, *Immigration* (New York: Macmillan, 1913), 302–304.

1.5. Contributions of Immigrants to the American Economy, 1850–1950

In looking back from 1950, William Bernard, executive director of the National Committee on Immigration Policy, brought to the attention of his readers the positive contributions of the foreign-born to the American economy through the first and particularly the second major waves of immigration. Bernard worked with his organization, with a degree of success, to make American immigration laws more open and more universal in the years following World War II. In doing so, he reminded the American public of the extensive contributions of immigrants to the American economy in the past.

The tremendous contributions made by immigrants to our national development are undeniable. . . .

Much of the hard labor required to convert our country from a vast area of undeveloped resources into a top-ranking industrial nation has been borne by immigrants and their descendants.

Realization of the great agricultural potentialities of the country has been due in no small measure to their efforts. . . .

Following in the wake of the first pioneers, many immigrant families of German, Scandinavian, Slavic, and other national strains have helped to extend the area of cultivation ever westward. Large portions of the Middle West and the West are now being tilled by descendants of these immigrant stocks. In the East many farms left idle by former native tenants, moreover, have been taken over and run profitably by Italian, Polish, and other immigrant families. The development of Pacific Coast agriculture has depended in part on crops from the Mediterranean imported by immigrants skilled in raising them, and the Japanese also brought to California exceptional talent in intensive cultivation and gardening. . . .

Much of the heavy and difficult work of building our continent-wide transportation system was likewise performed by the different new immigrant groups at various periods of our history. In the middle of the nineteenth century the Irish constituted a most important element in the laboring class. They took over a large part of the heavy work in the building of the Erie Canal and the other waterways which formed essential links in the transportation system of that era. In the construction of our vast system of railroads which had spanned the continent by the turn of the century, new laboring groups such as the Slavs and Italians worked along with the Irish. In the building of the far western railroads the Chinese were an important source of labor. . . .

A similar succession can be traced in the mining and metal industries. In general, the most recent immigrant groups have tended to hold the most arduous and lowest paid jobs, as the earlier comers advanced to more agreeable and profitable occupations. Thus the heavy work in the mining and metal industries which in earlier days was performed by English, Welsh, and other old-immigrant groups has been largely taken over by immigrants from Hungary, Poland, Italy, Yugoslavia, and other parts of eastern and southern Europe. In the early part of the century a large proportion of the Slavic immigrants were employed in the coal and iron industry, in the steel mills, and in mining.

Indeed, in the rapid industrial expansion between 1890 and 1910 the new immigration from southern and eastern Europe, which assumed such large proportions at this time, played an indispensable part. . . .

The United States Census Bureau in *A Century of Population Growth* estimated that during the nineteenth century immigrants contributed thirty million persons to the American population and during the same period added forty billion dollars to our wealth. . . .

Not only have immigrants contributed to our general economic growth and wealth but they have also brought to this country organizing ability, enterprise, scientific knowledge, and inventiveness, which speeded the tempo of our development and added immeasurably to the diversity of American life. . . .

The role of immigration in promoting industrial progress may be further suggested by the mention of the names of a few immigrants who have been outstanding leaders in the development of special industries: Andrew Carnegie (Scottish) played such a role in the steel industry, Samuel Slater (English) in the cotton-mill industry, John Jacob Astor (German) in the fur industry, Michael Cudahy (Irish) in the meat-packing industry, Frank Assman (Swedish) in can processing, and Henry Lomb, John J. Bausch, and Charles Lembke (all German) in the optical industry. Other leading immigrant figures in industry include Joseph Bulova (Czech) in the watch industry, James Butler (Irish) in chain groceries, Leo Baekeland (Belgian) in bakelite and velos, Giuseppe Tagliabue (Italian) in thermometers, Conrad Worra (German) in aluminum products, Charles L. Fleischmann (a Hungarian Jew) in yeast, David Sarnoff (a Russian Jew) in radio, Frederick Weyerhaeuser (German) in the lumber industry, and William S. Knudsen (Danish) the head of General Motors. Immigrant producers, actors, artists, and technical experts have played a very important part in the motion picture industry, the show business, the theater, music, and the other arts. If diversity of industry and specialization are necessary for a high standard of living, as the economists state, immigrants have contributed substantially to our present standard, considered the highest in the world. . . .

Competition between different elements in our population and their ways of living has stimulated new ideas and made for new inventions. Instead of being static and rigid we have changed with the times and forged ahead.

Source: William S. Bernard, ed., *American Immigration Policy: A Reappraisal* (New York: Harper and Brothers, 1950), 56–63, 66.

1.6. Late Twentieth-Century Immigrants Contribute to the Rise in Cost of Public Services and Benefits

---

As immigration increased in the post–World War II years, particularly after the 1965 immigration law, the impact of newcomers on the American economy again became an issue debated by the public and in Congress. In addition to purported negative effects of immigrants on the established American labor force, critics of immigration pointed to the foreign-born as a contributing factor in the rising cost of public benefits and services. This issue became a particular concern in the early 1990s in California with its large immigrant population and in the face of an economic downturn. During the debate in California that led to the passage of Proposition 187 which declared undocumented immigrants ineligible for education and certain other public services, Wayne Lutton, editor of The Social Contract, *focused on the public costs of immigrants in a 1992 article in his publication which advocates less open immigration.*

Economists George Borjas of the University of California-San Diego, and Stephen Trejo of the University of California-Santa Barbara, in their study, Immigrant Participation in the Welfare System, confirm the validity of the "widespread perception that unskilled immigrants are particularly prone to enter the welfare system, and that the entry of large numbers of these immigrants in the past two decades has increased taxpayer expenditures of income transfer programs." Data from the 1970 and 1980 Censuses indicate that immigrant welfare dependency rates have been rising steadily since the onset of the 1965 immigration revisions and have become significantly higher—both in absolute terms and relative to native-born American citizens. The 1990 Census documents increasing rates of welfare use by immigrants.

Professors Borjas and Trejo find that welfare use increases with the age of an immigrant more quickly than it does among native-born Americans. By law, immigrants are subject to deportation if they become a "public charge" during their first five years of residency in the U.S. While this provision is almost never enforced, the possibility may discourage some recent immigrants from applying for aid. Borjas and Trejo also discovered that "the process of assimilation leads immigrants into welfare rather than out of it. [Immigrant] assimilation involves the accumulation of information not only about labor market opportunities, but also about alternative opportunities available through the welfare system." Research conducted by Lief Jensen supports the conclusions reached by Borjas and Trejo. Writing in the Spring 1988 issue of International Migration Review, Professor Jensen noted that foreign-born residents of the United States were 56 percent more likely than native-born Americans to be living in poverty, 25 percent more likely to receive public aid, and to have an average per capita income from public assistance 13.6 percent higher than natives.

Welfare participation rates differ among immigrants. Those coming from less-developed countries and possessing skills that do not meet the requirements of a high-tech economy are much more likely to use welfare than are skilled immigrants from industrialized nations. The most recent census figures indicate that 29.3 percent of Vietnamese immigrants were on welfare, 25.8 percent of those from the Dominican Republic, 18 percent from Cuba, 12.4 percent from Mexico, all the way down to 4 percent from Denmark and 3.9 percent from Switzerland. Immigrants are participating in more than fifteen major federally- and state-financed services. The largest expense category is public education, kindergarten through high school. Thanks to a 1982 decision by the U.S. Supreme Court, taxpayers are required to educate the children of illegal aliens.

Uncompensated medical care provided to illegal aliens at publicly-supported hospitals follows education as the most costly burden to U.S. taxpayers. The average cost to taxpayers is $4700 per admission (Estimated Annual Costs of Major Federal and State Services to Illegal Aliens, Center for Immigration Studies).

Important cost elements that cannot be accurately estimated—but are no less real—are those general services used by all persons residing in an area, regardless of their citizenship, such as police and fire protection, the courts, parks and other public facilities, transportation, and environmental protection. The costs of all of these services rise as population grows.

Since 1970, U.S. immigration policies are responsible for an increase in our population of more than 27 million. Immigrants and their children—because of their high fertility rates—account for more than half of U.S. population growth since 1970. They are likely to contribute two-thirds of the anticipated increase through the remainder of the 1990s, according to demographer Leon Bouvier of Tulane University.

American baby boomers are having small families. But large-scale immigration has doubled U.S. population growth over what it would have been without immigration. Thus, a significant part of the rising costs of public services can fairly be attributed to immigration.

Source: Wayne Lutton, "Welfare Cost for Immigrants," *The Social Contract* (Fall 1992): 1–3. (www.thesocialcontract.com)

1.7. Immigrant Workers and Entrepreneurs Fuel Growth of California's High-Technology Industries

Silicon Valley, California's premier high-technology industrial hub, has attracted and employed many highly educated, skilled immigrants. The firms in this industry have lobbied Congress for more open immigration and for special admission status for im-

migrants with technological skills. Congressionally approved visas, most of which go to workers for the high-tech industry, have grown from 65,000 annually to 115,000 in 1998. Not only has immigration supplied employees but, according to a study by University of California, Berkeley, professor Anna Lee Saxenian, "Silicon Valley's New Immigrant Entrepreurs," many of these talented newcomers, particularly the Chinese and Indians, have started their own firms and now are major contributors to the American economy in sales, in the creation of new jobs, and in developing overseas business networks.

Analysis of census data shows that by 1990, one third of the high technology workforce's scientists and engineers in Silicon Valley were foreign-born. And of those foreign-born, almost two-thirds were Asian or Indian born. Clearly these statistics provide proof to the claim by some technology observers that "Silicon Valley is built on ICs." The reference to ICs are not integrated circuits or some other computer-related terminology, but rather to Indian and Chinese engineers and scientists who work in Silicon Valley.

Highly Educated Workers

These scientists and engineers are highly educated and earn advanced degrees at significantly greater rates than native-born students. While 31% of the native born high-tech workers in Silicon Valley hold graduate degrees, Saxenian (*AnnaLee Saxenian, "Silicon Valley's New Immigrant Entrepreneurs"*) found that 40% of the Chinese and 55% of the Indian-born technology workers had at least a master's degree. The phenomenon was not unique to Northern California; nationally the number of doctorates awarded to Chinese students tripled between 1990 and 1996, from 477 to 1680, and for Indian students the figure doubled, from 346 to 692.

However, despite being better educated, these foreign-born workers had the same earnings as their lesser educated native-born counterparts. To break through this apparent earnings limitation, many immigrants have chosen to form their own high-tech companies in Silicon Valley.

Immigrant Entrepreneurs

To understand the growing number of immigrant entrepreneurs in Silicon Valley, it is helpful to review the number of Chinese and Indian executives already working in high-tech companies. In 1998, Dun & Bradstreet found that 24% of Silicon Valley's high-tech companies had Chinese or Indian executives. Many of these foreign-born executives, facing the limitations on salary that Saxenian documented, have started their own high-tech firms in large numbers. In 1998, 2,001 Chinese-run and 774 Indian-run new businesses accounted for $16.8 ***billion*** in sales and over 58,000 jobs in Silicon Valley. . . .

Immigrants Creating Networks

Scholars have long noted that new immigrants begin their assimilation by forming networks with other recent immigrants, particularly those from their own homelands. Italian and German immigrants, for example, formed close-net communities in the early 1900s, combining resources when possible to build business associations, churches, and fraternal societies. In much the same way, today's Silicon Valley immigrants have done the same, forming local social and professional networks. Saxenian found, however, that unlike the associations of old, the new high-tech immigrants used networks to "enhance their own entrepreneurial opportunities as well as the dynamism of the regional economy."

The organizations formed do not act like traditional associations (e.g., a union or chamber of commerce). Rather, most are focussed on the professional and technical needs of the high-tech immigrant entrepreneur. Common activities for these new networks include seminars on typical American business topics such as writing a business plan, negotiation skills, and in some cases even the very "90s" topic of "stress management." The goal is often to show immigrant entrepreneurs that traditional ethnic business models, often tied to family relationships, do not work as well in the high-tech global workplace.

Interestingly, these modern networks bridge many divides that still exist for new immigrants. For example, the Chinese Software Professionals Association conducts its meetings in English, so immigrants of many regions and dialects can communicate in a common and business-friendly language. And as evidence of the Indian-American community's similar successes in working together and overcoming bigotry and intolerance in their homeland, Saxenian quotes author V.S. Naipaul: "Indians developed something [overseas] that they would have never known in India—a sense of belonging to an Indian community. This feeling of community could override religion and caste."

Success of High-Tech Immigrant Networks

These networks have combined with technology to allow immigrant entrepreneurs the ability to build international businesses that only a decade or two ago would have been solely possible for a large multinational corporation. By leveraging the strengths of American and overseas markets, Chinese and Indian-born executives are able to bring benefits to America and in many cases their homelands.

For example, Saxenian found that Taiwan-born immigrants have successfully tapped into Silicon Valley's design and development strengths and the Hsinchu, Taiwan area's manufacturing capacity and proximity to Asian markets to economically benefit both America and Taiwan.

Likewise, she discovered that Indian-born immigrants have successfully built 24-hour software development operations by exploiting the time difference between California and India.

Related to these global networks, Saxenian makes the interesting observation that Taiwan came through the recent Asian economic crisis far better than other Asian countries; she offers the hypothesis that the region's strong ties to Silicon Valley through high-tech immigrant networks deserves partial credit.

Conclusion

Saxenian concludes her study by noting that "the new immigrant entrepreneurs thus foster economic development directly, by creating new jobs and wealth, as well as indirectly, by coordinating the information flows and providing the linguistic and cultural know-how that promote trade and investment flows with their home countries." She argues that the successes of these skilled high-tech workers "suggests that California should resist the view that immigration and trade are zero-sum processes. We need to encourage the immigration of skilled workers, while simultaneously devoting resources to improving the education of native workers."

Source: American Immigration Law Foundation, "Skilled Immigrants and Silicon Valley," *Immigrant Policy Reports*, July 1999, 1–3. (www.ailf.org)

1.8. Immigrants Help Late Twentieth-Century Massachusetts Economy

On the East Coast as well as the West Coast, immigrants are contributing significantly to the vitality of the American economy. A year 2000 study, "The Changing Workforce: Immigrants and the New Economy in Massachusetts," discusses how newcomers are sustaining the manufacturing sector, are contributing meaningfully to the service industry, and are highly represented in professional occupations, particularly in science and engineering.

The image of a economically depressed New England, suffering from urban flight, closing factories, and dwindling population, has been indelibly printed on the American imagination since the 1970s. However, there is a new New England on the rise, fueled largely by immigration, that refutes the decades-old perception of a region losing ground in the modern era, according to a new study titled "The Changing Workforce: Immigrants and the New Economy in Massachusetts."

Massachusetts has always had a high percentage of immigrants among its population. In 1910, at the zenith of immigration to the U.S., 31.5 percent of all Massachusetts residents were foreign-born. This number peaked in 1920, with 1.088 million foreign-born residents living in the state. However, by 1970, the state's immigrant population, mostly retired and aging, had declined to less than 500,000 persons—less than half of the 1920 figure—and accounted for only 8.7 percent of the state's population. Massachusetts also began to experience a population loss due to domestic out-migration and a declining birth rate.

In the 1980s, however, immigrants from different parts of the globe began to settle in Massachusetts. By the time of the 1990 Census, only 37 percent of Massachusetts' immigrant population had roots in Europe, contrasting with immigration before 1970, when nearly 80 percent of foreign-born residents were from Europe and Canada. The new immigrants, from Asia, Latin America, and Puerto Rico, and living both in central cities and suburban developments, helped to offset the regional population loss and contribute to the workforce. In fact, if it were not for foreign immigration, the population of Massachusetts would actually be shrinking, and would have shrunk every decade since the 1970s. Of all the children in Massachusetts under 18, approximately one in four is either an immigrant or the child of an immigrant parent.

Immigrants from outside the United States have contributed in a substantial way to the growth of Massachusetts' residential labor force. Foreign immigrants were responsible for 82 percent of the net growth in the state's civilian labor force between the mid-1980s and 1997.

In addition, those newcomers who have come since 1990 are more likely than earlier immigrants to have a college or advanced degree. Due in large part to the universities in Massachusetts, more of that state's foreign-born residents are more highly educated than their national counterparts.

College degree or not, the labor force participation rate of immigrants versus native-born in Massachusetts is very close. Male immigrants are actually more likely to actively participate in the labor market than their native-born counterparts, both nationally and in Massachusetts. Interestingly, immigrants who seemingly face the most hurdles to gaining employment—those with only a high school diploma or less—are actually more active in the labor force than their native-born counterparts.

Importance to Manufacturing

The mills of Massachusetts are kept humming in large part by foreign-born workers. More immigrants are employed in the manufacturing sector in Massachusetts—22 out of every 100 employees—than in any other sector, including professional service industries. Despite the large number of manufacturing jobs lost in the last 15 years in Massachusetts, this sector continues to employ approximately half a million people and plays a disproportionately important role in the state economy because it generates a large portion of the goods that Massachusetts exports to other regions and nations. Immigrants are nearly twice as likely as native-born to be employed in the manufacturing industries, followed by the personal services industry, including household help, hairdressing salons and laundries. Immigrants are two to four times as likely as foreign born to be working in these areas.

On average, immigrant workers achieve annual earnings equal to 75 percent of the earnings of their native-born counterparts in Massachusetts. From 1995 to 1997, the median annual earnings of full-time, year-round immigrant workers was approximately $25,400, compared to $34,200 for native-born workers. However, the higher the educational attainment by immigrants, the more paycheck parity they achieve compared with native-born workers. Immigrant workers with a bachelor's or more advanced degree earned 94 to 100 percent of native-born counterparts, with a median annual earning of $46,000 per year.

Many Immigrants High-Skilled

Within the professional occupations, immigrants demonstrated attainment when compared to native-born professionals. Immigrants are more than twice as likely as native-born professionals to be university and college teachers. Just over 2 percent of all foreign-born workers held these positions, as opposed to less than one percent of native-born professionals. Additionally, foreign-born professionals are more likely than the native-born to be employed as engineers, physical scientists and computer scientists. The study also shows that immigrants become more upwardly mobile the longer they are in the U.S., with only 15 percent of those who had migrated to the U.S. before 1980 living below the poverty line, including the elderly, as opposed to a higher rate for immigrants who had arrived in thc 1980s.

Conclusion

As this report clearly shows, the face of Massachusetts is changing. Its immigrant population, and thus its future citizenry, is more ethnically diverse than ever before. These "new" immigrants are also more economically diverse than previous waves of the foreign-born, keeping the manufacturing sector alive, working in the service industries, and participating in highly-skilled jobs centered around Massachusetts' many universities. The newcomers with little or no education are more likely than native-born Americans to be employed in the labor force—they clearly want to and do work. While these newcomers to Massachusetts do face challenges—and the study contains recommendations to help meet those challenges—it clearly shows that short-term pain can equal long-term gain for both the immigrants who, over time, gain parity with the native-born, and with the citizenry, who gain in revitalized central cities and in keeping certain economic sectors upon which Massachusetts depends, such as manufacturing, alive. This study will surely contribute positively to an informed public debate within Massachusetts about the contributions that the changing workforce is bringing to the state.

Source: American Immigration Law Foundation, "Newcomers Help Massachusetts Economy," *Immigrant Policy Reports*, January 2000, 1–3. (www.AILF.org)

ANNOTATED SELECTED BIBLIOGRAPHY

Bernard, William, ed. *American Immigration Policy: A Reappraisal*. New York: Harper and Brothers, 1950. Presents material showing the economic benefits of immigration from the nineteenth century through the late 1940s.

Borjas, George. *Friends or Strangers: The Impact of Immigrants on the U.S. Economy*. New York: Basic Books, 1990. Stresses the negative impact of immigrants on the post–World War II American economy.

Briggs, Vernon M. *Mass Immigration and the National Interest*. Armonk, N.Y.: M. E. Sharpe, 1992. Discusses American immigration policy and congressional immigration legislation, primarily from the 1960s into the 1990s, particularly in terms of the nation's changing labor market.

Brown, Peter, and Henry Shue, eds. *The Border That Joins: Mexican Migrants and U.S. Responsibility*. Totowa, N.J.: Rowman and Littlefield, 1983. Essays discuss the history, attitudes, and economic push and pull of Mexican immigrants in regard to the United States.

Busey, Samuel. *Immigration: Its Evils and Consequences*. New York: De Witt and Davenport, 1856. Reprint, New York: Arno Press, 1969. Presents economic disadvantages of immigrants in America's first major wave of immigration.

Calavita, Kitty. *Inside the State: The Bracero Program, Immigration, and the I.N.S.* New York: Routledge, Chapman, and Hall, 1992. Concerns the beginning and growth of the Bracero program which brought, by contract, Mexican workers to the United States from 1942 to 1964.

Duignan, Peter, and L. H. Gann, eds. *The Debate in United States over Immigration*. Stanford, Calif.: Hoover Institution Press, 1998. Focuses on the economic impact of immigration at the turn of the twenty-first century.

Fairchild, Henry. *Immigration*. New York: Macmillan, 1913. Includes material on the negative effect of the second major wave of immigration on America.

Glazer, Nathan, ed. *Clamor at the Gates: The New American Immigration*. San Francisco: ISC Press, 1985. One section concerns immigrants and the economy which includes employment trends, wages, and immigrant entrepreneurship.

Hofstetter, Richard, ed. *U.S. Immigration Policy*. Durham, N.C.: Duke University Press, 1984. Much of this work is devoted to a variety of economic issues related to immigration.

Muller, Thomas, and Thomas Espenshade. *The Fourth Wave: California's Newest Immigrants*. Washington, D.C.: Urban Institute, 1985. Discusses the economic impact of post-1965 immigration on California, which has received the largest number of new immigrants.

Simon, Julian. *The Economic Consequences of Immigration*. Cambridge, Mass.: Basil Blackwell, 1989. Presents the positive contributions of immigrants to the American economy.

ORGANIZATIONS AND WEB SITES

Cato Institute: www.cato.org

Center for Immigration Studies: www.cis.org

Immigration Forum: www.immigrationforum.org

Social Contract: www.thesocialcontract.com

Urban Institute: www.urban.org

2

Should Humanitarian Concerns Dictate U.S. Immigration Policy?

With extensive space, a proclaimed freedom of religion, and a democratic form of government, the United States has been the haven for many people escaping the ravages of war and of nature; political, religious, and ethnic persecution; and totalitarian governments. From statements made by George Washington, through the nineteenth and early twentieth centuries, particularly in the decades since World War II, the United States has declared itself a humanitarian nation. However, many, perhaps most, Americans have over the years held that this value was not unlimited. Indeed, Americans have wrestled for generations with the question of how many and which immigrants should be permitted to come. And for all the rhetoric about welcoming "your tired, your poor, your huddled masses yearning to breathe free," Americans have been reluctant to take in too many newcomers who are poor, have health problems, and are markedly culturally different from "mainstream" Americans.

Through almost two centuries people came to the North American colonies of Great Britain with a mixture of economic and religious motivations. The strongly religious Puritans in New England and the Quakers in Pennsylvania hungered for land and vigorously engaged in commercial activity. Meanwhile the plantation owners in the South showed some interest in establishing Church of England parishes. Religious beliefs, together with influences from the eighteenth-century European Enlightenment, contributed a humanitarian dimension to the evolving American culture. While this was particularly manifested in concern for extended family members, neighbors, and those of one's own denomination or group, it often did not extend to "others." The Native Americans, whose land was coveted, were demonized; ethnocentric Englishmen manifested a dislike for the Germans and the Scotch-Irish; and Protestants were inhospitable to the religiously different minority Catholics and Jews.

Many of these attitudes were carried into the national period. George Washington, while speaking to a group of persons of Irish background at the end of the Revolutionary War in 1783, proclaimed that "the bosom of America is open to receive not only the Opulent and respectable Stranger, but the oppressed and persecuted of all Nations and Religions."[1] Still, in 1790, amid the first tremors of the French Revolution and slave unrest in Haiti, he signed a naturalization law passed by Congress that stated "that any alien, being a free white person . . . may be admitted to become a citizen."[2] This statute markedly restricted Washington's earlier welcome to persons of all nations, with race, a divisive factor already in the United States, now becoming a decisive factor in who might become a naturalized American. Within that important limitation, the country did provide a refuge for persons fleeing revolution and war in France, Ireland, and Haiti in the early years of the republic.

Then in the 1840s, with the nation's first major wave of immigration, primarily from Ireland and Germany, the humanitarianism of the American people was tested and strained. Not only were the numbers of newcomers unprecedented in the experience of the new nation, but, particularly with the Irish fleeing from famine in the late 1840s, many of these immigrants were poor, often desperately so, and ill. Americans were jarred by the newcomers' peasant backgrounds and class differences and the increasing cost of maintaining growing numbers in poorhouses and prisons. For many native-born Americans, living in an age of aggressive Protestant evangelism and expansion, the Roman Catholicism of many of the immigrants proved most disconcerting of all. It was one thing to be charitable to those in need who were seen in some way as your own kind, and another thing to be helpful to the poor, especially in large numbers, who were different.

From Maryland to Massachusetts, Americans worried about the costs of receiving so many poor people. The *Baltimore American*, reporting on the foreigners in the almshouses in the major American cities in 1835, wrote, "Would there not be a saving of expense if these five thousand and odd should be shipped back to their respective homes?"[3] In the following year a Massachusetts legislative committee petitioned the state's representatives in Washington "to use their endeavors to obtain the passage of a law by Congress to prevent the introduction of foreign paupers into this country."[4] The Reverend W. A. Lord, a New England divine, speaking on "National Hospitality" in regard to the wave of new immigrants in 1855, stated that "as the flood has increased in size, it has brought much of the dregs of European society" who "have but little claim upon our charity."[5]

Still others, in speeches and writings, called upon the more religious and humanitarian aspects of American society to welcome the newcomers and to aid those who were in distress. In 1797 Dr. Joseph Priestley, an emigré scientist living in Pennsylvania, reminded a group, gathered in Philadelphia to hear him speak on American character, that they or their "not very remote ancestors" had come from another country, that with the help of providence they had improved their circumstances, and that now "poor emigrants are entitled to assistance." In 1841 Samuel Goodrich, a pro-immigrant advocate, wrote, "Let us by no means join in the popular outcry against foreigners. . . . Let us rather receive them as friends, and give them welcome to our country. . . . Let our country be the asylum of the oppressed of all lands."[6]

In 1853 Edward Everett, a renowned orator, reminded his audience of the benefits to the country from immigration. "The constant influx into America of stout and efficient hands supplies the greatest want in a new country, which is that of labor, gives value to land, and facilitates the execution of every species of private enterprise and public work." Consequently, he urged generosity to those among the newcomers who were caught in poverty and illness. "Massachusetts and New York might do a worse thing with a portion of their surplus means than feed the hungry, clothe the naked, give home to the stranger, and kindle the spark of reason in the mind of the poor foreign lunatic."[7]

After the Civil War, and particularly with the advent of the second major wave of immigration after 1880, more varied religious, ethnic, and nonsectarian agencies developed specifically to aid immigrants. Among them were the Italian Welfare Society, the Immigrants' Protective League, and the Hebrew Immigrant Aid Society. But very little public assistance went to help immigrants adjust to a new land; indeed, Americans had a marked reluctance to use tax money to help the poor, in general, and the immigrant poor, in particular. Additionally, mainstream private charitable groups at this time made a distinction between the deserving and the undeserving poor, and most often the culturally different immigrants were designated as undeserving.

Public responsibility for processing immigrants rested on the states, rather than the federal government before 1891. Some states and municipalities made efforts to protect their citizens from arriving immigrants who carried diseases by instituting quarantine procedures. They also tended to handle immigrants roughly when they ran afoul of the law or sought public relief. A few states, like New York, which received the greatest share of immigrants in the nineteenth century, made some limited efforts to protect the newcomers. The New York Protection of Emigrants law enacted in 1848 attempted to stop the preying on the newly arrived by robbery and other schemes to relieve them of their money and belongings.

While such efforts as the New York law to protect immigrants from con men and robbers manifested aspects of American humanitarianism, counter tendencies also surfaced, particularly in dealing with people who were "more different." The Chinese, Japanese, and other Asians suffered very harsh treatment. Anti-Semitism and anti-Catholicism thrived during the wave of "new" immigration from the 1880s to World War I. Immigration restriction organizations like the American Protective Association appealed particularly to rural, small-town Americans fearful of an invasive urban culture they saw as "foreign." As the numbers of poor people coming to America rose so, too, did the agitation to limit their numbers. Francis Walker, a leading economist and president of the Massachusetts Institute of Technology, drawn to nativism by his fear of labor and social unrest and a replacing of native stock by new "inferior" immigrants, wrote in 1899 that

> Charity begins at home. . . . For one, I believe it is time that we should take a rest, and give our social, political, and industrial system some chance to recuperate. The problems which so sternly confront us to-day are serious enough, without being complicated and aggravated by the addition of some millions of Hungarians, Bohemians, Poles, south Italians, and Russian Jews.[8]

Walker's words were part of a growing anti-immigrant chorus which was putting increased pressure on the federal government to restrict the inflow of the foreign-born from Eastern and Southern Europe.

During the Progressive era, from the late nineteenth century through World War I, when many Americans turned to "the problem" of the cities and sought to purify everything from the water supply to government, reform took two very different positions in regard to the immigrants. Many of those who wanted a more rational, modernized politics were very critical of immigrants, particularly the poor, less educated ones who sustained patronage-wielding city bosses with their votes. On the other hand were the considerable number of reformers, particularly well-educated young people, including those who established and staffed settlement houses in the immigrant sections of the cities, who dedicated time and effort to improve the living and working conditions of poor immigrants and convert them, or at least their children, into dutiful "Americans." Settlement house workers, like Jane Addams and Lillian Wald, not only taught English and other subjects and provided social services to help immigrants to adapt to American middle-class values, but they proposed and fought for city and state legislation that would improve tenement living and factory working conditions. Such efforts led to the enactment of housing standards and fire protection, somewhat shorter hours, and more sanitary and safer conditions of work.

With the increased number of newcomers, the anti-immigration forces gained support and were able to persuade Congress to pass a literacy requirement in 1917. The entrance of the United States into World War I heightened American fears about immigrant loyalties and "hyphenated" Americans in the country and led to stepped up "Americanization" campaigns at work. Anti-immigrant fever teemed during the war, contributing to prohibition against alcohol, which was associated with Germans and Irish of doubtful loyalty, and calls for immigration restriction. After World War I, with a backlash against idealism, the restrictionists succeeded in having Congress limit the overall number of immigrants and, through quotas, to reduce markedly the numbers from Southern and Eastern Europe. Asians were given no quotas at all.

The harshness of these immigration laws arose in large part from a reemergence in the post–World War I years of the continuing role of race in America. Related was the conflicting attitudes among Americans about human nature. Reformers, who had made some headway in the Progressive years after the turn of the century, believed in the ability to reshape human behavior through a changed environment and education. Many of the restrictionists who gained increased influence by the 1920s believed in the durability of "character" traits in people—that nature not nurture ruled. Immigration concerns and policy were informed by that debate.

In 1929 the American people faced a major challenge. The Great Depression, which lasted through most of the 1930s, drained charitable resources domestically and prodded the withdrawal of humanitarian concern for immigrants. It was a decade in which more people left or were forced out of the United States than entered it. Deportations were particularly severe in the Southwest against Mexican "aliens" and even some citizens of Mexican background. This general attitude also hardened Americans in the face of the growing persecution of Jews in Germany. No special effort was made to assist refugees or potential refugees from Germany, and admittance was refused even to boatloads of persons, including many children, who reached American ports.

By the end of World War II, a shift in attitude began, particularly toward those who had suffered and fled from Germany and the Soviet Union. Through concerted efforts of American religious lobbies on Congress, special provisions were made to bring several hundred thousand displaced persons who were in camps in central Europe to the United States. By 1952, as the Cold War was developing, Congress showed its willingness to support a refugee policy, particularly for persons escaping from Communist countries. This policy saw its first major implementation when, following a failed revolution in Hungary in 1956, special provisions were made for many of the refugees from the conflict to enter the United States. They were given limited government assistance on arriving in the United States.

When large numbers of Cubans fled to the United States, beginning in 1959 with the rise to power of Fidel Castro, the American government developed a well-coordinated program of assistance to receive and settle these refugees. In the 1970s the United States again adjusted its immigration and refugee policies to accommodate a large number of allies and escapees from America's failed military endeavors in Southeast Asia, mostly from Vietnam but also some from Cambodia and Laos. In general, these were people who had worked with the American effort to stem the expansion of Communist forces in those countries. They too received some government assistance for resettlement in the United States. Other refugees came from Communist China and from the leftist regime in Nicaragua, and Jews came from the Soviet Union.

During the Cold War, persons persecuted by right-wing, but supposedly anti-Communist, dictatorships friendly to the United States were not given refugee status in this country; such was the fate of Salvadoreans and Haitians. Critics of this American policy, such as Alex Stepick, a professor of sociology and anthropology at Florida International University, asked, "Will foreign policy and covert racist concerns continue to predominate U.S. asylum policy, or will broad humanitarian concerns overcome the recent historical tradition?"[9] No clear policy followed. American officials did give some consideration to refugees from Iran after 1979 and some other Middle Eastern countries, which were not Communist but with whom the United States did not have good relations. Some limited number of persons were admitted who were refugees from natural disasters. But, through the 1970s, U.S. policy continued to favor refugees escaping from communism and to refuse those persons fleeing from poverty or political, cultural, or religious repression in non-Communist countries.

Under pressure from civil rights and humanitarian groups and triggered by a large new exodus from Cuba, the federal government enacted the Refugee Act of 1980. It stated that any person can qualify as a refugee in the United States who is fearful of returning to his or her country because of persecution "on account of race, religion, nationality, membership in a particular social group, or political opinion."[10] This law thus recognized persecution regardless of the ideology of a regime or its relations to the United States. The annual refugee limit was raised from some 17,000 to 50,000, and it continued the right of the attorney general to admit additional refugees in emergency situations. In actuality, according to the Federation for American Immigration Reform, "the lowest number of adjustments since then was 84,288 in FY'98. The number has consistently been well in excess of 100,000 since FY'91 and the average FY'80 to FY'96 has been above 110,000."[11]

With many millions of refugees throughout the world, among the questions facing the United States have been how many of these persons and which of them can or should be admitted into this country each year. In a commencement address given at Portland State University, Oregon, in June 1998, President Bill Clinton held that anti-immigrant attacks are "not only wrong, it's un-American." He lauded immigrants as "the most adventurous, the most innovative and the most industrious of people." The president added: "Let me state my view unequivocally: I believe new immigrants are good for America."[12] Dan Stein, executive director of the Federation for American Immigration Reform, retorted, "If the president is endorsing over 1 million a year in immigration, then what he's endorsing is urban sprawl, overcrowding, congestion, the destruction of our schools and a societal design that would be virtually unlivable for our grandchildren."[13]

Others in the last decades of the twentieth century have maintained that the United States is suffering from humanitarian overload and compassion fatigue. Lindsey Grant, a State Department official, wrote in 1988, "The natural and generous impulse of many Americans is to welcome the immigrant, particularly if they know him . . . I would argue that our conscience begin at home." He considers immigration to be threatening to the United States and no real solution to population problems abroad.[14]

Nevertheless, the advocates of an increased humanitarian American immigration policy have continued to voice their deeply felt concerns. Andrew Shacknove, a proponent of a more open American refugee policy, reminded his readers in 1988 that "few forms of human misery are equal to being refugees who by definition face a challenge to life or liberty that threatens their very survival." Morally, the United States in regard to refugees has "the duty to avoid depriving persons, including foreigners, of life and liberty, unless some compelling state interest justified doing so," and this principle is based on "our equal moral worth as human beings."[15]

There thus remains a controversy about America's humanitarian role in regard to potential immigrants and refugees. While most commentators maintain that generosity is a part of the American national character, most also hold that it is not unlimited. The question facing American policy makers and the general population is what portion of the many needy people worldwide can and should be admitted by the United States as immigrants and refugees. There are those who suffer from religious and political persecution, from natural disasters, and from lack of economic necessities and opportunities. Among the needy, do we give preference to those whose conditions are most dire, or those who are from friendly or unfriendly countries, or those who add diversity or do not add diversity to the United States, or those who bring skills the country needs?

NOTES

1. "George Washington to the Members of the Volunteer Association and Other Inhabitants of the Kingdom of Ireland Who Have Lately Arrived in the City of New York," in *The Writings of George Washington*, ed. John C. Fitzpatrick (Washington, D.C.: U.S. Government Printing Office, 1938), 27, 253–54.

2. *The Naturalization Act of 1790*, U.S. Statues, 1st Cong., 2d sess., 1, 103.

3. *Baltimore American*, October 3, 1835.

4. Massachusetts House or Representatives, "The Introduction into the United States of Paupers from Foreign Countries," 24th Cong., 1st sess. April 18, 1836, H. Doc. 219, 1–3.

5. W. A. Lord, *A Tract for the Times: National Hospitality* (Montpelier, Vt.: 1855), 21–44.

6. Samuel Griswold Goodrich, *Ireland and the Irish* (Boston, 1841), 111–17.

7. Edward Everett, "Discovery of America," June 1, 1853, in *Orations and Speeches* (Boston: Little, Brown, 1892), vol. 3, 213–16, 220–23.

8. Francis A. Walker, *Economics and Statistics* (New York: Henry Holt, 1899), vol. 2, 437–50.

9. Alex Stepick, "Haitian Boat People: A Study in the Conflicting Forces Shaping U.S. Immigration Policy," in *U.S. Immigration Policy*, ed. Richard R. Hofstetter (Durham, N.C.: Duke University Press, 1984), 196.

10. The Refugee Act of 1980, Section 101, in "Refugees and Asylum." *Issue Brief*, Federation for American Immigration Reform (FAIR), November 1999, 1 (www.fairus.org).

11. Ibid., 3.

12. Bill Clinton quoted in John Harris, "President Denounces Policies That 'Exclude Immigrants,' " *Washington Post*, June 14, 1998, A6.

13. Ibid.

14. Lindsey Grant, "How Many Americans?" in *U.S. Immigration in the 1980s: Reappraisal and Reform*, ed. David Simcox (Boulder, Colo.: Westview Press, 1988), 279–80.

15. Andrew E. Schacknove, "American Duties to Refugees: Their Scope and Limits," in *Open Borders? Closed Societies? The Ethical and Political Issues*, ed. Mark Gibney (Westport, Conn.: Greenwood Press, 1988), 131, 136.

DOCUMENTS

2.1. Call for the Deportation of Poor Immigrants in the 1830s

Many Americans were turned against a humanitarian concern for immigrants who were poor and in need of help by a strong resistance to taxes, a deep adherence to individualism, and a dislike of the foreign-born. The Baltimore American, *in 1835, reported on the increasing cost of almshouses, which were populated by a growing number of immigrants. They called for the deportation of foreign-born paupers.*

A principal subject of self-congratulation to Americans, in comparing their country with those of Europe, is the exemption we enjoy from the burden of a large pauper population—a burden oppressive from the moral evils attending it, as from the tax it inflicts on a community. By the unexampled facility which all foreigners, without distinction in character, enjoy in settling among us, we are in a fair way of being deprived of this cause of congratulation. In the almshouses of the four principal American cities, the foreign paupers exceed in number the native, and the same proportion exists in many other places.

The city government of Boston lately appointed an agent, Mr. Simonds, to visit the houses of industry, correction, and reformation in various parts of the northern and middle states. One of the results of his inquiries is that in the four almshouses of New York, Philadelphia, Baltimore, and Boston, there are 4,786 Americans and 5,303 foreigners. *Would there not be a saving of expense if these five thousand and odd should be shipped back to their respective homes?* . . . The paupers *ought* to be sent "home."

Source: Baltimore American, October 3, 1835.

2.2. Let America Be Hospitable to Poor Sufferers from Abroad

While the growing influx of poor Irish immigrants in the 1840s and 1850s drew much criticism from some Americans, there were others who out of general humanitarian and religious con-

cerns or out of a particular interest in the Irish themselves called upon Americans to extend to the newcomers "the hand of encouragement and sympathy." One of these, Samuel Goodrich, authored a book, Ireland and the Irish, *in 1841, in which he called for empathy and benevolence toward immigrants and the Irish in particular.*

Let us by no means join in the popular outcry against foreigners coming to our country, and partaking of its privileges. They will come, whether we will or no; and is it wise to meet them with inhospitality, and thus turn their hearts against us? Let us rather receive them as friends, and give them welcome to our country. Let us rather say, "The harvest before us is indeed great, and the laborers are few: come, go with us, and we will do thee good." Our hills, and valleys, and rivers, stretch from ocean to ocean, belting the entire continent of the New World; and over this rich and boundless domain, Providence has poured the atmosphere of liberty. Let these poor sufferers come and breathe it freely. Let our country be the asylum of the oppressed of all lands. Let those who come bent down with the weight of European tithes and taxation, here throw off the load, and stand erect in freedom. Let those who have dwelt in the chill shadows of the Castle of Ignorance, erected by kings, and fortified by priestcraft, come here, and be warmed by the free sunlight of knowledge. Let those whose limbs have been cramped by chains, those whose minds have been fettered by hereditary error, come here, and, seeing happiness, be permitted freely to pursue it.

Let us at least extend the hand of encouragement and sympathy to the Irish. Their story for centuries is but a record of sorrows and oppressions. . . .

Let us be especially guarded against two sources of prejudice, to which we are peculiarly liable. In the first place, in our personal experience, we are familiar with the most ignorant and unfortunate of the Irish nation. We see, in servile employments, those who have been exposed to all the debasing influences that degrade mankind. Is it fair to draw from these a standard by which to judge the whole people? Let us rather ask ourselves where there is another nation, who have been so long trampled down by oppression; who have been born in poverty and nursed in adversity; who have inherited little from the past but sorrow, and can bequeath nothing to the future but hope—where is there a people so wronged, that has yet preserved so many virtues? How gallantly, indeed, do Irish wit, and cheerfulness, and hospitality, and patriotism, ride on the wreck of individual hopes, and sparkle through the very waves of adversity!

Let us beware of prejudice from another source. We read English books, papers, and pamphlets. We read them under the inspiring influence of Britain's great name. Say what we may of that country, the British empire is a mighty power, and her literature is even more potent than her armies and her navies. It is by this she casts a spell over the world, and binds the nations in moral fetters. We see in the English people nearly the same exclusive love of country that burned in the bosom of the ancient Roman. This spirit animates every offspring of the English press. It is this which leads them to vindicate the tyranny of the government in Ireland, by portraying the Irish as an untamable race, deaf to reason, and only to be ruled by the harsh inflictions of power. Let us, Americans, see that our minds are not driven from the moorings of justice, by this sinister current in which they are placed. Influenced by such considerations as these, let us by all fair means bring about a good understanding between the Irish emigrants and society. Let us deal gently with them, even with their errors; and thus we shall win their confidence; thus they may be persuaded to take counsel of the good, the wise, and the virtuous, and not throw themselves into the arms of those who flatter their vices and minister to their passions, but to use and abuse them.

Let this reasonable and just policy mark our conduct towards the grown-up Irish among us; and in regard to their children, let us individually and collectively use our best endeavors to bestow upon them the benefits of education. But let us remember that even an attempt to educate the Irish will fail, if it be not founded in a recognition of the elements of their national character, quick perception, a keen sense of justice, and ready resentment of wrong. If over these, prejudice, suspicion, and pride, have thrown their shadows, let us adapt the instruction we would offer to the light they can bear. In this way, a numerous people may be redeemed from misery to happiness, and rendered a blessing instead of a curse to our country.

Source: Samuel Griswold Goodrich, *Ireland and the Irish* (Boston, 1841), 111–17.

2.3. America's Surplus in 1850s Should Help Support Immigrants in Need

As the influx of newcomers increased through the 1840s and 1850s into America's first major wave of immigration, nativist opposition became more vocal and more politically active. Edward Everett, a well-known, mid-nineteenth-century American orator, was one of a considerable number of Americans who rejected nativist attitudes. Referring to both religious dictums and secular examples he advocated that the people of the United States, out of their surplus and despite temporary incon-

veniences, should show benevolence toward strangers in need. Concern for immigrants was part of a pre–Civil War humanitarianism and American "exceptionalism" that included efforts for the better treatment of the blind and the insane, for temperance, and for the abolition of slavery.

Of late years, from three to four hundred thousand immigrants are registered at the several custom-houses, as arriving in this country in the course of a year. It is probable that a third as many more enter by the Canadian frontier. Not much less than two millions of immigrants are supposed to have entered the United States in the last ten years; and it is calculated that there are living at the present day in the United States five millions of persons, foreigners who have immigrated since 1790, and their descendants. . . .

[The] "Celtic Exodus," as it has been aptly called, is to all the parties immediately connected with it one of the most important events of the day. To the emigrants themselves it may be regarded as a passing from death to life. . . . the constant influx into America of stout and efficient hands supplies the greatest want in a new country, which is that of labor, gives value to land, and facilitates the execution of every species of private enterprise and public work.

I am not insensible to the temporary inconveniences which are to be set off against these advantages, on both sides of the water. Much suffering attends the emigrant there, on his passage, and after his arrival. It is possible that the value of our native labor may have been depressed by too sudden and extensive a supply from abroad; and it is certain that our asylums and almshouses are crowded with foreign inmates, and that the resources of public and private benevolence have been heavily drawn upon. These are considerable evils, but they have perhaps been exaggerated.

It must be remembered, in the first place, that the immigration daily pouring in from Europe is by no means a pauper immigration. On the contrary it is already regarded with apprehension abroad, as occasioning a great abstraction of capital. How the case may be in Great Britain and Ireland, I have seen no precise statement; but it is asserted on apparently good grounds, that the consumption and abstraction of capital caused by immigration from Germany amounts annually to . . . fifteen millions of our currency.

No doubt, foreign immigration is attended with an influx of foreign pauperism. . . . It is said, that, owing to some defect in our [Massachusetts] system or its administration, we support more than our share of needy foreigners. They are sent in upon us from other States. New York, as the greatest seaport, must be exposed also to more than her proportionate share of the burden. However the evil arises, it may no doubt be mitigated by judicious legislation; and in the meantime Massachusetts and New York might do a worse thing with a portion of their surplus means than feed the hungry, clothe the naked, give a home to the stranger, and kindle the spark of reason in the mind of the poor foreign lunatic, even though that lunatic may have been (as I am ashamed, for the credit of humanity, to say has happened) set on shore in the night from a coasting-vessel, and found in the morning in the fields, half dead with cold, and hunger, and fright.

But you say, "They are foreigners." Well, do we owe no duties to foreigners?

Source: Edward Everett, "Discovery of America," June 1, 1853, in *Orations and Speeches* (Boston: Little, Brown, 1892), vol. 3, 213–16, 220–23.

2.4. Reject Sentimental Charity for Immigrants Regarded as Inferior in the 1850s

For some Americans, including such religious leaders as the Reverend W. H. Lord, immigrants were too culturally and ethnically different to merit their humanitarian concern. Lord, writing in 1855, at the height of the nativist movement, justified his harshness by demonizing immigrants, agreeing with those who believed that they belonged to the "devil's regiment." This minister called on Americans to reject any "sentimental philanthropy" on behalf of poor immigrants.

[T]he questions arising out of the great influx of foreign population to our land, are of sufficient moral, social and religious consequence to demand the most careful investigation, and the utmost candor in discussion. . . . We must look at them in the light of the past; in the light of those general laws which have ever moulded and controlled the social and political forms and movements of our race. We must look at them as matters, whose decision is to affect the future more than the present; the countless millions of our posterity, more than ourselves; and the entire civilization of the world, more than the interests of any party, religious sect or national government. . . .

That the character of the emigrants, as a whole, has somewhat depreciated with the increase of their number is susceptible of easy proof. Formerly the emigration from the old countries was confined to that class which possessed both substance and intelligence, and were well fitted, after a suitable interval, to become useful and valuable citizens. But as the flood has increased in size, it has brought much of the dregs of European society, and its stream has been foul with the sediment and drift of the old world. Multitudes have been brought to the land, whose expatriation has been assisted by the selfish generosity of their various governments—those who "left their country for their country's good," and have but little claim upon our charity or hospitality. They are of a class most fitly designated by Carlyle as the "devil's regiments of the line," for whom he would neither build "model prisons," nor enclose them in the loving embrace of a sentimental philanthropy. Thus at the same time that this tide has been draining Europe of her peasantry and artizans, it has drawn in also, by the helping hand of foreign states, far too many criminals and paupers. These, like heavy and decaying substances, are for the most part stranded in the large cities where they land.

Source: W. A. Lord, *A Tract for the Times: National Hospitality* (Montpelier, Vt., 1855), 5, 21–44.

2.5. "Give Me Your Tired, Your Poor," 1880s

As America entered its second major wave of immigration in the 1880s, Emma Lazarus, a poet who wrote about the oppression of Jewish people abroad and worked with refugees in New York City, expressed her humanitarian concerns for immigrants in her 1883 sonnet "New Colossus." This poem was placed on the pedestal of the Statue of Liberty in 1886 and has remained a powerful symbol on behalf of American openness to poor immigrants "yearning to breathe free."

Not like the brazen giant of Greek fame,
With conquering limbs astride from land to land
Here at our sea-washed, sunset gates shall stand
A mighty woman with a torch, whose flame
Is the imprisoned lightening, and her name
Mother of Exiles. From her beacon-handed
Glows world-wide welcome; her mild eyes command
The air-bridged harbor that twin cities frame
"Keep, ancient lands, your storied pomp!" cries she
With silent lips. "Give me your tired, your poor,
Your huddled masses yearning to breathe free,
The wretched refuse of your teeming shore.

Send these, the homeless, tempest-tost to me,
I lift my lamp beside the golden door!"

Source: Emma Lazarus, "The New Colossus," 1883. Inscribed at the base of the Statue of Liberty. In Morris Schoppes, *Emma Lazarus, Selections from Her Poetry and Prose* (New York: Cooperative Book League, 1944), 40–41.

2.6. Reject Loathsome New Immigrants; Charity Begins at Home

While the new turn-of-the century immigration gained humanitarian concern from some Americans, it was subjected to strong opposition from others. Francis Walker, a leading American economist, president of the Massachusetts Institute of Technology, and a member of the anti-immigrant New England elite, regarded the large influx of newcomers from Southern and Eastern Europe as a poisoning of America by a degraded and beaten people. In his 1899 work Economics and Statistics, *he advocated turning away these immigrants to save the culture and unity of the United States. According to Walker, "Charity begins at home."*

The immigrant of the former time came almost exclusively from western or northern Europe. We have now tapped great reservoirs of population then almost unknown to the passenger lists of our arriving vessels. Only a short time ago, the immigrants from southern Italy, Hungary, Austria, and Russia together made up hardly more than one per cent of our immigration. To-day the proportion has risen to something like forty per cent, and threatens soon to become fifty or sixty per cent, or even more. The entrance into our political, social, and industrial life of such vast masses of peasantry, degraded below our utmost conceptions, is a matter which no intelligent patriot can look upon without the gravest apprehension and alarm. These people have no history behind them which is of a nature to give encouragement. They have none of the inherited instincts and tendencies which made it comparatively easy to deal with the immigration of the olden time. They are beaten men from beaten races; representing the worst failures in the struggle for existence. Centuries are against them, as centuries were on the side of those who formerly came to us. They have none of the ideas and aptitudes which fit men to take up readily and easily the problem of self-care and self-government, such as belong to those who are descended from the tribes that met under the oak trees of old Germany to make laws and choose chieftains.

Their habits of life, again, are of the most revolting kind. Read the description given by Mr. Riis, of the police driving from the garbage dumps the miserable beings who try to burrow in those depths of unutterable filth and slime in order that they may eat and sleep there! Was it in cement like this that the foundations of our republic were laid? What effects must be produced upon our social standards, and upon the ambitions and aspirations of our people, by a contact so foul and loathsome? . . .

For it is never to be forgotten that self-defense is the first law of nature and of nations. If that man who careth not for his own household is worse than an infidel, the nation which permits its institutions to be endangered by any cause which can fairly be removed is guilty, not less in Christian than in natural law. Charity begins at home; and while the people of the United States have gladly offered an asylum to millions upon millions of the distressed and unfortunate of other lands and climes, they have no right to carry their hospitality one step beyond the line where American institutions, the American rate of wages, the American standard of living, are brought into serious peril. All the good the United States could do by offering indiscriminate hospitality to a few millions more of European peasants, whose places at home will, within another generation, be filled by others as miserable as themselves, would not compensate for any permanent injury done to our republic. Our highest duty to charity and to humanity is to make this great experiment, here, of free laws and educated labor, the most triumphant success that can possibly be attained. In this way we shall do far more for Europe than by allowing its city slums and its vast stagnant reservoirs of degraded peasantry to be drained off upon our soil. Within the decade between 1880 and 1890 five and a quarter millions of foreigners entered our ports! No nation in human history ever undertook to deal with such masses of alien population. That man must be a sentimentalist and an optimist beyond all bounds of reason who believes that we can take such a load upon the national stomach without a failure of assimilation, and without great danger to the healthy life of the nation. For one, I believe it is time that we should take a rest, and give our social, political, and industrial system some chance to recuperate. The problems which so sternly confront us to-day are serious enough, without being complicated and aggravated by the addition of some millions of Hungarians, Bohemians, Poles, south Italians, and Russian Jews.

Source: Francis A. Walker, *Economics and Statistics* (New York: Henry Holt, 1899), vol. 2, 437–50.

2.7. United States in the Late Twentieth Century Must Increase Its Humanitarianism

In the decades following World War II, American humanitarianism and immigration again became a debated and contentious issue. Refugees became one focus in this debate. Long-standing humanitarian traditions were reinforced by civil rights and internationalist advocates in the latter half of the twentieth century. Andrew Shacknove, an authority on refugee issues, spoke for this influential sector of the nation in his 1988 essay "American Duties to Refugees," in which he argued, on moral grounds, for a more humanitarian, more open American policy toward persons fighting for survival as refugees from abroad.

Few forms of human misery are equal to being refugees, who by definition face a challenge to life or liberty that threatens their very survival. But refugees are not alone in their suffering. Their wanderings can also jeopardize the elemental welfare and security of their neighbors. Imperiled by mere geographic proximity, citizens of asylum states may confront an odious choice between the extremes of heroic personal sacrifice and the expulsion of refugees to life-threatening circumstances. Refugee migrations can even erode the security of entire regions, as the Lebanese tragedy attests. Thus preventing, containing, and managing refugee outflows is crucial not only to secure the basic survival of the refugee, but to insure the integrity of the national political community and the preservation of a minimum world order.

Before host states can formulate a response to such refugee emergencies, they must develop standards, both moral and political, by which policy can be evaluated. Clarity of purpose and direction in the conduct of refugee affairs is predicated on the establishment of first principles for the evaluation of current procedures and institutions and the crafting of preferred alternatives. Such principles derive directly from the just entitlements of both refugees and their American host communities. Lacking such principles or fundamental objectives, the United States will simply stagger from one disaster to another, divided internally by its inability to consolidate a domestic consensus and at odds internationally through any attempt to pass on the burden of assisting refugees to other states. From the Mariel debacle to the interdiction of Haitians on the high seas, from the rubble of El Salvador to the sanctuaries of Texas, recent history furnishes evidence of the need for first principles for the ordering of our refugee policy. When the government of the United States omits all consideration of just entitlements or the limits of obligation, when it turns away the destitute while aiding the celebrated, when it embitters its own citizens by requiring heroic sacrifices or disgraces them by perpetrating mean acts, the policy itself collapses under the weight of its own illegitimacy. . . .

The consuming objective of the refugee is immediate, raw survival. By definition, the refugee inhabits a wilderness of acute deprivation where life is jeopardized by an extreme threat to minimum security or subsistence. Such threats are posed primarily by the refugees' compatriots, but there are many other challenges to their elemental welfare. Too often, the refugees' flights seem to involve movement from one ring of hell to the next. State predation of chaotic social collapse are merely exchanged for piracy, *refoulement*, or squalid incarceration in the detention camps of a reluctant host state. The fact that such actions perpetuate rather than initiate a situation that threatens the security or subsistence of the refugee often renders them neither less lethal nor less immoral.

Our first duty to refugees is to avoid depriving them of their basic security, subsistence, and liberty unless some actual, proximate, and compelling interest of state is implicated. This is the principle of nondeprivation, whose ancient moral foundation is deeply rooted in the American ethic. It is particularly relevant in the now frequent instances in which refugees arrive directly at our borders and shores seeking asylum.

In the refugee context, the principle of nondeprivation means that there is a strong presumption against:

1. depriving others of their basic needs;
2. protecting persons who deprive others of their basic needs;
3. assisting persons who deprive others of their basic needs: and
4. perpetuating the deprivation of basic needs.

The duty to avoid depriving persons, including foreigners, of life and liberty, unless some compelling state interest justifies doing so, stems from our equal moral worth as human beings. The moral equality of persons is an indispensable premise of communal life in the United States. From our lofty ideals to our routine chores, from access to the courts and protection by the police to the impatient wait in the post office queue, we presume an equality of human worth. Moreover, the principle of equal human worth is the primary moral given of those states and international agencies central to the management of refugee affairs. The crucial financial donors to the United States High Commission for Refugees (UNHCR) and the private relief agencies, the major countries of overseas resettlement, and many, if not all, asylum states consider moral equality to be the cornerstone of their social relations. It is precisely when moral equality is altogether denied by the persecution of one political or religious group by another, the invasion of one state by another, or gross disparities of wealth that refugees are fostered.

Moral equality entails, at the least, a recognition of the elemental integrity of each human life. Recall that, as an empirical matter, life requires the satisfaction of minimum security and subsistence. The absence of security or subsistence is fatal; hence, such needs are basic. Therefore, all persons whose moral calculus rests upon the principle of equal human worth must avoid depriving others of their basic needs, avoid protecting or assisting those who do, or demonstrate some compelling reason why such deprivation is justified. These duties constitute the principle of nondeprivation. In the absence of some solid justification, to ignore this principle is to violate the moral minimum. . . .

The duty to avoid depriving others of life and liberty, like all other moral principles, is not absolute. Actions of state routinely involve moral conflict, and such conflict is often conspicuous in the refugee context. But when the government of the United States deprives a person, whether citizen or foreigner, of life or liberty, it bears the heavy burden of proving clearly that some crucial interest of state or of some group is at stake and that all less extreme actions are insufficient to meet that compelling interest.

Source: Andrew E. Schacknove, "American Duties to Refugees: Their Scope and Limits," in *Open Borders? Closed Societies? The Ethical and Political Issues*, ed. Mark Gibney (Westport, Conn.: Greenwood Press, 1988), 131, 136–38.

2.8. America Today Must Resist Humane Instincts to Third World Immigrants

In post–World War II America, a new influx of immigrants now worried those who have argued that the United States has been open to immigrants beyond what has been and will be the good of the nation. They have called for a limit on American humanitarianism. Lindsey Grant, a veteran of the foreign service and the Department of State coordinator for the "Global 2000 Report to the President" on worldwide environmental concerns, has emerged as a strong advocate of greater restrictions on immigration on environmental grounds. In his 1988 essay "How Many Americans?," Grant argued against "the generous impulse of many Americans . . . to welcome the immigrant," and he supported those who believe that the United States should reduce immigration, on moral grounds, for the benefit of America's poor and the future of the country's environment.

There is something of a dichotomy apparent.

Overwhelmingly, Americans say in opinion polls that they favor enforcement of our immigration laws and a scaling down of legal immigration.

On the other hand, one detects both among liberals and some libertarian conservatives a resistance to the idea of tougher controls on immigration.

The natural and generous impulse of many Americans is to welcome the immigrant, particularly if they know him. If people are crowded elsewhere, if they are driven from their livelihood by economic or political pressures, do we not owe them the chance we have had? Most immigrants seem attractive and hard-working. Why not welcome them?

This reaction arises from a peculiarly American mindset that leads us to universalize our experience. We assume a responsibility for everything and everybody, everywhere. The United States has been a continent and a frontier more than a nation-state. We are not accustomed to thinking in terms of limits. Japan and Europe have had longer experience with limits, as their restrictive immigration policies attest.

This American world conscience comes into conflict with other moral values that should be important to us. Are we to abandon the sense of obligation to our own poor? Are we to reconcile ourselves to a society in which the rich get richer and the poor get poorer? Do we have the right to pass on to our children an ecology that is living beyond its means, passing a progressively impoverished environment on to successive generations?

Each person must resolve this conflict for himself, but I would argue that our conscience begin at home. There are good reasons both altruistic and practical to help others, but in a nation-state system our nation has neither the authority nor the obligation to save them. The President is sworn by the Constitution to "promote the general welfare, and secure the blessings of liberty to ourselves and our posterity," not the world. As other countries periodically make clear, this limitation might not be altogether unpopular abroad.

There is another level to the moral issue. As Americans, we are entitled to believe that the immigrant is happier here than he would have been at home, but it is not so certain that the movement is of benefit to the vast majority who will (one must assume) stay behind. The "brain drain" robs Third World countries of talents they need; some countries such as India have bitterly resisted the drain. Similarly, migration to the U.S., if it provides a safety valve by draining off the articulate and restless, may simply defer the day when their countries address their own problems. And delay intensifies the problems.

The Third World contains 76 percent of the world's population. Even by an optimistic estimate, its growth alone during this quarter-century will be nearly twice the total population of the industrial world and nearly ten times that of the United States. To believe that a permissive view of immigration will significantly contribute to solving a problem of this scope is simply to engage in wishful thinking. Even if such a permissive attitude were shared throughout the industrial world (which it emphatically is not), migration could not accommodate the current surge of population. It must be dealt with, as China understands, at its origins.

To offer haven to the few who escape is to forget the many who cannot, and an expanding American population does not necessarily advance the common good. To those whose conscience stands in the way, I offer this suggestion: your humane instincts may be sending you the wrong message.

Source: Lindsey Grant, "How Many Americans?" in *U.S. Immigration in the 1980s: Reappraisal and Reform*, ed. David Simcox (Boulder, Colo.: Westview Press, 1988), 279–80.

ANNOTATED SELECTED BIBLIOGRAPHY

Beck, Roy. *Re-Charting America's Future*. Petoskey, Mich.: Social Contract Press, 1994. One section argues that humanitarian considerations must not deter the United States from limiting immigration.

Dinnerstein, Leonard. *America and the Survivors of the Holocaust: The Evolution of Displaced Persons Policy, 1945–1950*. New York: Columbia University Press, 1982. Examines how religious and humanitarian interests, following World War II, brought about awareness of the plight of Holocaust survivors and other displaced persons in Central Europe and lobbied for the passage of the legislation that brought some 400,000 of these person to the United States as refugees.

Gibney, Mark, ed. *Open Borders? Closed Societies? The Ethical and Political Issues*. Westport: Conn.: Greenwood Press, 1988. Discusses humanitarian concerns related to immigration policy and practice.

Gorman, Robert. *Mitigating Misery: An Inquiry into the Political and Humanitarian Aspects of U.S. and Global Refugee Policy*. Lanham, Md.: University Press of America, 1993. Deals with the numbers, selection, assistance, and settlement of refugees by the United States in the post–World War II era.

Hofstetter, Richard, ed. *U.S. Immigration Policy*. Durham, N.C.: Duke University Press, 1984. Discusses Haitian "boat people" and other humanitarian immigration issues.

Loescher, Gil, and John Scanlan. *Calculated Kindness: Refugees and America's Half-*

Open Door, 1945 to the Present. New York: Free Press, 1986. Discusses the humanitarian aspects of America's refugee policy.

Miller, Jake. *The Plight of Haitian Refugees*. New York: Praeger, 1984. Describes the conditions faced by Haitians in their homeland, the efforts of thousands of them to come to the United States, and their reception in this country.

Simcox, David, ed. *U.S. Immigration in the 1980s: Reappraisal and Reform*. Boulder, Colo.: Westview Press, 1988. Includes material on the immigrant and refugee humanitarian overload in the United States.

Williamson, Chilton. *The Immigration Mystique: America's False Conscience*. New York: Basic Books, 1996. Argues that those Americans who support immigration endanger the core identity of the nation which, the author contends, is based on an Anglo-Saxon Protestant culture.

Wyman, David. *The Abandonment of the Jews: America and the Holocaust, 1941–1945*. New York: Pantheon Books, 1984. Describes America's lack of humanitarian concern and action in regard to the Jewish population in Europe which was being exterminated by Nazi Germany.

ORGANIZATIONS AND WEB SITES

American Friends Service Committee: www.asfc.org

Federation for American Immigration Reform: www.fairus.org

Migration and Refugee Service: www.nccbuscc.org/mrs

Social Contract: www.thesocialcontract.com

3

Has Immigrant Diversity Been a Contribution or a Threat to America's Strength and Unity?

From the earliest years of the colonial period, British North America attracted diverse people, in terms of nationality, language, religion, culture, and class, but this diversity did not spread uniformly across the colonies. The New England provinces, for example, did not welcome diverse people and at times were outrightly hostile to religious dissenters who tried to settle there. Despite some African slaves and some variety of people, particularly in its ports, this region had a predominantly English Puritan population into the mid-eighteenth century. The Southern provinces, which were settled early by the English, looked for labor first to indentured servants primarily from the mother country and then to African slaves by the late seventeenth century. Some localities, especially ports like Charleston, received some diverse people, including French Huguenots and Swiss settlers, and the backcountry teemed with Scotch-Irish, Germans, and other settlers of varying faiths or, as some missionaries complained, no religion at all. However, throughout the colonial period, this region's population was primarily of British and African background.

The middle provinces attracted, and adapted to, a variety of people and thereby forecast what eventually became the predominant American population pattern. Parts of New York, New Jersey, and Pennsylvania had settlers from Sweden, including Finns, and from the Netherlands, including French Huguenots, Walloons, Frieslanders, and others, by the mid-seventeenth century, all of whom occupied the land before being conquered by the British. Most of these people remained and, though they retained distinctive churches, eventually became absorbed into the emerging Anglo-American culture of the colonies. To realize a profit, most of those in the middle provinces who received land grants under the British willingly sold land to Germans, Scotch-Irish, and immigrants from other countries. The port cities of New York, Perth Amboy, New Jersey, and Philadelphia attracted an even greater variety of people. When visiting New Amsterdam (New York) in 1643, Jesuit Father Isaac Jogues reported that some eighteen languages were spoken there and that there were already a number of religions present. "Besides the Calvinists there are in the colony Catholics, English Puritans, Lutherans, Anabaptists."[1]

While all these varied people did not always like and cooperate with one another, a considerable intermixture in business, government, and socializing did occur in the tightly bound geography of the middle colonies. Through these activities, with growing religious toleration, and through intermarriage, observers could talk about the residents of the middle provinces as being a new people, an emerging American people. J. Hector St. John de Crèvecoeur, an immigrant from France, observed this reality. In 1782 he wrote about "the mixture of English, Scotch, Irish, French, Dutch, Germans, and Swedes. From this promiscuous breed, that race now called Americans have arisen."[2]

Still, even in the middle colonies, the mixture, while striking to foreigners, was rather limited. It consisted primarily of persons with roots in Northern and Western Europe. The Native Americans and the Africans remained on the periphery of society. During the American Revolution, when the founding generation was preoccupied with defining an American identity and charting an American destiny, many writers ignored the diversity altogether as they strove for unity. One early leader, John Jay, writing in *The Federalist* in 1787 stated; "Providence has been pleased to give this one connected country to one united people, a people descended from the same ancestors, speaking the same language, professing the same religion."[3]

In the fifty years after the end of the revolution only a relatively small number of new immigrants arrived each year. Among them were refugees from revolutions in France, Ireland, and Haiti in the 1790s and also some number of English and Scots and additional Scotch-Irish and Catholic Irish. During the early political battles over the fear of the French Revolution spreading to the United States, which gripped the Federalist party in the 1790s, Congress passed laws making deportation of immigrants easier and naturalization harder. The more generous Jeffersonians let the laws lapse when they took power in 1801.

A major challenge to the nation in terms of diversity came with the first wave of mass immigration in the decades after 1840. The Irish and Germans who crowded into the ports on the East Coast of the United

States and into towns in the interior seemingly were people already "familiar." For more than a hundred years people with these backgrounds had come to North America and had been basically accepted or lived in such geographical isolation so as not to be a visible concern. What was new after 1840 was the large number of those who came, their concentration in cities, and, particularly for the Irish, their poverty. Native-born Americans feared that the culture of the country and especially the predominant Protestantism of the nation were threatened. Garrett Davis of Kentucky, in 1849, for example, denounced the fact that "a greatly increasing immigration is constantly pouring in upon us the hordes of Europe, with their hereditary national animosities, their discordant races, languages, and religious faiths, their ignorance and their pauperism, mixed up with a large amount of idleness, moral degradation and crime." He concluded that "this is the beginning of the conflict of races on a large scale." At this time the term "race" included ethnic differences.[4]

Despite a growing nativism in the 1840s and 1850s, a series of nativist and anti-Catholic riots which wracked American cities, and even the rise and brief success of the nativist, Know Nothing Party (a political organization, secretive in its early years, that was hostile to the political involvement of recent immigrants and Roman Catholics) in the 1850s, many Americans were willing to give the immigrants a fair chance. Some Americans saw much benefit to the nation from the growing diversity brought by immigration. The sum of their arguments was voiced by one Thomas Nichols in a lecture given in 1845, when he asserted that "the great physiological reason why Americans are superior to other nations in freedom, intelligence, and enterprise, is because they are the offspring of the greatest intermingling of races."[5] Ralph Waldo Emerson, one of the best-known writers of the time, wrote,

> I hate the narrowness of the Native American Party. . . . It is precisely opposite true wisdom. . . . In this continent—asylum of all the nations—the energy of Irish, Swedes, Poles, and Cossack, and all the European tribes—of the Africans, and of the Polynesians, will construct a new race, a new religion, a new state, a new literature, which will be vigorous as the new Europe which came out of the smelting pot of the Dark Ages.[6]

Greater contentiousness concerning diversity took place in America's newly acquired West Coast. Shortly after the United States seized California from Mexico in the Mexican American War of 1846–1848, gold was discovered there. The prospect of finding gold in California lured many Americans and hopefuls from Latin America, Europe, and China there. Anglo-Americans claimed California for themselves. They denigrated Mexicans and despised the Chinese. "Americans" injected discrimination into almost every aspect of public life and assaulted these newcomers, who were relegated to ghettos and often lacked recourse to the law to protect themselves. Following pressure from western labor and nativists, in 1882 Congress passed a law that excluded any further admission of Chinese laborers, the first group to be so treated. The justification for these actions, in the words of Senator James Slater in 1882, was,

> The Chinese are aliens, born in a foreign land, speak a foreign tongue, owe allegiance to a foreign government, are idolaters in religion, have a different civilization from ours, do not and will not assimilate with our people, come only to get money, and return, and they are inimical to our laws, evade them whenever and where they can.[7]

Despite ill treatment and the exclusion law, Chinese enclaves persisted in San Francisco and numerous towns in the West and elsewhere.

The second major wave of immigrants, after 1880, forced the United States to face a new test of its degree of openness. While immigrants continued to come from Germany, Ireland, Holland, Scandinavia, and Great Britain, the majority now came from places from which previously there had been very few immigrants. The largest numbers were from Italy, Poland, Austria-Hungary, and Russia, but large numbers also came from other parts of Southern and Eastern Europe, and some too from Turkey, Lebanon, Armenia, Syria, Japan, India, Korea, and the Caribbean. Included among these newcomers were many more Catholics; many Jews; a considerable number of Russian, Greek, and other Orthodox Christians; and a few Moslems and Buddhists. "Racially" and religiously the new immigration threatened to remake America into a new people—or so nativist Americans feared.

Some Americans, among them some religious leaders and settlement house workers, as well as many employers, welcomed this new diversity as a benefit to the nation with its vigorous supply of labor, cultural richness, and vitality. The Reverend Percy Grant, who had worked with French-Canadians, Portuguese, Hebrews, and Italians, spoke favorably about their adjustment to America and their promise for the future. Lillian Wald, director of the Henry Street Settlement in New York, wrote in 1915; "The immigrant brings in a steady stream of new life and new blood to the nation."[8]

The new immigration pushed Americans to consider their immigration history and their national character. While xenophobic writers like Madison Grant, whose *The Passing of the Great Race* (1916), which went through many editions, railed against the "barbarism" of the new immigrants and the degradation of American institutions and debilitation of American culture and "racial" vigor because of them, friends of immigration argued for the benefits the process made to American culture and vigor.[9] John Gavit, a pro-immigrant advocate, stated in the *Survey* in 1922,

> Each phase of immigration has been "the new immigration" at its time; each has been viewed with alarm; each has been described as certain to impair the physical quality of our people and destroy the standards of living and of citizenship. . . . Russian and Austrian, Greek, Roumanian, Portuguese, the latest comers, are in the midst of the same process.[10]

In another work that focused on the issue of the creation of a national culture, he wrote,

> We are in the midst of the making of the "American." It does not yet appear what he shall be, but one thing is certain, he is not to be of any particular type now distinguishable. Saxon, Teuton, and Kelt, Latin and Slav—to say nothing of any appreciable contribution by yellow and brown races as yet negligible in this aspect of the question—each of the races that we now know on this soil will have its share of "ancestorial" responsibility for the "typical America" that is to be.[11]

Even more voices opposed the new immigration, and they grew as the numbers of newcomers increased from the 1880s into the 1910s. Elite New Englanders saw the new people as a threat to the continued importance of America's Anglo-Saxon Protestant roots. Other Americans chimed in, recoiling from Southern and Eastern Europeans as being ethnically, culturally, mentally, and physically inferior, and thus threatening to lower American standards and values. Organized and popular anti-Semitism and anti-Catholicism flourished in the Midwest and elsewhere, and scientists, clergy, and college professors led a chorus of public concern that so many new and different people would dilute America's presumed ethnic and racial superiority.

Dr. Alfred Reed of the United States Public Health Service was a typical advocate of such thinking. He wrote about the new wave of immigrants in 1912, "The dregs and off-scourings of foreign lands, the undesirables of whom their own nations are only too eager to purge themselves, come in hosts to our shores."[12] Another doctor, Charles Woodruff, wrote about the new immigrants as "hordes of illiterates, 'scum of Europe,' 'paupers,' Hebrews, Poles, Slovaks, Croatians, Magyars, Italians, Syrians, who cannot understand the Aryan democracy."[13]

These two medical practitioners could find their anti-immigrant views supported by the findings of a cadre of newly emerging scientists in the United States dedicated to establishing the purported physical and biological superiority of Northern and Western European peoples.

Edward Lewis, a critic of immigration, in *America, Nation or Confusion: A Study of Our Immigration Problems* (1928), wrote,

> What then can we expect of the newer racial elements which, particularly since 1890, have poured in on us? They are far more alien to us than the Irish and the Germans. They are more backward races than those of North Europe. . . . Diversity of standards and traditions . . . operates to prevent the wholesome development of our national life on its cultural side.[14]

Among the groups whom Lewis would exclude were the Jews whom he criticizes for what he considers as their separateness. Professor E. A. Ross, looking forward from the early twentieth century with dismay, wrote,

> Already America has ceased to allure, as of yore, the British, the Germans and the Scandinavians; but it strongly attracts the Italians, Greeks and Slavs. By 1930, perhaps the opportunities left will have ceased to interest them, but no doubt, the Khivans, the Bokhariots, the Persians and the Afghans will regard this as the Promised Land. By 1950, even they will scorn the chances here, but then, perhaps the collies from overpopulated India will be glad to take an American wage.[15]

These attitudes resulted in pressure on Congress and a succession of presidents to make the nation less open to immigrants. First the categories of restrictions were increased; then, despite a number of presidential vetoes, a literacy requirement was legislated in 1917; and then in the particularly intolerant 1920s, in the National Origins Acts, Congress, with pseudo-scientific justification, made a substantial shift toward immigration restriction. The number of immigrants to be allowed to enter the country annually was limited, and within the limitations quotas were assigned by countries of origin. Basing the quotas on the percentage of persons from a country that were already resident in the United States, sizeable quotas were given to the Northern and Western European countries, and very low quotas were given to Southern and Eastern European countries. There were no quotas, thus full exclusion, for most Asian countries. The countries in the Western Hemisphere were not included in the quota system. As a result of these new laws, immigration markedly decreased in the 1920s. Then the Great Depression of the 1930s discouraged most new immigration and encouraged emigration and even forced deportations, particularly of Mexicans.

The experiences of World War II and its aftermath on the United States caused a changed view toward foreigners in general and immigrants in particular. A renewed, but not unlimited or unchallenged, openness toward immigrants surfaced. This began with the need for labor during the war with the Bracero program, which brought in by contract Mexican and Caribbean workers. An opening in 1943 toward China as an ally in the war was made by enacting a quota of 101 annually for that country. In 1946 India and the Philippines received the same quota. Religious groups pushed for a refugee policy that brought many displaced persons primarily from Eastern Europe to the United States after the war. In 1952 quotas were given to Korea and Japan. The Cold War extended special refugee status to Chinese, Hungarians, Cubans, Jews from the Soviet Union, and allied people from Southeast Asia.

The 1920s quota laws were still in effect in the years after World War II, despite strong criticism from many, including Presidents Harry S. Truman and John F. Kennedy. Conscious of the need for the United States to practice what it preached about democracy and opportunity during the Cold War, and of the need to expand civil rights at home, Truman said, "The idea behind this discriminatory policy was, to put it boldly, that Americans with English or Irish names were better people and better citizens than Americans with Italian or Greek or Polish names. . . . Such a concept is utterly unworthy of our traditions and our ideals."[16] Kennedy wrote, "Immigration policy should be generous; it should be fair; it should be flexible."[17]

Particularly through the pressure of foreign policy needs and the civil rights movement, the prejudicial quota system was repealed by the 1965 immigration law. This law and subsequent federal legislation, which increased the total number of immigrants allowed annually to be admitted to the United States, gave an equal 20,000 annual immigrant maximum to all countries and included a preference for family reunification and for persons with designated job skills. The result was a radical change in the continents from which most immigrants came to the United States in the years after 1965. The poverty and political upheavals of the Third World pushed people out just as the United States immigration policy opened up. Whereas, in the two centuries before that date, over 90 percent of the immigrants had come from Europe, since that date some 40 percent have come from Latin America, 40 percent from Asia, and only 10 percent from Europe. Another 10 percent have come from Africa and other places. Virtually every culture in the world is represented, and virtually every religion in the world is now practiced in the United States.

These changes have caused apprehension and opposition among many

Americans, partly because some degree of racism has continued in the United States. Additionally, Americans fear the dilution of traditional cultural values and a weakening of the country's unity through friction among groups and general divisiveness. For many, a general "uncomfortableness" with difference also explains uneasiness about the current immigration. In such a climate of fear and uneasiness, some newcomers have suffered verbal abuse, discrimination, and violence.

Anti-immigration attitudes have been fostered by a neo-nativist cadre of authors and newly founded and funded organizations. One such group is U.S. Border Control. Paul Roberts, a vigorous critic of the changing composition of American immigration, writing in the *Washington Times National Weekly* in 1999, called the nation's late twentieth-century immigration practice "the ethnic cleansing of European-Americans." He expressed the fear that "the United States will face ethnic divides that exceed those in Kosovo and the Balkans."[18] Another critic of late twentieth-century American immigration policy, Peter Brimelow, himself an immigrant from England and author of *Alien Nation*, protested in 1997 in an essay, "The Case for Limiting Immigration," that

> America's current immigration system is highly discriminatory. It has choked off immigration from Europe, the traditional homeland of Americans. It has allowed about a dozen mostly Third World countries to shoulder aside all others and monopolize legal immigration. . . . There is no precedent for a sovereign country undergoing such a rapid and radical transformation of its ethnic character in the entire history of the world.[19]

On the other hand, the new post-1965 wave of immigrants with their global diversity has garnered support from many Americans. Contributing to this openness has been the awareness that the earlier turn-of-the-century immigrants who some regarded as unassimilable have actually been acculturated. Further, America has become very engaged in international affairs; many Americans have fought against racism; again people have celebrated the vitality of new people; many have realized the role that the new people have been playing in making the United States more competitive in the increasingly economically interrelated world; and citizens have experienced continuing unity in diversity. From such thoughts and experiences a widespread realization of the positive aspects of current immigration has emerged. Ben Wattenberg, a strong proponent of the United States as the first universal nation, summed up the optimism of pro-immigration thought in 1991: "We are becoming what we had professed to be, the first universal nation, and we're very successful at it. It is very much in the American interest—

commercial, geopolitical, demographic and ideological—to encourage this tendency toward diversity."[20]

A varied population has been an aspect of America from the early colonial times to the present. It has generally been welcomed when the number of people from any one area has been relatively small. However, when many immigrants within a limited period of time have come from a single nation, linguistic group, religion, or culture, and particularly if they were poor and "different," their presence has caused a widespread feeling of unease and fear, and at times it has provoked hostility. Still, even at the height of surges in immigration, Americans have stepped forward to champion the vitality of diversity and reaffirm the confidence that American ideas and opportunities would work to integrate the newcomers into the national social and civic culture. The large influx of immigrants in the last decades of the twentieth century has brought the diversity of the world to America and has reopened the debate about positive and negative aspects of more increasingly different people in the United States.

NOTES

1. Quoted in Frederick Binder and David Reimers, *All the Nations under Heaven: An Ethnic and Racial History of New York City*, 4th ed. (New York: Columbia University Press, 1995), 5.
2. J. Hector St. John de Crèvecoeur, *Letters from an American Farmer* (1782; reprint, New York: E. P. Dutton, 1957), 37.
3. John Jay, The Federalist No. 2, October 31, 1787, in *The Federalist*, ed. Jacob Cooke (Middletown, Conn.: Wesleyan University Press, 1961), 9.
4. Garrett Davis, *Speech upon His Proposition to Impose Further Restrictions upon Foreign Immigrants* (Frankfort: Convention to Revise the Constitution of Kentucky, December 15, 1849).
5. Thomas L. Nichols, *Lecture on Immigration and Right of Naturalization* (New York, 1845), 21.
6. Quoted in Michael Le May, *From Open Door to Dutch Door: An Analysis of U.S. Immigration Policy since 1820* (New York: Praeger, 1987), 33.
7. *Congressional Record*, 47th Cong., 1st sess., 1882, 13: 1636.
8. Lillian Wald, *House on Henry Street* (New York: Henry Holt, 1915) 306.
9. Madison Grant, *The Passing of the Great Race* (New York: Charles Scribner's Sons, 1916).
10. John Palmer Gavit, *Survey* 42 (February 25, 1922).
11. John Palmer Gavit, *Americans by Choice* (New York: Harper, 1922).
12. Alfred C. Reed, "The Medical Side of Immigration," *Popular Science Monthly*, 80, 4 (April 1912): 383–392.
13. Quoted in Julius Drachsler, *Democracy and Assimilation: The Blending of Immigrant Heritages in America* (New York: Macmillan, 1920), 45.
14. Edward Lewis, *America, Nation or Confusion: A Study of Our Immigration Problems* (New York: Harper and Brothers, 1928), 288, 370–71.

15. Quoted in Drachsler, *Democracy and Assimilation*, 45–46.

16. Harry S. Truman, "To The House of Representatives," H. Doc. 520, *Congressional Record*, 82nd Cong., 2nd sess., 1952, 98: 8082–83.

17. John F. Kennedy, *A Nation of Immigrants* (New York: Harper and Row, 1964), 82.

18. Paul Craig Roberts, "The Ethnic Cleansing of European-Americans," *Washington Times National Weekly*, June 21–27, 1999 and www.usbc.org, 1.

19. Peter Brimelow, "The Case for Limiting Immigration," in *The Debate in the United States over Immigration*, Peter Duignan and Lewis Gann (Stanford, Calif.: Hoover Institution Press, 1997), 103, 108.

20. Ben J. Wattenberg, *The First Universal Nation* (New York: Maxwell Macmillan International, 1991), 46.

DOCUMENTS

3.1. An Increasingly Heterogeneous Population in the 1840s Might Endanger America

As the number of immigrants grew rapidly in the United States through the 1840s, fear that increasing diversity would harm the country arose among a significant portion of the population. This apprehension was expressed by Garrett Davis, a U.S. senator from Kentucky, in a speech he delivered at a convention to revise the constitution of his state in 1849. He declared that the then current wave of immigrants was too hetergenous, too unfit for American institutions, and that the newcomers were causing "discord and dissension," which, he believed, would lead to a war of races and religion in the nation. Davis supported a growing nativist movement in calling for restrictions on immigrants.

Why am I opposed to the encouragement of foreign immigration into our country, and disposed to apply any proper checks to it? Why do I propose to suspend to the foreigner, for twenty-one years after he shall have signified formally his intention to become a citizen of the United States, the right of suffrage, the birthright of no man but one native-born? It is because the mighty tides of immigration, each succeeding one increasing in volume, bring to us not only different languages, opinions, customs, and principles, but hostile races, religions, and interests, and the traditionary prejudices of generations with a large amount of the turbulence, disorganizing theories, pauperism, and demoralization of Europe in her redundant population thrown upon us. This multiform and dangerous evil exists and will continue, for "the cry is, Still they come!" . . .

England, many of the German powers, Switzerland, and other governments, have put into operation extensive and well-arranged systems of emigrating and transporting to America their excess of population, and particularly the refuse, the pauper, the demoralized, and the criminal. Very many who come are stout and industrious, and go to labor steadily and thriftily. They send their friends in the old country true and glowing accounts of ours, and with it the means which they have garnered here to bring, too, those friends. Thus, immigration itself increases its means, and constantly adds to its swelling tides. Suppose some mighty convulsion of nature should loosen Europe, the smaller country, from her ocean-deep foundations, and drift here to our coast, would we be ready to take her teeming myriads to our fraternal embrace and give them equally our political sovereignty? If we did, in a few fleeting years where would be the noble Anglo-American race, where their priceless heritage of liberty, where their free constitution, where the best and brightest hopes of man? All would have perished! It is true all Europe is not coming to the United States, but much, too much of it, is; and a dangerous disproportion of the most ignorant and worst of it, without bringing us any territory for them. . . . The question is, Shall they come and take possession of our country and our government, and rule us, or will we, who have the right, rule them and ourselves? I go openly, manfully, and perseveringly for the latter rule, and if it cannot be successfully asserted in all the United States, I am for taking measures to maintain it in Kentucky, and while we can. Now is the time—prevention is easier than cure. . . .

No well-informed and observant man can look abroad over this widespread and blessed country without feeling deep anxiety for the future. Some elements of discord and disunion are even now in fearful action. Spread out to such a vast extent, filling up almost in geometrical progression with communities and colonies from many lands, various as Europe in personal and national characteristics, in opinions, in manners and customs, in tongues and religious faiths, in the traditions of the past, and the objects and the hopes of the future, the United States can, no more than Europe, become one homogeneous mass—one peaceful, united, harmonizing, all self-adhering people. When the country shall begin to teem with people, these jarring elements being brought into proximity, their repellent and explosive properties will begin to act with greater intensity; and then, if not before, will come the war of geographical sections, the war of races, and the most relentless of all wars, of hostile religions. This mournful catastrophe will have been greatly hastened by our immense expansion and our proclamation to all mankind to become a part of us.

Source: Garrett Davis, *Speech of Hon. Garrett Davis upon His Proposal to Impose Further Restrictions upon Foreign Immigration: Delivered in the Convention to Revise the Constitution of Kentucky, December 15, 1849* (Frankfort, Ky., 1855), 7–11, 30–32.

3.2. Diversity of Population Strengthens United States

Despite a dread of diversity among some in the United States in the 1840s, others regarded diversity as a source of strength for the growing nation. Thomas Nichols, a New Englander and a doctor who had been, at first, critical of immigration, had come to believe that diversity and a mingling of blood gave a superiority to America's population over that of other nations. His thoughts meshed with those of the pre–Civil War reformers who believed in the capacity of people to change and improve. Nichols, in his 1845 Lecture on Immigration and Right of Naturalization, *spoke about the positive contribution that diverse immigrants had made to the United States.*

The questions connected with emigration from Europe to America are interesting to both the old world and the new—are of importance to the present and future generations. They have more consequence than a charter or a state election; they involve the destinies of millions; they are connected with the progress of civilization, the rights of man, and providence of God!

I have examined this subject the more carefully, and speak upon it the more earnestly, because I have been to some extent, in former years, a partaker of the prejudices I have since learned to pity. A native of New England and a descendant of the puritans, I early imbibed, and to some extent promulgated, opinions of which reflection and experience have made me ashamed. . . .

But while I would speak of the motives of men with charity, I claim the right to combat their opinions with earnestness. Believing that the principles and practices of Native Americanism are wrong in themselves, and are doing wrong to those who are the objects of their persecution, justice and humanity require that their fallacy should be exposed, and their iniquity condemned. It may be unfortunate that the cause of the oppressed and persecuted, in opinion if not in action, has not fallen into other hands; yet, let me trust that the truth, even in mine, will prove mighty, prevailing from its own inherent power!

The right of man to emigrate from one country to another, is one which belongs to him by his own constitution and by every principle of justice. It is one which no law can alter, and no authority destroy. "Life, liberty, and the pursuit of happiness" are set down, in our Declaration of Independence, as among the self-evident, unalienable rights of man. If I have a right to live, I have also a right to what will support existence—food, clothing, and shelter. If then the country in which I reside, from a superabundant population, or any other cause, does not afford me these, my right to go from it to some other is self-evident and unquestionable. The *right to live*, then, supposes the right of emigration. . . .

Emigration from various countries in Europe to America, producing a mixture of races, has had, and is still having, the most important influence upon the destinies of the human race. It is a principle, laid down by every physiologist, and proved by abundant observation, that man, like other animals, is improved and brought to its highest perfection by an intermingling of the blood and qualities of various races. That nations and families deteriorate from an opposite course has been observed in all ages. The great physiological reason why Americans are superior to other nations in freedom, intelligence, and enterprize, is because that they are the offspring of the greatest intermingling of races. . . .

It is not too much to assert that in the order of Providence this vast and fertile continent was reserved for this great destiny; to be the scene of this mingling of the finest European races, and consequently of the highest condition of human intelligence, freedom, and happiness; for I look upon this mixture of the blood and qualities of various nations, and its continual infusion, as absolutely requisite to the perfection of humanity. . . . Continual emigration, and a constant mixing of the blood of different races, is highly conducive to physical and mental superiority. . . .

From the very nature of the case, America gets from Europe the most valuable of her population. Generally, those who come here are the very ones whom a sensible man would select. Those who are attached to monarchical and aristocratic institutions stay at home where they can enjoy them. Those who lack energy and enterprize can never make up their minds to leave their native land. It is the strong minded, the brave hearted, the free and self-respecting, the enterprizing and the intelligent, who break away from all the ties of country and of home, and brave the dangers of the ocean, in search of liberty and independence, for themselves and for their children, on a distant continent; and it is from this, among other causes, that the great mass of the people of this country are distinguished for the very qualities we should look for in emigrants. The same spirit which sent our fathers across the ocean impels us over the Alleghanies, to the valley of the Mississippi, and thence over the Rocky mountains into Oregon.

For what are we not indebted to foreign emigration, since we are all Europeans or their descendants? We cannot travel on one of our steamboats without remembering that Robert Fulton was the son of an Irishman. We cannot walk by St. Paul's churchyard without seeing the monuments which admiration and gratitude have erected to Emmet, and Montgomery. Who of the thousands who every summer pass up and down our great thoroughfare, the North River, fails to catch at least a passing glimpse of the column erected to the memory of Kosciusko? I cannot forget that only last night a portion of our citizens celebrated with joyous festivities the birthday of the son of Irish emigrants, I mean the Hero of New Orleans!

Who speaks contemptuously of Alexander Hamilton as a foreigner, because he was born in one of the West India Islands? Who at this day will question the worth or patriotism of Albert Gallatin, because he first opened his eyes among the Alps of Switzerland—though, in fact, this was brought up and urged against him, when he was appointed special minister to Russia by James Madison. What New Yorker applies the epithet of "degraded foreigner" to the German immigrant, John Jacob Astor, a man who has spread his canvas on every sea, drawn to his adopted land the wealth of every clime, and given us, it may be, our best claim to vast territories!

Who would have banished the Frenchman, Stephen Girard, who, after accumulating vast wealth from foreign commerce, endowed with it magnificent institutions for education in his adopted land? So might I go on for hours, citing individual examples of benefits derived by this country from foreign immigration. . . .

I have enumerated some of the advantages which such emigration has given to America. Let us now very carefully inquire, whether there is danger of any injury arising from these causes, at all proportionable to the palpable good. . . .

Are foreigners coming here to overturn our government? Those who came before the Revolution appear to have been generally favorable to Republican institutions. Those who have come here since have left friends, home, country, all that man naturally holds dearest, that they might live under a free government—they and their children. Is there common sense in the supposition that men would voluntarily set about destroying the very liberties they came so far to enjoy?

"But they lack intelligence," it is said. Are the immigrants of today less intelligent than those of fifty or a hundred years ago? Has Europe and the human race stood still all this time? . . . The facts of men preferring this country to any other, of their desire to live under its institutions, of their migration hither, indicate to my mind anything but a lack of proper intelligence and enterprize. It has been charged against foreigners, by a portion of the whig press, that they generally vote with the democratic party. Allowing this to be so, I think that those who reflect upon the policy of the two parties, from the time of John Adams down to that of Mayor Harper, will scarcely bring this up as the proof of a lack of intelligence!

The truth is, a foreigner who emigrates to this country comes here saying, "Where Liberty dwells, there is my country." He sees our free institutions in the strong light of contrast. The sun seems brighter, because he has come out of darkness. What we know by hearsay only of the superiority of our institutions, he knows by actual observation and experience. Hence it is that America has had no truer patriots—freedom no more enthusiastic admirers—the cause of Liberty no more heroic defenders, than have been found among our adopted citizens. . . .

I have yet to learn that foreigners, whether German or Irish, English or French, are at all disposed to do an injury to the asylum which wisdom has prepared and valor won for the oppressed of all nations and religions. I appeal to the observation of every man in this community, whether the Germans and the Irish here, and throughout the country, are not as orderly, as industrious, as quiet, and in the habit of performing as well the common duties of citizens as the great mass of natives among us.

Source: Thomas L. Nichols, *Lecture on Immigration and Right of Naturalization* (New York: 1845), 3–4, 21, 24–32.

3.3. Chinese Immigrants: A Distinct Race and a Danger to American Society

One group that proved to be too different, culturally and racially, for most Americans of European background was the Chinese, who began, in the 1850s, to settle in considerable numbers primarily on the West Coast. The negative attitudes toward the Chinese, which started on the West Coast and then spread throughout the nation, were expressed in a House of Representatives report in 1892. The congressional contributors to this document regarded the Chinese as a "distinct race" and as a "source of danger" to the United States. They successfully called for a reenactment of the 1882 law excluding Chinese laborers from admission to the country. This exclusion lasted until the 1940s.

There is urgent necessity for prompt legislation on the subject of Chinese immigration. The exclusion act approved May 6, 1882, and its supplement expires by limitation of time on May 6, 1892, and after that time there will be no law to prevent the Chinese hordes from invading our country in number so vast, as soon to outnumber the present population of our flourishing States on the Pacific slope. . . .

The popular demand for legislation excluding the Chinese from this country is urgent and imperative and almost universal. Their presence here is inimical to our institutions and is deemed injurious and a source of danger. They are a distinct race, saving from their earnings a few hundred dollars and returning to China. This they succeed in doing in from five to ten years by living in the most miserable manner, when in cities and towns in crowded tenement houses, surrounded by dirt, filth, corruption, pollution, and prostitution; and gambling houses and opium joints abound. When used as cooks, farm-hands, servants, and gardeners, they are more cleanly in habits and manners. They, as a rule, have no families here; all are men, save a few women, usually prostitutes. They have no attachment to our country, its laws or its institutions, nor are they interested in its prosperity. They never assimilate with our people, our manners, tastes, religion, or ideas. With us they have nothing in common.

Living on the cheapest diet (mostly vegetable), wearing the poorest clothing, with no family to support, they enter the field of labor in competition with the American workman. In San Francisco, and in fact throughout the whole Pacific slope, we learn from the testimony heretofore alluded to, that the Chinamen have invaded almost every branch of industry; manufacturers of cigars, cigar boxes, brooms, tailors, laundrymen, cooks, servants, farmhands, fishermen, miners and all departments of manual labor, for wages and prices at which white men and women could not support themselves and those dependent upon them. Recently this was a new country, and the Chinese may have been a necessity at one time, but now our own people are fast filling up and developing this rich and highly favored land, and American citizens will not and can not afford to stand idly by and see this undesirable race carry away the fruits of the labor which justly belongs to them. A war of races would soon be inaugurated; several times it has broken out, and bloodshed has followed. The town of Tacoma, in 1887, banished some 3,000 Chinamen on twenty-four hours' notice, and no Chinaman has ever been permitted to return.

Our people are willing, however, that those now here may remain, protected by the laws which they do not appreciate or obey, provided strong provision be made that no more shall be allowed to come, and that the smuggling of Chinese across the frontiers be scrupulously guarded against, so that gradually, by voluntary departures, death by sickness, accident, or old age, this race may be eliminated from this country, and the white race fill their places without inconvenience to our own people or to the Chinese, and thus a desirable change be happily and peacefully accomplished. It was thought that the exclusion act of 1882 would bring about this result; but it now appears that although at San Francisco the departures largely exceed the arrivals, yet the business of smuggling Chinese persons across the lines from the British Possessions and Mexico has so greatly increased that the number of arrivals now exceed the departures. This must be effectually stopped.

Source: US Congress, House of Representatives, 52nd Cong, 1st session, Vol. 23, H. Rep 255, February 10, 1892.

3.4. Basic Character of the American People by the Early Twentieth Century Was Diversity

John Palmer Gavit wrote for the Survey *in 1922 in the midst of a widespread post–World War I reaction against immigrants and most things foreign and in the midst of congressional debates to limit overall immigration, very sharply restrict newcomers from Southern and Eastern Europe, and exclude those from most of Asia. The* Survey *was one of the leading magazines that reported on urban and other social issues. Gavit, the author of* Americans by Choice *(1922), believed that a basic characteristic of the American was diversity. He argued that the "new immigrants" from Southern and Eastern Europe would be acculturated into Americans as had been the earlier immigrants.*

Now, what is "an American"? What is it that makes a nation of us, if not a distinctive race? What is it that the immigrant joins, body and soul, when he becomes "an American"?

Every little while somebody arises with ashes upon his head and bemoans the threatened disappearance of what he calls "the American type." Perhaps we know what the expression may mean in New England—a combination of English, Scotch or Welsh, who in turn would be part Dane, Pict and Scot, Saxon, Normans and Celt; with perhaps a strain of French or maybe of Dutch. In Pennsylvania very likely it would be English Quaker—or Platt-Deutsch. The French-Spanish combination in the Gulf region, the Scandinavian or German in the Middle West and Northwest, the Spanish-Mexican along the Rio Grande and in Southern California, and so on, are "American" by a title as good as that of those who trace their descent from the Pilgrim fathers. We cannot isolate any physical characteristics; we cannot segregate any particular racial descent: one may search in vain for any definable hereditary mental or spiritual characteristic that will fit or typify all or even many.

Source: John Palmer Gavit, *Survey* 42, February 25, 1922.

3.5. Southern and Eastern European Immigrants Are Regarded as Inferior

While opposition to immigrants from Asia continued through the nineteenth century and into the twentieth century, many Americans also found the Eastern and Southern Europeans, who began to come to the United States in large numbers after 1880, unacceptably different. An eruption of Nordic superiority was given support, not only by journalists, but also in the purported scientific work of a significant number of sociologist, psychologists, and biologists. Julius Drachsler, a sociologist, reported in Democracy and Assimilation, *published in 1920, on the nega-*

tive views held on the diverse Slavic, Semitic, and Mediterranean immigrants who were then coming into the United States. The critics considered these newcomers to be "inferior racial groups and cultures." Such viewpoints, which received wide currency, contributed to federal legislation passed in the 1920s that established a quota system that greatly decreased Southern and Eastern European immigration to the United States.

[A]nother view is taken by some leading sociologists and biologists. The "new" immigration as contrasted with the "old," they urge, represents a distinctly different set of racial and cultural elements. The older groups were predominantly of the Baltic or Nordic race and Anglo-Saxon in culture, while the newcomers are overwhelmingly Slavic, Semitic, and Mediterranean. They tend to mass in separate foreign colonies, especially in the heart of the great industrial and commercial centers of America. The life in these colonies is in many respects almost self-sufficient. The immigrant, with newspapers printed in his own language, with his own churches or synagogues, his own social organizations, his own trading places, his own old-world political interests, tends to remain indifferent to the great, homogeneous American current. Racial and cultural differences are thus kept alive and constitute a perennial danger to the solidarity of the national mind. Illiteracy, yellow journalism, peonage, east spirit, low position of women, prostitution, congestion, pauperism, juvenile delinquency, separatist schools, "dirty" politics, are among the glaring evils arising from the over-population of the land by these undesirable newcomers. A brilliant exponent of this view is Professor Edward A. Ross. "The plain truth is" he writes, "that rarely does an immigrant bring in his intellectual baggage anything of use to us. The music of Mascagni and Debussy, the plays of Ibsen and Maeterlinck, the poetry of Rostand and Hauptmann, the fiction of Jokai and Sienkiewiez, were not brought to us by way of Ellis Island." But condemnations of the Eastern and South European immigrant are not limited to scintillating emotional outbursts. The calm, dispassionate science of statistics is called in to aid in the measurement of the relative social worth of these unwelcome guests. Thus, according to the calculations of one sociologist, the consecutive order of ten ethnic varieties in the United States according to their "mean rating" in all of ten selected personal traits, is as follows: 1. Native White Americans. 2. Germans. 3. English. 4. Polish and Russian Hebrews. 5. Scandinavians. 6. Irish. 7. French Canadians. 8. Austrian Slavs. 9. South Italians. 10. Negroes. The ratings are based upon the judgments of ten competent observers, among whom were sociologists, psychologists, journalists and social workers. The personal traits chosen were: physical vigor, intellectual ability, self-control, moral integrity, sympathy, coöperation, leadership, perseverance, efficiency, aspiration. He finds that "the Irish, Jews and native Americans appear to vary considerably in excellence, but the repeated low ranking of Negroes, Italians, Slavs, and French Canadians is remarkable. It may be said that Anglo-Saxon prejudice here prevails and it must be admitted that Negroes, Slavs or Latins were not represented in our list of observers. However, since American standards of judgment have been derived mainly from English and Teutonic sources, this order probably represents the relative conformity to our notions of excellence." . . .

If now these new immigrants begin to fuse with the old, the original stock will be diluted by having "sub-common" blood injected into its veins. The resulting race, being by heredity inferior to the old, will be culturally sterile. Considerations of cheap labor and rapid development of natural resources are then temporary and insignificant phases of the problem when compared with the possible biologic consequences. . . .

The problem of immigration will therefore not be satisfactorily solved unless it is clearly understood that at bottom it is a struggle between an older superior racial group and culture, and newer inferior racial groups and cultures, and that heroic measures must speedily be adopted to secure the supremacy of the former.

Source: Julius Drachsler, *Democracy and Assimilation: The Blending of Immigrant Heritages in America* (New York: Macmillan, 1920), 40–45.

3.6. New Immigrants Bring New Life and New Blood in the Early Twentieth Century

While many Americans criticized the turn-of-the-century immigrants, there were those who saw value in the newcomers and in the diversity that they were bringing to the nation. Among these were the mostly young, often college-educated, settlement house workers who lived in the midst of and worked with the "new" immigrants. One of these was Lillian Wald, the director of the Henry Street Settlement House in New York City. While she and others were not uncritical of aspects of immigrant life in America, many of them saw, as she wrote in 1915 in The House on Henry Street, *that the Southern and Eastern Europeans were bringing "a steady stream of new life and new blood to the nation."*

The immigrant brings in a steady stream of new life and new blood to the nation. The unskilled have made possible the construction of great engineering works, have helped to build bridges and roadways above and under ground. The number of skilled artisans and craftsmen among immigrants and the contribution they make to the cultural side of our national life are too rarely emphasized. Alas for our educational system! we must still look abroad for the expert cabinetmaker or stone-carver, the weaver of tapestry, or the artistic worker in metals, precious or base.

In another place I have spoken of the rise of certain needle trades from those of sweaters and sweaters' victims to a standardized industry, with an output estimated at hundreds of millions yearly. The industry of cloak and suit making has been to a large extent developed by the immigrants themselves. When the stranger looks upon the lofty buildings in other parts of the city, gigantic beehives with the swarms of workers going in and out, he seldom comprehends that great wealth has been created for the community by these humble workers.

The man who now stands at the gates of Ellis Island turns his socially trained mind toward the development of methods for the protection and assimilation of the immigrant after the gates have closed upon him. But the best conceived plans of this Commissioner of Immigration and others who have long studied the question will be fruitless unless, throughout the country, an intelligent and respectful attitude toward the stranger is sedulously cultivated.

In the early glow of our enthusiasm, when we were first brought in contact with the immigrant, we dreamed of making his coming of age—his admission to citizenship—something of a rite. Many who come here to escape persecution or the hardships suffered under a militaristic government idealize America. They bring an enthusiasm for our institutions.

Source: Lillian Wald, *House on Henry Street* (New York: Henry Holt, 1915), 306–7.

3.7. President Kennedy Calls for Repeal of Discriminatory Immigration Quotas

Following World War II, the external Cold War struggle and the domestic civil rights movement put pressure on the federal government to revise, in a more open and global way, the restrictive immigration legislation passed in the 1920s. The Irish Catholic John F. Kennedy, as a senator and then as president, was deeply concerned about immigrants and about America's immigration laws and policies. Many of his ideas on these matters were put forward in A Nation of Immigrants, *published posthumously in 1964. Kennedy praised immigrant diversity, criticized and called for a repeal of the restrictive national origins quota system, and advocated a more generous, fairer, and more flexible immigration policy. The important, pathbreaking 1965 immigration law, passed under President Lyndon Johnson, contained many of the ideas promoted by Kennedy.*

The Immigration and Nationality Act of 1952 undertook to codify all our national laws on immigration. This was a proper and long overdue task. But it was not just a housekeeping chore. In the course of the deliberation over the Act, many basic decisions about our immigration policy were made. The total racial bar against the naturalization of Japanese, Koreans and other East Asians was removed, and a minimum annual quota of one hundred was provided for each of these countries. Provision was also made to make it easier to reunite husbands and wives. Most important of all was the decision to do nothing about the national origins system.

The famous words of Emma Lazarus on the pedestal of the Statue of Liberty read: "Give me your tired, your poor, your huddled masses yearning to breathe free." Until 1921 this was an accurate picture of our society. Under present law it would be appropriate to add: "as long as they come from Northern Europe, are not too tired or too poor or slightly ill, never stole a loaf of bread, never joined any questionable organization, and can document their activities for the past two years."

Furthermore, the national origins quota system has strong overtones of an indefensible racial preference. It is strongly weighted toward so-called Anglo-Saxons, a phrase which one writer calls "a term of art" encompassing almost anyone from Northern and Western Europe. Sinclair Lewis described his hero, Martin Arrowsmith, this way: "a typical pure-bred-Anglo-Saxon American—which means that he was a union of German, French, Scotch-Irish, perhaps a little Spanish, conceivably of the strains lumped together as 'Jewish,' and a great deal of English, which is itself a combination of primitive Britain, Celt, Phoenician, Roman, German, Dane and Swede."

Yet, however much our present policy may be deplored, it still remains our national policy. As President Truman said when he vetoed the Immigration and Nationality Act (only to have that veto overridden): "The idea behind this discriminatory policy was, to put it boldly, that Americans with English or Irish names were better people and better citizens than Americans with Italian or Greek or Polish names. . . . Such a concept is utterly unworthy of our traditions and our ideals."

Immigration policy should be generous; it should be fair; it should be flexible. With such a policy we can turn to the world, and to our own past, with clean hands and a clear conscience. Such a policy would be but a reaffirmation of old principles. It would be an expression of our agreement with George Washington that "The bosom of America is open to receive not only the opulent and respectable stranger, but the oppressed and persecuted of all nations and religions; whom we shall welcome to a participation of all our rights and privileges, if by decency and propriety of conduct they appear to merit the enjoyment."

Source: John F. Kennedy, *A Nation of Immigrants* (New York: Harper and Row, 1964), 77–83.

3.8. Late Twentieth-Century Immigrants Threaten the Cultural Homogeneity of the United States

The immigration laws of 1965 and succeeding years have led to America's third major wave of immigration, one that has opened the United States to people from every nation in the world. This global diversity has aroused fear, discomfort, and opposition among a portion of America's citizenry, as heterogeneity did in the past. Paul Craig Roberts, a columnist, is one among a considerable number of writers who have given voice to this opposition. Roberts, in "The Ethnic Cleansing of European-Americans," in the June 1999 issue of the Washington Times National Weekly, *castigated American immigration policy for threatening "cultural homogeneity" in the United States. This article was reprinted on the Web site of the U.S. Border Control, an organization which advocates greater immigration restriction.*

Recently a federal judge wrote to me. The judge enclosed a list of new citizens for whom he had conducted a naturalization ceremony. He was astounded that among almost 100 new citizens there were only four or five Europeans.

Immigration policy has produced an extraordinary change in the ethnic composition of the U.S. population. Experts tell me it has been three decades since Europeans comprised a significant percentage of new citizens. In 1965 the Democrats, who lost the South, changed the immigration rules in order to build African, Asian and Hispanic constituencies that would vote Democratic.

In effect, native-born U.S. citizens are being "ethnically cleansed," not by violence but by their own immigration policy. With the United States taking in 1.2 million immigrants annually, and with that number again entering illegally, cultural homogeneity has been the casualty.

When I first came to Washington, D.C. 25 years ago, the only international looking people one saw were in the diplomatic community. Now it is every third person. A person can now duplicate the experiences of world travel by just touring the neighborhoods inside the D.C. Beltway. It is much the same in most cities.

Recent immigrants who favor the melting pot are themselves alarmed. Yeh Ling-Ling, the executive director of Diversity Alliance for a Sustainable America, believes we need a time-out from mass immigration in order to permit assimilation; otherwise, the United States will face ethnic divides that exceed those in Kosovo and the Balkans.

Source: Paul Craig Roberts, "The Ethnic Cleansing of European-Americans," *Washington Times National Weekly*, June 21–27, 1999, 1. www.usbc.org

3.9. Immigration Diversity Since World War II Has Strengthened America's Religious Traditions

There have been those in the United States who have applauded the increasingly variegated immigrant influx through the last half of the twentieth century as helping to vitalize America and to position it positively in an increasingly interrelated world. An aspect of this globalization, as Migration News of North America, *a pro-immigration publication, reported with approval in 1996, has been increased religious diversity in the United States. This report also showed that some of the traditional American religious denominations have been strengthened by the new wave of immigrants.*

Largely because of changes in immigration laws in 1965, the United States "is now the most religiously diverse country on earth," according to an article in the September–October, 1996 issue of Harvard magazine.

According to Professor Martin Marty of the University of Chicago, a religion has "six marks"—a system centered on a matter of deep meaning, socialization (believers tend to form communities), show a preference for symbolic language over everyday speech, use ceremonies (especially at birth, marriage and death), take a metaphysical view of life (there is more to the world than what one sees) and require behavioral adjustments (attending Sunday School or shunning pork).

Some social scientists consider that religious institutions to be [one] of the most important sources of social capital in the US—institutions that can create the social networks and norms that enable people to work together for common goals. Churches, in this view, teach people basic political skills—how to give a speech, organize a meeting, raise money and provide pools of friends and neighbors who can be recruited for civic activities.

Protestants. Many traditional Protestant denominations are welcoming immigrants and hope to thereby bolster declining membership.

It has not always been easy to integrate immigrants. The First United Methodist Church in Queens, New York was troubled in 1995 by divisions between Filipino immigrants and African Americans. The pastor of the church tried to bring in new lay ministers, but was removed by the Bishop, prompting some of the immigrant members to picket the Bishop's office. In Queens, churches that rely on immigrants who joined long ago are dying—one has 30 elderly Polish-American members, another only five German-American members.

The United Methodist Church has lost about two million members nationwide in 10 years. Membership is growing in communities with Korean, Caribbean, African and Asian immigrants.

Most Americans attend neighborhood churches and their attendance patterns reflect housing patterns. Martin Luther King in the 1960s asserted that 11 am on Sunday morning was the most segregated hour of the week, as African-Americans and whites went to separate churches. There are very few racially-integrated churches in the US.

Catholics. The Pope's October 1995 visit to New York highlighted the ethnic diversity of Catholic parishes brought about by continuing immigration. Churches built by German or Irish or Italian immigrants decades ago now celebrate Mass in Spanish or Polish. Mass is celebrated in New York area churches in 38 languages.

Before his 1995 visit, the Pope released a statement asking established residents to try to understand the circumstances of illegal immigrants. "The illegal immigrant," the Pope said, "comes before us like that stranger whom Jesus asks to be recognized." The Pope called for international cooperation to foster political stability and accelerate economic development so that people are not forced to migrate.

In an address to the United Nations in 1995 the Pope deplored the "fear of difference" that he said can lead to violations of human rights.

Catholic leaders make a point of saying that no passport or papers are required to enter their churches, thus reproving those with less welcoming attitudes to immigrants. Los Angeles Archbishop Roger Mahoney decried Prop. 187 in California in fall 1994 as a "social sin," and pastoral letters in New York and elsewhere remind listeners that Catholic teaching instructs that immigrants should be treated with hospitality.

A nationwide September 1995 poll conducted in English and Spanish found that about the same percentage of Catholics as respondents in general—28 percent—want immigration levels reduced.

There are an estimated 22 million Hispanic Catholics in the United States, about a third of the country's 66 million Catholics. About a fourth of the Hispanic Catholics were born outside the US.

California's Catholic priests are becoming more outspoken on issues such as affirmative action and prenatal care for undocumented immigrants, a major change from their previous behind-the-scenes lobbying efforts. A group of clerics representing the state's 12 dioceses met with elected officials in Sacramento in March, 1996.

According to a spokesperson, the group's advocacy is a mandate from the state's 5.6 million Hispanic Catholics whom they represent, and also reflects the church's traditional concern for the poor, elderly and children. The group became more outspoken after a November 1995 pastoral statement from the US Catholic Conference of Bishops that urged Catholics to become more active politically as a community conscience.

Islam. There are six to eight million Muslims in the US, including two million Black Muslims. The number of Muslims in the US is increasing rapidly through immigration and conversions. Islam, now with one billion adherents, is the world's fastest-growing religion.

Of the more than 1,200 mosques in the US, nearly 80 percent have been built within the past 12 years. The first theological school in the US to train Islamic imams opened in Virginia in 1996. In the past two years, six mosques have been damaged or destroyed by arson.

Experts say that Islam, with its clearly defined behavioral norms, is particularly appealing to American blacks living in neighborhoods where community and family life have been strained by poverty, crime and despair. Islam also provides an alternative for some blacks who associate Christianity with slavery and racism. For some, Islam is a bridge to their African roots—as many as 20 percent of the slaves transported to America may have been Muslims.

At a private Islamic school in Silver Spring, Maryland, girls who wear the hijab, or traditional Muslim head scarf, do not have to worry about teasing by their classmates. Islamic schools in the Washington, DC area are popular; most have long waiting lists. The American Muslim Council estimates that there are 200,000 Muslims in the Washington DC area and 1,500 pupils in Islamic schools. Many Muslim parents who cannot get their children into Islamic school opt to homeschool.

Some Muslims, both immigrant and American-born, are organizing to increase their political clout. Most are liberal on minority rights and immigration, but conservative in such matters as opposing sex and violence in movies and television. In California, home to the largest Muslim community in the US, most Muslims supported Republican Pete Wilson in the governor's race, but most opposed Prop. 187.

Source: Philip Martin, "Religion and Immigration," *Migration News, North America* 3, no. 12 (December 1996), 1–3, www.migration.ucdavis.edu.

ANNOTATED SELECTED BIBLIOGRAPHY

Brimelow, Peter. *Alien Nation: Common Sense about America's Immigration Disaster*. New York: Random House, 1995. Speaks strongly against diverse immigrants coming to the United States in the latter decades of the twentieth century; maintains that they are a danger to the nation.

de Crèvecoeur, J. Hector St. John. *Letters from an American Farmer*. London: Thomas Davies, 1782. Reprint, New York: E. P. Dutton, 1957. Describes, very positively, the variety of people in America, particularly in the Middle Atlantic region, at the time of the Revolutionary War.

Dublin, Thomas, ed. *Immigrant Voices: New Lives in America*. Urbana: University of Illinois Press, 1993. First-person accounts of immigrants from many different countries from the early nineteenth century to the latter part of the twentieth century.

Fuchs, Lawrence. *The American Kaleidoscope: Race, Ethnicity and the Civic Culture*. Hanover, N.H.: Wesleyan University Press, 1990. Presents the conflicts, accommodations, and contributions relating to differing immigrant groups in the history of the United States.

Gavit, John Palmer. *Americans by Choice*. New York: Harper, 1922. Reprint, Montclair, N.J.: Patterson Smith, 1971. Speaks positively about the many different new people arriving in the United States, during the second major wave of immigration, 1880–1920.

Grant, Madison. *The Passing of the Great Race*. New York: Charles Scribner's Sons, 1916. A vigorous voice against the diversity of the newcomers in the second wave of immigration in the United States and a warning to "Anglo Saxons" to close the door to the United States or be overwhelmed. The book, which went through many editions significantly influenced immigration restriction legislation after World War I.

Haines, David. *Refugees in the United States: A Reference Handbook*. Westport, Conn.: Greenwood Press, 1985. Describes background and settlement of each of the major refugee groups that came to the United States between 1960 and the early 1980s.

Kennedy, John F. *A Nation of Immigrants*. New York: Harper and Row, 1964. Positive account of the contribution of diverse foreign-born people to the development of the United States.

Reimers, David. *Still the Golden Door: The Third World Comes to America*. 2nd ed., New York: Columbia University Press, 1992. Discusses the very diverse Third World immigrants—legal, by contract, and undocumented—who have entered the United States from before World War II through the 1980s.

Ross, Edward A. *The Old World in the New*. New York: Century Co., 1914. Very negative position in regard to the new and different immigrants coming to the United States in the years after 1880.

Stolarik, Mark, ed. *Forgotten Doors: The Other Ports of Entry to the United States*. Philadelphia: Balch Institute Press, 1988. A collection of essays on immigration, particularly from 1880 to 1930, through the ports of Baltimore, Boston, Los Angeles, Miami, New Orleans, Philadelphia, and San Francisco.

Takaki, Ronald. *Strangers from a Different Shore: A History of Asian Americans*. Boston: Little, Brown, 1989. An account of the origins and settlement of Asian immigrants and their reception by the Americans who were already resident in the United States.

Ungar, Sanford. *Fresh Blood: The New American Immigrants*. New York: Simon and

Schuster, 1995. A sympathetic examination of the post–World War II immigrants, the communities that they have established, and the issues that they have faced. Discusses the treatment of these newcomers by the American people.

U.S. Immigration Commission, 1907–1911. *Report*. 41 vols. Washington, D.C.: U.S. Government Printing Office, 1911. An extensive investigation of a wide variety of aspects of turn-of-the-century immigration.

Warne, Frank. *The Immigration Invasion*. New York: Dodd, Mead and Company, 1913. The large influx of Southern and Eastern European immigrants in the early twentieth century is creating a diversity that threatens American institutions and the racial and ethnic composition of the nation.

Wattenberg, Ben J. *The First Universal Nation*. New York: Maxwell Macmillan International, 1991. A positive viewpoint on the variety of new immigrants who have come to the United States since World War II.

ORGANIZATIONS AND WEB SITES

Americans for Immigration Control Foundation: www.cfw.com

Federation for American Immigration Reform: www.fairus.org

Immigration Forum: www.immigrationforum.org

Migration and Refugee Services: www.nccbuscc.org/mrs

Migration News of North America: www.migration.ucdavis.edu

National Council of La Raza: www.nclr.org

National Network for Immigration and Refugee Rights: www.nnirr.org

Project USA: www.ProjectUSA.org

Social Contract: www.thesocialcontract.com

U.S. Border Control: www.usbc.org

4

Has Immigration Affected the Quality of the Environment?

The environmental movement in the United States arose primarily in the post–World War II era. While there was an early and has been a long continuing concern about crowding and pollution in the cities, the predominant American outlook has been shaped by the nation's great territorial expanse and an abundance of natural resources and the need for people to develop both of them. Not until the second half of the twentieth century did concerns about a too rapid growth of population, a degradation of the environment, and negative consequences from development become major issues hitched to questions about immigration policy.

In the colonial period and through the nineteenth century, the abundance of land was a major factor in attracting immigrants to America. The extensive and expanding territory of the United States encouraged a general openness to immigration as a means of developing the country. As A. Woodbury, in an article published in *The New Englander* in 1855, wrote, "We have plenty of land yet unoccupied, and there is no danger as yet of crowding one another. Eight persons to a square mile give us a really sparse population," as compared to the 207 inhabitants per square mile in Europe at that time. Woodbury continued, "While we have so much land, which it is utterly impossible for us to use or occupy, the crowded population of Europe should annually send off immense numbers to find a home in the western world.... We are glad that they come."[1] Virginia governor Henry Wise, in 1856 in the *Richmond Examiner*, also argued for continued open immigration; the country's two billions of unimproved acres, he observed "might be made to add to our national wealth, by cultivation and population."[2] Such was the confidence in America's ability to absorb immigrants as the frontier beckoned.

While a considerable number of those who did come were attracted to and had the resources to obtain land for farming, an increasing number settled in the nation's growing cities where economic opportunities burgeoned amid the "market revolution." There also were those who came to America with such limited resources that they could not afford to travel beyond the port cities in which they had arrived from Europe.

The growth of cities worried those who regarded it as a threat to the dominance of rural power and values. In 1800 Thomas Jefferson wrote; "I view great cities as pestilential to the morals, the health and the liberties of man."[3] When an economic depression hit America, *Niles' Weekly Register* reported in 1819, "The tide of emigration still set to the United States. . . . We regret that it is so. . . . Our population in most of the maritime districts and in some parts of the interior also, seems too thick—there are too many mouths to consume what the hands can find business to do."[4]

The fears of growing and congested cities markedly increased after 1840. The introduction of the railroad and the steamship accelerated the growth of cities as economic centers, and new mill towns prospered along the rivers where water power could be readily harnessed. Steam power enabled more factories to locate in cities. These urban areas and their workplaces were fed by the inflow of large numbers of newcomers in America's first major wave of immigration. Tens of thousands of people, many of them very poor, searched out housing, which was inadequate and often wretched. Many health problems plagued the newcomers as growing amounts of sewage fouled the water supply and made the city pipes seem "rotten."

While technology helped alleviate some of these problems by the end of the nineteenth century, others were worsened as the number of immigrants grew even larger in the years after 1880. A city like New York with a population of some 40,000 in 1800 had grown over 25 times to over a million people (together with Brooklyn) by 1860, and then, after the consolidation of Brooklyn and the other boroughs into greater New York in 1898, to five million by 1900. Urban congestion helped fuel the surge of anti-immigrant protestations in the 1850s and again at the turn of the century. Anti-urban views merged with anti-immigrant ones as the population rose.

In 1914 Edward Ross, a professor of sociology at the University of Wisconsin, and a major critic of immigration, linked the social and political ills of cities to the immigrants crowding into them.

> Not least among the multiplying symptoms of social ill health in this country is the undue growth of cities. . . . The proportion of American stock steadily diminishes while the foreign stock increases its representation until in the great cities it constitutes nearly three-fourths of the population. . . . Congestion, misliving, segregation, corruption, and confusion are seen in motley groups like Pittsburgh, Jersey City, Paterson, and Fall River.[5]

Railroads and trolleys began to pull urban people out of the core city areas to suburban localities, and growth in the use of the automobile after 1920 markedly accelerated this movement. Although this phenomenon decreased the population in the central cities, it added a new problem there because automobiles contributed heavily to growing air pollution. This transformation of the transportation system, particularly in metropolitan regions, led to greater economic and social segregation—isolating the middle class from immigrants and blacks and making them seem even more foreign. It was easier to blame the physical deterioration of the cities on the poor who continued, often out of necessity, to live there.

Expanding industry through the early and mid-twentieth century also increased the pollution of air and water. While some people voiced concern over the environmental costs of industrial and transportation expansion before 1940, only after World War II did a growing awareness of and concern about the deteriorating environment take hold. This concern gave birth to a movement, with support from a wide variety of grassroots public interest groups, that would result in a vast array of new laws and agencies.

Many in the environmental movement came to focus on the growing human population worldwide and in the United States as a basic cause of the depletion of natural resources and the degradation of nature. Unless population growth was checked, they argued, it would endanger the quality and perhaps even the survival of human life. They regarded expanding population as increasing crowding with a resulting greater pollution of air and water; as leading to the destruction of wilderness places, wetlands, and farmland; and as draining limited natural resources. Not only did they want to limit human reproduction in the United States, but they also wanted to restrict sharply—some even to put a moratorium on—immigration.

The influential Sierra Club was one of the first environmental groups to call for a limit on immigration. Although there have been dissenting voices in this organization, it has continued to show concern about the negative impact of immigration on the environment, and it has been joined in this by other environmental groups, including Negative Population Growth, the Izaak Walton League, and Population-Environment Balance. Nick Ervin, the conservation chairperson of the San Diego Sierra Club, wrote in 1993, "Immigration into the United States means higher consumption rates globally and higher fertility rates nationally."[6] David Simcox, the director of the Center for Immigration Studies, in 1992 wrote in *Elephants in the Volkswagen: Facing the Tough Questions about Our Overcrowded Country*:

> Immigration under current law and practice directly accounts for 32 percent of national population growth. . . . If the United States is to begin to reverse its population growth, net immigration of 300,000 or less is imperative. But as annual entries have crept up since the 1960s, we have come to see as the norm a net inflow of newcomers of at least twice that number.[7]

Richard Lamm, a former governor of Colorado and an active anti-immigration advocate, wrote for *Social Contract* in 1997: "The United States is no longer an empty continent that can absorb endless pools of labor. . . . It is time to close down the age of mass immigration. It has served us well in the past. It does not make public sense for the future."[8] The Federation for Immigration Reform (FAIR), a strong activist group advocating a reduction in immigration, has expressed much concern about the future of the American environment. In 1998 they asserted,

> [N]o amount or kind of conservation efforts can succeed in reducing overall resource consumption and pollution if population does not level off. . . . Our population hasn't leveled off, and isn't expected to begin to level off for even the next fifty years. Why? Because of immigration. . . . All Americans who are committed to preserving the environment should include immigration reduction as part of the action agenda they support.[9]

Proponents of continued and even more open immigration have urged Americans to realize that human reproduction in the United States has been decreasing over the years, as it has in a number of other affluent urban industrialized nations, and that the population here has not been fully replacing itself. Some of these pro-immigration advocates have argued that if the United States is to continue to have its high standard of living and wants to include therein a greater percentage of Americans who are now below the poverty line, the economy has to continue to grow. This growth would require a replacement of the declining birthrate by immigration, particularly young immigrant workers. These advocates have argued that an open immigration policy is needed for a prosperous American future. They maintain that science and technology already have begun to decrease the danger of pollution and to increase farm and industrial productivity.

Franklin Abrams, a representative voice among those who demographically regard immigration as an asset and not a danger to America's future, wrote in 1984 in *U.S. Immigration Policy*:

> The advocates of zero population growth complain that immigration now accounts for 50% of U.S. population growth. They neglect to mention, however, that the principal reason for this percentage is that the U.S. birth rate has declined to less than the replacement level. . . . Under current fertility trends . . . net immigration of 800,000 per year would be necessary to prevent a decline in population. . . . Furthermore, when compared to Europe, the United States is relatively uncrowded. For example, France—not the most densely populated country in Europe—is four times as densely populated as the United States.[10]

Peter Francese, president of *American Demographics Magazine*, strongly supported the proponents of a more open immigration when in 1990 he wrote,

> [T]here are powerful demographic forces at work in the United States that virtually mandate federal policy be changed to permit more immigration than we have now. The rapid increase in the number of very elderly people, combined with declining numbers of young adults and a record low population growth rate, will put this nation in a demographic vise. . . . By continuing to restrict immigration tightly we shoot ourselves in both feet. In the short run, our productive capacity is crippled by worker shortages, and in the long run, we will be hobbled by high dependency ratios—too many elderly dependents for too few workers. . . . The United States needs to admit more immigrants now.[11]

Advocates for more open immigration accuse some environmental groups of being a cover for persons who do not care for the race and ethnicity of current immigrants and want to stop their coming into the country. In May 2001, the California-based Political Ecology Group reported that by "using alarmist arguments about U.S. population growth, anti-immigrant organizations are actively courting environmentalists and urging them to support an immigration moratorium. . . . These groups are exploiting people's valid fears about environmental degradation to foment a hateful anti-immigrant atmosphere. . . . This scapegoating draws attention away from the real corporate causers of environmental problems and divides immigrants and environmentalists when we need to be working together."[12]

Two major forces are currently in conflict in the United States: the environmental movement and continuing immigration. The environmentalists are concerned about vanishing open space, wilderness areas, and wetlands; about the depletion of natural resources; about dangers of pollution to clean air and clean water; and in general about the future quality of life. Population growth is regarded as a key threat to all these aspects of the environment. While the environmentalists have gained a wider hearing for their arguments nationwide, they have not succeeded in pressuring Congress into lowering the number of immigrants legally accepted into the United States annually. One of the reasons for this lack of success has been that proponents of economic growth, in the face of a declining birthrate, have argued that immigration remains important to help supply current and future workforce needs. In particular, the prosperity of the latter 1990s into the twenty-first century has absorbed immigrant workers, has increased the demand for them, and has lessened, for the time, some of the effectiveness of those advocating for increased immigration restriction. If, however, there is an economic downturn, the environmentalists likely will gain allies in their fight for a reduction of the number of immigrants permitted to enter the country.

NOTES

1. A. Woodbury, "The Moral of Statistics," *New Englander* 13, 1855, 189–91.
2. Quoted in James Hambleton, *A Biographical Sketch of Henry A. Wise* (Richmond, Va.: 1856), 321–24.
3. Thomas Jefferson to Benjamin Rush, September 23, 1800, in *The Writings of Thomas Jefferson*, ed. Andrew Lipscomb and Albert Bergh (Washington, D.C.: Thomas Jefferson Memorial Association of the United States, 1904), vol. 10, 173.
4. "Too Many Immigrants," *Niles' Weekly Register* 17, September 18, 1819, 36.
5. Edward A. Ross, *The Old World in the New* (New York: Century, 1914).
6. Nick Ervin, "Immigration and the Environment," *Wild Earth*, 3, no. 2 (Summer 1993): 77.
7. David Simcox, "Sustainable Immigration, Learning to Say No," in *Elephants in the Volkswagen: Facing the Tough Questions about Our Overcrowded Country*, ed. Lindsey Grant (New York, W. H. Freeman, 1992), 168, 170.
8. Richard Lamm, "A New Question for Makers of Public Policy," *Social Contract*, Fall 1997. (www.thesocialcontract.com)
9. FAIR, "The Immigration—Population—Environment Connection," *Issue Brief*, October 1998. (www.fairus.org)
10. Franklin Abrams, "American Immigration Policy: How Strait the Gate?" In *U.S. Immigration Policy*, ed. Richard Hofstetter (Durham, N.C.: Duke University Press, 1984), 109, 116.
11. Peter Francese, "Aging America Needs Foreign Blood," *Wall Street Journal*, March 27, 1990, 20.

12. "Immigration & Environmental Campaign," San Francisco: Political Ecology Group. www.peg@peg.org

DOCUMENTS

4.1. More Immigrants Are Entering the United States in 1819 Than the Country Can Support

In the early nineteenth century the Niles' Weekly Register *was an important newspaper in the United States. It was much concerned about the economic downturn in 1819. Even though immigration was relatively small compared to what it became after 1840, this newspaper reported public fear that America had more immigrants than the economy could support. This concern reflected, environmentally, a lack of confidence in the ability of America's natural resources to support a growing population. A similar concern would be expressed during each economic downturn in the nation's history.*

The tide of emigration still sets to the United States. Never before perhaps, except in the last year, did so many persons from Europe reach our shores to take up their abode with us, at this advanced state of the season, as are now arriving. We regret that it is so. Hundreds, perhaps we might say thousands of them, will be incumbrances on us during the ensuing winter; for many tens of thousands of our own people, accustomed to sustain themselves by their labor, will be out of employment, unless some extraordinary event shall take place.

We have always until just now greeted the stranger on his arrival here with pleasure. There was room enough for all that would come, and industry was a sure road to a comfortable living, if not to independence and wealth. We were glad of the addition which they made to our population, and of the impulse which they gave to the capacity of production, thus advancing our country to its weight of power and extent of resources which the patriot delights to anticipate, but which also every one desired to see realized. Now, however, our population in most of the maritime districts and in some parts of the interior also, seems too thick—there are too many mouths to consume what the hands can find business to do; and that hitherto sure refuge of the industrious foreign emigrant, the western country, is overstocked by the domestic emigration. Certainly, the present system cannot last long, and the time *must* come when home industry will be encouraged and protected, in all its branches. If this were the case, all would be busy, money would circulate freely, and happiness abound.

It appears that a good many persons who recently arrived from England, being disappointed in their prospects of employment, are on their return home. We have thought that some such were occasionally reshipped, under sanction and perhaps at the cost of the British government, that they might check emigration. But this cannot be suspected now. The poor people are truly alarmed at the prostration of things presented to them, and will rather depend upon the resources they have been accustomed to, than suffer poverty in a land of strangers. Still those who have a little money, may certainly do better with it here than at home.

It is reported, that to relieve themselves of the support of their paupers, many such will be sent to the United States by the church-wardens, etc., of England! It will therefore become the state authorities to be careful to take the proper securities of those who bring passengers, that they will not become chargeable on the public.

Source: "Too Many Immigrants," *Niles' Weekly Register* 17, September 18, 1819, 36.

4.2. No Danger of Crowding from Immigration in the United States with Its Extensive Unoccupied Land in the 1850s

---

In 1855, in the midst of strong nativist opposition to the large number of newcomers then entering the United States, A. Woodbury, a proponent of expanding immigration, expressed the opinion of those in the country who recognized that immigrants were an important asset to the economic growth of the United States. Environmentally, Woodbury voiced optimism that America's extensive space and natural resources could well support a growing population, including the influx of many new immigrants.

It will be seen at once that we have plenty of land yet unoccupied, and there is no danger as yet of crowding one another. Eight persons to a square mile give us a really sparse population. The case in Europe is considerably different. There, the smallest degree of density is to be found in the kingdom of Sweden and Norway, where the population numbers 4,645,007, and where there are but 15.83 inhabitants to a square mile. The largest degree is to be found in Belgium, with a population of

4,426,202, and a density of 388.60 to a square mile. Eight countries in Europe, namely, Austria, France, Great Britain and Ireland, Prussia, Belgium, Denmark, Holland, and Switzerland, have an average density of 207 inhabitants to a square mile. It is not surprising that, while we have so much land, which it is utterly impossible for us to use or occupy, the crowded population of Europe should annually send off immense numbers to find a home in the western world, where there is so much room for them, and such ample accommodations. We are glad that they come. We would welcome them and give them on our soil a free and happy home. We deprecate, to the utmost, that dog-in-the-manger policy which would attempt to prevent their using what we ourselves do not want, and cannot improve.

While we are on this branch of our subject, let us see to what extent this foreign element is mingled into our population. In the whole country, out of a white population of 19,553,068 in 1850, there were but 2,240,581 foreign born persons. The number may have increased to about 3,000,000 by the present time of writing. This is a ratio of about 9 per cent of the aggregate population. This population was divided in 1850 into 1,239,464 males, and 1,001,117 females. Such is the extent. It seems to us not a very formidable array of numbers.

Whatever danger there is to be apprehended from the mixture of foreigners with the native population, it certainly does not arise from the number of foreigners. For that is comparatively small. Does it come from the number of votes which they are able to throw, in a hotly contested election? By the tables presented in a speech delivered by Hon. N. P. Banks, of Massachusetts, during the late session of Congress, we find that, at the last presidential election, out of a canvass of 1,931,024 votes in fourteen states, giving a majority of the electoral vote, the foreign vote numbered just 258,548, or in a proportion of one to seven and a fraction. In these states there was then a foreign population of 1,763,497. The proportion of the number of voters to the population is nearly the same with the proportion of foreign voters to the whole number of votes cast. In these fourteen states it is found that of the whole foreign population 856,480 were Irish born, who were mostly Catholics. Of the remainder, nearly 1,000,000, a large proportion must be Protestants, or at least not Catholics. Assuming that seven is the ratio, we have for the sum total, in these states, of Irish voters, Catholic and Protestant, 122,354. We are very apt to hear of "millions of foreigners," and of "a half-million of Catholic voters, ignorant, superstitious, and semi-civilized, controlling our elections," and the like. We suggest that a little caution on this score, and a stricter adherence to facts, in such a discussion as the nation happens now to be engaged in, would by no means be amiss. We do not see a great deal of danger in the number of foreign voters. We apprehend that there is more to be feared from native demagogues.

Source: A. Woodbury, "The Moral of Statistics," *New Englander* 13, 1855, 189–91.

4.3. Immigration Contributes to Crowding and Social Problems in Early Twentieth-Century Cities

Environmental concerns during the second major wave of immigration, in the years after 1880, focused mostly on massive crowding in America's rapidly expanding cities. As millions of Southern and Eastern European immigrants, together with migrants from rural states, settled in urban areas, congestion became a major problem. Health officials, critics from rural America, and reformers warned about the impact of crowding on the spread of diseases and the growth of pollution. Many called for a restriction on immigration, including Edward Ross, an outspoken professor of sociology at the University of Wisconsin, who expressed his fears about the negative environmental effects of immigration on urban congestion and problems in The Old World in the New, *published in 1914.*

Not least among the multiplying symptoms of social ill health in this country is the undue growth of cities. A million city-dwellers create ten times the amount of "problem" presented by a million on the farms. Now, as one traverses the gamut that leads from farms to towns, from towns to cities, and from little cities to big, the proportion of American stock steadily diminishes while the foreign stock increases its representation until in the great cities it constitutes nearly three-fourths of the population. In 1910 the percentage distribution of our white population was as follows:—

	Native White Stock	Foreign Stock	Foreign-Born
Rural districts	64.1	20.8	7.5
Cities 2,500–10,000	57.5	34.5	13.9
Cities 10,000–25,000	50.4	42.0	14.4
Cities 25,000–100,000	45.9	46.7	20.2
Cities 100,000–500,000	38.9	53.4	22.1
Cities 500,000 and over	25.6	70.8	33.6

It is not that the immigrants love streets and crowds. Two-thirds of them are farm bred, but they are dropped down in cities, and they find it easier to herd there with their fellows than to make their way into the open country. Our cities would be fewer and smaller had they fed on nothing but country-bred Americans. The later alien influx has rushed us into the thick of urban problems, and these are gravest where Americans are fewest. Congestion, misliving, segregation, corruption, and confusion are seen in motley groups like Pittsburgh, Jersey City, Paterson, and Fall River rather than in native centers like Indianapolis, Columbus, Nashville, and Los Angeles.

Source: Edward A. Ross, *The Old World in the New* (New York: Century, 1914), 239–40.

4.4. Post–World War II Immigration Causes Population Growth and Environmental Degradation

---

In the decades since World War II Americans became more aware of the need to protect the environment. These were the years of the nation's third major wave of immigration, which raised concerns that the immigrant contribution to a growing population endangers the American environment. The Federation for American Immigration Reform (FAIR) has been a leading organization urging increased restrictions on immigration in the United States. In one of its "Issue Brief," *entitled "Why Environmentalists Support Immigration Reform," published in 1999, FAIR maintained that immigrants are a major cause of American population growth which has been leading to "environmental degradation" in the United States.*

As one of the world's most populous and consumptive nations, the United States has a particular responsibility to curb its environmental degradation. To some degree, this can be done through changing our society's consumptive habits. But no amount of lifestyle changes will be able to compensate for an ever-growing population.

The United States has a population growth rate that is anomalously high among industrialized nations. If there is no change in our population growth, the population of this country in 2050 will be nearly 50 percent larger than it is now. That many more people will result in that much more pressure on the environment. For us, key to gaining control over and reversing environmental degradation is stabilizing population. . . .

Since 1970 our population has grown by about 68 million people. Almost half of that growth came from post-1970 immigrants and their descendants. If we do not lower the level of immigration, we will add 130 million people to our population size in the next fifty years—80 million (60 percent) of whom will be post-1995 immigrants and their descendants.

Because immigration is the driving force behind present U.S. population increase, limiting immigration is the key to slowing population growth, stabilizing our population, and reining in our environmental degradation. Limiting immigration can be accomplished practically and humanely by adhering to the following principles.

- Move from a system of expansive 'chain migration' to one of discrete 'nuclear family' migration.
- Support an enforceable cap on overall annual immigration of about 200,000.
- Deduct the immediate relatives of an immigrant in the year the primary immigrant is admitted for residence.
- Admissions under any special, new, or temporary programs (such as amnesties, paroles, or lotteries) should count toward the overall cap, and other admissions reduced accordingly.
- Enact a blanket moratorium on future immigration (other than spouses and minor children of U.S. citizens) in order to eliminate the backlog and to get a fresh start.
- Explain these groundrules clearly to the primary immigrant before he/she enters the U.S.

With such changes, the level of immigration would begin to match the level of emigration, and we would develop a 'migration equilibrium' under which immigration would contribute to our economy and society, but not to our population growth. Through reform, immigration can become consistent with our environmental priorities.

We must act now. The environmental pressures caused by immigration-driven population growth are not merely a future possibility; they are a present reality. The daily news teems with tales of the effects of immigration on host communities. Runaway population growth affects not merely the big cities that traditionally receive immigration, but also smaller and more rural communities, which are now receiving both direct immigration and a 'secondary migration' of natives fleeing the effects of that population growth. Stories of urban sprawl and the destruction of the surrounding farmland are rife in the media, and a feeling grows that there is nowhere to run from environmental degradation.

As tempting as it may be to stick our heads in the sand and busy ourselves with more politically acceptable aspects of the problem, we must tackle the immigration aspect as well. Until recently, environmental groups have had little problem either making the connection between immigration and the environment or taking a stance against population growth. For example, in its 1979 publication Handbook on Population Projections, the Sierra Club noted that "for almost fifteen years, the Sierra Club has acknowledged that population growth is the cause of all environmental problems." Since 1965, the year the immigration law was changed in such a way as to unintentionally generate the current high levels of immigration, the Sierra Club has beaten a steady thirty-year drumbeat on the need to limit environmental degradation by limiting population growth and immigration. . . .

The key to maintaining a dynamic stability in any system is equilibrium. For our country to achieve a balance with nature we must accomplish a dynamic stability in our own population. In the United States, that means achieving migration equilibrium where the number of people entering our society balances with the number of people leaving it. Environmentalists owe it to themselves and to posterity to endorse efforts to reach that equilibrium through reforming legal immigration and ending illegal immigration. Difficult though that may seem, it is not nearly so difficult as it will be to deal with the consequences of ignoring the issue.

Source: Scipio Garling, "Why Environmentalists Support Immigration Reform," *Issue Brief*, FAIR, November 1999. (www.fairus.org)

4.5. U.S. Environment Improves in the Late Twentieth Century as Immigration and Population Increase

---

Population growth is at the center of the debate about America and the world's environmental future. While some Americans base opposition to immigration on the grounds that it increases the U.S. population and thus contributes to greater consumption and danger to the environment, others point to the fact that the established American population is not reproducing itself through births and thus immigration is needed for economic growth and national security. There also are those who maintain that increased population stimulates technological advances which leads to an improvement of the environment. This argument is advanced in the report below taken from immigration advocate Julian Simon's The Ultimate Resource *and published by the Washington-based Cato Institute, an influential, pro-immigration think tank and research organization.*

Does adding immigrants to the population cause greater natural resource scarcity for natives? Does immigration cause degradation of the environment? . . .

Supplies of Natural Resources

In the very short run, an additional person necessarily causes increased cost, higher prices, and increased scarcity. But the long-term trends for virtually every raw material (including energy) are toward sharply lower prices and increasing availability. These trends have occurred during periods of increasing population. That is, natural resources over the long run have been getting less scarce rather than more scarce, as indicated by the fundamental economic measure of cost.

This process is counterintuitive. Here is a brief description of the process that brings it about: (1) An immigrant-swelled increased population leads to greater use of natural resources than otherwise. (2) Prices of raw materials then rise. (3) The price rise and the resultant fear about scarcity impel individuals to seek new lodes of raw materials, new production technologies, and new substitutes for the resources. (4) Eventually the price of the service or the resource in question—for example, the price of energy whether produced from wood, coal, oil, or nuclear power—falls lower than it was before the temporary scarcity began. This process requires some time and is quite indirect. Yet this process has been the mainspring of economic progress for 5,000 years.

In short, increased demand eventually leads to supplies greater than would have existed otherwise, rather than to the scarcity that simple Malthusian theory expects.

This process even applies to land. Increased agricultural productivity has led to much former farmland no longer being profitable to farm, with resulting increases in forest and recreational areas, especially in the South and in the Northeast.

Cleanliness of the Environment

The basic trends in U.S. environmental quality are positive, accompanying (though not necessarily caused by) increases in population. The cleanliness of the water we drink in the United States has been improving in past decades by every reasonable measure of quantity and purity. The air, too, has been getting less polluted.

So the weight of the evidence suggests that, though additional people cause more pollution in the short run, in the long run additional people lead to less pollution, strange as that may sound at first to the noneconomist. . . .

Conclusion

As population size and average income have increased in the United States, the supplies of natural resources and the cleanliness of the environment have improved rather than deteriorated. These data do not by themselves prove a causal connection. But they offer very strong evidence that there is not a causal connection in the other direction; more people do not imply deterioration.

Source: "Immigration: The Demographic and Economic Facts, Effects on Natural Resources and the Environment" (Cato Institute and the National Immigration Forum, November 17, 2000), 1–3. (www.cato.org)

ANNOTATED SELECTED BIBLIOGRAPHY

Beck, Roy. *Re-Charting America's Future.* Petoskey, Mich.: Social Contract Press, 1994. Deals with the negative effect on the environment from the impact of immigration on the growing population in the United States.

Bouvier, Leon. *Peaceful Invasion: Immigration and Changing America.* Lanham, Md.: University Press of America, 1992. Discusses the negative aspects of population growth in the United States and the impact of immigration on this growth.

———, and Lindsey Grant. *How Many Americans? Population, Immigration and the Environment.* San Francisco: Sierra Club Books, 1994. Discusses the relationship between immigration and population growth, and calls for greater control of immigration.

Grant, Lindsey. *Elephants in the Volkswagen: Facing the Tough Questions about Our Overcroweded Country.* New York: W. H. Freeman and Company, 1992. Sees population growth, including immigration, as a threat to the environment of the United States.

Hardin, Garrett. *Living within Limits: Ecology, Economics and Population.* Oxford: Oxford University Press, 1993. Makes a strong statement in behalf of reducing population growth; calls for a control on compassion which involves a limit of immigration.

Lammn, Richard, and Gary Imhoff. *The Immigration Time Bomb: The Fragmenting of America.* New York: E. P. Dutton, 1985. Warns that America is receiving too many immigrants and that this will have a negative effect on the country's environment.

Levine, Herbert. *Immigration.* Austin, Tex.: Raintree Steck-Vaughn, 1998. Includes essays, pro and con, on the issue, "Is the United States Admitting Too Many Immigrants?"

Mills, Nicolaus. *Arguing Immigration: The Debate over the Changing Face of America.* New York: Simon and Schuster, 1994. Contains pro and con articles concerning the impact of immigration on the environment in the United States.

Muller, Thomas, and Thomas Espenshade. *The Fourth Wave: California's Newsest Immigrants.* Washington, D.C.: Urban Institute, 1985. Discusses the environmental impact, positive and negative, of the post–World War II large influx of immigrants into California, which has become a major destination for newcomers, particularly from Latin America and Asia.

Simox, David, ed. *U.S. Immigration in the 1980s: Reappraisal and Reform.* Boulder, Colo.: Westview Press, 1988. Includes material on the negative impact of immigration on the environment in the United States.

Simon, Julian. *Population Matters: People, Resources, Environment, and Immigration.* New Brunswick, N.J.: Transaction Publishers, 1990. Discusses the relation of America's population needs to environmental concerns and argues for a more open immigration policy.

ORGANIZATIONS AND WEB SITES

Carrying Capacity Network: www.carryingcapacity.org

Center for Immigration Studies: www.cis.org

Immigration Debate: www.ImmigrationDebate.com

National Network for Immigration and Refugee Rights: www.nnirr.org

National Population Growth: www.npg.org

Sierra Club: www.sierraclub.org

U.S. Numbers: www.NumbersUSA.com

II

Immigration and National Identity

5

How Does Immigration Affect National Identity?

In the process of forming the new United States with an already diverse population, the founding generation used ideas to help bind its people into a nation, ideas expressed to a large extent in the Declaration of Independence and the Constitution. From such ideas a civic culture emerged that valued liberty, established an increasingly participatory democracy, included a bill of rights, and fostered open economic opportunity. These ideals were expected to integrate a citizenry with multiple ethnic and religious backgrounds into a vital new people.

The idea that America promised to remake Old World peoples into a new people echoed in writings of the revolutionary age. At the outset of the Revolutionary War, in 1776, Thomas Paine, a rebel propagandist, saw as a strength for the future of the new nation and its politics the fact that "this new world hath been the asylum for the persecuted lovers of civil and religious liberty from *every part* of Europe."[1] J. Hector St. Jean de Crèvecoeur, in *Letters from an American Farmer* in 1782, wrote,

> What then is the American, this new man? He is either an European, or the descendant of an European, hence that strange mixture of blood, which you will find in no other country. . . . He is an American, who, leaving behind him all his ancient prejudices and manners, receives new ones from the new mode of life he has embraced, the new government he obeys. . . . Here individuals of all nations are melted into a new race of men, whose labours and posterity will one day cause great changes in the world.[2]

At the same time, some of the new nation's leaders, particularly but not only the Federalists (members of a political party favoring a strong national government), believed that those of British descent were the best, perhaps the only, people capable of carrying forward America's republican principles. This was a position held by John Jay, a leader of the Federalist Party, and Alexander Hamilton. Hamilton, the former secretary of the treasury and himself an immigrant from the Caribbean, in 1802, following the Federalists' defeat in recent elections, in part due to the work of foreign-born radicals who escaped revolution in the Old World to nurture it in America, stated that "the safety of the republic depends essentially on the energy of a common national sentiment . . . and love of country which will almost invariably be found to be closely connected with birth, education, and family." Hamilton feared the impact of immigrants on the new American political system: "They will . . . entertain opinion on government congenial with those under which they have lived; or, if they should be led hither from a preference to ours, how extremely unlikely is it that they will bring with them that temperate love of liberty, so essential to real republicanism."[3] In 1781 Thomas Jefferson expressed similar fears in *Notes on the State of Virginia*. To him, American liberty was founded in the English constitution, and he thought that immigrants raised in countries with absolute monarchies would infuse into American politics "their spirit, warp and bias its direction, and render it a heterogeneous, incoherent, distracted mass."[4] The Federalists in Philadelphia regarded Irish immigrants as politically unreliable because they supported the rival Democratic-Republican Party.

Even after the demise of the Federalist Party and the extension of the electorate to the "common man"—that is, to nearly universal white male suffrage, under the Jacksonian Democrats in the 1830s—many voices still expressed fear that a considerable portion, perhaps most, of the large number of immigrants who arrived in America after 1830 were unfit to participate in a democratic government because of their experience with a hierarchical religion and type of government in the countries where they were born and raised. According to the critics, persons who were Catholic and under the domination of a pope and an ecclesiastical hierarchy and those who were brought up in countries dominated by monarchies or other authoritarian rulers lacked the experience of freedom to be constructive members of America's civic culture. Nativists took to the polls in the 1830s and 1840s, but the Know-Nothing Party, which advocated greater restrictions on naturalization, citizenship, and political participation for immigrants, enjoyed the greatest, though short-lived success, during the 1850s when the "famine Irish" and many German Catholics seemingly threatened to swamp American cities with poverty and "disorder."

One of the early nativists was the inventor Samuel Morse. As early as

1835, he became exercised about the increase in the number of Catholics. Morse viewed them—particularly the bishops, priests, and most of all, the Jesuits—as a major threat to American political institutions.

> Already have foreigners increased in the country to such a degree, that they justly give us alarm. . . . The greater part of the foreigners in our population is composed of Roman Catholics. . . . Politicians on both sides have propitiated . . . priests, to obtain the votes of these people. . . . Jesuits are at work upon the passions of the American community, managing in various ways to gain control.[5]

Such ideas fed fears of foreign "corruption" of American republican institutions and of foreign "intrigue" to overthrow democracy. They also spurred nativists to organize. One such group known as the Native Americans proclaimed at its initial national convention held in Philadelphia in 1845:

> It is an incontrovertible truth that the civil institutions of the United States of America have been seriously affected, and that they now stand in imminent peril from the rapid and enormous increase of the body of residents of foreign birth, imbued with foreign feelings, and of an ignorant and immoral character, who receive, under the present lax and unreasonable laws of naturalization, the elective franchise and the right of eligibility to political office. . . . We recommend the immediate organization of the truly patriotic native citizens throughout the United States, for the purpose of resisting the progress of foreign influence in the conduct of American affairs.[6]

Although the nativists enjoyed only limited success at the polls in the 1840s, their warnings helped stir violence against immigrants and Catholics. Indeed, the 1840s was perhaps America's most violent decade as anti-Irish, anti-Catholic, and anti-black riots erupted across urban America.

But the immigrants kept coming in ever greater numbers. In turn, nativists stepped up their call for action. In 1856, when the Native Americans, then better known as the Know-Nothings, were at the height of their political strength, Samuel Busey, a doctor, in his book *Immigration: Its Evils and Consequences*, wrote,

> So far as a knowledge of our institutions is concerned the entire foreign population may be, and should be classed as ignorant, illiterate and uneducated; for the experience of the past, has most clearly proved that their ignorance of Republican institutions con-

> stitutes the most grievous and dangerous evil of foreign immigration.[7]

Supporters of immigrants countered by reminding critics that foreign-born newcomers to the United States were freely choosing liberty and a democratic form of government in coming to America and that the country's experience over many decades showed that persons of different religions and national and ethnic backgrounds had become loyal citizens and had participated constructively in America's civic culture. Typical of this view was a New York State Assembly Select Committee on Resident Aliens report published in 1848 in which the committee concluded,

> To all those foreigners, who in good faith desire to assume the political rights and duties of American citizens, we wisely offer cordial welcome, and every facility for investing themselves with all the rights and privileges of our republican brotherhood. . . . All experience and observation has shown that there are no truer American citizens than the children of those who came among us as aliens.[8]

Anti-Catholic, nativist attacks galvanized Catholics into a defense of their faith and of their fidelity to American principles. In 1855 Martin Spalding, the Catholic bishop in Louisville, Kentucky, reacted strongly against the attacks of the Know-Nothings on the political integrity of Catholic citizens. To the charge that they stood apart from Protestants and voted as a separate bloc, he answered, "This charge is groundless, both in its facts and in its inferences. . . . Whenever it is a question of state policy, they (the Catholics) can have no interests different from those of their fellow-citizens. The laws which will be good for the latter, will be good for them." He further wrote, "Never since the foundation of the republic has it been heard of that the Catholic bishops or clergy have taken an active part in conducting the proceeding of political conventions, or in fomenting political excitement, in the name of the religion of peace and love."[9]

During the 1850s Americans debated furiously over the future of the republic. Slavery was already threatening to tear the union apart. Nativism also loomed as a threat to a unified republic, but friends of liberty rallied to the immigrants' side. An editorial published in *Putnam's Monthly* in 1855 stated, "What is America, and who are Americans? . . . The real American . . . is he . . . who, abandoning every other country and foreswearing every other allegiance, gives his mind and heart to the grand constituent ideas of the Republic."[10] In the same magazine, the poet Parke Godwin warned the nation of possible dire consequences of excluding a large immigrant population from political participation.

> As a doctrine . . . what does Know-Nothingism propose? The political disability of vast numbers of men, on the ground of race or religion. Can anything be more intolerant, narrow, or bigoted? . . . Debar the half-million of emigrants who annually reach our shores from the elective franchise, and what would be the effect? Why, the growth, in the very midst of the community, of a vast disfranchised class—of an immense body of political lepers—of men having an existence apart from their fellow-men, not identified with them, not incorporated with society; and consequently tempted on all sides to conspire against it, to prey upon it, and to keep it in disorder.[11]

While the Know-Nothings did win local elections and gain seats in various state legislatures, they did not succeed in restricting the naturalization of immigrants or their access to the American political process. The slavery controversy soon swamped the nativists and interrupted the debate on American character in relation to immigration. The Civil War fundamentally recast the republican order and promised a "new birth of freedom" for blacks. That promise also reopened the question of what role immigrants might play in a reconstructed union. Still the question of whether only Anglo-Saxons or Northern Europeans were qualified to make the new American political system function effectively or whether the ideals of this system would best be fulfilled by persons who were committed to freedom whatever their ethnic or racial background continued to be debated.

The major wave of immigration that came after 1880 renewed debates on the ability of America to absorb so many "new people." The concern was that a large inflow of people, now from Southern and Eastern Europe as well as from the Middle East, Japan, and the Caribbean, were unfit to participate in American civic and political life. In the increasingly race-conscious late nineteenth century, Anglo-Saxons claimed superior intellect and heritage, but, worried about being overwhelmed by the new immigrants, they begrudgingly included the more acculturated Germans and the Irish into the accepted social groupings. They also asserted that the new immigrants were unfit for self-government. Those who held this position pointed to the authoritarian regimes and religions in the countries from which most of the immigrants were coming, indicted them for their limited education, unfamiliar customs, foreign language, and poverty; and utilized supposed "science" to prove their lesser intellectual ability. In addition, many of these self-proclaimed defenders of American ideals harbored and often outrightly expressed strong racial, ethnic, and religious prejudices.

One such spokesperson was John Commons, an influential labor economist, who, in a 1903 article "Races and Democracy," argued that the democratic form of government in the United States had its origins when "that race, the so-called Anglo-Saxon, developed them out of its own insular experience unhampered by inroads of alien stock." He continued, "These are the basic qualities which underlie democracy—intelligence, manliness, cooperation. If they are lacking democracy is futile. Here is the problem of races, the fundamental division of mankind. Race differences are established in the very blood and physical constitution." From this he concluded that any groups and races judged to have "mental or moral defects" were unfit for participatory democracy.[12]

The critics of the new immigrants considered them a threat to American identity. Henry Fairchild, a professor of sociology at New York University, wrote in *The Melting-Pot Mistake* in 1926: "Unrestricted immigration was . . . slowly, insidiously, irresistibly eating away the very heart of the United States. What was being melted in the great Melting Pot, losing all form and symmetry, all beauty and character, all nobility and usefulness, was the American nationality itself."[13]

Many anti-immigrant advocates also feared the growing strength of the Democratic Party through its success in attracting and representing ethnic and immigrant voters into well-structured urban political organizations, except in Philadelphia where the ruling political machine was Republican. Political reformers and good government groups, advocating a more rational political system, one more controlled by middle-class interests, attacked city bosses who combined corruption with some welfare for the poor. The reformers, who frequently ignored the interests of the poor, condemned immigrants for what they considered herd mentality in their support for the urban political machines. Rural leaders and spokespersons, who saw their area of the country losing political power were also often critical of immigrants who contributed to the growing population and wealth of the nation's cities. These critics further decried the saloons and crime in the urban areas.

Thus, many regarded the new immigrants as a divisive force in the United States, who, if allowed to continue to come in the millions, would subvert the ideals for which America was held to be the world's best hope for a better future. Indicative of such thinking was Frank Warne's influential book *The Tide of Immigration* (1916) in which he wrote, "America is one thing, and America overlaid or interlarded with large slices of the most ignorant and unreliable portions of Europe is another." He was concerned about Jews, Slavs and "un-American immigrants from southern Europe." Warne continued, "[T]he time has come when some restrictive plan must be devised and planned. . . . It has passed beyond the range of purely economic discussion and entered a field wherein all Americans must unite to grapple with a serious threat against the solidarity of the Nation."[14]

Those who spoke in behalf of the immigrants' choice of liberty and the strength of American ideals in bringing together people of varied ethnic and religious backgrounds emphasized the elasticity and resiliency of American democracy and the strength the republic gained from immigrant "contributions." Supreme Court Justice Louis Brandeis, the first Jewish appointee to the Court, attested to such values. In a speech given in Boston in 1915 on "True Americanism," he stated,

> *E pluribus unum*—out of many one—was the motto adopted by the founders of the Republic. . . . They were also convinced, as we are, that in America, under a free government, many people would make one nation. . . . America . . . has always declared herself for equality of nationalities as well as for equality of individuals. It has therefore, given like welcome to all the peoples of Europe. . . . America has believed that each race had something of peculiar values which it can contribute to the attainment of those high ideals for which it is striving.[15]

Brandeis hardly had the last word on this topic; indeed, he was a voice in the face of retreat as the forces of nativism pushed through the highly restrictive National Origins Acts of the 1920s and a new Ku Klux Klan bullied immigrants, Catholics, Jews, and blacks in many Midwestern, Western, and Southern states.

Despite considerable pressure, those who spoke in behalf of immigrants and the fact that diversity could strengthen the nation's democratic ideals succeeded in holding off the anti-immigrant forces, until anti-foreign attitudes were strengthened by World War I and its xenophobic aftermath. These factors led to legislation requiring immigrant literacy in 1917 and a limit on total immigration and the ethnically and racially skewed quota and exclusion regulations in the 1920s. There were those who argued that these restrictions were contrary to America's fundamental civic ideals, ideals that were essential to the nation's identity and unity, but they were a minority voice after World War I. Robert Wagner of the New York State legislature and later a U.S. senator in 1929 asked, "Are we going to legislate on the assumption that this is an Anglo-Saxon country, or are we going to learn from all history that minorities are never reconciled to such decisions, and that in that direction lies strife and disunion?"[16] However, before these regulations went into effect, many millions of the new people had arrived in the second wave of immigration and most were on their way to becoming American citizens.

The antidemocratic aspects of the immigration quota system continued to be challenged, particularly in light of America's engagement in World War II against the racist policies of Nazi Germany and then during the Cold War against the totalitarian practices of the Soviet Union. Americans pointed to the contradictions in their own country's professed freedom of movement, speech, and religion and its racist-oriented immigration exclusion and racial segregation at home. The Holocaust reminded critics of immigration exclusions of the dangers of "scientific racism" and the need to stand up for basic freedoms. William Bernard, executive director of the National Committee on Immigration Policy, wrote in 1950,

> The doctrine of American nationalism as an exclusively Anglo-Saxon creation has been identified with anti-democratic forces in our history from the early decades of the nineteenth century. . . . It is difficult to explain the prodigious literature . . . which endeavors to show that the "new" immigrant is inferior from a biological point of view without to some extent regarding it as an attempt to rationalize our departure from the principles of a democratic society. . . . The development of Fascism and Nazism in Europe and the interrelation between their doctrines and native American movements revealed a new threat to our democratic institutions. . . . So long as the National Origins Law (the quota system) remains the law of our country with its specific discriminations against certain ethnic groups, the movements which foment group hatred and undermine democracy will have a potent weapon at their command.

According to Bernard,

> experience has shown that democratic society may produce a type of solidarity superior to that found in a society based on forced conformity. The test of two world wars should offer conclusive proof of the resources for unity to be found in the diversified composition of the American nation. A healthy nationalism thrives not on isolation but through continuous contacts with the peoples of other nations.[17]

Through the 1950s and into the 1960s the criticism increased against the quota system. For one thing, immigrants and their descendants from the turn of the century, whom some people had judged as unfit for America's civic culture, were in the post–World War II decades fully participating in the country's democratic processes, including the holding of numerous city, state, and national offices. They were now better positioned to make the case against quotas as unfair and undemocratic. In many places, including the halls of Congress, they pressed steadily for revisions throughout the 1950s and 1960s. In addition, the quotas came under attack during the civil rights movement as having their origin in prejudice and racism. Immigration reform became part of the "rights revolution" of the 1960s, which led to the passage of major civil rights bills in 1964 and 1965 and the cultural and political awakening of women, homosexuals, and other minorities. Calls for the reform of the immigration system came from many of the nation's leaders, including Presidents Harry S. Truman and John F. Kennedy. Kennedy wrote, "The impact of immigration has been broadly to confirm the impulses in American life demanding more political liberty and more economic growth. . . . Every ethnic minority, in seeking its own freedom, helped strengthen the fabric of liberty in American life."[18]

These combined pressures led to the passage of the 1965 immigration law, which increased the number of immigrants to be admitted into the country annually, did away with quotas, and assigned an equal 20,000 maximum number of immigrants annually for each country in the world. On signing this bill at the Statue of Liberty in New York harbor, President Lyndon Johnson, speaking of quotas, stated, "Today, with my signature, this system is abolished." Instead, the new law "says simply that from this day forth those wishing to emigrate to America shall be admitted on the basis of their skills and their close relationship to those already here." Johnson continued, "Our beautiful America was built by a nation of strangers. From a hundred different places or more, they have poured forth . . . joining and blending in one mighty and irresistible tide. The land flourished because it was fed from so many sources—because it was nourished by so many cultures and traditions and peoples." The president thought that the new law would provide greater future immigration opportunity for "people from all the countries of the globe."[19]

As a result of this legislation and of America's postwar refugee policies, immigration increased dramatically, especially from Asia and Latin America. These new people in the United States represented many different races and ethnicities, and they came with a wide range of new and different cultures, religions, languages, cuisines, education, music, and attitudes toward life, family, and government. Population profiles of the United States from the 1970s through the year 2000 revealed a nation ever more diverse and an ever-shrinking white, European-origin portion of the total citizenry.

Despite the civil rights movement, a considerable number of Americans in the last decades of the twentieth century were still uncomfortable with people who were different from those who were considered the mainstream in the United States. They resurrected earlier nativist arguments on the supposed unfitness of new and "darker" people for American civic responsibility. Many of these critics believed that a large portion of the newcomers, by race and ethnicity, did not have the education, experience, intelligence, and temperament to become part of the American civic culture, to practice liberty constructively, or to be able to contribute positively to the democratic process. They feared that they would become a marginal, disruptive, divisive force in American society and would subvert the country's ideals, values, and identity. These critics of the newly opened American immigration policy called for more restrictions and smaller numbers in behalf of maintaining as much of a Caucasian mainstream as possible. They claimed to have support among the American general public.

The politics of immigration policy was especially rancorous in the American West where large numbers of new immigrants sought work and reshaped the regional culture. Worried about immigrant use of public resources and reordering politics, the nativists called for English-only education and tighter control of the nation's borders. Representative of such people's fears was the argument of a former governor of Colorado, Richard Lamm, who wrote,

> Massive immigration involves serious and profound social and cultural dangers. . . . Civilizations rise and civilizations fall—and there are certain universal pathologies that characterize the fall of history's civilizations. Ethnic, racial and religious differences can become such a pathology; they can grow, fester and eventually splinter a society. . . . I believe that America's culture and identity are threatened by massive levels of legal and illegal immigration.[20]

On the other hand were those who believed that the great majority of the new immigrants coming to the United States prized liberty and the American political ideals. They believed that the new immigrants would bring greater vitality to American life and would enrich the country with cultural diversity. The pro-immigrant groups felt that America's ideals and civic culture were strong enough to bring a unity to this diversity and that this unity with more global components would be increasingly effective in the increasing internationalized world.

Peggy Noonan, a speech writer for Presidents Ronald Reagan and George H. W. Bush, wrote in 1991, "Immigration is affirmation, proof that we are still what we used to be, a haven for the bold and striving dispossessed." She quoted English Prime Minister Margaret Thatcher: "Americans and Europeans sometimes forget how unique the United States is. . . . No other nation has been built upon an idea—the idea of liberty. Whether in flight from persecution or poverty [immigrants] have welcomed American values and opportunities. And America herself has bound them to her with powerful bonds of patriotism and pride."[21] Lawrence Fuchs, the executive director of the staff of the federal Select Commission on Immigration and Refugee Policy, quoted a reporter at a New York Liberty Weekend: "[T]he Indian news dealer, the Haitian cabbie, the Greek cook—with their energy and their dreams, they nourish and redeem a nation's soul."[22]

Thus, extending from the first years of the nation into the twenty-first century, Americans have debated whether U.S. citizenship is based more on ideas and ideals melded into a civic culture or on race and ethnicity. Consequently, and particularly at the times of large-scale immigration, some Americans have feared that many newcomers from multiple nations, religions, cultures, and classes could not be effectively integrated into that citizenship. Others have believed that the inflow of multifarious immigrants and the efforts to incorporate them into the American society and body politic have been the actual validation of the ideals in the civic culture. In the midst of the major flow of immigrants in the last decades, the twentieth century into the twenty-first century, the concerns about race, ethnicity, the ideals of the civic culture and political participation have continued, particularly in relation to newcomers from Third World countries.

NOTES

1. Thomas Paine, *Common Sense* (1776), in *The Norton Anthology of American Literature*, 4th ed. (New York: W. W. Norton, 1995), 328.
2. de Crèvecoeur, *Letters from an American Farmer*, 39.
3. Alexander Hamilton, "Examination of Jefferson's Message to Congress of December 7th, 1801," Paper 8, January 12, 1802, in *Works of Alexander Hamilton*, ed. Henry Cabot Lodge (New York: G. P. Putnam's Sons, 1885–1886), vol. 8, 288–89.
4. Quoted in ibid., January 7, 1802, vol. 7 284–85.
5. An American (Samuel Finley Breese Morse), *Imminent Dangers to the Free Institutions of the United States through Foreign Immigration, and the Present State of the Naturalization Laws* (New York: E. B. Clayton, 1835), nos. 4–5, 11–16.
6. *Address of the Delegates of the Native American National Convention, Assembled at Philadelphia, July 4, 1845, to the Citizens of the United States*, Philadelphia, 1845, 2–9.
7. Samuel Busey, *Immigration: Its Evils and Consequences* (New York: De Witt and Davenport, 1856), 129.
8. *Report of Select Committee on Allowing Resident Aliens to Hold Real Estate*, New York Assembly Document No. 168, 1848, 1–5.
9. Martin J. Spalding, *Miscellanea: Comprising Reviews, Lectures, and Essays, on Historical, Theological and Miscellaneous Subjects* (Louisville, Ky.: 1855), xlviii, lii–lviii.
10. "Who Are Americans?" Editorial, *Putnam's Monthly* 5, May 1855, 533–40.
11. Parke Godwin, "Secret Societies—The Know-Nothings," *Putnam's Monthly* 5, January 1855, 95–97.
12. John Commons, "Races and Democracy," *Chautauquan* 38, September 1903, 33–35.
13. Henry Pratt Fairchild, *The Melting-Pot Mistake* (Boston: Little, Brown, 1926), 208–20.
14. Frank Warne, *The Tide of Immigration* (New York: D. Appleton, 1916), 108–110.

15. Louis D. Brandeis, "True Americanism," *Boston City Record*, July 10, 1915.

16. Quoted in William Bernard, ed., *American Immigration Policy, A Reappraisal* (New York: Harper and Brothers, 1950), 270.

17. Ibid., 148–53.

18. Kennedy, *A Nation of Immigrants*, 64–65.

19. Lyndon B. Johnson, "Remarks on Immigration Law," *Congressional Quarterly* 23, October 1965, 2063–64.

20. Richard D. Lamm and Gary Imhoff, *The Immigration Time Bomb: The Fragmenting of America* (New York: E. P. Dutton, 1985), 76–77.

21. Peggy Noonan, "Why the World Comes Here," *Readers Digest*, July 1991, 39–42.

22. Lawrence Fuchs, *The American Kaleidoscope: Race, Ethnicity and the Civic Culture* (Hanover, N.H.: Wesleyan University Press, 1990), 371.

DOCUMENTS

5.1. Ethnically Diverse Americans in 1780s Form a New Nation Founded on Freedom and Opportunity

French-born J. Hector St. John de Crèvecoeur lived in New York at the time of the birth of the new nation. He was struck by the diversity and the melding of the population, particularly in the middle Atlantic states. Crèvecoeur saw a new people being formed—the Americans, who were unified, not by blood ties, but by an allegiance to a new government founded on the ideas of freedom and opportunity. His observations are found in his classic Letters from an American Farmer, *first published in 1782 and since reprinted many times.*

What then is the American, this new man? He is either an European, or the descendent of an European, hence that strange mixture of blood, which you will find in no other country. I could point out to you a family whose grandfather was an Englishman, whose wife was Dutch, whose son married a French woman, and whose present four sons have now four wives of different nations. *He* is an American, who leaving behind him all his ancient prejudices and manners, receives new ones from the new mode of life he has embraced, the new government he obeys, and the new rank he holds. He becomes an American by being received in the broad lap of our great *Alma Mater*. Here individuals of all nations are melted into a new race of men, whose labours and posterity will one day cause great changes in the world. Americans are the western pilgrims, who are carrying along with them that great mass of arts, sciences, vigour, and industry which began long since in the east; they will finish the great circle. The Americans were once scattered all over Europe; here they are incorporated into one of the finest systems of population which has ever appeared, and which will hereafter become distinct by the power of the different climates they inhabit. The American ought therefore to love this country much better than that wherein either he or his forefathers were born. Here the rewards of his industry follow with equal steps the progress of his labour; his labour is founded on the basis of nature, *self-interest*; can it want a stronger allurement? Wives and children, who before in vain demanded of him a morsel of bread, now, fat and frolicsome, gladly help their father to clear those fields whence exuberant crops are to arise to feed and to clothe them all: without any part being claimed, either by a despotic prince, a rich abbot, or a mighty lord. Here religion demands but little of him; a small voluntary salary to the minister, and gratitude to God; can he refuse these? The American is a new man, who acts upon new principles: he must therefore entertain new ideas, and form new opinions. From involuntary idleness, servile dependence, penury, and useless labour, he has passed to toils of a very different nature, rewarded by ample subsistence—This is an American.

Source: J. Hector St. John de Crèvecoeur, *Letters from an American Farmer* (London: Thomas Davies, 1782; reprint, New York: E. P. Dutton, 1957), 39–40.

5.2. Immigrants Endanger American Republican Institutions in Early National Period

Alexander Hamilton was born in the West Indies, educated in New Jersey and New York, served as one of George Washington's aides-de-camp in the American Revolutionary War, and was the first secretary of the treasury in the Washington administration. He was a leader in the Federalist Party in the 1790s and the architect of the new nation's economic policy. Ever concerned about political stability as a basis for economic development, he feared that immigrants would bring the ideas of the French Revolution to the United States and thus supported the passage of the Alien and Sedition laws in 1798. Fears of immigrant political loyalty informed much political discussion in the 1790s. When Thomas Jefferson and his Democratic-Republican Party gained the presidency in 1800 and then supported immigration, Hamilton reminded his rival that he himself had earlier feared that immigration would harm the new American republican institutions. Hamilton insinuated that Jefferson changed his mind only because the votes of foreign-born citizens had helped him in his electoral victory. These critiques were included in Hamilton's "Examination of Jefferson's Message to Congress of December 7th, 1801."

"The next most exceptionable feature in the message, is the proposal to abolish all restriction on naturalization, arising from a previous residence. In this the President is not more at variance with the concurrent maxims of all commentators on popular governments, than he is with himself. The 'Notes on Virginia' are in direct contradiction to the message, and furnish us with strong reasons against the policy now recommended. The passage alluded to is here presented. Speaking of the *population* of America, Mr. Jefferson says: "Here I will beg leave to propose a doubt. The present desire of America, is to produce rapid population, by as great *importations of foreigners* as possible. *But is this founded in good policy*? Are there no inconveniences to be thrown into the scale, against the advantage expected from a multiplication of numbers, by the *importation of foreigners*? It is for the happiness of those united in society, to harmonize as much as possible, in matters which they must of necessity transact together. Civil government being the sole object of forming societies, its administration must be conducted by common consent. Every species of government has its specific principles. Ours, perhaps, are more peculiar than those of any other in the universe. *It is a composition of the freest principles of the English Constitution*, with others, derived from natural right and reason. To these, nothing can be more opposed than the maxims of absolute monarchies. Yet from such, we are to expect the *greatest number of emigrants. They will bring with them the principles of the governments they leave, imbibed in their early youth; or if able to throw them off, it will be in exchange for an unbounded licentiousness, passing as is usual, from one extreme to another. It would be a miracle were they to stop precisely at the point of temperate liberty. Their principle with their language, they will transmit to their children.* In proportion to their numbers, *they will share with us in the legislation.* They will infuse *into it their spirit, warp and bias its direction, and render it a heterogeneous, incoherent, distracted mass.* I may appeal to experience, during the present contest, for a verification of these conjectures; but if they be not certain in event, are they not possible, are they not probable? *Is it not safer to wait with patience for the attainment of any degree of population desired or expected?* May not our government be more homogeneous, *more peaceable, more durable?* Suppose twenty millions of republican Americans, thrown all of a sudden into France, what would be the condition of that kingdom? If it would be more turbulent, less happy, less strong, we may believe that the addition of half a million of foreigners, to our present numbers, would produce a similar effect here." . . .

But if gratitude can be allowed to form an excuse for inconsistency in a public character—*in the man of the people*—a strong plea of this sort may be urged in behalf of our President. *It is certain,* that had the late election been decided entirely by native citizens, had foreign auxiliaries been rejected on both sides, the man who ostentatiously vaunts that the *door of public honor and confidence have been burst open to him,* would not now have been at the head of the American nation. Such a proof, then, of virtuous discernment in the oppressed fugitives had an imperious claim on him to a grateful return and, without supposing any very uncommon share of *self-love,* would naturally be a strong reason for a revolution in his opinions.

Source: Alexander Hamilton, "Examination of Jefferson's Message to Congress of December 7th, 1801," in *Works of Alexander Hamilton*, ed. Henry Cabot Lodge (New York: G. P. Putnam's Sons, 1885–1886), vol. 8, 284–88.

5.3. Nativists Fear Immigration in the 1840s Undermines Politics of Self-Government

With the marked increase in immigration, particularly from Germany and Ireland, after 1840, anti-immigrant sentiment grew in the United States. Nativists feared that the large numbers of newcomers were a threat to America's republican institutions. This opposition to the foreign-born began to take political form in a number of states. In 1845 a national convention of Native Americans met in Philadelphia, where the assembled nativists called for a restriction on immigration and particularly on the participation of the foreign-born in American politics. The Native Americans, later known as the Know Nothings, gained national political strength but crested in the mid-1850s, after which the slavery controversy eclipsed nativist concerns.

We, the Delegates elect[ed] to the first National Convention of the Native American body of the United States of America, assembled at Philadelphia, on the 4th of July, A.D. 1845, for the purpose of devising a plan of concerted political action in defence of American institutions against the encroachments of foreign influence, open or concealed, hereby solemnly, and before Almighty God. . . .

The influx of a foreign population, permitted after little more than a nominal residence, to participate in the legislation of the country and the sacred right of suffrage, produced comparatively little evil during the earlier years of the Republic; for that influx was then limited by the considerable expenses of a transatlantic voyage, by the existence of many wholesome restraints upon the acquisition of political prerogatives, by the constant exhaustion of the European population in long and bloody continental wars, and by the slender inducements offered for emigration to a young and sparsely peopled country, contending for existence with a boundless wilderness, inhabited by savage men. Evils which are only prospective rarely attract the notice of the masses, and until peculiar changes in the political condition of Europe, the increased facilities for transportation, and the madness of partisan legislation in removing all effective guards against the open prostitution of the right of citizenship had converted the slender current of naturalization into a torrent threatening to overwhelm the influence of the natives of the land, the far-seeing vision of the statesman, only, being fixed upon the distant, but steadily approaching, cloud.

But, since the barriers against the improper extension of the right of suffrage were bodily broken down, for a partisan purpose, by the Congress of 1825, the rapidly increasing numbers and unblushing insolence of the foreign population of the worst classes have caused the general agitation of the question, "How shall the institutions of the country be preserved from the blight of foreign influence, insanely legalized through the conflicts of domestic parties?" Associations under different names have been formed by our fellow citizens, in many States of this confederation, from Louisiana to Maine, all designed to check this imminent danger before it becomes irremediable, and, at length, a National Convention of the great American people, born upon the soil of Washington, has assembled to digest and announce a plan of operation, by which the grievance of an abused hospitality, and the consequent degradation of political morals, may be redressed, and the tottering columns of the temple of Republican Liberty secured upon the sure foundation of an enlightened nationality.

In calling for support upon every American who loves his country pre-eminently, and every adopted citizen of moral and intellectual worth who would secure, to his compatriots yet to come amongst us, the blessings of political protection, the safety of person and property, it is right that we should make known the grievances which we propose to redress, and the manner in which we shall endeavor to effect our object.

It is an incontrovertible truth that the civil institutions of the United States of America have been seriously affected, and that they now stand in imminent peril from the rapid and enormous increase of the body of residents of foreign birth, imbued with foreign feelings, and of an ignorant and immoral character, who receive, under the present lax and unreasonable laws of naturalization, the elective franchise and the right of eligibility to political office. . . .

In former years, this body was recruited chiefly from the victims of political oppression, or the active and intelligent mercantile adventurers of other lands; and it then constituted a slender representation of the best classes of the foreign population well fitted to add strength to the state, and capable of being readily educated in the peculiarly American science of political self-government. Moreover, while welcoming the stranger of every condition, laws then wisely demanded of every foreign aspirant for political rights a certificate of practical good citizenship. Such a class of aliens were followed by no foreign demagogues—they were courted by no domestic demagogues; they were purchased by no parties—they were debauched by no emissaries of kings. A wall of fire separated them from such a baneful influence, erected by their intelligence, their knowledge, their virtue and love of freedom. But for the last twenty years the road to civil preferment and participation in the legislative and executive government of the land has been laid broadly open, alike to the ignorant, the vicious and the criminal; and a large proportion of the foreign body of citizens and voters now constitutes a representation of the worst and most degraded of the European population—victims of social oppression or personal vices, utterly divested, by ignorance or crime, of the moral and intellectual requisites for political self-government.

Source: Address of the Delegates of the Native American National Convention, Assembled at Philadelphia, July 4, 1845, to the Citizens of the United States, Philadelphia, 1845, 2–9.

5.4. Immigrants in the 1850s Are Ready to Embrace Liberty and Political Participation

Immigration was debated furiously during the 1850s. Parke Godwin, a poet and a major contributor to Putnam's Monthly, *wrote during the height of the nation's first major wave of immigration about the anti-immigrant Know Nothing Party, as the Native American Party came to be called. In 1855, in an article titled "Secret Societies—the Know-Nothings," Godwin charged that this party claimed to be protecting America's political institutions by the use of un-American principles. The author called native and immigrant people true Americans, based not on ethnicity, but on adherence to "the American idea." Godwin further pointed out that should the Know Nothings succeed in depriving the foreign-born of the opportunity for political participation, this could cause them to be a danger to American unity and institutions.*

As a doctrine,. . . . what does Know-Nothingism propose? The political disability of vast numbers of men, on the ground of race or religion. Can anything be more intolerant, narrow, or bigoted? Did the old priestly or warlike tyrannies, which man has been writhing under these centuries back, lend themselves to a meaner dominion than this would assert for our young Republic? The fetid and defunct dynasties which have become a loathsome remembrance to men, which were terrible fungi in their day, and a reproach for ever, grew from roots like these it is now proposed to plant in our soil. We that have made it our song ever since we were born, that here humanity had at last found a home, that here all the antiquated distinctions of race, nationality, sect, and caste, were merged in the single distinction of manhood—that here man was to be finally recognized as man, and not as Jew or Gentile, as Christian or Mohammedan, as Protestant or Catholic—we, who have made the world ring with self-glorifications of the asylum of the oppressed of all creeds and nations, of the city of refuge to all the weary exiles of freedom, "whom earth's proud lords, in rage or fear, drive from their wasted homes," we are now asked to erect political barriers, to deal out political excommunication as narrow, as mean, as selfish, and as unwarrantable as ever debased the elder governments.

That a preparatory residence and discipline should be required of foreigners, before their incorporation into the State, is reasonable; the extent and nature of such social quarantine may also be conceded to be a question for discussion; but the total exclusion of aliens from citizenship for the future is so monstrous a meanness that one is loath to entertain the conception. It is such an utter and unequivocal surrender of nearly every peculiarity of our institutions, that it would not merely lay all the new comers under ban, but denationalize ourselves! The cry is, "America for Americans," and we agree to it heartily, but what is America, and who are Americans? "He is not a Jew," saith the apostle, "who is one outwardly," and America, in the same sense, is not a certain measurable area of territory, nor the American every miserable biped that happens to be born upon it. American is the cognomen of a nation of men, and not of a collection of arable acres; and Americans are not simply the individual Indians, negroes, and whites who first saw light between Passamaquoddy and Pensacola but all who are Americans inwardly—who are built up on the American idea, who live in the true sentiment of democracy, whose political "circumcision is of the heart, in the spirit and not in the letter, and whose praise is not of men but of God." These are the true Americans, wherever they chanced to be born—whether Turk, Russian, Milesian, or Choctaw, and are infinitely to be preferred to the unthinking and virulent natives whose Americanism sinks no deeper than their skins, and had no existence before their flabby little bodies were first swaddled. America to the Americans, surely—not to the spurious, skin-deep, apparitional Americans, but to the real men worthy of the name!

We are apt to suppose, in projecting these exclusions, that the persons shut out are the only persons seriously affected by them, but that is a woeful mistake. He that commits injustice, he that perpetrates meanness, suffers from it as badly as he that is the direct victim. Curses, like young chickens, says the familiar old proverb, always come home to roost. Debar the half-million of emigrants who annually reach our shores from the elective franchise, and what would be the effect? Why, the growth, in the very midst of the community, of a vast disfranchised class—of an immense body of political lepers—of men having an existence apart from their fellow-men, not identified with them, not incorporated with society; and consequently tempted on all sides to conspire against it, to prey upon it, and to keep it in disorder.

Source: Parke Godwin, "Secret Societies—The Know-Nothings," *Putnam's Monthly* 5, January 1855, 95–97.

5.5. Immigrants in 1850s Regarded as "Politico-Religious" Foes of the Ideals of Native-Born Americans

In the midst of the first major wave of immigration in the United States the New York Mirror *in 1855 expressed strong nativist sentiments in an article on America for the Americans. This publication was critical of the numbers of immigrants, their poverty, their religion, their foreign cultures and associations, and particularly the fact that they were active politically and thus had more influence on government than was to the liking of some native-born citizens. This article labels immigrants as a "politico-religious foe."*

Well, why not? Is there another country under the sun, that does not belong to its own native-born people? Is there another country where the alien by birth, and often by openly boasted sympathy, is permitted to fill the most responsible offices, and preside over the most sacred trusts of the land? Is there another country that would place its secret archives and its diplomacy with foreign states, in other than native hands—with tried and trusty native hearts to back them? Is there another country that would even permit the foreigner to become a citizen, shielded by its laws and its flag, on terms such as we exact, leaving the political franchise out of sight? More than all else, is there a country, other than ours, that would acknowledge as a citizen, a patriot, a republican, or a safe man, one who stood bound by a religious oath or obligation, in political conflict with, and which he deemed temporarily higher than, the Constitution and Civil Government of that country—to which he also professes to swear fealty?

America for the Americans, we say. And why not? Didn't they plant it, and battle for it through bloody revolution—and haven't they developed it, as only Americans could, into a nation of a century and yet mightier than the oldest empire on earth? Why shouldn't they shape and rule the destinies of their own land—the land of their birth, their love, their altars, and their graves; the land red and rich with the blood and ashes, and hallowed by the memories of their fathers? Why not rule their own, particularly when the alien betrays the trust that should never have been given him, and the liberties of the land are thereby imperilled?

Lacks the American numbers, that he may not rule by the right of majority, to which is constitutionally given the political sovereignty of this land? Did he not, at the last numbering of the people, count seventeen and a half millions, native to the soil, against less than two and a half millions of actually foreign-born, and those born of foreigners coming among us for the last three-quarters of a century? Has he not tried the mixed rule, with a tolerance unexampled, until it has plagued him worse than the lice and locust plagued the Egyptian? Has he not shared the trust of office and council, until foreign-born pauperism, vice and crime, stain the whole land—until a sheltered alien fraction have become rampant in their ingratitude and insolence? Has he not suffered burdens of tax, and reproach, and shame, by his ill-bestowed division of political power?

America for the Americans! That is the watchword that should ring through the length and breadth of the land, from the lips of the whole people. America for the Americans—to shape and to govern; to make great, and to keep great, strong and free, from home foes and foreign demagogues and hierarchs. In the hour of Revolutionary peril, Washington said, "Put none but Americans on guard to-night." At a later time, Jefferson wished "an ocean of fire rolled between the Old World and the New." To their children, the American people, the fathers and builders of the Republic, bequeathed it. "Eternal vigilance is the price of liberty!"—let the American be vigilant that the alien seize not his birthright.

America for the Americans! Shelter and welcome let them give to the emigrant and the exile, and make them citizens in so far as civil privileges are concerned. But let it be looked to that paupers and criminals are no longer shipped on us by foreign states. Let it be looked to that foreign nationalities in our midst are rooted out; that foreign regiments and battalions are disarmed; that the public laws and schools of the country are printed and taught in the language of the land; that no more charters for foreign titled or foreign charactered associations—benevolent, social or other—are granted by our Legislatures; that all National and State support given to Education, have not the shadow of sectarianism about it. There is work for Americans to do. They have slept on guard—if, indeed, they have been on guard—and the enemy have grown strong and riotous in their midst.

America for the Americans! We have had enough of "Young Irelands," "Young Germanys," and "Young Italys." We have had enough of insolent alien threat to suppress our "Puritan Sabbath," and amend our Constitution. We have been a patient camel, and borne foreign burden even to the back-breaking pound. But the time is come to right the wrong; the occasion is ripe for reform in whatever we have failed. The politico-religious foe is fully discovered; he must be squarely met, and put down. We want in this free land none of this political dictation. . . . Our feeling is earnest, not bitter. The matters of which we have written are great and grave ones, and we shall not be silent until we have aided in wholly securing *America for the Americans!*

Source: New York Mirror, in *The Wide-Awake Gift: A Know-Nothing Token for 1855*, ed. "One of 'Em" (New York: 1855), 40–43.

5.6. Contrary to Critics, Catholic Immigrants Are Loyal to American Political Ideals

As the number of Irish and German immigrants grew after 1840, an important aspect of nativist opposition to the foreign-born was a fear that a cohesive, hierarchical religious force, Catholicsm, would undermine American republican political ideals. Catholics countered with reminders that Catholics had served with Washington in winning independence from Great Britain and had promoted American interests thereafter. One of the leading American Catholic ecclesiastical officials in the 1850s, Martin Spalding, a bishop in Louisville, Kentucky, wrote that Catholics in the United States fully supported the American political system and that in fact they were a force for uniting diverse peoples within the nation.

[W]e are further told, that Catholics in this country stand aloof from their Protestant fellow-citizens, and form a virtually separate society, having neither feelings nor interests in common with others. . . .

Catholics, especially those of foreign birth, vote together [we are told] and vote for a particular political party; the liberties of our country are therefore [said to be] endangered from this constantly augmenting foreign influence. This charge is groundless, both in its facts and in its inferences. . . .

Much has been said and written of late years about the "foreign vote." Both parties, on the eve of elections, have been in the habit of courting "foreigners" who have thus, against their own choice and will, been singled out from the rest of the community and placed in a false and odious position by political demagogues for their own vile purposes. That they have been thus severed from their fellow-citizens, and insulted with the compliment of their influence as a separate body, has not been so much their fault, as it has been their misfortune. From the successful party they have generally received—with a few honorable exceptions—little but coldness *after* the election; while from the party defeated, they have invariably received nothing but abuse and calumny. So they have been, without their own agency, placed between two fires, and have been caressed and outraged by turns. Any appeal made to them by politicians, in their character of religionists or foreigners, and not in that of American citizens, is manifestly an insult, whether so intended or not; and we trust that Catholics will always view such appeals in this light. Whenever it is question of state policy, they can have no interests different from those of their fellow-citizens. The laws which will be good for the latter, will be good for them: at least they can live under any system of equal legislation which will suit the Protestant majority, with whom they cheerfully share all the burdens of the country. . . .

Never since the foundation of the republic has it been heard of that the Catholic bishops or clergy have taken an active part in conducting the proceedings of political conventions, or in fomenting political excitement, in the name of the religion of peace and love. They are not, and never have been, either abolitionists or free-soilers, ultraists or politico-religious alarmists. Nor have they ever ventured, either collectively or individually, to address huge remonstrances to Congress, threatening vengeance in the name of Almighty God, unless certain particular measures were passed or repealed! . . .

But [we are told] they are foreigners in feeling and in interest, and they still prefer their own nationality to ours. We answer first, that if this their alleged feeling be excessive, and if it tend to diminish their love for the country of their adoption, it is certainly in so far reprehensible. But where is the evidence that this is the case? Has their lingering love for the country of their birth—with its glowing memories of early childhood and ripening manhood, of a mother's care and a sister's love—interfered in aught with their new class of duties as American citizens? Has it prevented their sharing cheerfully in the burdens, in the labors, and in the perils of the country? We believe not. Instead of their being unconcerned and indifferent, their chief fault, in the eyes of their enemies, lies precisely in the opposite—in their taking *too much* interest in the affairs of the Republic. We answer, in the second place, that this natural feeling of love for the country of their birth, growing as it does out of that cherished and honorable sentiment which we denominate patriotism, will, in the very nature of things, gradually diminish under the influence of new associations, until it will finally be absorbed into the one homogeneous nationality; and thus, the evil—if it be an evil—will remedy itself. The only thing which can possibly keep it alive for any considerable time would be precisely the narrow and proscriptive policy adopted in regard to citizens of foreign birth by the Know Nothings and their sympathizers. The endeavor to stifle this feeling by clamor and violence will but increase its intensity.

We answer thirdly, that the influence of Catholicity tends strongly to break down all barriers of separate nationalities, and to bring about a brotherhood of citizens, in which the love of our common country and of one another would absorb every sectional feeling. Catholicity is of no nation, of no language, of no people; she knows no geographical bounds; she breaks down all the walls of separation between race and race, and she looks alike upon every people, and tribe, and caste. Her views are as enlarged as the territory which she inhabits; and this is as wide as the world. Jew and gentile, Greek and barbarian; Irish, German, French, English, and American, are all alike to her. In this country, to which people of so many nations have flocked for shelter against the evils they endured at home, we have a striking illustration of this truly Catholic spirit of the church. Germans, Irish, French, Italians, Spaniards, Poles, Hungarians, Hollanders, Belgians, English, Scotch, and Welch; differing in language, in national customs, in prejudices—in everything human—are here brought together in the same church, professing the same faith, and worshiping like brothers at the same altars! The evident tendency of this principle is to level all sectional feelings and local prejudices, by enlarging the views of mankind, and thus to bring about harmony in society, based upon mutual forbearance and charity.

Source: Martin J. Spalding, *Miscellanea: Comprising Reviews, Lectures, and Essays, on Historical, Theological and Miscellaneous Subjects* (Louisville, Ky.: 1855), xlviii, lii–lviii.

5.7. Turn-of-the-Century Immigrants Accused of Lowering Intelligence of the American Electorate and Endangering Solidarity of the Nation

In the midst of the second major wave of immigration in the late nineteenth century through the early twentieth century, nativists accused the "new immigrants" from Southern, Central, and Eastern Europe of "lowering the intelligence of the electorate." One charge nativists made was that immigrants brought disruption to public life and disruption to business with their socialist, anarchist, and communist ideas. Although wildly exaggerated, the labor radicalism of some immigrants seemed to nativists to be an indictment of all. In 1912 the New York Evening Sun, *a major conservative newspaper, expressed such fears of immigrants in-*

volved with labor advocacy and worried that they endangered the "solidarity of the Nation."

America is one thing, and America overlaid or interlarded with large slices of the most ignorant and unreliable portions of Europe is another. And the indeterminate factor in the coming years—the coming issue—is the question of how much further we can permit free, unsifted immigration. Our current immigration both raises the most serious problems now forming for governmental solution, and also, by lowering the intelligence of the electorate, furnishes the gravest hindrance to their solution. The sudden eruption of the gaunt figure of syndicalism in our labor troubles is the most ominous sign of the times. We have had our strikes a-plenty in the past, but the first considerable development of an actually revolutionary spirit comes today, and comes, as lately at Lawrence and now at Paterson, among the un-American immigrants from southern Europe.

The question is not one to be settled in a day or in a year. We shall doubtless have it with us for a long while to come. But we think the time is ripe for a very serious debate upon the problem and actually for a beginning of restrictive measures. The first brute need for hands to lay open an unexplored continent has unquestionably passed. Such need as remains must be balanced against the paramount need for minds to govern a highly developed nation.

The time has come when some restrictive plan must be devised and planned. The question admits of no division between capitalist and laborer. It has passed beyond the range of purely economic discussion and entered a field wherein all Americans must unite to grapple with a serious threat against the solidarity of the Nation.

Source: New York Evening Sun, March 28, 1912.

5.8. Opposition to Political Participation on Basis of Ethnicity or Race Contrary to Ideals of American Democracy

---

Louis D. Brandeis, one of the most influential early twentieth-century justices on the United States Supreme Court, in an oration in Boston in 1915 spoke on the meaning of Americanism. He did so as the country was experiencing one of its largest waves of immigration. He stressed its roots in the ideas of liberty, equal opportunity, and the brotherhood of man, and held that these were essential components of American democracy. Brandeis further maintained that these ideals supported the welcome of immigrants and opposed those who would limit citizenship and political participation by ethnicity or race.

Ladies and Gentlemen: *E pluribus unum*—out of many one—was the motto adopted by the founders of the Republic when they formed a union of the thirteen States. To these we have added, from time to time, thirty-five more. The founders were convinced, as we are, that a strong nation could be built through federation. They were also convinced, as we are, that in America, under a free government, many peoples would make one nation. Throughout all these years we have admitted to our country and to citizenship immigrants from the diverse lands of Europe. We had faith that thereby we could best serve ourselves and mankind. This faith has been justified. The United States has grown great. The immigrants and their immediate descendants have proved themselves as loyal as any citizens of the country. Liberty has knit us closely together as Americans. . . .

What are the American ideals? They are the development of the individual for his own and the common good; the development of the individual through liberty, and the attainment of the common good through democracy and social justice. . . . But what is there in these ideals which is peculiarly American? Many nations seek to develop the individual man for himself and for the common good. Some are as liberty-loving as we. Some pride themselves upon institutions more democratic than our own. Still others, less conspicuous for liberty or democracy, claim to be more successful in attaining social justice. And we are not the only nation which combines love of liberty with the practice of democracy and a longing for social justice. But there is one feature in our ideals and practices which is peculiarly American. It is inclusive brotherhood.

Other countries, while developing the individual man, have assumed that their common good would be attained only if the privileges of citizenship in them should be limited practically to natives or to persons of a particular nationality. America, on the other hand, has always declared herself for equality of nationalities as well as for equality of individuals. It recognizes racial equality as an essential of full human liberty and true brotherhood, and that it is the complement of democracy. It has, therefore, given like welcome to all the peoples of Europe.

Democracy rests upon two pillars: one, the principle that all men are equally entitled to life, liberty, and the pursuit of happiness; and the other, the conviction that such equal opportunity will most advance civilization. Aristocracy, on the other hand, denies both these postulates. It rests upon the principle of the superman. It willingly subordinates the many to the few, and seeks to justify sacrificing the individual by insisting that civilization will be advanced by such sacrifices.

The struggles of the eighteenth and nineteenth centuries both in peace and in war were devoted largely to overcoming the aristocratic position as applied to individuals. In establishing the equal right of every person to development it became clear that equal opportunity for all involves this necessary limitation: each man may develop himself so far, but only so far, as his doing so will not interfere with the exercise of a like right by all others. Thus liberty came to mean the right to enjoy life, to acquire property, to pursue happiness in such manner and to such extent only as the exercise of the right in each is consistent with the exercise of a like right by every other of our fellow-citizens. . . .

America, dedicated to liberty and the brotherhood of man, rejected the aristocratic principle of the superman as applied to peoples as it rejected it as applied to individuals. America has believed that each race had something of peculiar values which it can contribute to the attainment of those high ideals for which it is striving. America has believed that we must not only give to the immigrant the best that we have, but must preserve for America the good that is in the immigrant.

Source: Louis D. Brandeis, "True Americanism," *Boston City Record*, July 10, 1915.

5.9. President Lyndon Johnson Celebrates Passage of 1965 Immigration Law

Lyndon B. Johnson, who assumed the presidency on the death of John F. Kennedy, was elected president in his own right in 1964 amid the civil rights movement and the Cold War, both of which brought sharp critical attention to the prejudices inherent in the national origins quota system enacted in the 1920s. Just as he pressed for major civil rights legislation to end racial segregation and to enfranchise blacks, Johnson pushed for repeal of restrictive immigration laws. He was instrumental in the passage of the 1965 immigration act which opened up the United States to a more equal influx of people from all countries of the world. The president, significantly, celebrated the passage of this immigration law, the most important in the post–World War II era, at the base of the Statute of Liberty.

This bill that we sign today is . . . one of the most important acts of this Congress and of this Administration. For it does repair a very deep and painful flaw in the fabric of American justice. It corrects a cruel and enduring wrong in the conduct of the American nation. . . . [T]his measure that we will sign today will really make us truer to ourselves both as a country and as a people. It will strengthen us in a hundred unseen ways. . . .

This bill says simply that from this day forth those wishing to emigrate to America shall be admitted on the basis of their skills and their close relationship to those already here.

This is a simple test, and it is a fair test. Those who can contribute most to this country—to its growth, to its strength, to its spirit—will be the first that are admitted to this land.

The fairness of this standard is so self evident that we may well wonder that it has not always been applied. Yet the fact is that for over four decades the immigration policy of the United States has been twisted and has been distorted by the harsh injustice of the National Origins Quota System.

Under that system the ability of new immigrants to come to America depended upon the country of their birth. Only three countries were allowed to supply seventy percent of all the immigrants. Families were kept apart because a husband or a wife or a child had been born in the wrong place. Men of needed skill and talent were denied entrance because they came from southern or eastern Europe or from one of the developing continents. This system violated the basic principle of American democracy—the principle that values and rewards each man on the basis of his merit as a man. It has been un-American in the highest sense because it has been untrue to the faith that brought thousands to these shores even before we were a country.

Today, with my signature, this system is abolished.

We can now believe that it will never again shadow the gate to the American nation with the twin barriers of prejudice and privilege.

Our beautiful America was built by a nation of strangers. From a hundred different places or more, they have poured forth into an empty land—joining and blending in one mighty and irresistible tide.

The land flourished because it was fed from so many sources—because it was nourished by so many cultures and traditions and peoples.

And from this experience, almost unique in the history of nations, has come America's attitude toward the rest of the world. We, because of what we are, feel safer and stronger in a world as varied as the people who make it up—a world where no country rules another and all countries can deal with the basic problems of human dignity and deal with those problems in their own way.

Now, under the monument which has welcomed so many to our shores, the American nation returns to the finest of its traditions today. The days of unlimited immigration are past. But those who do come will come because of what they are, and not because of the land from which they sprang.

When the earliest settlers poured into a wild continent there was no one to ask them where they came from. The only question was: Were they sturdy enough to make the journey, were they strong enough to clear the land, were they enduring enough to make a home for freedom, and were they brave enough to die for liberty if it became necessary to do so.

And so it has been through all the great and testing moments of American history. This year we see in Vietnam men dying—men named Fernandez and Zajac and Zelinko and Mariano and McCormick.

Neither the enemy who killed them nor the people whose independence they have fought to save ever asked them where they or their parents came from. They were all Americans. It was for free men and for America that they gave their all, they gave their lives and selves.

By eliminating that same question as a test for immigration the Congress proves ourselves worthy of those men and worthy of our own traditions as a nation. . . .

Over my shoulder here you can see Ellis Island, whose vacant corridors echo today the joyous sounds of long-ago voices.

And today we can all believe that the lamp of this grand old lady is brighter today—and the golden door that she guards gleams more brilliantly in the light of an increased liberty for the people from all the countries of the globe.

Thank you very much.

Source: Lyndon B. Johnson, "Remarks on Immigration Law," *Congressional Quarterly 23*, October 1965, 2063–64.

5.10. Large Influx of New Immigrants Called a Threat to American Culture, Identity, and Cohesiveness

Richard Lamm was a three-term governor of Colorado as the post-1965 major wave of immigration gained momentum. He considered the influx of large numbers of newcomers, particularly the Hispanics, as a threat to American culture, identity, and cohesiveness. He put forward his ideas with coauthor Gary Imhoff in The Immigration Time Bomb, *published in 1985. With this book, in numerous speeches, and during various appearances on television, Lamm became a major spokesperson for new restrictions on immigration and for a major effort to institute English-only education.*

I love America, and I want to save and preserve it. To most people, that sentence would seem a bland and noncontroversial bit of flag-waving. But when the subject is immigration, a lot of people would object to it strenuously. When confronted with the social stresses and strains that large-scale immigration place on our country, some people just want to ignore them, want to deny that they exist. Others are less well disposed to the culture and the mores of the United States and don't believe that we should save and preserve them.

Let me say it directly: massive immigration involves serious and profound social and cultural dangers. . . .

I believe that America's culture and national identity are threatened by massive levels of legal and illegal immigration. Admittedly, there are good historical reasons that some people remain complacent in the face of massive migration. After all, there were adjustment difficulties in earlier periods of peak migration, but the fears of Americans that migrants would permanently change the basis of American culture were unjustified, as were their fears that migrants and their children would not assimilate. And the yearly inflow of immigrants to the United States composes a lower percentage of our total population today than it did in the 1910s. Therefore, it is easy to assume that we're unjustified if we worry about the social effects of large-scale migration today.

I know that earlier large waves of immigrants didn't "overturn" America, but there are at least five reasons not to be complacent, reasons to believe that today's migration is different from earlier flows. First, the yearly inflow of immigrants is a small portion of our society's total population, but immigrants are not evenly dispersed throughout the country. They settle in a few big cities, and they constitute large proportions of those cities. The culture of Kansas and Nebraska is not much affected by the small influxes of migrants they receive, but the cultures of Miami, Florida; Los Angeles, California; and Washington, D.C., have been and are increasingly affected, visibly and markedly.

Second, the peak migration years of the 1910s were ended in 1921 by a new immigration law that set annual ceilings on migration levels. The peak immigration years of the 1970s and 1980s are continuing—and there is not now any plan that promises to end them. The migration stream of the 1910s would not have been assimilated had it continued unabated, had it been augmented by decades of followers.

Third, earlier flows of immigrants were well mixed by language groups, and no single group predominated. As Michael Teitelbaum pointed out in an influential article: "While there were substantial concentrations of a particular language group in past decades (e.g., 28 percent German-speaking in 1881–90 and 23 percent Italian-speaking in 1901–10), previous immigration flows generally were characterized by a broad diversity of linguistic groups ranging from Chinese to Polish to Spanish to Swedish. Furthermore, those concentrations that did occur proved to be short-lived." But, Teitelbaum points out, today's migration stream is quite different: "The INS reports that, in the period 1968–77, approximately 35 percent of all legal immigrants to the United States were Spanish-speaking. If one adds to this figure plausible estimates of Spanish-speaking illegal immigrants, it becomes clear that over the past decade perhaps 50 percent or more of legal and illegal immigrants to the United States have been from a single foreign-language group." And this concentration shows no sign of changing in and of itself at any time in the near future.

Source: Richard D. Lamm and Gary Imhoff, *The Immigration Time Bomb: The Fragmenting of America* (New York: E. P. Dutton, 1985), 76–79.

5.11. Late Twentieth-Century Immigrants Identify with Ideals of Liberty and Opportunity

Peggy Noonan, a political commentator and a speech writer for Presidents Ronald Reagan and George H. W. Bush, has been an interested observer of the large influx of new people to the United States in the last decades of the twentieth century. In an article, "Why the World Comes Here," published in Reader's Digest *in 1991, she focused on the fact that immigrants are the Americans who most consciously have chosen this country, chosen its identifying ideals of liberty and opportunity.*

America is experiencing the biggest influx of immigrants since the great wave that ended in the 1920s, the one that brought the grandparents and great-grandparents of the baby boomers who are now, demographically, America. Here in New York these new immigrants, many of them shopkeepers, run a whole level of the city. It is the level that works.

Recently, I heard from a friend who had been thinking about this historic wave of immigration. The facts of the wave are clear—6.3 million newcomers legally immigrated to the United States from 1980 through 1989, most of them from Asia, Mexico, and the Caribbean. The people I grew up with, the European ethnics, are cresting. It's becoming a new America. . . .

In many ways, immigrants know what Americanism is better than we do. They've paid us the profoundest compliment by leaving the land of their birth to come and spend their lives with us. And they didn't come here to join nothing, they came to join something—us at our best, us as they imagined us after a million movies and books and reports from relatives. They wanted to be part of our raucous drama, and they wanted the three m's—money, mobility, meritocracy. . . .

Immigrants and longtimers alike must realize that America is a special place, something new in history. Margaret Thatcher referred to this in her first major speech after leaving Downing Street. "Americans and Europeans sometimes forget how unique the United States is," she said. "No other nation has been built upon an idea—the idea of liberty. Whether in flight from persecution or poverty, [immigrants] have welcomed American values and opportunities. And America herself has bound them to her with powerful bonds of patriotism and pride."

We are in a profound economic transition, from a nation of car makers and steelworkers to a nation of communications and service workers. We're trying to make a transition from being a great nation to being a different kind of great nation. No other country has asked itself to do that. To succeed, we must draw from our newcomers the toughness and resilience of spirit that have nurtured our America since its birth.

Source: Peggy Noonan, "Why the World Comes Here," *Readers Digest* 139, July 1991, 39–42.

ANNOTATED SELECTED BIBLIOGRAPHY

Billington, Ray. *The Protestant Crusade, 1800–1860: A Study of the Origins of American Nativism*. New York: Macmillan, 1938. Treats early nineteenth-century opposition to immigration, particularly the fear that the growing number of Catholics threatened republican ideals and Protestant domination.

Busey, Samuel. *Immigration: Its Evils and Consequences*. New York: De Witt and Davenport, 1856. Reprint, New York: Arno Press, 1969. Expresses strong opposition to the considerable impact of the new foreign-born on American politics and government during the first major wave of immigration in the United States.

Commons, John. *Races and Immigrants in America*. New York: Macmillan, 1907. Reprint, New York: Augustus M. Kelley, 1967. Presents immigration from Southern and Eastern Europe at the turn of the century as a danger to American democracy.

de Crèvecoeur, J. Hector St. John. *Letters from an American Farmer*. London: Thomas Davies, 1782. Reprint, New York: E. P. Dutton, 1957. Observes that, already in the late eighteenth century, Americans are forming a new identity based on the ideas of freedom and economic opportunity.

Daniels, Roger. *Asian America: Chinese and Japanese in the United States since 1850*. Seattle: University of Washington Press, 1988. Details the harsh treatment of Asian immigrants over the decades by Americans who reacted very negatively to their racial and cultural differences.

Fuchs, Lawrence. *The American Kaleidoscope: Race, Ethnicity and the Civic Culture*. Hanover, N.H.: Wesleyan University Press, 1990. Gives an account of the succession of immigrant people struggling over the decades to become incorporated into the American civic culture, based on liberty, political participation, and economic advancement.

Gavit, John Palmer. *Americans by Choice*. New York: Harper, 1922. Reprint, Montclair, N.J.: Patterson Smith, 1971. Discusses how immigrants, drawn to

America for its freedom and opportunities, strengthen the country's basic ideals.

Harles, John. *Politics in the Lifeboat: Immigrants and the American Democratic Order.* Boulder, Colo.: Westview Press, 1993. Examines the political rights of immigrants and their political impact on the United States.

Higham, John. *Strangers in the Land: Patterns of American Nativism, 1860–1925.* New Brunswick, N.J.: Rutgers University Press, 1955. Details the increase of racially and ethnically oriented anti-immigrant forces in American society during the second major wave of immigration, from the 1880s into the 1920s.

Kennedy, John F. *A Nation of Immigrants.* New York: Harper and Row, 1964. Immigrants regarded as central to American identity and vitality.

Millman, Joel. *The Other Americans: How Immigrants Renew Our Country, Our Economy and Our Values.* New York: Viking Press, 1997. Regards large number of late twentieth-century immigrants from Third World countries as hard working and as strengthening American values.

Perea, Juan, ed. *Immigrants Out! The New Nativism and the Anti-Immigrant Impulse in the United States.* New York: New York University Press, 1997. Details resistance to the increase of the foreign-born in America's late twentieth-century third major wave of immigration on the basis of national identity and citizenship.

Pozzetta, George, ed. *Nativism, Discrimination and Images of Immigrants.* Vol. 15, *American Immigration and Ethnicity.* New York: Garland Publishing, 1991. Collection of articles discusses opposition by some Americans to a variety of immigrant groups from the colonial period to 1950.

Solomon, Barbara. *Ancestors and Immigrants: A Changing New England Tradition.* Cambridge, Mass.: Harvard University Press, 1956. Details the rise of anti-immigration activities among the New England elite in the late nineteenth century and the formation of the Immigration Restriction League.

Strong, Josiah. *Our Country.* New York: Baker and Taylor, 1885. A widely read anti-immigrant tract.

Takaki, Ronald. *A Different Mirror: A History of Multicultural America.* Boston: Little, Brown, 1993. Records the struggle of successive waves of immigrant groups to gain acceptance in American society and the opposition they had to face.

Ziegler, Benjamin. *Immigration: An American Dilemma.* Boston: D. C. Heath, 1953. Includes excerpts of articles, positive and negative, on the impact of immigrants on American political life.

ORGANIZATIONS AND WEB SITES

National Council of La Raza: www.nclr.org

National Immigration Forum: www.immigrationforum.org

Project USA: www.ProjectUSA.org

Social Contract: www.thesocialcontract.com

6

What Are the Arguments For and Against English-Only and Bilingual Education?

Through settlement and conquest along the North American coast, the British in the seventeenth century established not only government, but also their culture, laws, religion, and language. English was a vital part of communication and identity for the colonial people. However, other languages were in use. Among the conquered people, like the Dutch, non-English language persisted into and through the eighteenth century. In addition, immigrants from a variety of countries spoke many languages in the polyglot evolving port cities and in rural areas where people from the same background clustered. In the "German counties" in the backcountry of Pennsylvania and Virginia, for example, German was spoken in commerce, church, and society into the nineteenth century.

English-speaking colonial leaders, including Benjamin Franklin, in the mid-1700s were critical of the growing number of German immigrants who came into British North America, particularly Pennsylvania, and continued to speak their own language. In 1755 Franklin expressed a fear that the Germans "will never adopt our language."[1] Although Franklin later retreated from his concerns about German language maintenance and loyalty, troubled relations between English and German speakers remained for some time.

Through the nineteenth into the twentieth century, the English language became increasingly identified with the United States as a nation, even as, perhaps in part because, the influx of immigrants brought an increasing variety of other languages. In the first major wave of immigrants after 1840, it was primarily the large number of Germans who spoke a different language. In German-dominated rural communities and urban neighborhoods, like the "over the Rhine" area of Cincinnati, German was the predominant means of discourse within families and in churches and social organizations. Controversy arose when some of the Germans wanted their language to be used in the schools and in government. To accommodate the Germans, bilingual education was established in many Midwestern towns and cities. By 1900 some 6 percent of American elementary school students were being taught in the German language. Many Germans in the first generation and most among the second generation did learn English, especially in the urban areas. On a smaller scale, mostly on the West Coast, there were enclaves where Chinese was the predominant language, and areas, mainly in the Southwest, where Spanish was spoken.

With the second mass wave of immigration after 1880, a larger portion of immigrants spoke an even greater number of different languages. Sections existed in almost all of the major cities and portions of smaller communities, as well as some rural areas, where little or no English was spoken; rather, the languages of communication were Italian, Russian, Yiddish, Japanese, Hungarian, Swedish, Greek, Spanish, and many others.

Such language diversity and persistence raised a concern about effective communication within the nation and about the economic and social opportunities for the immigrants. This apprehension was often expressed in particularly harsh terms. During World War I, especially, English was an important mark of patriotism. In a nation of immigrants, a common language was vital to bind people together. During the war stepped-up Americanization programs at work sites emphasized English language instruction for workers' safety, efficiency, and production. Meanwhile, superpatriots, worried about the loyalties of the foreign-born among them, demanded loyal use of the English language from all. The German language, in particular, came under severe attack. In 1917 Governor W. L. Harding of Iowa proclaimed,

> The official language of the United States and the state of Iowa is the English language. . . . Therefore . . . English should and must be the only medium of instruction in public, private, denominational or other similar schools. . . . Conversations in public places, on trains and over the telephone should be in the English language. . . . Let those who cannot speak or understand the English language conduct their religious worship in their homes.[2]

The "Hate the Hun" campaign of the war succeeded in "purging" America of much of the overt German culture and almost ended German language instruction everywhere in the schools.

Even before the war, many communities, schools, settlement houses, and other organizations had developed English instruction programs for the newcomers. Again, while there was extensive maintenance of the mother tongue among the immigrants, most did attempt to learn at least some English, and most of the children of the immigrants attained English proficiency.

Beginning in the late 1880s, language, in terms of literacy, took on a new role in the contentious struggle concerning overall immigration policy. For some, an advocacy for literacy was based on the realization that being able to read and write were skills that would enhance the immigrants' employability and upward mobility and would contribute to their fuller and more effective participation in the civic culture of their communities and of the country. Some advocates argued for literacy in English, but the legislation that was proposed, beginning in the 1890s, would base admission to the country on an immigrant's literacy in at least one language, not necessarily English.

The main impetus for this legislation came not from those who wanted to benefit individual immigrants, but from those who believed a literacy requirement would curtail immigrants they considered undesirable, that is most of those coming from Southern and Eastern Europe and from Asia where literacy rates were low. Senator Henry Cabot Lodge of Massachusetts, who became a spokesperson for those who wanted to protect what they considered the traditional culture and ethnicity of the country, spearheaded this legislation in Congress. In 1896 Lodge stated,

> This bill is intended to amend the existing law so as to restrict still further immigration to the United States. . . . The first section excludes from the country all immigrants who cannot read and write either their own or some other language. . . . The illiteracy test will bear most heavily upon the Italians, Russians, Poles, Hungarians, Greeks, and Asiatics, and very lightly or not at all, upon English-speaking emigrants or Germans, Scandinavians, and French. In other words, the races most affected by the illiteracy test are those whose emigration to this country has begun within the last twenty years and swelled rapidly to enormous proportions, races with which the English-speaking people have never hitherto assimilated, and who are most alien to the great body of the people of the United States.[3]

Congressman John Burnett in 1908 declared, "It is against those of a different race from us that my principal objection is aimed. . . . I favor this restriction [the literacy test] because it appears to me to be the only practicable way in which any people of an undesirable race can be excluded."[4]

The advocacy for the literary test met resistance from those who opposed immigration restrictions. Ethnic organizations, business interests, and humanitarian and religious groups—those who saw value in continued open immigration—argued against the anti-immigration goals of the supporters of the literacy test. A spokesperson for these interests, John Gavit, a strong pro-immigration advocate, wrote, "The educational test assures not safety as to character. The ability to speak, read, and write English or any other language . . . are little in the way of assurance of loyalty or usefulness as a citizen."[5] Representative Halvor Steenerson of Minnesota, a state with many immigrants, asserted in Congress in 1906, "Nothing has been shown that connects inability to speak English with any of the evils complained of."[6] Frank Thompson, superintendent of the Boston public schools, wrote, "While it is regrettable that there is so large a number of non-English-speaking immigrants among us, it is also surprising and pleasing that the greater proportion of our foreign-born have sought and acquired that which we have not forced upon them."[7] Henry L. Mencken, in *The American Language*, in 1919, gave much attention to the contributions of the immigrants' foreign tongues to English in the United States. "Every fresh wave of immigrants has brought in new . . . words, and some of them have become so thoroughly imbedded in the language that they have lost their air of foreignness, and are used to make derivatives as freely as native words."[8]

Nevertheless, the literacy test was passed by both houses of Congress several times only to be vetoed by Presidents Grover Cleveland, William Howard Taft, and Woodrow Wilson. In 1897 Cleveland called the proposed literacy law "a radical departure from our national policy relating to immigrants." He referred to the contributions of "millions of sturdy and patriotic adopted citizens" to the "stupendous growth" of the nation. Cleveland continued, "It is said, however, that the quality of recent immigration is undesirable. The time is quite within recent memory when the same thing was said of immigrants who, with their descendants, are now numbered among our best citizens." He rejected the bill as "unnecessarily harsh and oppressive."[9] Taft vetoed a 1913 literacy bill because it "violates a principle that ought, in my opinion, to be upheld in dealing with our immigration."[10] Wilson in 1915 also labeled the literacy bill "a radical departure from the traditional and long-established policy of this country." He believed it limited asylum and asserted that "it excludes those to whom the opportunities of elementary education have been denied, without regard to their character, their purposes, or their natural capacity."[11]

In 1917 Congress succeeded in overriding Wilson's veto, and the literacy requirement became law. It did not, however, seem to be particularly effective in slowing the flow of immigrants from Southern and

Eastern Europe in the aftermath of World War I. Congress then turned to quotas, which achieved more fully and directly deep cutbacks in immigration from Southern and Eastern Europe and ended immigration from most of Asia.

With the third wave of immigration after World War II, language again became a contested issue, especially in states with a large Spanish-speaking population. One expression of the politics of language has been the rise of the English-only movement, which has fought for laws requiring English to be considered the official language in public business. They and others also have been critical of bilingual education in schools. The English-only movement has revived some of the same issues heard in the earlier literacy debate. Its proponents feel that, even more than at the turn of the twentieth century, literacy and particularly facility in English are important to the economic and social success of current immigrants in the United States. There also has been a concern about the unity of the nation because there are areas in the country, of considerable size, in which an increasing number of people speak Spanish.

In 1985 Richard Lamm, a former governor of Colorado, with Gary Imhoff, in *The Immigration Time Bomb*, argued, "Our language embodies everything we believe, every aspect of our concepts and our culture. English is the glue. It holds our people together; it is our shared bond. . . . In America, language integration is an integral part of political integration, an integral part of our national cohesiveness."[12] When he was a U.S. senator, S. I. Hayakawa, a linguist and former college president from California, introduced a proposed amendment to the Constitution to make English the official language of the country. "English unites us as Americans—immigrants and native-born alike. Communicating with each other in a single, common tongue encourages trust, while reducing racial hostility and bigotry."[13]

As a result of the English-only movement, official English legislation has been considered in forty-seven states and enacted in seventeen of them. The proposed constitutional amendment lagged because it did not address a major issue in parts of the country, because many of the immigrants were learning English voluntarily, and because ethnic and other pro-immigrant groups opposed it. Lawrence Fuchs, executive director of the staff of the Select Commission on Immigration and Refugee Policy, in *The American Kaleidoscope*, characterized advocates of the amendment as having "an anxiety that the immigrants would Hispanicize them, just as Benjamin Franklin had worried in his own time that immigrants would 'Germanize us'."[14] Martin Ford, a concerned citizen, brought historical perspective to the issue, in a letter written to the *Washington Post* in February 1999 in which he stated, "Proponents of 'English-only' laws portray the controversy over the increased use of Spanish as unprecedented. . . . But the history of the German language in this country argues otherwise."[15]

Opponents of the English-only movement believe that it, like the earlier literacy movement, has been a rallying point for some persons whose main interest has been to limit or exclude many or all of the new immigrants for racial, ethnic, or cultural reasons. Representative of this opposition, Arturo Madrid, a spokesperson for Hispanic policy concerns, in an article "Official English: A False Policy Issue," wrote in 1990,

> The English-only movement taps into and is informed by deeply rooted fears: fear of persons who are different from the majority population and fear of change. . . . There is no historical basis for the thesis that English, or language itself, holds this society together. . . . Contrary to popular belief, American society never enjoyed a golden age in which we all spoke English, we never were all one linguistically. The history of the United States is one of bi- and multi-lingualism. . . . What makes us a great nation is the power and the creativity of our demographic diversity.[16]

Another controversy has arisen around the question of bilingual education. Its original purpose was to help in the education of English-deficient immigrant students. At least part of their schooling was to be in their native language, so that they could learn some subject content while they were learning English. It was meant to be a temporary bridge until English proficiency was achieved. Bilingual education has received federal government funding and has gained support in New York, New Jersey, and other states.

At the same time, considerable opposition to bilingual education has arisen. Its critics have claimed that for most, or at least many, students it is an ineffective way of gaining English proficiency and, indeed, that it actually hinders or prevents the learning of English for some students. Other educators refute these contentions, holding that poor learning for some students is due primarily to other causes. The research seems to be mixed, but, through ballot initiatives, the proponents of English-only education have forced limitations on bilingual education in key states such as California.

Rosalie Porter, the director of the Institute for Research in English Acquisition and Development in Amherst, Massachusetts, in a 1998 article published in the *Atlantic Monthly*, reported that "bilingual education has heightened awareness of the needs of immigrant, migrant and refugee children," and that among newcomers it has aided "parental understanding of American schools and . . . parental involvement in school activities." An organization that is critical of bilingual education, U.S. English, agrees that "in some localities where bilingual teachers are available, a program of short-term instruction that uses the child's home language to help him for the first few months would seem acceptable." The disagreements come on the efficacy of bilingual education. According to Porter, "The accumulated research of the past thirty years reveals almost no justification for teaching children in their native languages to help them learn either English or other subjects."[17] David Reimers, a historian who has studied recent immigration, stated in a 1999 *Focus* interview:

> There are plenty of studies, but alas they often have different results. A major problem for all of these programs . . . is that the burden of educating children falls on local communities that often lack resources. Indeed, even in communities where the will is strong, it is difficult to find qualified teachers with language skills.[18]

Some supporters of bilingual education advocate more extended bilingual education in order to enhance a student's skill in his or her native language together with knowledge and appreciation of his or her native culture, as well as learning English and American culture. They believe that bilingual education will help, culturally and politically, to strengthen ethnic communities, which often find themselves disadvantaged in an alienating environment. Eduardo Hernandez-Chavez, in his article "Language Maintenance, Education and Philosophies of Bilingualism in the United States," spoke for many, particularly Hispanics, when he advocated the teaching "of the ethnic language in such a way that it is maintained strong within the community."[19]

Opponents of these goals of bilingual education claim that it succeeds in attaching students overly to the culture of the country they have left and does not give them enough knowledge and appreciation of American culture. They believe that bilingual education works against acculturation and thus is a divisive force in American society. It is on these grounds that U.S. English is in "direct opposition" to bilingual education. They support "the primacy of national unity . . . above the claims of ethnic-group identity."[20] This organization, together with others opposed to bilingual education, has fought its adoption in states and school districts and has worked for a rollback in California, Arizona, New York, and other states.

Language maintenance among immigrants and acquisition of English competency by them have been a source of ongoing concern among both citizens and newcomers throughout the history of the United States. These issues have been very much alive in the post–World War II era. Pressure has been exerted by a segment of American society on the new wave of immigrants to attain quickly an ability to communicate in English as an aspect of rapid integration into mainstream life. Others have advocated a more humane, more gradual immigrant transition, including English acquisition, and argue for the value of maintenance of the language and culture of the newcomers' countries of origin. The rapid integrationists want a more mandated use of English for immigrants; the gradualists believe that American liberty and economic opportunity will motivate the immigrant voluntarily to learn English. While there continues to be pressure from English-only advocates as the nation moves into the twenty-first century, their message seems to have less urgency in the country as the prosperous economy seeks additional workers and as a large portion of the new immigrants and their children have been acquiring English language skills.

A sharper controversy has arisen and continues on the efficacy of bilingual education to serve the best interests of English-deficient immigrant students. Rapid integrationists regard it as a less efficient means of learning English and as a support for divisive multiculturalism. They often support such methods as language immersion for recently arrived students. Cultural pluralists consider bilingualism an adequate means for learning English, a superior way for newly arrived students to learn other subjects, and a support for cultural continuity in ethnic communities. The research on bilingual education for learning English has been mixed and often negative. Bilingualism in the schools continues to have strong support from those who teach it and from many ethnic, and particularly Hispanic, organizations. General popular opinion as seen in polls and in voting has turned increasingly against bilingual education. Some polls report that even ethnics, including some Hispanics, oppose this type of school program. Consequently, there has been a vote in California to ban bilingual education in the schools. In New York City, following a year 2000 study and hearing in which there were mixed reactions to this type of education, the suggestion has been made that bilingual education be continued, but that parents of English-limited students be given the choice of a bilingual, English as a second language, or English-immersion program for their children.

NOTES

1. Benjamin Franklin, *Observations concerning the Increase of Mankind, Peopling of Countries, &c.* (Tarrytown, N.Y.: William Abbatt, 1918).
2. W. L. Harding, "Proclamation about Language," Des Moines, Iowa, May 23, 1918.
3. Henry Cabot Lodge, *Congressional Record,* 54th Cong., 1st sess., 1996, 28: 2817–20.
4. Quote in Edward Lewis, *America Nation or Confusion: A Study of Our Immigration Problem* (New York: Harper and Brothers, 1928), 9.
5. John Palmer Gavit, *Americans by Choice* (New York: Harper, 1922), 410.
6. Halvor Steenerson, *Congressional Record,* 59th Cong., 1st sess., 1906.

7. Frank Thompson, "The School as the Instrument for Nationalization Here, and Elsewhere," in *Immigration and Americanization: Selected Readings*, ed. Philip Davis (Boston: Ginn, 1920), 590.

8. H. L. Mencken, *The American Language: An Inquiry into the Development of English in the United States, 1919*, 3rd ed. (New York: Knopf, 1923, 103–113.

9. Grover Cleveland, "Veto Message" (1897), *Congressional Record*, 54th Cong., 2nd sess., Senate Document 185.

10. William Howard Taft. "Veto Message" (1913), *Congressional Record*, 62nd Cong., 2nd sess., Senate Document 1087, 1–4.

11. Woodrow Wilson, "Veto Message" (1915) *Congressional Record*, 65th Cong, 3rd sess., 52: 2481–82 and House Document 1527, 3–4.

12. Lamm and Imhoff, *The Immigration Time Bomb*, 99, 121.

13. S. I. Hayakawa, "Bilingualism in America: English Should Be the Only Language," *USA Today Magazine*, July 1989.

14. Fuchs, *The American Kaleidoscope*, 461.

15. Martin Ford, "The German Language in America," Letters to the Editor, *Washington Post*, February 23, 1999, A18.

16. Arturo Madrid, "Official English: A False Policy Issue," *Annals*, AAPSS, March 1990, 62–65.

17. Rosalie Pedalino Porter, "The Case against Bilingual Education," *Atlantic Monthly* 281, no. 5 (May 1998): 28–39.

18. David Reimers, "Immigration and American Values," *Focus on Law Studies* (Spring 1999): 2. (www.abanet.org/publiced/focus/immvalues.html)

19. Quoted in Gary Imhoff, "The Position of U.S. English on Bilingual Education," *Annals*, AAPSS, March 1990, 56.

20. Ibid., 63.

DOCUMENTS

6.1. Public Use of All Foreign Languages Banned by Governor of Iowa during World War I

There have been many occasions over the decades when Americans have objected to the use of a language other than English by immigrants. One example, during the emotional tension caused by World War I, when all things German were suspect, was the proclamation by Governor W. L. Harding of Iowa, banning the public use of all foreign languages in his state, even for religious services.

A Proclamation

To the people of Iowa:

Whereas, our country is engaged in war with foreign powers; and

Whereas, controversy has arisen in parts of this state concerning the use of foreign languages;

Therefore, for the purpose of ending the controversy and to bring about peace, quiet and harmony among our people, attention is directed to the following, and all are requested to govern themselves accordingly.

The official language of the United States and the state of Iowa is the English language. Freedom of speech is guaranteed by federal and state constitutions, but this is not a guaranty of the right to use a language other than the language of the country—the English language. Both federal and state constitutions also provide that "no laws shall be made respecting an establishment of religion or prohibiting the free exercise thereof." Each person is guaranteed freedom to worship God according to the dictates of his own conscience, but this guaranty does not protect him in the use of a foreign language when he can as well express his thought in English, nor entitle the person who cannot speak or understand the English language to employ a foreign language, when to do so tends, in time of national peril, to create discord among neighbors and citizens, or to disturb the peace and quiet of the community.

Every person should appreciate and observe his duty to refrain from all acts or conversation which may excite suspicion or produce strife among the people, but in his relation to the public should so demean himself that every word and act will manifest his loyalty to his country and his solemn purpose to aid in achieving victory for our army and navy and the permanent peace of the world.

If there must be disagreement, let adjustment be made by those in official authority rather than by the participants in the disagreement. Voluntary or self-constituted committees or associations undertaking the settlement of such disputes, instead of promoting peace and harmony, are a menace to society and a fruitful cause of violence. The great aim and object of all should be unity of purpose and a solidarity of all the people under the flag for victory. This much we owe to ourselves, to posterity, to our country, and to the world.

Therefore, the following rules should obtain in Iowa during the war:

First. English should and must be the only medium of instruction in public, private, denominational or other similar schools.

Second. Conversation in public places, on trains and over the telephone should be in the English language.

Third. All public addresses should be in the English language.

Fourth. Let those who cannot speak or understand the English language conduct their religious worship in their homes.

This course carried out in the spirit of patriotism, though inconvenient to some, will not interfere with their guaranteed constitutional rights and will result in peace and tranquility at home and greatly strengthen the country in battle. The blessings of the United States are so great that any inconvenience or sacrifice should willingly be made for their perpetuity.

Therefore, by virtue of authority in me vested, I, W. L. Harding, governor of the State of Iowa, commend the spirit of tolerance and urge that henceforward the within outlined rules be adhered to by all, that petty differences be avoided and forgotten, and that, united as one people with one purpose and one language, we fight shoulder to shoulder for the good of mankind.

In testimony whereof I have hereunto set my hand and caused to be affixed the great seal of the State of Iowa.

Done at Des Moines, this twenty-third day of May, 1918.

Source: W. L. Harding, "Proclamation about Language," Des Moines, Iowa, May 23, 1918.

6.2. Literary Test Will Deter Poorly Educated Immigrants from Entering the United States

Henry Cabot Lodge was one of the most influential U.S. senators in the late nineteenth and early twentieth centuries. His family, with colonial roots, was among the intellectual elite of New England. Lodge had a doctorate in political science from Harvard. He regarded himself as a defender of the tradition of Anglo-Saxon culture in the United States, which he thought threatened by the large influx of poorly educated Southern and Eastern European immigrants after 1880. Lodge wanted restrictions enacted against these newcomers, and he proposed a literacy test for admission to the country to achieve this end. Lodge was instrumental in the development of the Immigration Restriction League, an elitist New England organization founded in 1894 and dedicated to the enactment of the literacy test. His 1896 speech supporting a literacy test bill in Congress was part of a battle which continued until it succeeded in 1917.

Mr. President, this bill is intended to amend the existing law so as to restrict still further immigration to the United States. Paupers, diseased persons, convicts, and contract laborers are now excluded. By this bill it is proposed to make a new class of excluded immigrants and add to those which have just been named the totally ignorant. The bill is of the simplest kind. The first section excludes from the country all immigrants who cannot read and write either their own or some other language. The second section merely provides a simple test for determining whether the immigrant can read or write, and is added to the bill so as to define the duties of the immigrant inspectors, and to assure to all immigrants alike perfect justice and a fair test of their knowledge. . . .

The illiteracy test will bear most heavily upon the Italians, Russians, Poles, Hungarians, Greeks, and Asiatics, and very lightly, or not at all, upon English-speaking emigrants or Germans, Scandinavians, and French. In other words, the races most affected by the illiteracy test are those whose emigration to this country has begun within the last twenty years and swelled rapidly to enormous proportions, races with which the English-speaking people have never hitherto assimilated, and who are most alien to the great body of the people of the United States. On the other hand, immigrants from the United Kingdom and of those races which are most closely related to the English-speaking people, and who with the English-speaking people themselves founded the American colonies and built up the United States, are affected but little by the proposed test. These races would not be prevented by this law from coming to this country in practically undiminished numbers. These kindred races also are those who alone go to the Western and Southern States, where immigrants are desired, and take up our unoccupied lands. The races which would suffer most seriously by exclusion under the proposed bill furnish the immigrants who do not go to the West or South, where immigration is needed, but who remain on the Atlantic Seaboard, where immigration is not needed and where their presence is most injurious and undesirable. . . .

Mr. President, more precious even than forms of government are the mental and moral qualities which make what we call our race. While those stand unimpaired all is safe. When those decline all is imperiled. They are exposed to but a single danger, and that is by changing the quality of our race and citizenship through the wholesale infusion of races whose traditions and inheritances, whose thoughts and whose beliefs are wholly alien to ours and with whom we have never assimilated or even been associated in the past. The danger has begun. It is small as yet, comparatively speaking, but it is large enough to warn us to act while there is yet time and while it can be done easily and efficiently. There lies the peril at the portals of our land; there is pressing in the tide of unrestricted immigration. The time has certainly come, if not to stop, at least to check, to sift, and to restrict those immigrants. In careless strength, with generous hand, we have kept our gates wide open to all the world. If we do not close them, we should at least place sentinels beside them to challenge those who would pass through. The gates which admit men to the United States and to citizenship in the great Republic should no longer be left unguarded.

Source: Congressional Record, 54th Cong., 1st sess., 1896, 28, 2817–20.

6.3. There Is No Relation between Literacy and Good Moral Character

Congressman Halvor Steenerson came from Minnesota, a state with a heavy, particularly Scandinavian, immigrant population. In a debate held in the House of Representatives in June 1906, in the midst of the second major wave of American immigration, Steenerson spoke against a proposed literacy requirement for the naturalization of immigrants. He argued that there was no relation between literacy and the good moral character of an immigrant.

The qualifications that we have required of people in the past who intend to become citizens is that they be men of good moral character and that they are attached to the principles of the Constitution of the United States. . . . They may be men of good moral character and attached to the principles of the Constitution, and yet be unable to comply with this requirement. Ability to *write* the English language. . . . If, for instance, an elderly man like President Fallières of France should decide to emigrate to the United States, he cannot be naturalized, because in all probability he would not be able to learn the English language within five years; whereas Count Boni de Castellane, who has undoubtedly had opportunities in the past ten years of learning the English language, could be naturalized, because he could speak and write English. . . .

It is not from the immigrants who come here to settle on our public domain, who come here to abide permanently and to build homes and raise families, that we may expect frauds upon our election laws or danger to our free institutions. Such immigrants should not be denied citizenship because of inability to speak and write English. They may, notwithstanding, be as loyal and as patriotic as any. Nothing has been shown that connects inability to speak English with any of the evils complained of. There is no relation of cause and effect between them. The frauds and perjury against naturalization laws were committed by persons proficient in English.

Source: Halvor Steenerson, *Congressional Record*, 59th Cong., 1st sess., 1906, 408.

6.4. Presidents Cleveland, Taft, and Wilson Veto Literacy Test Legislation

In reaction to the large flow of post-1880 newcomers to the United States, primarily from Southern and Eastern Europe, anti-immigrant proponents persuaded Congress to consider a bill that would exclude the foreign-born who could not read and write English or some other language. This proposed legislation was enacted by Congress in 1897, 1913, and 1915, but it was vetoed by three different presidents; Grover Cleveland, William Howard Taft, and Woodrow Wilson. Cleveland praised immigrant contributions to the United States and called the literacy requirement a "radical departure from our national policy." Taft regarded the proposed law as a violation of principle in regard to immigrants. Wilson wrote that the bill was contrary to the United States as an asylum and as a land of opportunity. He believed that it disregarded the character and natural capacity of immigrants. When this bill was passed again by Congress in 1917, Wilson again vetoed it, but the legislature passed it over his veto.

Grover Cleveland

To the House of Representatives: I hereby return without approval House bill No. 7864, entitled "An act to amend the immigration laws of the United States."

By the first section of this bill it is proposed to amend section 1 of the act of March 3, 1891, relating to immigration by adding to the classes of aliens thereby excluded from admission to the United States the following:

"All persons physically capable and over 16 years of age who cannot read and write the English language or some other language. . . ."

A radical departure from our national policy relating to immigrants is here presented. Heretofore we have welcomed all who came to us from other lands except these whose moral or physical condition or history threatened danger to our national welfare and safety. Relying upon the zealous watchfulness of our people to prevent injury to our political and social fabric, we have encouraged those coming from foreign countries to cast their lot with us and join in the development of our vast domain, securing in return a share in the blessings of American citizenship.

A century's stupendous growth, largely due to the assimilation and thrift of millions of sturdy and patriotic adopted citizens, attests the success of this generous and free-handed policy which, while guarding the people's interests, exacts from our immigrants only physical and moral soundness and a willingness and ability to work.

A contemplation of the grand results of this policy cannot fail to rouse a sentiment in its defense, for however it might have been regarded as an original proposition and viewed as an experiment, its accomplishments are such that if it is to be uprooted at this late day its disadvantages should be plainly apparent and the substitute adopted should be just and adequate, free from uncertainties, and guarded against difficult or oppressive administration.

It is not claimed, I believe, that the time has come for the further restriction of immigration on the ground that an excess of population overcrowds our land.

It is said, however, that the quality of recent immigration is undesirable. The time is quite within recent memory when the same thing was said of immigrants who, with their descendants, are now numbered among our best citizens.

A careful examination of this bill has convinced me that for the reasons given and others not specifically stated its provisions are unnecessarily harsh and oppressive, and that its defects in construction would cause vexation and its operation would result in harm to our citizens.

The White House, March 2, 1897.

"Veto Message" (1897) *Congressional Record*, 54th Congress, 2nd Session, Senate Document 185.

William H. Taft

To the Senate: I return herewith, without my approval, S. 3175.

I do this with great reluctance. The bill contains many valuable amendments to the present immigration law which will insure greater certainty in excluding undesirable immigrants.

The bill received strong support in both Houses and was recommended by an able commission after an extended investigation and carefully drawn conclusions.

But I cannot make up my mind to sign a bill which in its chief provision violates a principle that ought, in my opinion, to be upheld in dealing with our immigration. I refer to the literacy test. For the reasons stated in Secretary Nagel's letter to me, I cannot approve that test.

The White House, February 14, 1913.

"Veto Message" (1913), *Congressional Record*, 62nd Congress, 2nd Session, Senate Document 1527, 3–4.

Woodrow Wilson

To the House of Representatives: It is with unaffected regret that I find myself constrained by clear conviction to return this bill (H. R. 6060, "An act to regulate the immigration of aliens to and the residence of aliens in the United States") without my signature. . . .

In two particulars of vital consequence this bill embodies a radical departure from the traditional and long-established policy of this country, a policy in which our people have conceived the very character of their Government to be expressed, the very mission and spirit of the Nation in respect of its relations to the peoples of the world outside their borders. It seeks to all but close entirely the gates of asylum which have always been open to those who could find nowhere else the right and opportunity of constitutional agitation for what they conceived to be the natural and inalienable rights of men; and it excludes those to whom the opportunities of elementary education have been denied, without regard to their character, their purposes, or their natural capacity.

Restrictions like these, adopted earlier in our history as a Nation, would very materially have altered the course and cooled the humane ardors of our politics. The right of political asylum has brought to this country many a man of noble character and elevated purpose who was marked as an outlaw in his own less fortunate land, and who has yet become an ornament to our citizenship and to our public councils. The children and the compatriots of these illustrious Americans must stand amazed to see the representatives of their Nation now resolved, in the fullness of our national strength and at the maturity of our great institutions, to risk turning such men back from our shores without test of quality or purpose. It is difficult for me to believe that the full effect of this feature of the bill was realized when it was framed and adopted, and it is impossible for me to assent to it in the form in which it is here cast.

The literacy test and the tests and restrictions which accompany it constitute an even more radical change in the policy of the Nation. Hitherto we have generously kept our doors open to all who were not unfitted by reason of disease or incapacity for self-support or such personal records and antecedents as were likely to make them a menace to our peace and order or to the wholesome and essential relationships of life. In this bill it is proposed to turn away from tests of character and of quality and impose tests which exclude and restrict, for the new tests here embodied are not tests of quality or of character or of personal fitness, but tests of opportunity. Those who come seeking opportunity are not to be admitted unless they have already had one of the chief of the opportunities they seek, the opportunity of education. The object of such provisions is restriction, not selection.

The White House, January 28, 1915.

"Veto Message" (1915), *Congressional Record*, 63rd Cong., 3rd session, 2481–2 and House Document 1527, 3–4.

6.5. Learning English Should Be Required of Those Applying for Citizenship

---

Richard Lamm was a three-term governor of Colorado as the post-1965 major wave of immigration was gaining momentum. He was concerned about the influx of large numbers of newcomers, particularly Hispanics, many of whom continue to speak Spanish, and he warned America about the dangers to national cohesiveness. According to Lamm, language is a key to national unity; it is a basic element of American citizenship. While he urged immigrants to learn English and schools to teach English, his real solution was an American policy which reduced the number of immigrants admitted into the country. Lamm put forward his ideas with coauthor Gary Imhoff in The Immigration Time Bomb, *published in 1985.*

Official federal government policies that encourage bilingual and bicultural education delay the assimilation of new immigrants. Of course, such was not the intent of the federal educational bureaucrats who designed bilingual programs or of the members of Congress who voted for them, but that is the result.

I believe that it makes no sense for the government to discourage foreign-language speakers from speaking English. I am concerned about the dangers of countries in which two language groups clash. I think about the problems caused by Quebec's separatist movement, founded upon the French language. I think about the tensions even within peaceful multilingual countries: the cantonization of Switzerland and the division of Belgium. Language is clearly the cause of some of the world's most severe tensions and disputes. And I know that the United States makes few demands upon its new citizens, has few common elements shared by all Americans—and the English language is the greatest of these common elements.

Our language embodies everything we believe, every aspect of our concepts and our culture. English is the glue. It holds our people together; it is our shared bond. We cannot communicate with those who do not share our language; we are reduced to signs and charades. Likewise, migrants to the United States who do not know English also have an attachment to their languages that goes beyond mere sentiment. Giving up a language to speak another is not like changing hairstyles or clothes styles in order to fit in with a new society. Giving up a language—even learning a new language just to use in the public sphere, among strangers—is giving up part of oneself. The problem of splintered Miami is that Cuban and other Latin immigrants insist on the right to live their lives in Spanish words and in Spanish concepts, and English-speaking Americans react to the rejection of America and its language by the immigrants who were welcomed here and live here (and who call English-speaking Americans "Anglos" in our own country). In this era of massive immigration, it is everybody's problem. . . .

The English language is a basic element of American citizenship. I don't mean to say that anyone who speaks English with an accent is un-American, or to imply that those who do not speak English are unwelcome here. But I do say, along with S. I. Hayakawa, that "the language we share is at the core of our identity as citizens, and our ticket to full participation in American political life. We can speak any language we want at the dinner table, but English is the language of public discourse, of the marketplace, and of the voting booth." . . .

In America, language integration is an integral part of political integration, an integral part of our national cohesiveness. And it is notable that we as a country have been unsuccessful in integrating many Hispanic—particularly Mexican—immigrants into our political and cultural life. . . .

Learning English to become a citizen is a perfectly reasonable requirement that benefits both our society and migrants themselves. It is no kindness to ourselves or to migrants to pretend that English is unnecessary in this country. It is no kindness to Hispanic immigrants to add to their present ability to listen to the radio, watch television, vote, or get educated in Spanish. Americanization is not an illiberal or a xenophobia process. Through Americanization we reach out to migrants and welcome them fully within our society, and migrants reach out to us and enter fully into our society. Indeed, it is the very essence of paternalism to claim that any group of nationality of migrants is unable to become American. We think that America is a great country with a rich culture—and migrants who come here, who choose this country, must think so too, or they would not have undertaken the difficult job of uprooting themselves from their homes and moving to a foreign land. If immigrants do not feel that they are fully a part of this society, as American as everyone else, then we are failing. We should reexamine the methods we use to integrate immigrants into our country and the goals of those methods. Languages are social cement. If bilingual-bicultural education encourages a feeling of separateness and difference among its students, it is simply inappropriate for this country.

And if Americanization is breaking down, we should examine the process of immigration itself. One very good reason that immigrant groups may not be accommodating themselves to this country may be that the pace of immigration into certain cities and states is too rapid, that the continuing immigration stream is preserving the separatism of migrant groups. Both acculturation and immigration, after all, are demographic processes. They can be measured by numbers. We ignore those numbers at our peril. We cannot willfully pretend that those numbers have no relevance to our country, that America is uniquely immune to profound demographic change.

Source: Richard D. Lamm and Gary Imhoff, *The Immigration Time Bomb: The Fragmenting of America* (New York: E. P. Dutton, 1985), 99–124.

6.6. The Official English Movement Is Divisive and Contrary to American Practice

Arturo Madrid, a faculty member and an administrator at the University of Minnesota and a founder of the Tomas Rivera Center for the study of Hispanic policy issues, has been a strong critic of the post-1965 official English movement. He considers it divisive, anti-immigrant, contrary to past American practice, and not in the current best interests of the nation.

Making English the official language of the United States is a false policy issue. The principal argument of its proponents, namely, that the use of languages other than English fragments American society and debilitates the nation, is spurious at best. Moreover, there is little basis to their claim that the use of English is declining and that its status is threatened. Rather than promoting the mastery and use of English, the advocates of English-only policy seek instead to impose an official language of state on the American population. Rather than encouraging civic assimilation and participation, they would limit the benefits of citizenship to English speakers.

The English-only movement taps into and is informed by deeply rooted fears: fear of persons who are different from the majority population and fear of change. Change is threatening and results in protectionist behavior. The economic change American society has been undergoing over the past two decades has resulted in the resurgence of economic protectionism. Demographic protectionism has characterized American immigration policy throughout history and became acute during the 1980s. The movement to give English official status is a manifestation of linguistic protectionism and is inseparable from the dark and exclusionary underside of demographic protectionism. Not surprisingly, it manifests xenophobic and nativist tendencies.

There is no historical basis for the thesis that English, or language itself, holds this society together. On the contrary, the attempts to impose English on the American population have served historically to divide the nation. Language policy has been an instrument of control, used to exclude certain groups from participating fully in America's institutions as well as to deny them the rights and benefits that accrue to members of this nation. The most pernicious historical example of this was the de jure and de facto denial of English-language literacy to American Indians as well as to the population of African and Mexican origins. So-called literacy tests were used to keep nonwhites from voting until the 1963 Voting Rights Act. The most outrageous current example is the absence of a national policy to teach English to non-English speakers.

Contrary to popular belief, American society never enjoyed a golden age in which we all spoke English; we never were all one linguistically. The history of the United States is one of bi- and multi-lingualism. At the time of the Declaration of Independence, for example, a significant proportion of the population spoke German. The founders of the American nation wisely chose not to single out English as the national or official language. While cognizant of the need for a common language, they did not propose that English officially displace other languages. For the most part they pursued the goals of maintaining the use of languages other than English and of enabling those who did not speak English to learn it. No mention of language choice, for instance, is made in the Declaration of Independence or in the United States Constitution. Far more important as forces to unify the nation were individual rights, freedoms, and protections; governmental and societal tolerance for cultural, linguistic, and religious diversity; democratic representation; and unfettered commerce.

ASSESSING THE THREAT

How should we judge the supposed threat of societal fragmentation and linguistic anarchy? The answer lies in facts rather than perceptions. Despite the propaganda of those who promote English-only policies, English is the language of state and the common language of the U.S. population. In the absence of up-to-the-minute, comprehensive national data, all concerned parties must perforce turn to the U.S. census, which documents that 98 percent of American residents in 1980 felt they spoke English "well" or "very well." Even in California, the most culturally and linguistically heterogeneous state, 94 percent of the population spoke English. . . .

One of the principal strengths of American society has been its tradition of struggle against discrimination, exclusivity, and xenophobia. What makes the United States so attractive to people the world over are the protections and opportunities it offers. What makes us a great nation is the power and the creativity of our demographic diversity. If the unity and strength of American society are at issue, then our energies need to be directed at language policies that empower all citizens rather than punish some. Instead of succumbing to the rhetoric of those who equate patriotism with speaking English and strength with demographic homogeneity, let us insist on the primacy of literacy, on the power of our diversity, and on the participation of all our citizens in the institutions of our society.

Source: Arturo Madrid, "Official English: A False Policy Issue," *Annals*, AAPSS, March 1990, 62–65.

6.7. Bilingual Education Does Not Enhance Students' Learning of English

---

Bilingual education has been promoted for immigrant children of the post-1965 era as a humane and effective way of learning content at school while acquiring English language skills. It has become a politically volatile issue because this type of education has been funded, at least in part, by the federal government and because it has been hailed as a means of sustaining ethnic communities. Rosalie Pedalino Porter, director of the Institute for Research in English Acquisition and Development (READ) in Amherst, Massachusetts, in a May 1998 article published in Atlantic Monthly, *pointed out some of the achievements of bilingual education but concluded that, in its main objectives, it has failed, since, she claims, it has not enhanced the learning of students in "English or other subjects" who have been in bilingual programs.*

Bilingual education is a classic example of an experiment that was begun with the best of humanitarian intentions but has turned out to be terribly wrongheaded. To understand this experiment, we need to look back to the mid-1960s, when the civil-rights movement for African-Americans was at its height and Latino activists began to protest the damaging circumstances that led to unacceptably high proportions of school dropouts among Spanish-speaking children—more than 50 percent nationwide. Latino leaders borrowed the strategies of the civil-rights movement, calling for legislation to address the needs of Spanish-speaking children—Cubans in Florida, Mexicans along the southern border, Puerto Ricans in the Northeast. In 1968 Congress approved a bill filed by Senator Ralph Yarborough, of Texas, aimed at removing the language barrier to an equal education. The Bilingual Education Act was a modestly funded ($7.5 million for the first year) amendment to the Elementary and Secondary Education Act of 1965, intended to help poor Mexican-American children learn English. At the time, the goal was "not to keep any specific language alive," Yarborough said. "It is not the purpose of the bill to create pockets of different languages through the country . . . but just to try to make those children fully literate in English."

English was not always the language of instruction in American schools. During the eighteenth century classes were conducted in German, Dutch, French, and Swedish in some schools in Pennsylvania, Maryland, and Virginia. From the mid nineteenth to the early twentieth century, classes were taught in German in several cities across the Midwest. For many years French was taught and spoken in Louisiana schools, Greek in Pittsburgh. Only after the First World War, when German was proscribed, did public sentiment swing against teaching in any language but English.

These earlier decisions on education policy were made in school, church, city, or state. Local conditions determined local school policy. But in 1968, for the first time, the federal government essentially dictated how non-English-speaking children should be educated. That action spawned state laws and legal decisions in venues all the way up to the Supreme Court. No end of money and effort was poured into a program that has since become the most controversial arena in public education.

In simplest terms, bilingual education is a special effort to help immigrant children learn English so that they can do regular schoolwork with their English-speaking classmates and receive an equal educational opportunity. But what it is in the letter and the spirit of the law is not what it has become in practice. Some experts decided early on that children should be taught for a time in their native languages, so that they would continue to learn other subjects while learning English. It was expected that the transition would take a child three years.

From this untried experimental idea grew an education industry that expanded far beyond its original mission to teach English and resulted in the extended segregation of non-English-speaking students. In practice, many bilingual programs became more concerned with teaching in the native language and maintaining the ethnic culture of the family than with teaching children English in three years. . . .

Bilingual education has heightened awareness of the needs of immigrant, migrant, and refugee children. The public accepts that these children are entitled to special help; we know that the economic well-being of our society depends on maintaining a literate population with the academic competence for higher education and skilled jobs. The typical complaint heard years ago, "My grandfather came from Greece [or Sicily or Poland] and they didn't do anything special for him, and he did okay," no longer figures in the public discussion.

Bilingual education has brought in extra funding to hire and train paraprofessionals, often the parents of bilingual children, as classroom aides.

Promoting parental understanding of American schools and encouraging parental involvement in school activities are . . . also by-products of bilingual education. Workshops and training sessions for all educators on the historical and cultural backgrounds of the rapidly growing and varied ethnic communities in their districts result in greater understanding of and respect for non-English-speaking children and their families. These days teachers and school administrators make an effort to communicate with parents who have a limited command of English, by sending letters and school information to them at home in their native languages and by employing interpreters when necessary for parent-teacher conferences. In all these ways bilingual education has done some good.

But has it produced the desired results in the classroom? The accumulated research of the past thirty years reveals almost no justification for teaching children in their native languages to help them learn either English or other subjects—and these are the chief objectives of all legislation and judicial decisions in this field. Self-esteem is not higher among limited-English students who are taught in their native languages, and stress is not higher among children who are introduced to English from the first day of school—though self-esteem and stress are the factors most often cited by advocates of bilingual teaching.

Source: Rosalie Pedalino Porter, "The Case against Bilingual Education," *Atlantic Monthly* 281, no. 5 (May 1998): 28–39.

ANNOTATED SELECTED BIBLIOGRAPHY

Adams, Karen, and Daniel Brink, eds. *Perspectives on Official English*. New York: Mouton de Gruyter, 1990. Presents various perspectives on the movement to make English the official language of the states and the country during the 1980s.

Crawford, James, ed. *Bilingual Education: History, Politics, Theory, and Practice*. Trenton, N.J.: Crane, 1989. Origins, development, politics, court cases, and effectiveness of bilingual education.

———. *Language Loyalties: A Source Book on the Official English Controversy*. Chicago: University of Chicago Press, 1992. Viewpoints on the efforts to make English the official language.

De la Pena, Fernando. *Democracy or Babel: The Case for Official English*. Washington, D.C.: U.S. English, 1991. Presents the argument that official English is needed for the unity of the nation in behalf of an organization, U.S. English, which is a strong supporter of this position.

Gleason, Philip. *Speaking of Diversity: Language and Ethnicity in Twentieth Century America*. Baltimore, Md.: Johns Hopkins University Press, 1992. A history and analysis of language retention by ethnic groups over the past one hundred years.

Krashen, Stephen, and Douglas Biber. *On Course: Bilingual Education's Success in California*. Sacramento: California Association for Bilingual Education, 1988. A very positive portrayal of bilingual education in California.

Lamm, Richard, and Gary Imhoff. *The Immigration Time Bomb: The Fragmenting of America*. New York: E. P. Dutton, 1985. Argues for the need for immigrants to know English for their own good and for the good of the nation.

Mencken, H. L. *The American Language: An Inquiry into the Development of English in the United States, 1919*, 3rd ed. New York: Knopf, 1923. Describes the many contributions of the different immigrant groups in the United States to the expansion of the American English language.

Porter, Rosalie Pedalino. *Forked Tongue: The Politics of Bilingual Education*. New York: Basic Books, 1990. Contends that research shows that bilingual education, despite some benefits, is ineffective as a method for helping students learn English.

Pozzetta, George, ed. *Ethnicity, Ethnic Identity, and Language Maintenance*. Vol. 16, *American Immigration and Ethnicity*. New York: Garland Publishing, 1991. Concerns the issue of continued foreign language usage among various ethnic groups in the United States.

Tatalovich, Raymond. *Nativism Reborn? The Official English Language Movement and the America States*. Lexington: University Press of Kentucky, 1995. Relates the official English movement to the rebirth of a nativist opposition to immigration in the latter part of the twentieth century.

ORGANIZATIONS AND WEB SITES

English Language Advocates: www.elausa.org
Focus on Law Studies: www.abanet.org/publiced/focus
National Council of La Raza: www.nclr.org
Social Contract: www.thesocialcontract.com
U.S. English: www.US-English.org

7

Assimilation or Cultural Diversity?

Over the decades immigrants to the United States have come from almost every country in the world. They have arrived here with the culture, religion, customs, and language of their different places of origin. Even when they make strong efforts to become citizens of the United States and become Americanized and even when they are well received and are successful economically and socially, they cannot totally shed the ways into which they were born and raised in their country of origin. More than that, a large portion of immigrants see in their inherited culture important values and traditions; a familiarity, comfort, and psychological support that aids them in the living of their lives here; and a way of remaining connected with family and friends left behind. For the majority of immigrants who arrive poor and often are shunned by mainstream Americans, some harshly so, they find in their cultures and in their associations with others of like background the only defense they have against a largely alienating environment in the new country. This is especially true for those who may not want to remain here for their entire lives, and it is particularly true for those who come here specifically to work, often doing hard manual labor in isolating circumstances, as sojourners for a limited amount of time.

Some Americans over the years have been understanding of ethnic retentions among immigrants. They regard them as natural and helpful to people new to America. Some also consider the immigrants' cultural retentions as valuable for increasing variety and choice and adding vitality to American life and culture. They are confident that cultural differences can coexist with national unity or that these differences will gradually blend into and strengthen an ever-evolving American culture. Some Americans who do not care for some ethnic retentions, tolerate others. They might accept religious differences but not cultural ones, or accept cultural ones but object to languages other than English being spoken outside of the home. Some strongly dislike and object to almost any degree of ethnic retention, feel uncomfortable with diversity, want only English spoken, are afraid of ethnic tensions and friction, and find unity safe only in uniformity. Varying points of view in regard to acculturation and assimilation have persisted throughout the history of the nation, not only between longer resident Americans and immigrants, but also at times among immigrants themselves.

The issue of acculturation has most often been a matter of widespread concern when the numbers from any one country have been very large, when many of them have been poor, and when they have been regarded as particularly different from the majority of settled citizens. In the decades from the early eighteenth century through the 1880s, the largest focus was on the multitudinous immigrants from Germany and Ireland and the less numerous, but more distinct newcomers from China.

The issue of acculturation and assimilation is older than the republic. Benjamin Franklin in 1755 complained about the large number of Germans who had settled in Pennsylvania. Calling them "Palatine Boors," he wrote that they "are generally the most stupid of their own nation." Franklin continued, "Why should Pennsylvania founded by the English, become a colony of Aliens, who will shortly be so numerous as to Germanize us instead of our Anglifying them, and will never adopt our language or customs, any more than they can acquire our complexion." He conceded, however, that "their industry and frugality are exemplary. They are excellent husbandmen, and contribute greatly to the improvement of a country."[1] Later in his life, after the Germans had been settled for more time, Franklin took an overall more positive attitude toward this immigrant group.

As the nation formed and struggled to define itself in law and culture, the question of the immigrants' place in this process emerged. Again, the focus was on the Germans because of their large numbers. Their relative prosperity and their successful absorption into the body politic made the Germans a good example of the redeeming powers of American republicanism. Commenting on what made an American, French-born J. Hector St. John de Crèvecoeur observed in 1782 that in America a German boor can become a freeholder. Pennsylvania owed to the Germans "some share of its prosperity; to their mechanical knowledge and patience it owes the finest mills in all America, the best teams of horses, and many other advantages. The recollection of their former poverty . . . never quits them as long as they live."[2] In 1789 a Philadelphia physician and civic leader, Benjamin Rush, echoed Crèvecoeur's sentiments: "The State of Pennsylvania is so much indebted for her prosperity and reputation to the German part of her citizens." He praised their productivity and their interest in education and religion and noted that, while they conversed with each other mostly in German, most of the men were able to speak English.[3] Mathew Carey, a political economist, writing in favor of immigration in 1796 added, "Those Germans to whom Pennsylvania owes so much with respect to agriculture, improvements, industry and opulence, were transplanted from the most despotic soils. Here they became meliorated, and have furnished some of the most active and zealous friends and supporters of American's independence."[4]

The other early large group of immigrants was the Irish. On the average, they were poorer than the Germans in the 1840s and 1850s, had a larger percentage of Catholics among them, and had many critics. Suspicions among many in the United States about the ability of the immigrants from Ireland to adapt to American ways drew on stereotypes of the Irish current in popular English literature which portrayed them as sunk in ignorance, indolence, and barbarity.

Moral reformers were among the most vocal in criticizing the Irish, accusing them of habits of intemperance and rowdyism and noting their devotion to a "foreign" church. One of those who looked negatively on the Irish immigrants and the prospects for their acculturation into the American population was the influential journalist Edwin Godkin, who wrote in 1859,

> The prodigious influx of Irish during the last twenty years has created a large Irish class, apart from the rest of the people, poor, ignorant, helpless, and degraded, contemned by the Americans, used as tools by politicians of all parties, doing all the hard work and menial duties of the country, and filling the jails and almshouses, almost to the exclusion of everybody else. . . . More incongruous elements it would be difficult to bring together than the jolly, reckless, good-natured, passionate, priest-ridden, whiskey-loving, thriftless Paddy, and the cold, shrewd, frugal, correct, meeting-going Yankee. . . . The mass of Celts is now too large and unwieldy for American temperament to permeate it.[5]

Such views proliferated in national magazines and fixed in the minds of many the idea that the Irish birth traits were immutable.

More positive about the outlook for the integration of the Irish into the general citizenry was the influential writer Edward Everett Hale. While recognizing that there were problems with the Irish, particularly among those who crowded into the cities, he wrote in 1852 in *Letters on Irish Emigration* that "there is no reason for despair." The integration of these newcomers "goes on to a much greater extent than is generally supposed," particularly among the larger number who are "scattered up and down, in smaller localities through the land."[6] Thomas Nicholas, a physician, writing during the American Civil War when questions of the Irish immigrants' loyalty to the Union arose, following the New York City draft riots of 1863, declared,

> The Irish in America have been a source of wealth and strength. One can hardly see how the heavy work of the country could have been done without them. . . . Politics, also, have been a little benefit to them. . . . By a kind of instinct the Irish have attached themselves almost universally to the democratic party. They got the idea that it was the party of popular rights, the anti-aristocratic party, the liberal party. . . . Why Irishmen . . . are so much more assimilable than Englishmen, I cannot pretend to say. . . . This is curiously true of Irishmen. In the second generation they are more American than the Americans.[7]

While both the Germans and the Irish acculturated to American ways, the process was not accomplished without difficulty. Many in both groups went to rural areas and small towns, but large numbers had settled in growing cities by the mid-nineteenth century where they crowded into ethnic neighborhoods. Such enclaves provided a measure of group economic and psychic support and protection against harassment and violence from native-born Americans. Hard work; a difficult economic struggle against poverty; release through drink for many; suffering from accidents, disease, and early death; some crime; the rise of political boss rule; and the growth of Catholicism marked these neighborhoods. Some Americans, influenced by the widespread antiurban bias of the predominantly rural nation, argued that many, perhaps most, of the new immigrants who congregated together in cities could not and should not be assimilated into American social and civic life. They feared that the large number of Germans would form permanent foreign-speaking enclaves and that the Irish would remain outside the mainstream with their peasant background, deep poverty, and persistent commitment to the widely detested hierarchical Roman Catholic Church.

Opposition to the immigrants hindered, but did not eliminate, economic opportunities in the expanding nation, and it slowed, but did not prevent, most newcomers from embracing this country and its civic culture. In the process, differences arose within the different groups themselves on the ways best to proceed in this new land. In terms of education, the immigrants debated whether their children should be sent to public schools with their Protestant orientation or establish parochial schools and what should be the language of instruction in the schools.

Likewise, in the "immigrant" churches questions arose as to the language of the sermons and worship and to who "owned" the churches—the people of the parishes or the church hierarchy. In entering civic life, immigrants and their children argued over whether members of one's group should fight rebuffs in attempting to join city fire companies or establish their own; what their stance should be in regard to political issues in the former home country; what kinds of newspapers the group should support; and how the group should respond politically to protect the interests and welfare of its people.

When in 1861 the Civil War tore apart the United States, the new ethnic groups experienced much turmoil. Many Germans and the Irish rallied to the Union cause (and some to the Confederacy); others hesitated to join the army. Ethnic and religious differences separated the largely Protestant, Anglo-Saxon Republicans from the Irish and some German workers and contributed to scattered violent resistance. In several Northern areas immigrants feared and resisted being used as cannon fodder, especially after the emancipation of slaves seemed to advance the interests of blacks. Foreign-born residents continued to feel economically vulnerable. Still, the very real sacrifices made by many immigrants in the bloody war, and the nursing and charity work done by Catholic nuns among soldiers of all faiths, gained some reluctant acknowledgment from the general population that the newcomers might benefit the nation. Economic progress; an increase in skill levels, particularly among second-generation ethnics; a more effective use of the vote; and a new influx of immigrants who were even more different, as well as the presence of the freed African Americans, meant that the Germans and the Irish became increasingly accepted and acculturated by the end of the nineteenth century. This acculturation, together with the increase in "darker" people in the general population, made the Irish and Germans seem more "white" to the older-line Anglo-Saxons. In the process the Germans and the Irish contributed to the ever-evolving American culture with new foods, among which were the frankfurter and the hamburger, new ways of celebrating holidays like Christmas, new types of music, and the slow, reluctant, but crucially important, acceptance that one could be faithful to a religion other than Protestant and still be a contributing member of America's civic culture.

Most Americans in the nineteenth century regarded the Chinese, who settled primarily on the West Coast, as racially and culturally too different as well as inferior and could and should not be incorporated into the nation's citizenry. While there was some acculturation among the Chinese immigrants, it was greatly hindered by an opposition from Americans which was at times violent, markedly discriminatory laws, an aggressive narrowing of economic opportunities, strong efforts to prevent the development of families, exclusion from the possibility of citizenship and political participation, and forced ghettoization.

After 1880, the arrival of large numbers of new immigrants from Eastern and Southern Europe, Japan, the Middle East, and the Caribbean renewed fears that the country was being inundated with people who could not and should not be melded into American society. Many believed that these people, as well as the imperialistically conquered Puerto Ricans and Filipinos after 1898, with their strange languages, customs, limited education, and cultural and racial differences, were particularly unfitted to be American citizens. Sharp voices of alarm were heard from New England intellectuals, urban workers, rural farmers, reformers, and others calling for limiting and halting the new immigration.

Criticism and opposition also arose within religious, ethnic, and racial groupings. Irish Catholics, beginning to move into middle-class respectability but still with a rather rigorous attachment to the official church, were often unwelcoming and resistant to Italian Catholics with a more relaxed attachment to the church and to eastern European Catholics, some of whom had strange liturgies and married priests. Already established German Jews were uncomfortable with and critical of the practices of the Yiddish-speaking, shtetl-oriented, poorer, Orthodox Jews coming into the United States from Eastern Europe. Resident urban African Americans came into competition and some degree of friction with newly arrived blacks from the Caribbean, who had a more entrepreneurial bent, an accented English, and a different religious orientation. These variations resulted in demands among the newcomers for their own language parishes, for separate synagogues, and for different clubs and associations. Friction also broke out across immigrant and ethnic groups—Irish and Jewish, Polish and Italian, Russian and German—as they competed for work, space, and respect.

Older line Americans, who founded and joined such organizations as the American Protective Association and the Immigration Restriction League, formed the front line of opposition to immigration and expressed the fear that the "new immigrants" could not adapt to American society. They argued that the new, post-1880 immigrants were biologically, mentally, politically, racially, and morally unfit to be acculturated into American society. Although they did not fully subscribe to the Social Darwinism notion of "survival of the fittest," these nativists tended to ground their arguments on race in the biological, psychological, and social sciences. The anti-immigrant forces pressured Congress into passing a growing number of restrictions on immigrants to be monitored by the federal government at stations like Ellis Island. The restrictionists thought that only newcomers who could be quickly and fully assimilated into the mainstream society should be admitted into the country. They did not think that most of the Southern and Eastern Europeans, and certainly not the Asians, could be so assimilated.

One of the restrictionists who used social science to bolster his anti-immigrant stance was sociologist Henry Fairchild. In 1926, in *The Melting-Pot Mistake,* he asserted that, since the "new immigrants" had been brought up in an "authoritative spiritual tradition and social environment" which "is dissimilar in most respects, and absolutely contradictory and inconsistent in many respects, to the American nationality" and since those in each group tended to settle close together, they would "find assimilation hardly even a remote possibility."[8] The social sciences were used in multiple ways. While Fairchild and some other social scientists focused on links between immigrants and crime, delinquency, and other urban disorders, other scholars and activists sought in the social sciences methods to help "Americanize" the foreign-born.

Some of the turn-of-the-century newcomers were sojourners who did return to their native lands, but the majority of those who came in the second wave of immigration sought naturalization and citizenship. Some strove to assimilate as fully and as quickly as possible to get ahead and to gain acceptance; some simply liked their new country. Mary Antin, a young Jewish immigrant woman who wrote *The Promised Land* in 1912, for example, felt very much at ease in New York public schools and readily identified with American national symbols.[9] However, most in this new wave of immigration, like most of the earlier Irish and Germans, needed a more gradual acculturation. Thus, they also, at first, settled in ethnic neighborhoods, formed Old World associations, spoke in the languages they knew, read foreign language newspapers, adhered to inherited religious faiths, and followed familiar and meaningful customs and traditions; however, at the same time, they entered the American economy, were influenced by American society and ideals, and became involved in the American political process.

Some native-born Americans, including persons, working in settlement houses, immigrant aid societies, and other humanitarian organizations and some religious groups, tolerated the new immigrants' need for Old World retentions—to a point. They supported ethnic festivals, athletic events, and cultural performances; enjoyed varied new foods; and provided economic, education, health, and social assistance. These citizens worked hard to develop Americanization programs, teaching English, nutrition, ways of organization for better working conditions, and participation in the democratic process. They believed that the new immigrants, like earlier immigrants, could and would acculturate and contribute positively to American society.

In the face of growing criticism of the new immigrants and of increasing pressure for immigration restriction laws, some insightful observers, native and foreign-born, attempted to communicate a more positive view of the acculturation process. One of these was a Jewish American, Israel Zangwill, who in his 1909 play, *The Melting-Pot*, wrote,

> America is God's Crucible, the great Melting-Pot where all the races of Europe are melting and reforming . . . Germans and Frenchmen, Irishmen and Englishmen, Jews and Russians—into the Crucible with you all! God is making the American . . . the real American has not yet arrived. He is only in the Crucible, I tell you—he will be the fusion of all races.[10]

Zangwill saw an acculturation process in which the American was being formed not into an Anglo-Saxon, but into a new person incorporating contributions from all the different native and immigrant groups. E. A. Goldenweiser, an expert in charge of city inquiry for the U.S. Immigration Commission, wrote in the *Survey* in 1911 "that foreign colonies in large cities are not stagnant, but are constantly changing their composition, the more successful members leaving for better surroundings, until finally the entire colony is absorbed in the melting pot of the city."[11]

Observing and acknowledging the helpfulness of ethnic enclaves, particularly when immigrants first arrived in this county, and valuing the culture brought to America by the different ethnic groups which survived in the face of hostility from mainstream citizens, a number of ethnics and others sympathetic to the foreign-born supported acculturation, neither as assimilation nor as a full melting, but as a process in which ethnic differences could be maintained and integrated into a national unity based on shared ideals. They held that the positive aspects of varied ethnic cultures were important not only for the ethnic people themselves but also for the resulting diversity, which enriched the whole nation.

An early proponent of this understanding of acculturation was Randolph Bourne, a thoughtful analyst of immigration, who in 1916 described the settlement of the foreign-born in the United States as a type of transnationalism. He thought of America as a "world-federation in miniature," as "the peaceful living side by side, with character substantially preserved, of the most heterogeneous people under the sun." He maintained that "the attempt to weave a wholly novel international nation out of our chaotic America will liberate and harmonize the creative power of all these people and give them a new spiritual citizenship."[12]

This view of immigrant acculturation was supported by a Jewish intellectual, Horace Kallen. He called it "cultural pluralism" in his 1924 book *Culture and Democracy in the United States*. Kallen saw "the American people . . . (as) a mosaic of people." He held that "democracy involves not the elimination of difference, but the perfection and conservation of differences. It aims through Union, not uniformity, but at variety, at a one out of many. . . . It involves a give and take between radically different types, and a mutual respect and mutual cooperation based on mutual understanding."[13]

In the years before World War II, the ideal of immigrant acculturation as cultural pluralism attained little interest in mainstream America. It was in the postwar years, with the civil rights movement and a greater appreciation of the value of the cultures of diverse peoples, that cultural pluralism found considerable support. The publication of *Beyond the Melting Pot* in 1963 by Daniel Moynihan and sociologist Nathan Glazer, in which they presented a positive view of ethnic retentions, garnered much attention.[14] It helped fuel an ethnic revival in which Michael Novak, a national columnist, became a major voice with his *The Rise of the Unmeltable Ethnics* in 1979.[15]

While most second- and third-generation turn-of-the-century immigrants continued into the post–World War II years to associate with their ethnic heritage, they also had become increasingly Americanized. The children and grandchildren of the Southern and Eastern European immigrants, who many had predicted to be unassimilable, had extended their schooling and improved their job skills, which enabled them to move up the economic ladder, and many married outside of their ethnic group. In World War II they manifested a strong patriotism, and many gave their lives for the United States, which added to their identification with American values and national interests. In the postwar years, these ethnic people played a growing role in America's political life, and their increasing visibility as big city mayors, governors, and members of Congress made palpable not only the "ethnic" assimilation into American civic life, but also the more inclusive "democratic" character of the American civic culture that immigrants and their children had helped to forge.

There began to be insightful observers of this acculturation process. Stanley Aronowitz, a labor historian and activist, wrote in 1972 about the decline of ethnicity in American political and social life; sociologist Herbert Gans declared that most of what was left of ethnicity was merely symbolic; and social historian Richard Alba in 1985 proclaimed "the twilight of ethnicity among Americans of European ancestry." Not only had German ethnicity almost disappeared and Irish ethnicity visibly decreased, ethnicity, according to Alba, was fading markedly also among those people whose ancestors came at the turn of the century. He reported that the Italian "group's cultural distinctiveness has paled to a feeble version of its former self." Alba talked about the high degree of intermarriage and the growing educational attainment of Americans of Italian descent. "Core values have been overwhelmed by a common American culture." This process was also occurring with other European, turn-of-the-century ethnic groups, and Alba heralded the "emergence of a new ethnic group, one defined by ancestry from anywhere on the European continent."[16]

Since World War II, a new major wave of immigration has been bringing a globally diverse population to the United States, and, with this influx, questions of assimilation and acculturation have arisen anew. Many Americans have expressed the fear that at least some of the new immigrants, most notably those from Third World countries, are too different from the previous European immigrants, particularly when they come in large numbers and settle in clusters, to be integrated into American society. Mark Krikorian, executive director of the Center for Immigration Studies, writing in 1998 for U.S. Border Control, an organization critical of current immigration, stated the concern of many "that over the next 25 years the projected difference in ethnic/racial composition across states will be striking and unlike anything that existed before in the country's history." He was convinced that the large numbers and the clustering of the new immigrants would hinder "assimilation and Americanization." Krikorian, additionally, saw the widespread support for multiculturalism in the United States, not unlike earlier cultural pluralism, as a threat to "a common civic culture"; "today's immigration is the pure oxygen that allows the multicultural fire to burn hot."[17] These fears are often linked with negative reactions to other changes in American society and its values since the 1960s: altered race relations, feminism, gay rights, and moral relativism. Rachel Moran from the University of California, Berkeley Law School, in the spring 1999 issue of *Focus*, expressed concern about the future of national solidarity: "Immigrants today arrive already stratified by education, income, and wealth." Furthermore, "immigrant children who are most in need find themselves in districts that often have the least resources. . . . The dangers of segmented assimilation are real."[18]

Optimistic perceptions about the acculturation of the new immigrants run counter to the doomsday perspective of the restrictionists. Senator Edward Kennedy, in testimony before Congress in 1965, stated, "Another fear is that immigrants from nations other than those in northern Europe will not assimilate into our society. The difficulty with this argument is that it comes 40 years too late. Hundreds of thousands of such immigrants have come here in recent years, and their adjustment has been notable." He referred to the high rate of employment, business ownership, and home ownership among these newcomers. "By every standard of assimilation these immigrants have adjusted faster than any previous group."[19] Douglas Massey, a sociologist at the Population Studies Center, University of Pennsylvania, in his article "Dimensions of the New Immigration to the United States and the Prospects for Assimilation," reported on a variety of late twentieth-century studies of intermarriage for Asians and Hispanics and concluded that "significant and growing exogamy seems to characterize most of the new immigrant groups.... Once intermarriage occurs, all other types of assimilation are held to follow.... It represents the ultimate indication of a group's social acceptability and assimilability."[20]

A year 2000 report, "From Newcomers to New Americans: The Successful Integration of Immigrants," in *Meet the Forum* related that in 1990, within twenty years of their arrival in the United States, some 60 percent of immigrants lived in owner-occupied housing, and that within ten years of arriving, more than 75 percent spoke English well or very well. "Contemporary immigrant families overwhelmingly do what newcomers have always done: slowly, often painfully, but quite assuredly, embrace the cultural norms that are part of life in the United States."[21] Lawrence Fuchs quoted Laura Martinez of El Paso, Texas, a naturalized Mexican American, who said, "Becoming a U.S. citizen does not mean you may not take pride in your culture or be proud of your roots or love your people.... It simply means that you are now loyal to this wonderful country that is full of opportunities and you will support the Constitution."[22]

Throughout the decades of the American past a crucial question facing both settled citizens and immigrants has been the extent and the manner of the integration of newcomers into American society. In the post–World War II era, in the midst of the nation's third major wave of immigration, this issue has again gained much salience and public attention. Acculturation of new immigrants has been taking place at different rates and in different ways for different groups. Many, particularly the well-educated, come with a knowledge of English and American ways or learn them quickly. They very often become integrated into American workplaces, institutions, and neighborhoods. Others, generally the less affluent, who live in ethnically concentrated areas, tend to acculturate more slowly. They hold on to their language and customs longer. In some ways this retention has been assisted by the fact that American society in general has become more accepting of the values of culturally different people, by the fact that some ethnic communities continue to receive a steady stream of newly arrived immigrants, and by the fact that transportation makes it easier for many people to visit their former homelands. Still there is much mobility and as the foreign-born make economic progress, they tend to move out of poorer ethnic enclaves to less congested, more diverse areas. Even within ethnic communities, Americanization takes place in the schools, the media, and the general culture. In the process a dialectic between ethnic retentions and Americanization has redefined what it is to be "American," as the melting of cultures, values, and ways of the new immigrants blend into an ever-evolving America.

NOTES

1. Benjamin Franklin, *Observations concerning the Increase of Mankind, Peopling of Countries, &c.* (Tarrytown, N.Y.: William Abbatt, 1918).

2. de Crèvecoeur, *Letters from an American Farmer*, 55–57.

3. Benjamin Rush, "An Account of the Manners of the German Inhabitants of Pennsylvania" (1789), in *Proceedings and Addresses of the Pennsylvania-German Society*, vol. 19, 40.

4. Mathew Carey, "Thoughts on the Policy of Encouraging Migration," in *Miscellaneous Trifles in Prose* (Philadelphia, 1796), 110–24.

5. Rollo Ogden, ed., *Life and Letters of Edwin Lawrence Godkin* (New York: Macmillan, 1907), vol. 1, 181–84.

6. Edward Everett Hale, *Letters on Irish Emigration* (Boston, 1852), 47–58.

7. Thomas L. Nichols, *Lecture on Immigration and Right of Naturalization* (New York, 1845).

8. Henry Pratt Fairchild, *The Melting-Pot Mistake* (Boston: Little, Brown, 1926), 208–20.

9. Mary Antin, *The Promised Land* (Boston: Houghton Mifflin, 1912; reprint, Princeton, N.J.: Princeton University Press, 1985).

10. Israel Zangwill, *The Melting-Pot Drama in Four Acts* (New York: Macmillan, 1909).

11. E. A. Goldenweiser, "Immigrants in Cities," *Survey*, January 1, 1911, 602.

12. Randolph Bourne, "Trans-National America," *Atlantic Monthly* 118, July 1916, 93–95.

13. Horace Kallen, *Culture and Democracy in the United States* (New York: Boni and Liveright 1924): 61.

14. Nathan Glazer and Daniel Moynihan, *Beyond the Melting Pot: The Negroes, Puerto Ricans, Jews, Italians, and Irish of New York City* (Cambridge, Mass.: Harvard University Press, 1963).

15. Michael Novak, *The Rise of the Unmeltable Ethnics* (New York: Macmillan, 1972).

16. Richard Alba, "The Twilight of Ethnicity among Americans of European Ancestry: The Case of Italians," *Ethnic and Racial Studies* 8, no. 1. (January 1985): 152–53.

17. Mark Krikorian, "Will Americanization Work in America?" *Freedom Review*, Fall 1997, (http://www.cis.org/articles/1997/Freedom_Review.html)

18. Rachel Moran, "Immigration and American Values," *Focus on Law Studies* (Spring 1999): 3–4. (www.abanet.org/publiced/focus/immvalues.html).

19. *Congressional Record*, 89th Cong. 1st sess., 1965, 3: 24, 228.

20. Douglas Massey, "Dimensions of the New Immigration to the United States and the Prospects for Assimilation," *Annual Review of Sociology* 7 (1981): 70–72.

21. "From Newcomers to New Americans: The Successful Integration of Immigrants," *Meet the Forum*, January 18, 2000, 1. (www.immigrationforum.org/fromnewcomers.htm)

22. Fuchs, *The American Kaleidoscope*, 270.

DOCUMENTS

7.1. Eighteenth-Century Immigrants Assimilated Well

In the eighteenth century a very considerable number of Germans came to North America, particularly to Pennsylvania. Since many of them settled close together and retained their language and customs, some English-speaking residents feared that these immigrants would not be acculturated into the existing society and might be disloyal to it. In 1796 Mathew Carey, an economist and editor, in "Thoughts on the Policy of Encouraging Migration," answered a critic of immigration. Carey asserted that the eighteenth-century immigrants were being assimilated well into the life of the new United States and that they should be welcomed to the nation.

Amidst an exuberant variety of fanciful and new-fangled opinions, lately obtruded on the public, and defended with all the dexterity that casuistry can afford, there is none more absurd than that of those persons who decry and endeavour to prevent the migration of Europeans to America. A paragraphist, in one of the late papers, in support of such conduct, tells us that "water and oil may as easily be made to unite as the subjects of monarchies with the citizens of the republics of America." . . .

This *sage* politician asks in a triumphant style, "How few of the men who have come among us since the peace, have assimilated to our manners and government?" With much more foundation and justice may it be demanded, how few are they who have not thus assimilated themselves? . . . Had "the subjects of monarchies," who have given this genius so much uneasiness, been excluded from these shores, the aborigines would have possessed them to this day unmolested. . . . Those Germans to whom Pennsylvania owes so much with respect to agriculture, improvements, industry, and opulence, were transplanted from the most despotic soils. Here they became meliorated, and have furnished some of the most active and zealous friends and supporters of America's independence. The same will hold equally true of those numerous swarms of Irishmen, who both before and during the arduous struggle, came into this country—Their valour and conduct were displayed by sea and land—and history will bear the most honorable testimony of their heroism.

What then becomes of the random assertions of this writer? What end can he propose to answer but to divide the people of this country, and create dissensions and ill blood between the old citizens, and those who are on every occasion spoken of with a kind of supercilious and impertinent obloquy and contempt as *new comers—new comers?* Are not the unhappy divisions between constitutionalists and republicans, enough to impede and prevent the welfare and happiness of the state? Must more distinctions and differences be created, in order to counteract the efforts of true patriots to promote the common good? . . . Surely, then, he must be a most dangerous enemy to this country, who endeavours to excite jealousy and disunion here, from which so many evil consequences must naturally and inevitably arise. Let all such persons meet with the detestation and scorn they merit. Let the Americans, to use the words of this paragraphist, "give a preference to our old citizens," whenever their merit and abilities entitle them to it. But should the *new comer* be found to possess those qualities in a higher degree, let him not be exposed to neglect, abuse, or scurrility, merely because, actuated by a love of liberty, he has given this country a preference to his own, and abandoned his friends and relatives to coalesce with the inhabitants of America, who, as General Washington declares in his farewell address, "Have opened an asylum for the oppressed and distressed of all nations." . . .

Sage policy requires America to hold out every possible encouragement to industrious persons to migrate here, with their acquirements, their property, and their families? What then shall we say of those who are incessantly heaping scurrility and abuse on them? The answer is obvious. They must be either ignorant, illiberal, and mean persons: or those who have some selfish or party purpose to answer by such a vile conduct.

Source: Mathew Carey, "Thoughts on the Policy of Encouraging Migration," in *Miscellaneous Trifles in Prose* (Philadelphia, 1796), 110–24.

7.2. Many Irish Integrated into American Society by 1852

Edward Everett Hale, a New England Unitarian minister and author, in the midst of the first major wave of immigration in 1852, wrote that while many Irish crowded together in cities, the majority of them had spread throughout the United States and were in the process of being acculturated into the American society. Hale urged his countrymen to welcome the Irish and the government to aid them because he regarded them as a benefit to the nation. His ideas met much resistance from the general citizenry; hostility remained strong toward the Irish through the 1850s and did not subside to any considerable extent until after the Civil War.

It is true, that to attain the full use of this gift [immigration], the emigrant must be cared for. In other words, the country must open its hand to receive the offering of Europe. . . . The stranger cannot serve the country while he is a stranger. He must be a part of it. He must, for the purpose we seek, profit by the measure of its civilization. He must be directed by its intelligence. His children must grow up in its institutions. He must be, not in a clan in a city, surrounded by his own race. That is only to try a little longer the experiment which for centuries has failed. He must plunge, or be plunged, into his new home.

And, therefore, as I have intimated already, private action and public policy in this matter should unite to "stimulate the absorbents," that each little duct, the country through, may drink its share, of those drops which some do not taste at all, of the perpetual Westward flood, as it comes in.

There is no reason for despair about this. The process goes on to a much greater extent than is generally supposed. It is true we hear most of the clanned Irish in the large cities. . . . They are the only part of the emigration from whom we can hear much. But, from a hasty comparison of memoranda, I should say that there were not more than 120,000 of Irish birth in New York city, 30,000 in Boston, 30,000 in Philadelphia, 10,000 in Baltimore, 10,000 in Providence, 3,000 in Lowell.

Of Pittsburgh, Cincinnati, and St. Louis, I cannot speak; but I doubt if in any other place in America, there is a larger clan than the least of these.

The total of these, say 250,000, leaves nearly 2,000,000 Irish-born emigrants, who have been scattered up and down, in smaller localities, through the land.

So much has been done. Every consideration of humanity and policy demands that, by every means the process should be carried farther, out to the least subdivision possible.

Private men may do their duty to the emigration, by employing, training, teaching, and directing the emigrant; even to the point of making work on purpose to employ him. He, who takes the newest comer does most. . . . She who teaches a servant girl to read does a great deal. The family which adopts an orphan of the foreign blood does more than its share. For, as I have said, the proportion as yet is but eight emigrants to every hundred natives.

The State should stop at once its effort to sweep them back. It cannot do it. It ought not to do it. It should welcome them; register them; send them at once to the labor-needing regions; care for them if sick; and end, by a system, all that mass of unsystematic statutes which handles them as outcasts or Pariahs.

The Federal Government, having all the power, should use it; not growling in its manger, as it does, and only hindering those, upon whom, in its negligence, the duty falls.

And Nation, State, or man should feel that the Emigration is the greatest instead of the least element of our material prosperity; an element which should brace us to meet and handle any difficulties, real or fancied, which it may bring to our institutions of politics or of religion.

Source: Edward Everett Hale, *Letters on Irish Emigration* (Boston, 1852), 47–58.

7.3. Differences Between Yankees and Irish Immigrants Will Prevent the Irish from Acculturating

In expressing the feelings of many native-born Americans, Edwin Godkin, a well-known journalist, was outspokenly critical of the large number of Irish immigrants who had come to the United States in the 1840s and 1850s. In a letter in 1859, Godkin wrote about the marked difference between the American "Yankee" and the Irish "Paddy." Since the Irish were settling close together in the growing cities, he feared that they would not be acculturated into the American milieu.

Smith O'Brien has been travelling through the country and devoting a good deal of attention *en passant* to the condition of his countrymen. I do not think he will find in it much that is very encouraging. The great mass of them have not, so far as I can see, very materially improved their condition, socially at least, by emigration. Physically, they are perhaps better off, though even in this respect their life in the large cities is pretty much what it is in London and Dublin. They earn larger wages, but everything is dearer. The few that have a little capital and move West get on well. There is no prejudice against Irishmen as Irishmen which offers the least impediment to their prosperity, but the creed and mode of life and habits of the American public as they may be supposed to have descended from Cromwell's Ironsides. More incongruous elements it would be difficult to bring together than the jolly, reckless, good-natured, passionate, priest-ridden, whiskey-loving, thriftless Paddy, and the cold, shrewd, frugal, correct, meeting-going Yankee. There was a time when the Irish emigration was small, and purely American influence predominated in the country—when the Irishman, at least of the second generation, lost most of the traces of his origin, and was absorbed into the American population. But that time has passed. The prodigious influx of Irish during the last twenty years has created a large Irish class, apart from the rest of the people, poor, ignorant, helpless, and degraded, contemned by the Americans, used as tools by politicians of all parties, doing all the hard work and menial duties of the country, and filling the jails and almshouses, almost to the exclusion of everybody else. Were the emigrants Protestants, I think the American church organization, which is immensely powerful, would be brought to bear on them. The religious public would feel itself responsible for their condition, and community of faith and strong religious sympathies would probably wipe out all traces of the old Puritan contempt for the "Irish papist." But, unhappily, to other divisions between the new-comers and the old inhabitants is added the crowning and damning one of difference of creed. The churches take but little interest in the half-barbarous stranger for whom the priest is waiting on the shore the moment he leaves the ship; and the speculative New Englander, who has been bred in a theological atmosphere, where intellect has been sharpened ever since he learnt to speak by controversy on "fixed fate, free will, foreknowledge," feels little brotherhood for poor Paddy, who never discussed a point of doctrine in his life. Fifty years ago, however, the Paddy would have been surrounded by a purely American society, and with his usual adaptability would soon have converted himself into a tolerable likeness of "a Descendant of the Pilgrims." Now this is no longer possible. As soon as he arrives he is lost in the crowd of his countrymen, who encompass him in such numbers that his glimpses of American manners, morals, and religion are few and faint.

The priests do all in their power to encourage this clannishness and keep their flocks apart from the American population. They refuse, as far as possible, to allow the Irish children to attend the common schools. Archbishop Hughes is vehemently opposed even to emigration to the West, because there the emigrants are scattered and isolated, and less able to resist the insidious advances of heresy. All the influence he possesses is exerted in keeping them together in masses in the large towns, where, though their life is miserable, their earnings precarious, and their dwellings squalid and unhealthy, their spiritual wants are more closely attended to. The result is that the line of demarcation between the English colonist and the "mere Irish" of the seventeenth century in Ireland was hardly more strongly marked than that which today separates the Irish American from the native American, political inequalities of course excepted. Emigration, instead, as is commonly supposed in England, of effacing all distinction, has traced it more deeply. The mass of Celts is now too large and unwieldy for American temperament to permeate it; and I despair of any change for the better, until the supply of the raw material from the old country is so checked as to allow the supply we already possess to become scattered and the native element to work upon it more freely.

Source: Rollo Ogden, ed., *Life and Letters of Edwin Lawrence Godkin* (New York: Macmillan, 1907), vol. 1, 181–84.

7.4. "Foreign Colonies" Keep Early Twentieth-Century Immigrants from Melding into American Society

As a second major wave of immigration, after 1880, brought millions of newcomers mostly from Southern and Eastern Europe, there again arose critics who argued that the new foreign-born could not be successfully acculturated into the American people. One of the leading spokespersons for these critics was a prominent sociologist, Henry Pratt Fairchild. In 1926 in The Melting-Pot Mistake, *he declared that the "new immigrants" not only differed markedly from the earlier ones, but that they formed "foreign colonies" that kept them from melding into American society which itself was experiencing increased, divisive "class differentition."*

In the discussion of naturalization it was stated that the average immigrant of a century ago could hardly help coming in contact with true Americans and participating in genuine American life. Today, just the reverse is true. The typical immigrant of the present does not really live in America at all, but, from the point of view of nationality, in Italy, Poland, Czecho-Slovakia, or some other foreign country. Let us look into the causes of this situation, and examine the barriers that keep the foreigner out of America. . . . [T]he great majority of immigrants come here as members of the wage-earning class, and most of them remain so. Most of them, also, are poor. So in their efforts to penetrate the stream of Americanizing influences they have to face the handicap not only of alien origin and character, but also of an inferior economic status and absolute poverty. To cap the climax, the differentiation of occupations had gone so far that to-day a large number of callings are almost completely given over to foreign workers, often of specific national groups. They have become "Wop labor," "Hunkie labor," "Kike labor," etc. Consequently the foreigner, not to speak of associating with "upper class" Americans, does not even have the opportunity of mingling with genuine Americans in his own walk of life. The typical immigrant of to-day is not only hired, paid, and fired by a person scarcely less foreign than himself, but he also works side by side and shoulder to shoulder with a group of persons who are usually "greeners" like himself and quite frequently members of his own nationality.

A second great cause of the change in the conditions of assimilation is found in the altered type of the immigrants themselves, as already pointed out in the distinction between the old and the new immigration. The typical immigrants of the first one hundred years of our national life came from the same nationalities as the ancestors of the native Americans. The change that they had to undergo in order to be assimilated was the same change that the ancestors of their associates had passed through. Herein lies one of the significant applications of the fact, established at some length in earlier pages, that the American nationality was in all essential respects closely akin to the English nationality, and not far remote from the nationalities of the countries of northwestern Europe. To-day, the immigrants represent as diverse and inharmonious nationalities as are to be found among all the branches of the white race. The transformation necessary for assimilation is therefore both more sweeping and more difficult. Even if our modern immigrants had equal opportunities of contact with genuine Americans to those of two or three generations ago—a supposition, as we have seen, contrary to fact—they would still have a vastly more arduous road to travel before they could justly claim the title "American." Faced, as they are, with virtually insuperable barriers to association, they find assimilation hardly even a remote possibility.

The outstanding fact in this connection is that as a result of a century and a half of immigration there have been built up within the physical boundaries of what is called America extensive and deeply entrenched offshoots of numerous foreign nationalities. These are most conspicuous, and probably most frequent, in our great cities, and any one who has participated in any form of social case work has inevitably become familiar with them. But they exist in equally well-developed forms in the less crowded sections of the country devoted to agriculture, mining, and other extractive pursuits. In a certain section of Nebraska, a generation ago, one could drive for miles without meeting an adult who could speak English, and "Dutch Bohunk" was a customary epithet of opprobrium among the native American children of the town. Similar situations exist all over the land, furnishing conclusive refutation of the common argument that "distribution" can be relied upon to solve all the evils of immigration.

These "foreign colonies," as they are commonly called, are living evidences of the tenacity of nationality. They show how vigorously every individual clings to his own original national traits, how choice and dear they seem to him, and how difficult it is for him to change them even if he wishes. There are many sections of the United States in which even the third generation of immigrants does not speak English.

The persistence of nationality, and the revolutionary nature of the transformation involved in a change of nationality, can hardly be comprehended by one who has never been called upon to undergo such a process.

Source: Henry Pratt Fairchild, *The Melting-Pot Mistake* (Boston: Little, Brown, 1926), 208–20.

7.5. New Immigrants Move Out of Ethnic Neighborhoods and Become Absorbed in the Cities

In 1911 E. A. Goldenweiser, an expert in charge of the City Inquiry for the U.S. Immigration Commission, wrote an article for Survey, *a leading journal on contemporary social issues. In it he stated the "new immigrants" did form "foreign colonies" in American cities, but that for individual newcomers these were only a temporary settlements in the process of their Americanization. Goldenweiser maintained that when immigrants gained an economic footing, they tended to move out of these congested neighborhoods for better areas and became "absorbed in the melting pot of the American city."*

Seven cities were included by the Federal Immigration Commission in its study of conditions: New York, which with its hundreds of thousands of tenement houses and with an equal number of pages describing their evils is preeminently the congested city; Chicago, which in lifting itself out of a swamp left behind many a basement where the poor seek shelter, and many a yard which is dry only in the hottest season; Philadelphia, with its network of narrow alleys with surface drainage, its three-room houses with insufficient water supply and sanitary equipment, in a word, with its "horizontal tenement houses"; Boston, where "Americans in process" succeed each other in the restricted area of the North and the West Ends, and where the one-family dwelling, converted for the use of several households, emphasizes the rapid change of conditions; Cleveland, which awoke to find itself one of the leading cities in America and has not had time to think of the necessity of protecting itself from the slum; Buffalo, with its enormous colony of Poles who have come from farms in Europe and have to learn the solution of the problem of existence in a city; and Milwaukee, the most foreign city of them all, where there is no limit of space, and where in spite of that, economic pressure frequently results in crowding of houses on a lot and of persons in a house. . . .

[W]hen the immigrant becomes accustomed to American conditions, when he has gained a firm economic footing, when his children have gone to American schools, the desire for better surroundings overcomes the economic and racial reasons for remaining in congested districts. The stream of emigration from the foreign colonies in large cities is continuous; some move uptown when they marry, some seek new places to establish their own business; others look for cleaner streets, and still others follow the current for no conscious reason. The older immigrants do not often form colonies in American cities any longer, and the newer arrivals clearly tend to follow the example of their predecessors in congested districts, gradually scattering over the city of residence and often leaving that city altogether.

In conclusion, I wish to say that this study has not touched the general problem of the distribution of immigrants and their concentration in cities. What it has done is to show that the immigrants in cities in a large majority of cases live a clean and decent life, in spite of all the difficulties that are thrown in their way by economic struggle and municipal neglect. The study strongly indicates that racial characteristics are entirely subordinate to environment and opportunity in determining that part of the immigrant's mode of life which is legitimately a matter of public concern; and finally, it shows that foreign colonies in large cities are not stagnant, but are constantly changing their composition, the more successful members leaving for better surroundings, until finally the entire colony is absorbed in the melting pot of the American city. The population of congested quarters constantly changes, but the quarters themselves remain congested and will remain so as long as new immigrants continue to arrive in large numbers. It is vitally important for the city to keep her crowded quarters clean and her tenement houses sanitary; but it is just as important that the public understand that congested quarters of large cities are temporary receptacles of newly arrived immigrants, rather than stagnant pools of filth, and vice, and destitution.

Source: E. A. Goldenweiser, "Immigrants in Cities," *Survey*, January 1, 1911, 596–602.

7.6. Theodore Roosevelt Criticizes Hyphenated Americans Who Retain Their Culture

In a speech given in 1915, during the second major wave of immigration in the United States and with World War I threat-

ening to bring Old World hostilities to America, former president Theodore Roosevelt held that openness should be extended to the "new immigrants" but demanded of them full assimilation. He was highly critical of immigrants who sought to retain the culture of the country of their origin. Roosevelt called them hyphenated Americans and stated that "there ought to be no room for them in this country."

We of the United States need above all things to remember that, while we are by blood and culture kin to each of the nations of Europe, we are also separate from each of them. We are a new and distinct nationality. We are developing our own distinctive culture and civilization, and the worth of this civilization will largely depend upon our determination to keep it distinctively our own. Our sons and daughters should be educated here and not abroad. We should freely take from every other nation whatever we can make of use, but we should adopt and develop to our own peculiar needs what we thus take, and never be content merely to copy. . . .

There is no room in this country for hyphenated Americanism. When I refer to hyphenated Americans, I do not refer to naturalized Americans. Some of the very best Americans I have ever known were naturalized Americans, Americans born abroad. But a hyphenated American is not an American at all. This is just as true of the man who puts "native" before the hyphen as of the man who puts German or Irish or English or French before the hyphen. Americanism is a matter of the spirit and of the soul. Our allegiance must be purely to the United States. We must unsparingly condemn any man who holds any other allegiance. But if he is heartily and singly loyal to this Republic, then no matter where he was born, he is just as good an American as any one else.

The one absolutely certain way of bringing this nation to ruin, of preventing all possibility of its continuing to be a nation at all, would be to permit it to become a tangle of squabbling nationalities, an intricate knot of German-Americans, Irish-Americans, English-Americans, French-Americans, Scandinavian-Americans or Italian-Americans, each preserving its separate nationality, each at heart feeling more sympathy with Europeans of that nationality, than with the other citizens of the American Republic. The men who do not become Americans and nothing else are hyphenated Americans; and there ought to be no room for them in this country. The man who calls himself an American citizen and who yet shows by his actions that he is primarily the citizen of a foreign land, plays a thoroughly mischievous part in the life of our body politic. He has no place here; and the sooner he returns to the land to which he feels his real heart-allegiance, the better it will be for every good American. There is no such thing as a hyphenated American who is a good

American. The only man who is a good American is the man who is an American and nothing else. . . .

For an American citizen to vote as a German-American, an Irish-American, or an English-American, is to be a traitor to American institutions; and those hyphenated Americans who terrorize American politicians by threats of the foreign vote are engaged in treason to the American Republic. . . .

The foreign-born population of this country must be an Americanized population—no other kind can fight the battles of America either in war or peace. It must talk the language of its native-born fellow-citizens, it must possess American citizenship and American ideals. It must stand firm by its oath of allegiance in word and deed and must show that in very fact it has renounced allegiance to every prince, potentate, or foreign government. It must be maintained on an American standard of living so as to prevent labor disturbances in important plants and at critical times. None of these objects can be secured as long as we have immigrant colonies, ghettos, and immigrant sections, and above all they cannot be assured so long as we consider the immigrant only as an industrial asset. The immigrant must not be allowed to drift or to be put at the mercy of the exploiter. Our object is not to imitate one of the older racial types, but to maintain a new American type and then to secure loyalty to this type. We cannot secure such loyalty unless we make this a country where men shall feel that they have justice and also where they shall feel that they are required to perform the duties imposed upon them. The policy of "Let alone" which we have hitherto pursued is thoroughly vicious from two standpoints. By this policy we have permitted the immigrants, and too often the native-born laborers as well, to suffer injustice. Moreover, by this policy we have failed to impress upon the immigrant and upon the native-born as well that they are expected to do justice as well as to receive justice, that they are expected to be heartily and actively and single-mindedly loyal to the flag no less than to benefit by living under it.

Source: Theodore Roosevelt, "Americanism," address before the Knights of Columbus, Carnegie Hall, New York, October 12, 1915.

7.7. Immigrant Acculturation Should Be a Cultural Pluralism, Not a Melting Pot

Randolph Bourne, a thoughtful analyst of American immigration, in his 1917 article "Trans-National America," called for acceptance of the "new immigrants" and declared them an essential part of a new, emerging America. He envisioned American nationalism as a "cosmopolitan federation of national colonies." The United States, in his mind, was a model for a new world internationalism, a transnationalism. Bourne's ideas were expanded upon by Horace Kallen in the 1920s as cultural pluralism and to some extent by the multiculturalists in post-1965 America.

The failure of the melting-pot, far from closing the great American democratic experiment, means that it has only just begun. Whatever American nationalism turns out to be, we see already that it will have a color richer and more exciting than our ideal has hitherto encompassed. In a world which has dreamed of internationalism, we find that we have all unawares been building up the first international nation. The voices which have cried for a tight and jealous nationalism of the European pattern are failing. From that ideal, however valiantly and disinterestedly it has been set for us, time and tendency have moved us further and further away. What we have achieved has been rather a cosmopolitan federation of national colonies, of foreign cultures, from whom the sting of devastating competition has been removed. America is already the world-federation in miniature, the continent where for the first time in history has been achieved that miracle of hope, the peaceful living side by side, with character substantially preserved, of the most heterogeneous peoples under the sun. . . .

Indeed, it is not uncommon for the eager Anglo-Saxon who goes to a vivid American university to-day to find his true friends not among his own race but among the acclimatized German or Austrian, the acclimatized Jews, the acclimatized Scandinavian or Italian. In them he finds the cosmopolitan note. In these youths, foreign-born or the children of foreign-born parents, he is likely to find many of his old inbred morbid problems washed away. These friends are oblivious to the repressions of that tight little society in which he so provincially grew up. He has a pleasurable sense of liberation from the state and familiar attitudes of those whose ingrowing culture has scarcely created anything vital for his America of today. He breathes a larger air. In his new enthusiasms for continental literature, for unplumbed Russian depths, for French clarity of thought, for Teuton philosophies of power, he feels himself citizen of a larger world. He may be absurdly superficial, his outward-reaching wonder may ignore all the stiller and homelier virtues of his Anglo-Saxon home, but he has at least found the clue to that international mind which will be essential to all men and women of good will if they are ever to save this Western world of ours from suicide. His new friends have gone through a similar evolution. America has burned most of the baser metal also from them. Meeting now with this common American background, all of them may yet retain that distinctiveness of their native culture and their national spiritual slants. They are more valuable and interesting to each other for being different, yet that difference could not be creative were it not for this new cosmopolitan outlook which America has given them and which they all equally possess. . . .

Only America, by reason of the unique liberty of opportunity and traditional isolation for which she seems to stand, can lead in this cosmopolitan enterprise. Only the American—and in this category I include the migratory alien who has lived with us and caught the pioneer spirit and a sense of new social vistas—has the chance to become that citizen of the world America is coming to be, not a nationality but a trans-nationality, a weaving back and forth, with the other lands, of many threads of all sizes and colors. Any movement which attempts to thwart this weaving, or to dye the fabric any one color, or disentangle the threads of the strands, is false to this cosmopolitan vision. . . . How are we likely to get the more creative America—by confining our imaginations to the ideal of the melting-pot, or broadening them to some such cosmopolitan conception as I have been vaguely sketching? . . .

No Americanization will fulfill this vision which does not recognize the uniqueness of this trans-nationalism of ours. The Anglo-Saxon attempt to fuse will only create enmity and distrust. The crusade against 'hyphenates' will only inflame the partial patriotism of trans-nationals, and cause them to assert their European traditions in strident and unwholesome ways. But the attempt to weave a wholly novel international nation out of our chaotic America will liberate and harmonize the creative power of all these peoples and give them the new spiritual citizenship, as so many individuals have already been given, of a world.

Source: Randolph Bourne, "Trans-National America," *Atlantic Monthly* 118 (July 1916): 92–97.

7.8. Degree of Acculturation High among Post–World War II Immigrants

In 1965, amid the civil rights movement and pressure for a more open and fairer immigration and refugee policy, Edward M. Kennedy, U.S. senator from Massachusetts and brother of the recently assassinated President John F. Kennedy, advocated a major new immigration law that would end the quota system passed in the 1920s. In making his case, he praised the high degree of acculturation among America's post–World War II foreign-born. The "proof" of "assimilation" of the earlier im-

migrants helped open the door for new immigrants when Congress ended the quota system with the 1965 Immigration Reform Act.

Another fear is that immigrants from nations other than those in northern Europe will not assimilate into our society. The difficulty with this argument is that it comes 40 years too late. Hundreds of thousands of such immigrants have come here in recent years, and their adjustment has been notable. At my request, many voluntary agencies that assist new immigrants conducted lengthy surveys covering people who have arrived since the late 1940's. The results would be most gratifying to any American. I have only found five cases of criminal complaints involving immigrants in our studies of many thousands. Unemployment rates among these people are much lower than the national average; business ownership between 10 percent and 15 percent higher; home ownership as high as 80 percent in one city and averaging about 30 percent elsewhere. Economic self-sufficiency after approximately 4½ months from the date of arrival. By every standard of assimilation these immigrants have adjusted faster than any previous group.

In whatever other definition we wish to give to assimilate, we would find our new residents doing well. Family stability is found to be excellent; cases of immigrants on public welfare are difficult to find; 85 to 95 percent of those eligible have become naturalized citizens, and so forth.

The fact is, Mr. President, that the people who comprise the new immigration—the type which this bill would give preference to—are relatively well educated and well to do. They are familiar with American ways. They share our ideals. Our merchandise, our styles, our patterns of living are an integral part of their own countries. Many of them learn English as a second language in their schools. In an age of global television and the universality of American culture, their assimilation, in a real sense, begins before they come here.

Source: Edward Kennedy, U.S. Senate, *Congressional Record*, 89th Cong., 1st sess., 1965, 3: 24,228.

7.9. Late Twentieth-Century Immigrants Become Part of a Multicultural America which Is Hindering Their Assimilation and Contributing to Divisiveness

As people from all over the world came to America in the nation's third wave of immigration, following the 1965 Immigration Reform Act, some nativists doubted their ability to acculturate into American society. A leader among these pessimists, Mark Krikorian, the executive director of the Center for Immigration, has been an outspoken critic of the post-1965 immigration. In 1998 he wrote "Will Americanization Work in America?" for Freedom Review, *a periodical supporting greater immigration restrictions. Krikorian has been concerned about the large number of the new immigrants; however, even more, he fears that they are becoming a part of a multicultural America that is hindering assimilation and is contributing to divisiveness in the United States.*

Our country is experiencing the largest sustained wave of immigration in history, which, barring changes in legislation, will continue indefinitely. The Immigration and Naturalization Service (INS) gave out more than 900,000 green cards last year, enabling immigrants to live permanently in the United States and eventually qualify for citizenship. In addition, the INS estimates that more that 400,000 long-term illegal immigrants settled here last year. The total number of immigrants, about 25 million, represents close to 10 percent of our total population. . . .

Today's immigrant population of 25 million is twice the level of 1910. Although this represents a somewhat smaller percentage of the population than during prior waves of mass immigration (10 percent versus 15 percent), the proportion has doubled in less than 30 years. What's more, numbers alone matter a great deal with regard to assimilation and Americanization. Larger numbers, regardless of their share of the total population, can slow acquisition of English, for instance. This is not only for the obvious reason of less immigrant interaction with individual English-speakers, but also because greater numbers create the critical mass needed to support businesses, schools, newspapers, magazines, and radio and television stations that cater almost exclusively to immigrants, thus helping perpetuate independent immigrant subcultures. . . .

Not only are today's immigrants more clustered geographically, but they are also more concentrated ethnically. In one sense today's immigrant flow is more diverse than ever before, in that significant numbers of people come from all continents and races. But in a more important sense it is considerably less diverse than prior waves because a single ethnic/language group so dominates the flow. In 1996, 36 percent of legal immigrants were from Spanish-speaking countries. Mexico was the number-one source, sending more than three times as many people as number-two Philippines, and Spanish-speaking countries (Mexico, Cuba or the Dominican Republic) were the top sources of immigrants to five of the big-six immigrant states (California, New York, Florida, Texas and Illinois).

In addition, more than 70 percent of the five million illegal aliens estimated to live in the United States are from Spanish-speaking countries.

All told, more than 50 percent of all foreign-born people who have arrived in the United States since 1970 are Spanish speakers. . . .

The Hispanic domination of immigrant flow has no precedent in our history. While Germans accounted for 28 percent of the 1881–1890 flow, and Italians 23 percent of the 1901–1910 flow, such concentrations were transitory, with a wide variety of ethnic/language groups accounting for significant portions of the immigrant stream. But with today's permanent Hispanic majority among immigrants, one ethnic group can predominate in schools, neighborhoods, even metropolitan areas, one of the consequences of which is a reduced need for English to transcend a babel of immigrant languages.

High immigration, concentrated geographically and ethnically, should also affect the marriage market by creating the conditions for a lower rate of intermarriage than would otherwise have occurred in those ethnic communities reinforced by immigration. . . .

The change in the source countries of immigration also works against assimilation, as certain countries in Asia and Latin America have become the primary sources, with Europe accounting for only 16 percent of new immigrants in 1996. These developments in themselves are not as troubling as some immigration critics believe. Americans of European, Asian and Latin American descent seem willing enough to intermarry, belying fears of non-white immigrants inherent unassimilability, and pointing to the potential amalgamation of the immigrant stock.

But what makes the shift in the source countries problematic is that it began just as our country was embarking on a campaign to reinforce and subsidize ethnic separatism through affirmative action, bilingualism, and multiculturalism. These ideas had existed before—Horace Kallen, after all, promoted "cultural pluralism" during the last wave of immigration, and bilingual education for the children of German immigrants was widespread in the nineteenth century. . . .

In the past, these divisive notions ran up against a strong sense of shared national identity, a confident Americanism which demanded more than a minimalist contract obliging citizens to drive on the right side of the road and vote every other November. Today's insecure, tentative, apologetic approach to national identity in general, and to the assimilation of immigrants in particular, has encouraged these latent tendencies toward national balkanization.

Here we arrive at the fundamental problem: aside from the other dubious effects of mass unskilled immigration, aside from the anti-assimilationist nature of current immigration policy, does our society have what it takes to Americanize a large and continuing flow of strangers from overseas? Put differently, is it prudent for a nation which cannot agree on the meaning of its own history to welcome new citizens from outside? . . .

An immigrant flow that is consistently large, regionally and ethnically concentrated, eligible upon arrival for affirmative action, and, to top it all off, largely poor and uneducated, is an ideal constituency for the multicultural state. Of course, the assault on America's identity and values of the past three decades would have occurred regardless of immigration. But today's immigration is the pure oxygen that allows the multicultural fire to burn hot. Until the air supply is restricted, attempts at rebuilding a common civic culture will be unsuccessful.

Source: Mark Krikorian, "Will Americanization Work in America?" *Freedom Review*, Fall 1997. (http://www.cis.org/articles/1997/freedom_review.html)

7.10. Intermarriage of Post–World War II Immigrants with Majority Population Indicates Rapid, Pervasive Assimilation

Douglas Massey, a prominent sociologist and member of the Population Studies Center at the University of Pennsylvania, reported in 1981 on the high degree of intermarriage of Asian and Latin American immigrants with the majority population and suggested that a continuing pattern over time has been toward assimilation of all groups. Sociologists have held that a critical measure of intermarriage is "perhaps the most conclusive, objective indicator of the degree of assimilation" of an immigrant people.

According to Murguia & Frisbie (1977:374), "the frequency with which members of a minority intermarry with the majority population is perhaps the most conclusive, objective indicator of the degree of assimilation of the minority." Once intermarriage occurs, all other types of assimilation are held to follow automatically (Gordon 1964:81); and thus it represents the ultimate indication of a group's social acceptability and assimilability, with respect either to another group or to society at large.

Studies among Asian groups indicate that exogamy [marriage outside one's own group] increases over the generations and across time. Thus there has been a long secular increase in rates of intermarriage for Chinese and Japanese Americans in this century (Lind 1967; Tinker 1973; Kikumura & Kitano 1973; Glick 1970; Burma et al 1970; Parkman & Sawyer 1967; Montero 1980b). Similarly, Gurak & Kritz (1978) report that in 1970, exogamous marriages involving Japanese and Chinese males increased significantly between the first and second generations. In recent years, intermarriage rates for these two minorities have been in the neighborhood of 50% and above (Tinker 1973; Kikumura & Kitano 1973;

Monahan 1977; Montero 1980b). Thus findings indicate a pattern of widespread marital assimilation among two racial minorities that were at one time considered "unassimilable" by US society.

Although information on other Asian groups is less complete, they seem to be following the paths of the Japanese and Chinese (Parkman & Sawyer 1967). Glick (1970) reports that outmarriages by Koreans in Hawaii increased steadily from the early 1900s to the present, and Gurak & Kritz (1978) report a pronounced increase in exogamy between first and second generations Filipino males. As of 1970, intermarriage by persons of Filipino and Korean ancestry appeared to be close to the 50% level characteristic of the Chinese and Japanese minorities (Glick 1970; Monahan 1977).

Secular and intergenerational increases in exogamy also typify Hispanic groups. Among Catholics of Spanish origin sampled in 1963, the rate of outgroup marriage increased from 13% of marriages in the first generation to 24% in the second (Alba 1976). In a 1970 national sample, Cubans were found to be most rapidly assimilating, with the rate of outgroup marriage among males climbing from 16% to 74% between the first two generations (Gurak & Kritz 1978). The same New York sample revealed intergenerational increases in exogamy for South Americans (48% to 92%), Dominicans (37% to 77%), and Central Americans (52% to 95%). Even controlling for the small size of these groups, the increases were significant.

Mexican Americans have also shown a long secular increase in exogamy, stretching all the way back to 1850 (cf Panunzio 1942; Zeleny 1944; Gonzalez 1967; Mittlebach & Moore 1968; Bean & Bradshaw 1970; Murguia & Frisbie 1977). In more traditional areas of Mexican settlement in the southwest, such as Albuquerque or San Antonio, this increase has been slow. However, in more cosmopolitan urban centers like Los Angeles, changes have been more rapid (Grebler et al 1970). In the 1970s, over 30% of Spanish surnamed persons in California chose non-Spanish surnamed mates (Schoen & Nelson 1978).

Mexican American intermarriage increases sharply between generations. In 1974. Schoen & Nelson (1978) found exogamy to increase from around 13% among the foreign born to roughly 40% among those born in the United States. Using 1963 data from Los Angeles, Grebler et al (1970) found intermarriage increased from 13% in the first generation to 23% in the second, to 31% in the third. Moreover, while Mexican Americans were generally most likely to choose a spouse of the same generational background, by the second generation they were more likely to marry an Anglo than a first generation immigrant from Mexico, and by the third were more likely to marry an Anglo than *either* a first or second generation Mexican. In other words, the social distance between generations of Mexican Americans is in some cases greater than that between Mexicans and Anglos (Mittlebach & Moore 1968; Grebler et al 1970).

Outmarriage among Hispanics also increases with social class. In their Los Angeles data, Grebler et al. (1970) report a steady rise in exogamy with increasing occupational status. Such a relationship has also been found to hold for Cubans. South Americans, Central Americans, and Dominicans in New York (Fitzpatrick & Gurak 1979). Both Grebler et al (1970) and Fitzpatrick & Gurak (1979) cite evidence to suggest that Hispanic females often use marriage as a means of upward mobility, choosing husbands of a higher socioeconomic status than themselves.

Outside of New York City, patterns of Puerto Rican intermarriage are similar to those of other Spanish groups (cf Parkman & Sawyer 1967; Glick 1970; Gurak & Kritz 1978); but within this city (where the majority of Puerto Ricans live), the group displays a remarkable rate of endogamy [marriage within one's own group] (70%), which shows no tendency to decline between generations. These results persist even when controlling for the large size of this population, and represent a striking reversal of trends reported by Fitzpatrick (1966), who found New York's Puerto Rican population well on the way to marital assimilation during the 1950s. However, Puerto Ricans do exhibit an increase in exogamy with increasing occupational status, suggesting that their low level of marital assimilation may relate to their standing as the most disadvantaged of all Hispanic groups.

While significant and growing exogamy seems to characterize most of the new immigrant groups, several researchers have noted a tendency for outgroup marriages to cluster within culturally or racially similar groups (Parkman & Sawyer 1967; Kikumura & Kitano 1973; Leon 1975; Gurak & Kritz 1978; Fitzpatrick & Gurak 1979). Specifically, the new immigrants exhibit some tendency to maintain endogamy within "Asian" and "Hispanic" clusters, producing a "double melting pot" analogous to the "triple melting pot" Kennedy (1944) noted among European immigrants (i.e. Catholic-Protestant-Jew). However, such a pattern probably represents an intermediate stage in the process of marital assimilation (Leon 1975). Intermarriage across cluster boundaries and to the core Anglo population is significant and increases over the generations.

Source: Douglas Massey, "Dimensions of the New Immigration to the United States and the Prospects for Assimilation," *Annual Review of Sociology* 7 (1981): 70–72.

ANNOTATED SELECTED BIBLIOGRAPHY

Alba, Richard. *Ethnic Identity: The Transformation of White America*. New Haven, Conn.: Yale University Press, 1990. An account of how immigrants, particularly those with a European background, despite efforts at retention, have increasingly lost their ethnic identity and have become more and more a part of the American mainstream culture.

Bourne, Randolph. *War and the Intellectuals*. New York: American Union against Militarism, 1917. An early argument for immigrant and ethnic acculturation in the United States as cultural pluralism, which for Bourne was a reality. He saw America becoming a transnational ideal.

Carlson, Robert. *The Quest for Conformity: Americanization through Education*. New York: Wiley, 1975. Contends that schools were used to foster immigrant assimilation rather than achieve a melting pot or cultural pluralism.

de Crèvecoeur, J. Hector St. John. *Letters from an American Farmer*. London: Thomas Davies, 1782. Reprint, New York: E. P. Dutton, 1957. He was one of the first, in the second half of the eighteenth century, to label the mixture of foreign-born people from different European backgrounds in America as a melting pot.

D'Innocenzo, Michael, and Joseph Sirefman, eds. *Immigration and Ethnicity: American Society—"Melting Pot" or "Salad Bowl."* Westport, Conn.: Greenwood Press, 1992. Discusses the experiences of immigrants, their ethnic identity, and the future of ethnicity in the United States.

Drachsler, Julius. *Democracy and Assimilation*. New York: Macmillan, 1920. Observes and supports the acculturation of the "new" immigrants, contrary to the opinion of many of his anti-immigrant comptemporaries.

Edmonston, Barry, and Jeffrey Passel, eds. *Immigration and Ethnicity: The Integration of America's Newest Arrivals*. Washington, D.C.: Urban Institute Press, 1994. Discusses the integration of post-1980 immigrants into American society.

Fuchs, Lawrence. *The American Kaleidoscope: Race, Ethnicity and the Civic Culture*. Hanover, N.H.: Wesleyan University Press, 1990. Discusses the process, difficulties, and successes of acculturation among the succession of immigrant groups in the United States from the colonial period to the 1980s.

Glazer, Nathan, and Daniel Moynihan. *Beyond the Melting Pot: The Negroes, Puerto Ricans, Jews, Italians, and Irish of New York City*. Cambridge, Mass.: Harvard University Press, 1973. Concerns ethnic retentions and impediments to acculturation among a number of major ethnic and racial groups in New York City in the early 1970s.

Gleason, Philip. "The Melting Pot: Symbol of Fusion or Confusion." *American Quarterly* 16 (Spring 1964): 20–46. Analyzes the melting pot as a symbol of acculturation in the United States to the early 1960s.

Gorden, Milton. *Assimilation in American Life: The Role of Race, Religion, and National Origins*. New York: Oxford University Press, 1964. Analyzes the interplay in immigrant acculturation and intergroup relations among the processes of Anglo-Conformity, the Melting Pot, and Cultural Pluralism.

Haines, David, ed. *Refugees as Immigrants: Cambodians, Laotians and Vietnamese in America*. Totowa, N.J.: Rowman and Littlefield, 1989. Focuses on the adjustment of these Southeast Asian newcomers to life in the United States.

Hondagneu-Sotelo, Pierrette. *Gendered Transitions: Mexican Experiences of Immigration*. Berkeley: University of California Press, 1994. Studies a group of mostly undocumented Mexican immigrants and the role of gender in the process of their settlement in the United States.

Hoskin, Marilyn. *New Immigrants and Democratic Society: Minority Integration in Western Democracies*. New York: Praeger, 1991. Deals with immigrants from Third World countries, their cultural retentions, their efforts at acculturation, and how they are received in their places of settlement.

Kallen, Horace. *Culture and Democracy in the United States*. New York: Boni and Liveright, 1924. One of the formative voices in seeing and advocating immigrant acculturation as cultural pluralism toward the end of America's second major wave of immigration.

Light, Ivan, and Bhachu Parminder, eds. *Immigration and Entrepreneurship: Culture, Capital and Ethnic Networks*. New Brunswick, N.J.: Transaction Publishers, 1993. Discusses a number of current immigrant groups and how entrepreneurship plays an important role in both continuing aspects of their background culture and in becoming participants in American life.

Novak, Michael. *The Rise of the Unmeltable Ethnics*. New York: Macmillan, 1972. Stresses those aspects of ethnic life that remained outside of the American mainstream as of the early 1970s and points to issues related to Eastern European "ethnics."

Salins, Peter. *Assimilation, American Style*. New York: Basic Books, 1997. A positive voice for the historical process by which immigrants, in general, have been integrated into American society, while maintaining some degree of ethnic retention.

Wheeler, Thomas, ed. *The Immigrant Experience: The Anguish of Becoming an American*. New York: Dial Press, 1971. Personal accounts of difficulties on coming to the United States from a number of immigrants from different, but mostly European, backgrounds.

ORGANIZATIONS AND WEB SITES

American Immigration Control Foundation: www.cfw.com

Focus on Law Studies: www.abanet.org/publiced/focus

Migration and Refugee Service: www.nccbuscc.org/mrs

National Immigration Forum: www.immigrationforum.org

U.S. Border Control: www.usbc.org

III

Immigration and the Public Order

8

Does Immigration Pose a Threat to National Security?

The security of the United States has been a concern of American citizens and a duty of the government throughout the nation's history. External forces, as well as such internal conflicts as the Civil War, have posed major threats to the security of the country. Alleged threats, which had no real basis in actuality or at best were problematic, have also raised concerns about the loyalty of people in America. Immigration has at various times been the subject of public debate in relation to national security, in terms of individual and group loyalties.

In the 1790s, Americans worried about the fragility of the new republic amidst the French Revolution and the Napoleonic Wars, which threatened to draw the new nation into European conflicts. They were concerned that persons who came to the United States from other countries could endanger national security. In 1798 the Federalist-dominated Congress, fearful of French immigrants who might involve the United States in the "radical" French Revolution, passed the Alien and Sedition laws, which included the provision

> that it shall be lawful for the President . . . to order all such aliens as he shall judge dangerous to the peace and safety of the United States, or shall have reasonable grounds to suspect are concerned in any treasonable or secret machinations against the government thereof, to depart out of the territory of the United States.[1]

The Federalist-controlled government vigorously enforced the law, which drove some "radicals" from America and threatened to silence the opposition press. In the succeeding Democratic Republican administration of Thomas Jefferson, the Alien and Sedition Acts were allowed to expire, but the administration kept a wary eye on emigrés from Haiti. Southerners especially feared that immigrants from Haiti, where slaves had overthrown French rule, would bring influences that would unsettle the American slave system.

In the early national period, many in the predominantly Protestant population of the United States linked America's concept of liberty and republican form of government with Anglo-American Protestantism. The sense of the Puritan "mission" had carried over into the more general idea of a virtuous republic and a redeemer nation. Americans prided themselves on their special place in history. Such was the basis for American exceptionalism, distinct from and opposed to the authoritarian Catholicism of European monarchies. As Irish and German immigrants began to increase the number of the Catholic faithful, clergy, and churches in the United States after 1830, Anglo-American Protestant fears of Catholic subversion surfaced. At the same time, Americans generally nursed fears of secret societies. Long fed on ideas of conspiracy, such as the supposed British conspiracy to undermine freedoms in America in the 1760s and 1770s, Americans readily swallowed notions of a vast new conspiracy of Catholics and Old World autocrats to corrupt and disrupt the democratic experiment in the United States. One of the most notable spokesmen concerning these fears was the inventor Samuel Morse. In 1835 he wrote *Imminent Dangers to the Free Institutions of the United States through Foreign Immigration*, in which he denounced Catholic immigrants, priests, bishops, and, especially, Jesuits as participants in a "Foreign Conspiracy" on behalf of the reactionary Austrian monarchy. He felt that this regime was "compelled by self-preservation to attempt our destruction—they must destroy democracy." Morse advocated that, for the protection of the United States and its institutions from destruction by the immigrants, "the law of the land be so changed, that no foreigner who comes into the country . . . shall ever be entitled to the right of suffrage."[2]

As even larger numbers of Irish and German Catholic immigrants entered the United States in the years after 1840, the apprehensions of Morse became part of the anti-immigrant fears of the nativist Know Nothing Party. This party, which emerged in the mid-1850s, showed considerable, though brief, political strength before the slavery issue drove the nativists from the national political stage. The political nativists believed, in the words of historian John Higham, "that some influence originating abroad threatened the very life of the nation from within."[3] The nativists were especially alarmed at the growth and spread of Catholic churches and schools. In response to the nativists' fears, the Catholic bishop of Louisville, Kentucky, quoted an early 1850s article published in the *Boston Post* which stated,

> It is said that the we shall be overrun with foreigners; that they will rise upon native citizens and overpower them; that Catholicism will prevail and deprive America of its liberties. . . . Of our now thirty millions of population one million only are from Ireland. . . . Now, cannot this immense preponderance of Protestantism and of Americanism take care of itself? Is it not perfectly preposterous to suppose for a moment that the Irish Catholics will ever attempt to "rise," as the phrase is, with such an enormous disparity against them?[4]

The Catholic Church responded to nativism with a vigorous defense of religious freedom, and it also built schools, asylums, hospitals, and other institutions to insulate Catholics from Protestant incursions. Such responses only heighten nativists' fears of Catholic immigrant conspiracies.

In the 1860s, the important role played by immigrants, and in particular Germans and Irish, in the winning Union war effort softened nativism. During the Civil War the immigrants' production, military service, and lives lost marked an important and, for most citizens, a recognized contribution to national security. Catholics reminded Americans of their service. In the words of Bishop Martin Spalding, the

> "foreigners" have filled our army and navy; they have fought our battles; they have leveled our forests . . . filled our cities with operatives and mechanics; they have dug our canals, built our turnpikes and railroads . . . in a word, they have, in every way, largely contributed towards enhancing the wealth and increasing the prosperity of the Republic.[5]

In the latter part of the nineteenth century and into the twentieth century, immigrants continued to assist American strength and security by contributing to growing agricultural productivity and by supplying much of the labor for the country's rapidly growing transportation and utility infrastructure, urban construction, and factory output, which catapulted the country into the position of being the world's leading industrial nation.

While opposition to European immigrants abated to a considerable extent in the years after the Civil War, virulent anti-Chinese sentiment rose. Opposition began on the West Coast, where most of the little more than 100,000 Chinese settled in the decades after 1850. They were attracted by the discovery of gold in California, and they worked on the railroads, in factories, and on farms. Increasingly, the Chinese were attacked as labor competition and as culturally and racially unassimilable. A fear of the "yellow peril" spread across the country. A *New York Times* editorial in 1865 stated, "[I]f there were to be a flood-tide of Chinese population—a population befouled with all the social vices, with no knowledge or appreciation of free institutions or Constitutional liberty, with heathenish souls and heathenish propensities . . . we should be prepared to bid farewell to republicanism and democracy."[6] In 1879 President Rutherford Hayes expressed support for legislation to curtail the flow of Chinese immigrants into the United States. A Chinese exclusion law was passed in 1882.

With the onset of America's second major wave of immigration after 1880, voices again warned about the threat of the large numbers of newcomers, now heavily from Southern and Eastern Europe, to American security and culture. There was talk and fear of a need to protect the United States from an "invasion" by inferior people who would overwhelm the "native" population and its "superior" culture. Additionally, there developed a fear of socialists and anarchists, even though their number among the immigrants was very small. Anarchists were added to the growing list of persons who were not to be admitted to the country.

The outbreak of World War I soon brought outspoken attacks against all things German, and after the United States declared war on Germany, Americans feared that German immigrants would be more loyal to Germany than to their adopted country. Anti-German feeling was fanned and took the form of "Hate the Hun" campaigns against everything German, from language instruction to street names. Again fears of "foreign enemies within" fostered nativism. There also was much criticism of Irish immigrants for their support of Ireland's rebellion for freedom from America's ally England and for the reluctance of some Irish to support the American war effort because doing so aided Great Britain. Nevertheless, the war effort received strong support from most immigrant and ethnic groups in the United States, and they again contributed significantly to national security in time of crisis. Julius Drachsler, in *Democracy and Assimilation* written in 1920, reported that with America's entrance into World War I, among immigrants, "organization of 'loyalty leagues' grew apace. Passage of resolutions of 'unflinching loyalty to our country, the United States of America' became part of the regular order of business of every immigrant social organization." On May 12, 1917, some four hundred foreign-language publications sent their support to President Woodrow Wilson stating that immigrants "are anxious to show their gratitude to the land of their adoption and their complete loyalty to its government by making such sacrifices as may be properly expected at this time from all true patriots." To make sure immigrants became Americans and did not follow the tugs of Old World political loyalties, businesses, settlement houses, and public agencies conducted vigorous wartime Americanization campaigns and launched a successful drive to enact Prohibition as a means of "cleaning up America."[7]

A xenophobic reaction to America's involvement in the war and a fear among many about the success of the Bolsheviks (Communists) in the 1917 Russian Revolution resulted, in the name of national security, in the imprisonment and deportation of a number of immigrants who were not yet citizens but were judged to be radicals. Far from swinging left, many in the nation became more conservative after the war. Some of them, through a revival of the Ku Klux Klan and other such organizations, regarded themselves as the defenders of Americans of pioneer stock—Nordic Americans—and lashed out against "the hyphenates" and anyone suspected of importing European radicalism. They used the license to hate immigrants from the wartime anti-German hate campaigns to strike at Jews, Catholics, and blacks. There also continued the influence of earlier anti-immigrant writings like Madison Grant's *The Passing of the Great Race* (1916) in which he portrayed the "new immigrants" as a threat to the security of America's culture and population.[8]

President Warren G. Harding, who spoke out in behalf of the blacks in the South, in *Our Common Country* (1921), was at the same time very critical of "Americans of foreign birth" who spoke on behalf of various foreign interests during the Versailles Peace negotiations and at other times. "Meddling is not only dangerous to us, because it leads us into entanglements against which Washington warned us, but it also threatens an America divided in her own household."[9] The National Origins Acts of the 1920s settled the matter for the time by promising to keep out the "wrong" kinds of immigrants. Immigration slowed and prosperity returned by the mid-1920s. Americans felt "safer" and turned to the diversions of the Jazz Age and away from organized nativism.

In the 1930s, the Great Depression threatened the economic security of the nation. In addition to discouraging immigrants from coming to the United States in any numbers, this time of economic downturn motivated some to pressure poor immigrants to leave the country and force the government to deport others. These actions affected several hundred thousand persons of Mexican birth residing in the American Southwest. Here the issue was less national security than the economic health of "native" Americans.

The next major external threat to the security of the United States came from the Axis powers—Germany, Italy, and Japan—in World War II. When the United States entered the war, old fears of enemy subversion reappeared. The government engaged in selected detention of suspect aliens among the immigrant and ethnic Germans and Italians in America, but the effort was spotty and bore no resemblance to the widespread anti-German campaigns of World War I. The United States stressed that it was fighting Nazism and the German government, rather than the German people, who were viewed as victims themselves of Nazi oppression. In fact, the American war effort was aided by refugees from

Nazism, particularly Jews, who made important contributions to the United States in science and the arts.

To Japanese Americans, primarily on the West Coast, however, the war brought forced dispossession of their homes, farms, and businesses and incarceration in detention camps. Long-standing racial antipathy to Japanese Americans and envy at their industry burst forth with the attack on Pearl Harbor in 1941. These intense prejudices, as well as fears of subversion and sabotage, blinded people to the basic loyalty of these Americans to the United States. There was strong support when the federal government rounded up some 110,000 Japanese American adults and their children, many of whom were citizens, and, contrary to their civil rights, transported them to isolated interior desert and mountain camps. The great majority of the Japanese Americans in Hawaii, however, were not forced to leave their homes for such camps because they were so important to the economic vitality of that territory.

There is no record of any espionage being conducted by any Japanese American during the war. In fact, a considerable number of Japanese aided the war effort in work for American military intelligence in the Pacific and in fighting units in Europe. Still, the negative attitude toward Japanese Americans hardly abated during the war. Even the Supreme Court, in *Korematsu v. United States* in 1944, rejected a Japanese American plea for their civil rights and upheld the internments as justified by the wartime national interest. Three justices objected to the government's actions as based on racial prejudices. The nation, after the war, apologized to the Japanese Americans, and Congress voted a small compensation for those who suffered incarceration.[10]

Overall, as in past wars, ethnic and immigrant Americans played an important part during World War II through their extensive sacrifices made in the military and their efforts performed on the home front. Immigrants helped increase production with new methodologies and new inventions, particularly in the machine tool industry. Their contributions were important in assisting military intelligence and were critical in winning the race with Germany to develop atomic weapons. William Bernard, the executive director of the National Committee on Immigration Policy, in 1950, wrote about the contributions of immigrants to protecting the security of the United States during World War II:

> The record of service of the foreign-born and of aliens was outstanding proof of the strength of their devotion to their adopted country. . . . A total of more than 300,000 foreign-born persons served in the Army during this war. . . . A special type of war service was rendered by the refugee scientists, scholars, industrialists, technicians and other experts. . . . The distinguished record of such

> units as the all-Japanese-American 442d Regiment Combat Team proved that our minorities stood ready to defend our democracy.[11]

In films and public speeches, the loyalty and service of American immigrants were common themes. Indeed, the very "diversity" of the U.S. population and the ability of the United States to assimilate so many people who shared the beliefs of democracy became almost a commonplace theme in wartime and immediate postwar popular culture.

Following the war, a growing rivalry with the Soviet Union posed the major threat to American security, especially when the Soviets acquired "the bomb" and communism seemed to be spreading rapidly across the globe. During the Cold War, there developed a nuclear arms race in which immigrants assisted the United States, particularly in the development of the military's missile delivery system, but the very involvement of so many immigrants aroused concern about their loyalties. Fears of subversion grew in the hothouse of anticommunism. Worries, with anti-Semitic overtones, about Communist infiltration of American schools, Hollywood, and even churches marked the postwar era and led to black lists (lists of persons who are disapproved, fairly or unfairly, and as a result suffer some penalty or exclusion), the vilifying hearings of the House Un-American Activities Committee, and attacks by Senator Joseph McCarthy. To counter the alleged Communist threat, Congress, in 1952, passed a law that excluded any immigrant who was a Communist or had been associated in the past with any Communist or Communist-leaning organization.

The post-1965 wave of immigration, which gave preferences to some newcomers with designated skills, brought many talented scientists and engineers to the United States, some of whom have been employed in sensitive military research and production. Even as (indeed because) they have been making contributions to American security, there is a concern that some of them might be leaking information to other nations. Such fears have led to several investigations and purges of scientific programs, most recently the 1999 allegations of the unauthorized use of classified computer files at the Los Alamos National Laboratory with possible links to China.

Security concerns also have focused on the growth of terrorism among persons belonging to groups and movements that regard themselves as disadvantaged in various parts of the world. America's opposition to Fidel Castro's turn to communism in Cuba in the late 1950s brought fear in the United States that his regime would inflict terrorist attacks on this country. As oil reserves have drawn U.S. interests into the Middle East at the same time the United States has chosen to be the principal supporter of the new state of Israel, the United States has become a target of terrorism abroad and, some fear, through immigrants, in America itself. Indeed, terrorism increasingly has become a means of waging war at low cost and has exposed the ever more far-flung American military and economic interests abroad to attack. In the 1990s terrorism came to the United States. According to Allan Brownfeld,

> The lethal bombing at the World Trade Center in New York on February 26, 1993, is stirring widespread concern about the ability of the American society to prevent terrorist attacks. . . . The ability of Pakistanis and others from troubled Third World countries to easily enter the United States illustrates what many are describing as an immigration "crisis" that has reached "out of control" levels.[12]

Such attacks by foreigners or immigrants are limited, more, including the most destructive ones, such as the bombing of the federal government building in Oklahoma City in 1995, have been undertaken by native-born American citizens. However, the stereotype of Arabs and Muslims as the authors of violence has succeeded in making many Americans feel insecure and has brought stress to the growing number of peaceful Arab Americans and Muslim Americans in the United States.

Fears of "invasion" have been especially pronounced in America's "sun belt." Inadequately guarded borders supposedly allow an increased flow of drugs and a flood of immigrants, including many poor undocumented ones, which has become a national security issue for the United States. Americans who fear such consequences want more stringent laws and a more militarized border. Opponents to these proposals assert that the numbers now coming, legal and undocumented, represent a small percentage of the total population, less than in earlier waves of immigration, and that these immigrants make important contributions to American economic strength and many have fought loyally in U.S. military actions in Korea, Vietnam, the Middle East, Somalia, and Kosovo. Additionally, some industries, particularly those involved in advanced technology, have argued for and have employed many immigrants, including undocumented ones, contending that they are very important in the continued ability of many American firms to manufacture products key to American prosperity and security.

In the wake of a third major wave of immigration since 1965, the sheer numbers of newcomers and their cultural and racial differences have heightened nativist fears of sabotage, terrorism, and a general erosion of "American" culture and unity. Those who welcome immigration insist that such fears are exaggerated and often fueled by prejudices, and that, in fact, immigrants strengthen the security of the United States by bolstering the American economy and by serving loyally and effectively in the nation's armed forces. In the aftermath of the Cold War, with the United States regarded as "the great power" in the world, questions of national security have become more complex and contested. The vulnerability of American people, property, and interests, as a consequence of reactions to U.S. power, has made Americans newly wary of immigrant loyalty and the presence of foreigners. At the same time the value of immigrants to the United States in the new world economy has opened the possibility that the strength they add to American security will become so visible as to curtail the new nativism.

NOTES

1. *The Alien Act of 1798*, U.S. Statutes, 5th Cong. 2d sess., vol. 1, 570–71.

2. An American (Samuel Finley Breese Morse), *Imminent Dangers to the Free Institutions of the United States through Foreign Immigration, and the Present State of the Naturalization Laws* (1835; reprint, in new edition, New York, 1854), 23–39.

3. John Higham, *Strangers in the Land: Patterns of American Nativism, 1860–1925* (New Brunswick, N.J.: Rutgers University Press, 1955), 4.

4. Martin Spalding, *Miscellanea, Comprising Reviews, Lectures, and Essays, on Historical, Theological and Miscellaneous Subjects* (Louisville, Ky., 1855), xlviii, lii–lviii.

5. Ibid.

6. *New York Times*, 1865, in Stuart Miller, *The Unwelcome Immigrant: The American Image of the Chinese, 1785–1882* (Berkeley: University of California Press, 1969), 170.

7. Drachsler, *Democracy and Assimilation*, 20–22, 40–45.

8. Grant, *The Passing of the Great Race*.

9. Warren G. Harding, *Our Common Country* (Indianapolis: Bobbs-Merrill, 1921), 161–65.

10. Fuchs, *The American Kaleidoscope*, 229, 403.

11. Bernard, *American Immigration Policy*, 148–53.

12. Allan C. Brownfeld, "One Answer to Terrorism: Control Entry of Illegal Aliens," *Human Events*, March 20, 1993, 10.

DOCUMENTS

8.1. Immigrants Endanger American Liberties in 1830s

Samuel Morse, an early American inventor of note, was outspoken on behalf of an American exceptionalism based on Protestantism and republican values. Thus, even while immigration was relatively light in the first four decades of the nineteenth century, in 1835 he expressed bitter opposition to a gradual increase in foreign-born Irish and German Catholics in the United States. Morse believed that among these immigrants were agents of European, Catholic, monarchical governments, particularly Austria, which aimed to subvert American republican institutions. Further, he was convinced that the Catholic immigrants were subservient to their priests, and especially to Jesuits, who in propagating their autocratic church endangered American liberties and ideals. Morse compared the foreign-born Americans in the 1830s unfavorably with a nonhistorical, idealized image of earlier immigrants. Morse's nativism and anti-Catholicism had wide currency in his day and beyond.

Emigrants . . . have nurtured their foreign feelings and their foreign nationality to such a degree, and manifested such a determination to create and strengthen a separate and a foreign interest, that the American people can endure it no longer, and a direct hostile interest is now in array against them. This is an effect natural from such a cause; it is one long predicted in the hope of averting the evil. If evil is the consequence, the writer at least washes his hands of the guilt. The name and character of foreigner has, by this conduct of emigrants and their advocates, become odious, and the public voice is becoming louder and louder, and it will increase to unanimity, or at least so far as real American feeling pervades the hearts of Americans, until its language will be intelligible and audible even to those deaf ears, who now affect neither to hear, nor to heed it. . . . It is that anomalous, nondescript . . . thing, neither foreigner nor native, yet a moiety of each, now one, now the other, both or neither, as circumstances suit, against whom I war; a naturalized *foreigner*, not a naturalized citizen; a man who from Ireland, or France, or Germany, or other foreign lands, renounces his native country and adopts America, professes to become an American, and still, being received and sworn to be a citizen, talks (for example) of Ireland as "his home," as "his beloved country," resents anything said against the Irish as said against him, glories in being Irish, forms and cherishes an Irish interest, brings hither Irish local feuds, and forgets, in short, all his new obligations as an American, and retains both a name and a feeling and a practice in regard to his adopted country at war with propriety, with decency, with gratitude, and with true patriotism. I hold no parley with such contradictions as Irish fellow-citizens, French fellow-citizens, or German fellow-citizens. With as much consistency might we say *foreign natives*, or *hostile friends*. But the present is no time either for compliment or nice discrimination. When the country is invaded by an army, it is not the moment to indulge in pity towards the deluded soldiers of the various hostile corps, who act as they are commanded by their superior officers. It is then no time to make distinctions among the officers, lest we injure those who are voluntarily fighting against us, or who may be friends in the enemy's camp. The first thing is to bring the whole army to unconditional surrender, and when they have laid down their arms in a body, and acknowledged our sovereignty, then good fellowship, and courtesy, and pity will have leisure to indulge in discriminating friends from foes, and in showing to each their respective and appropriate sympathies.

We have now to resist the *momentous* evil that threatens us from *Foreign Conspiracy*. The Conspirators are in the *foreign importations*. Innocent and guilty are brought over together. We must of necessity suspect them all. That we are most seriously endangered, admits not of the slightest doubt; we are experiencing the natural reaction of European upon American principles, and it is infatuation, it is madness not to see it, not to guard against it. A subtle attack is making upon us by foreign powers. The proofs are as strong as the nature of the case allows. They have been adduced again and again, and they have not only been uncontradicted, but silently acquiesced in, and have acquired fresh confirmation by every day's observation. The arbitrary governments of Europe—those governments who keep the people in the most abject obedience at the point of the bayonet, with Austria at their head, have combined to attack us in every vulnerable point that the nation exposes to their assault. They are compelled by self-preservation to attempt our destruction—they must destroy democracy. It is with them a case of life and death, they must succeed or perish. If they do not overthrow American liberty, American liberty will overthrow their despotism. . . . Will you despise the cry of danger? Well, be it so. Believe the foreign Jesuit rather than your own countrymen. Open wide your doors. Yes, throw down your walls. Invite, nay allure, your enemies. Enlarge your almshouses and your prisons; be not sparing of your money; complain not of the outrages in your streets, nor the burden of your taxes. You will be repaid in praises of your toleration and liberty. What though European despots have compelled you to the necessity of employing your lives in toiling and providing for their outcast poor, and have caused you to be vexed, and your habit outraged by the expatriated turbulence of their cities, instead of allowing you to rejoice in the prosperity, and happiness, and peaceful neighborhood of your own well-provided, well-instructed children. . . .

What were the circumstances of the country when laws so favourable to the foreigner were passed to induce him to emigrate and settle in this country? The answer is obvious. Our early history explains it. In our national infancy we needed the strength of *numbers*. Powerful nations, to whom we were accessible by fleets, and consequently also by armies, threatened us. Our land had been the theatre of contests between French, and English, and Spanish armies, for more than a century. Our numbers were so few and so scattered, that as a people we could not unite to repel aggression. The war of Independence, too, had wasted us. We wanted *numerical strength*; we felt our weakness in numbers. *Safety*, then, national *safety*, was the motive which urged us to use every effort to increase our population, and to induce a foreign emigration. Then foreigners seemed all-important, and the policy of alluring them hither, too palpable to be opposed successfully even by the remonstrances of Jefferson. We could be benefited by the emigrants, and we in return could bestow on them a gift beyond price, by simply making them citizens. Manifest as this advantage seemed in the increase of our numerical strength, Mr. Jefferson looked beyond the advantage of the moment, and saw the distant evil. . . . Now, if under the most favourable circumstances for the country, when it could most be benefited, when numbers were most urgently needed, Mr. Jefferson could discover the evil afar off, and protest against encouraging foreign immigration, how much more is the measure to be deprecated, when circumstances have so entirely changed, that instead of *adding strength* to the country, immigration *adds weakness*, weakness physical and moral! And what overwhelming force does Mr. Jefferson's reasoning acquire, by the vast change of circumstances which has taken place both in Europe and in this country, in our earlier and in our later condition. *Then* we were few, feeble, and scattered. *Now* we are numerous, strong, and concentrated. *Then* our accessions by immigration were real accessions of strength from the ranks of the learned and the good, from the enlightened mechanic and artisan, and intelligent husbandman. *Now* immigration is the accession of weakness, from the ignorant and the vicious, or the priest-ridden slaves of Ireland and Germany, or the outcast tenants of the poorhouses and prisons of Europe. And again: *Then* our beautiful system of government had not been unfolded to the world to the terror of tyrants; the rising brightness of American Democracy was not yet so far above the horizon as to wake their slumbering anxieties, or more than to gleam faintly, in hope, upon their enslaved subjects. *Then* emigration was natural, it was an attraction of affinities, it was an attraction of liberty to liberty. Emigrants were the proscribed for conscience's sake, and for opinion's sake, the real lovers of liberty, Europe's loss, and our gain. . . . Now emigrants are selected for a service to their tyrants, and by their tyrants; not for their affinity to liberty, but for their mental servitude, and their docility in obeying the orders of their priests. They are transported in thousands, nay, in *hundreds of thousands*, to our shores, to our loss and Europe's gain. Again, I say, let . . . the law of the land be so changed, that no foreigner who comes into the country after the law is passed shall ever be entitled to the right of suffrage. This is just ground; it is practicable ground; it is defensible ground, and it is safe and prudent ground; and I cannot better close than in the words of Mr. Jefferson: "The time to guard against corruption and tyranny is before they shall have gotten hold on us; it is better to keep the wolf out of the fold, than to trust to drawing his teeth and talons after he has entered."

Source: An American (Samuel Finley Breese Morse), *Imminent Dangers to the Free Institutions of the United States through Foreign Immigration, and the Present State of the Naturalization Laws* (1835; reprint, New York: 1854), 23–29.

8.2. Immigrants in First Half of Nineteenth Century Support American Laws

Martin Spalding, the Catholic Bishop of Louisville, Kentucky, was a vigorous defender of his fellow religionists as loyal to America and its political system. Writing in 1855, in the midst of a major wave of Irish and German immigration and of a strong nativist negative reaction to them, Spalding quoted from an article published in the Boston Post, *which pointed to the peaceful acceptance by the Irish of American laws and to the preposterousness of the accusations that the Irish, a small part of the total population, would, or could, overthrow the government and institutions of the United States. Such Catholic defenses became standard as the Church responded to nativism and anti-Catholicism by appealing to American religious freedom and by galvanizing Catholics and immigrants to stand by their faith.*

It is said that we shall be overrun with foreigners; that they will rise upon native citizens and overpower them; that Catholicism will prevail and deprive America of its liberties. These assertions have been reiterated so often that thousands really fear such results. Take the former apprehension, and let facts, so far as they bear on the question of physical force, say how groundless that fear is. In the first place, for the whole time we have been a nation, it is a fact that no such attempt has been made; and if it ever should be made, such is the admirable working of our institutions, that the rule of a mob is utterly out of the question. Permanent success, even where the foreign population outweighs the native population, is an impossibility; for the whole force of the country would at once be invoked to suppress such a rule. In the next place, consider the utter folly, want of foresight, and suicidal policy of such an attempt, if it should ever be made. Of our now thirty millions of population one million only are from Ireland; of the thirty-eight thousand churches that the census of 1850 shows as being in the country, the Catholic are set down at one thousand two hundred and twenty-one; and of the eighty-seven millions of church property, the Catholics have nine millions. Now, cannot this immense preponderance of Protestantism and of Americanism take care of itself? Is it not perfectly preposterous to suppose for a moment that the Irish Catholics will ever attempt to "rise," as the phrase is, with such an enormous disparity against them? It is due, it is but bare justice, to our foreign population to say, that not only has there been no attempt at rising, but their conduct—save only in cases when heated by liquor or otherwise excited—has been almost invariably that of peaceable citizens, submissive to the laws. They have a right to have such a certificate, as to the past, to stand in their favor; and when we consider their position among us, we believe there is no more danger of their "rising" than there is of the falling of the stars.

Source: Martin Spalding, *Miscellanea, Comprising Reviews, Lectures, and Essays, on Historical, Theological and Miscellaneous Subjects* (Louisville, Ky., 1855), lii–liii.

8.3. Immigrant and Ethnic Organizations Pledge Loyalty to United States at Beginning of World War I

Julius Drachsler, an assistant professor of economics and sociology at Smith College, represented the minority of pro-immigration Americans who in the post–World War I years tried unsuccessfully to stem the growing pressure for legislation to restrict greatly the admission of immigrants. In Democracy and Assimilation, *in 1920, he wrote about the benefits of immigrants to the United States and to its security. He reported on resolutions made by many immigrant and ethnic organizations, including one from some 400 foreign-language publications, proclaiming loyalty to the United States as the country entered into World War I. These groups pledged their members, many of whom were foreign-born, to serve in the military and to aid in production and other home-front war efforts.*

It is needless to recount here the circumstances that were the immediate causes of the entrance of the United States into the world war (April 6, 1917), except to point out, that in no small measure they added to the growing feeling of uneasiness and suspicion with respect to the large body of foreign-born in the country. So keenly conscious were many of the immigrant leaders of the precarious position of their fellow-nationals that the foreign-language press, perhaps the most suspected of all immigrant institutions, felt it necessary to make a public declaration of absolute loyalty and allegiance to America. In a remarkable resolution addressed to the President of the United States and signed by representatives of almost four hundred foreign-language publications on May 12, 1917, they expressed themselves in the following unmistakable terms:[1]

> To the President of the United States.
>
> We, the undersigned, publishers of foreign language newspapers, circulating among eighteen millions of people who have left their native lands to enjoy the blessings of citizenship in the United States, knowing full well what is in the hearts of these people, assure you, Mr. President, that they cordially welcome the opportunity now offered them, in common with their fellow-Americans, to assist the enlightened citizenship of other nations in establishing more firmly throughout the world the great principles of democracy. They are proud of having contributed in considerable measure to the agricultural, industrial and commercial greatness of the United States, the benefits of whose prosperity they have shared. They are anxious to show their gratitude to the land of their adoption and their complete loyalty to its government by making such sacrifices as may be properly expected at this time from all true patriots. They are willing and eager to offer themselves, according to their qualifications, for military duty, for employment in field or factory, or for other service with the object of helping as far as they can to uphold your hands in the present crisis. They will cheerfully contribute from their resources in the fullest possible measure to meet the extraordinary financial needs of the government and in all other ways will earnestly cooperate to maintain the country's honor and to insure the triumph of a cause that is destined to bring about a lasting international peace.

The declaration of war by Congress seemed to have silenced all dissenting voices. Henceforth there was only one goal for all loyal Americans, a complete and crushing victory over the arrogant German war-machine. Among the immigrants, the psychological characteristics of the pre-war period were brought into still stronger relief. Organization of "loyalty leagues" grew apace. Passage of resolutions of "unflinching loyalty to our country, the United States of America" became part of the regular order of business of every immigrant social organization. Spontaneous requests were made by Czecho-Slovaks, Poles, Jews, Armenians, to the government to organize foreign legions as distinct fighting units in the American army, while the international composition of the American expeditionary forces was pointed out as proof of the unanimity of spirit among the native and the foreign born. Relief campaigns for sufferers in the war zones were inaugurated on a scale unimaginable before the War. Nor were patriotic societies, and the government slow to take advantage of the rising tide of feeling among the foreign-born and to harness this dynamic sentiment to urgent national tasks that had to be carried through as pre-conditions of final victory.

[1]Declaration of Foreign Language Newspapers. "To Woodrow Wilson, President of the United States, a Declaration by the American Foreign Language Newspapers, presented by the American Association of Foreign Language Newspapers, May 12, 1917." Among the signers were representatives of publications in the following languages: Bohemian, Slovak, Polish, Yiddish, Italian, Croatian, Swedish, French, Serbian, Slovenian, Flemish, Dutch, Syrian, Finnish, Norwegian, Danish, Ukrainian, Lithuanian, Roumanian, Portuguese, Japanese, Ruthenian, Chinese, Spanish, Korean.

Source: Julius Drachsler, *Democracy and Assimilation* (New York: Macmillan, 1920), 20–22.

8.4. Immigrant Advocacy of Original Country's Interests Might Entangle United States in European Conflicts

Warren G. Harding elected president of the United States in 1920, had been a senator and a member of the U.S. Senate Foreign Relations Committee, which became concerned about immigrant loyalties during World War I. Harding reported, in Our Common Country *in 1921, that, in congressional hearings related to the peace treaty at the end of World War I, spokespersons from American immigrant and ethnic groups advocated in behalf of the interests of their countries of origin. This future president echoed ideas on American isolationism that went back to the early days of the republic when he warned that such advocacy was a threat to the nation's security because it encouraged American entanglements in "Old World" conflicts and brought about dissension and division at home.*

It was my official duty to sit with the Senate Committee on Foreign Relations when it was hearing the American spokesmen for foreign peoples during the peace conference at Paris. Under the rules we could give hearing only to Americans, though many whom we had no right to hear sought to bring their appeal to the Senate as though it possessed some sense of justice which had no voice at Paris. We heard the impassioned appeals of Americans of foreign birth on behalf of the lands from which they came—where their kinsfolk resided. No one doubted their sincerity; no one questioned their right to be interested. But for me there was a foreboding, a growing sense of apprehension.

How can we have American concord; how can we expect American unity; how can we escape strife, if we in America attempt to meddle in the affairs of Europe and Asia and Africa; if we assume to settle boundaries; if we attempt to end the rivalries and jealousies of centuries of Old World strife? It is not alone the menace which lies in involvement abroad; it is the greater danger which lies in conflict among adopted Americans.

This is the objection to the foreign policy attempted, not with the advice and consent of the Senate, but in spite of warning informally uttered. America wants the good-will of foreign peoples, and it does not want the ill-will of foreign born who have come to dwell among us. . . .

That policy, my countrymen, is a bad policy. It is bad enough abroad, but it is even more menacing at home. Meddling abroad tends to make Americans forget that they are Americans. It tends to arouse the old and bitter feelings of race, or former nationality, or foreign ancestry, in the hearts of those who ought never to be forced to turn their hearts away from undivided loyalty and interest given to 'America first.'

I want America on guard against that course which naturally tends to array Americans against one another. I do not know whether or not Washington foresaw this menace when he warned us against entangling alliances and meddling abroad, but I see it, and I say to you that all America must stand firm against this dangerous and destructive and un-American policy. Meddling is not only dangerous to us, because it leads us into entanglements against which Washington warned us, but it also threatens an America divided in her own household, and tends to drive into groups seeking to make themselves felt in our political life, men and women whose hearts are led away from 'America First' to 'Hyphen First.'

Source: Warren G. Harding, *Our Common Country* (Indianapolis: Bobbs-Merrill, 1921), 161–65.

8.5. Immigrants Contributed to American Security Through Efforts and Sacrifices in Two World Wars

William Bernard was the executive director of the National Committee on Immigration Policy, a post–World War II organization that advocated more open and fairer American immigration legislation, including a repeal of the 1920s national quota system. Bernard, in building the case for more open immigration, detailed the contributions of the foreign-born to America's security through their extensive efforts and sacrifices in World War I and World War II. The beneficial actions of immigrants that he cited were consistent with their contributions to America in earlier wars and continued through the nation's military engagements in the last half of the twentieth century.

War may be said to be the acid test of the integration of immigrant groups into the American nation. The testimony of two world wars is eloquent with respect to the patriotism and loyalty of the foreign-born and alien population. The blood of aliens and of naturalized and native-born Americans has flowed together on battlefields all over the world.

Let us recall the relation of the immigrant to America at the time of the First World War. . . .

In the reports of the Provost Marshal General, the patriotism of these "Americans by choice" won high commendation:

> Thousands of non-declarant aliens of co-belligerent and even of neutral origin welcomed the opportunity to take up arms against the arch-enemy of all; the records of correspondence in this office contain eloquent testimony to this spirit. The figures of alien classification indicate this, and the local boards report explicitly that the number of non-declarant aliens waiving their exemptions was very large (191,491). . . .
>
> The great and inspiring revelation here has been that men of foreign and of native origin alike responded to the call to arms with a patriotic devotion that confounded the cynical plans of our arch-enemy and surpassed our own highest expectations. No man can peruse a muster roll from one of our camps or the casualty lists from a battlefield in France without realizing that America has fulfilled one of its highest missions in breeding a spirit of common loyalty among all those who have shared the blessings of life on its

> free soil. No need to speculate how it has come about; the great fact is demonstrated that America makes Americans.

With the experience of the First World War behind the nation, the loyalty of the foreign born in America was largely taken for granted in the recent conflict. The first proof of the immigrants' devotion came even before the opening shots had been fired in defense of Pearl Harbor. The conversion of America's peace-time industries to an arsenal for democracy could hardly have been accomplished without the help of the foreign born. In Detroit's key industries, for example, one-third of the workers were aliens—many of them expert toolmakers. . . .

As in the First World War, the record of service of the foreign born and of aliens was outstanding proof of the strength of their devotion to their adopted country. With the outbreak of war the Selective Service Act included all aliens in its registration and after September, 1942, permitted the induction even of enemy aliens if their personal history proved them acceptable to the land or naval forces. Altogether 109,000 non-citizens served in the United States Army between July 1, 1940, and June 30, 1945. Of these, 30,000 were aliens from enemy countries. A total of more than 300,000 foreign-born persons served in the Army during the same period. . . .

Especially striking were the contributions to the war effort on the part of the refugees who had come here seeking a haven from Nazi persecution. They were already geared to the necessity of fighting for a democratic way of life, and they became conspicuous as blood donors and in many other phases of the civilian war effort. They also rendered unique services for which they alone were qualified.

> A special type of war service was rendered by the refugee scientists, scholars, industrialists, technicians, and other experts, either directly in government service or through the universities and private industries. Because of their intimate knowledge of the languages, industries, public utilities, and governments of enemy countries—a knowledge not matched by that of native Americans—there was a great demand for their services. . . . The detailed knowledge possessed by these experts was effectively utilized in both military and economic warfare as for example in bombing operations by revealing the location of hidden munitions plants and by advising with regard to the timing of bombing operations so they would be most effective. . . .
>
> The Army availed itself of the services of several thousand German citizens now here who had expert technical knowledge of the water plants, telephone systems, etc., in German cities.

In the armed forces the refugees also had an outstanding record. Their eagerness to enter service was especially conspicuous; many tried to volunteer before they were drafted, although as aliens they were not permitted to do so. Frequently refugees in the armed services were given special assignments where knowledge of the language and terrain of the enemy-occupied countries was required. Many were decorated for special acts of bravery. And many made the supreme sacrifice for their new homeland and for liberty.

But the tales of heroism belong to no one special group. First-, second-, and third-generation immigrants fought alongside of other Americans in the Pacific and the European theaters in the air, on the seas, and on the land. Their names were listed in the rolls of the injured, the missing, and the dead. The distinguished record of such units as the all-Japanese-American 442d Regimental Combat Team proved that our minorities stood ready to defend our democracy.

Source: William S. Bernard, ed., *American Immigration Policy: A Reappraisal* (New York: Harper and Brothers, 1950), 148–53.

8.6. Late Twentieth Century Criminal Aliens Seen as a Threat to Public Safety and National Security

The Federation for American Immigration Reform (FAIR), an influential organization advocating restriction on immigration, in an Issue Brief, *entitled "Criminal Aliens," reported on the problems, numbers, and costs to states and to the federal government of immigrants who are criminals. It proclaimed this issue to be a public safety and a national security matter in late twentieth-century America. While the evidence indicates that criminals among immigrants are and should be a concern to Americans, it should be noted that there are criminals in almost all large groups of people and that the percentage of criminals among immigrants in the United States is small.*

Criminal aliens—non-citizens who commit crimes—are a growing threat to public safety and national security, as well as a drain on our scarce criminal justice resources. The World Trade Center bombing, the CIA shooting, the *Golden Venture* smuggling ring, and the growth of the Russian mafia are but a few examples of the fact that we are not doing a good job in screening out aliens who commit crimes. Congress all but ignored the substantial role criminal aliens are playing in the growing crime problem facing our country until 1996, when the number of deportable crimes was increased. However, the persistent nature of the criminal alien problem indicates that, without significant border and asylum reform to close the door to illegal and fraudulent entry, the criminal alien problem will only worsen.

The Magnitude of the Problem:

In 1980, our federal and state prisons housed fewer than 9,000 criminal aliens. By the end of 1994, these same prisons housed over 59,000 criminal aliens. Other aliens not included in this total include immigrants who have become U.S. citizens (not included in the federal prison data), aliens being held for trial and some awaiting deportation but not convicted in the United States. . . .

What Are the Costs to the Taxpayer?

In the federal prisons, the average cost of incarceration in 1994 was $21,300 per year. The taxpayer is, therefore, paying over $450 million this year in prison expenses apart from the other criminal justice system costs. In addition, the federal government has begun to reimburse heavily alien-impacted states for some of the costs of illegal alien prisoners in their state prisons. For Fiscal Year 1996, Congress appropriated $300 million for this program.

What Is the Burden on the States?

The New York State Senate Committee on Cities estimates that the annual criminal justice costs for criminal aliens in New York is $270 million. The Committee has called for a national moratorium on immigration to help alleviate this problem.

According to the Illinois Governor's Office, Illinois spends over $40 million per year for the incarceration of criminal aliens. This does not include the costs of arresting and prosecuting these aliens. . . .

Why Do We Face This Persistent Problem?

Despite the Border Patrol making over a million apprehensions last year, they estimate they miss two or more illegal border crossers for every apprehension. Most enter for short periods, but the INS estimates a net increase of about 150,000 a year from illegal border crossers who stay. An additional net increase of 150,000 results from persons who enter legally as nonimmigrants and then violate their status. . . . We are not carefully controlling entry through the side door used by persons requesting asylum. These persons enter the country under false pretenses and then claim they would be persecuted if sent home. Asylum applicants who seek this status at a port of entry generally have not been screened for eligibility to enter the country as either immigrants or nonimmigrants. Although we know nothing about their criminal or political activities before they came, their health or their ability to become productive members of our society, they often are admitted into the country and told their case will be reviewed later. Only a small share of asylum claimants are found eligible for that status. Yet we have over half a million asylum claimants in the country right now, some of whom have never been screened despite having entered years ago.

What Can Be Done?

- First, we must secure our borders. Denying jobs to illegal aliens is important to that effort.
- Second, we must make the criminal conviction of an alien a one-way ticket to deportation and permanent exclusion from the United States.
- Asylum applicants should be screened expeditiously and excluded if their claims are not credible. Even if they appear to have credible claims, they should be detained until background checks are done.
- Other corrective measures include greater INS and local government cooperation to identify criminal aliens, additional detention facilities for those in deportation proceedings and improved data bases and screening procedures to identify deported aliens if they try to return here either overtly or surreptitiously.

Source: "Criminal Aliens," *Issue Brief*, FAIR, December 1998, 1–3. (http://fairus.org/html/04110608.htm)

ANNOTATED SELECTED BIBLIOGRAPHY

Bernard, William S., ed. *American Immigration Policy, A Reappraisal*. New York: Harper and Brothers, 1950. Written in the aftermath of World War II, stresses the contributions of immigrants during that war and in the development, over the years, of America's growing strength.

Billington, Ray. *The Protestant Crusade, 1800–1860: A Study of the Origins of American Nativism.* New York: Macmillan, 1938. Discusses how Protestants and others regarded the increasing number of Roman Catholics in early nineteenth-century America as a threat to the country's established religious and political institutions.

Drachsler, Julius. *Democracy and Assimilation*. New York: Macmillan, 1920. Following World War I, recognizes immigrants' support for the United States during that conflict and their value to the prosperity and security of the country.

Harding, Warren G. *Our Common Country*. Indianapolis: Bobbs-Merrill, 1921. Immigrant advocacy of interests in their countries of origin causes divisions in the United States and endangers the nation's security.

Luebke, Frederick. *Bonds of Loyalty: German-Americans and World War I.* DeKalb: Northern Illinois University Press, 1974. Discusses the loyalty of German American immigrants and ethnic people in the face of harsh treatment from the American public during World War I.

Lynn-Jones, Sean, and Steven Miller, eds. *Global Dangers: Changing Dimensions of International Security.* Cambridge, Mass.: MIT Press, 1995. Includes material on dangers to security and stability from international migration of peoples.

Miller, John C. *Crisis in Freedom: The Alien and Sedition Acts.* Boston: Little, Brown, 1951. Examines the fear, in the 1790s, particularly among Federalists, for the security of the new American republican institutions from immigrants coming from revolutionary France.

Teitelbaum, Michael, and Myron Weiner, eds. *Threatened Peoples, Threatened Borders: World Migration and U.S. Policy.* New York: Norton, 1995. Treats American policies, including those relating to security, in the face of the extensive international migration of people in the late twentieth century.

Weiner, Myron, ed. *International Migration and Security.* Boulder, Colo.: Westview Press, 1993. Examines the impact of the movement of people across international boundaries on different security issues in a variety of nations.

Ziegler, Benjamin. *Immigration: An American Dilemma.* Boston: D. C. Heath, 1953. Includes information on security considerations in the 1952 Walter-McCarran Immigration Bill and President Harry Truman's veto message.

ORGANIZATIONS AND WEB SITES

American Immigration Control Foundation: www.cfw.com

Cato Institute: www.cato.org

Immigration Forum: www.immigrationforum.org

U.S. Border Control: www.usbc.org

9

How Have Immigration Issues Affected U.S. Foreign Policy?

The way in which the United States selects and receives immigrants and the way in which the nation treats them after their arrival affect America's relations with other countries. Immigration policy has been and is a part of American foreign policy.

In the late eighteenth and early nineteenth centuries, England attempted to protect her initial advantage in the early stages of industrialization by trying to prevent her citizens with knowledge of new mechanization from emigrating. The fact that Americans welcomed and even recruited English mechanics and others with technological knowledge to come to Rhode Island, New Jersey, and other places in the United States to establish and work in textile mills added to the strained relations between Great Britain and this country. Paul Wiers, in an article entitled "International Implications of American Immigration Policy," quoted a London newspaper in 1816 stating, "Fears were expressed over the ruinous drain of the most useful part of the population of the United Kingdom."[1] Additionally, in the late 1790s, the Federalists in the administration of President John Adams, fearing French immigrants with equalitarian and other radical political ideas with which they did not agree, and at a time when the country was engaged in a quasi-war with France, enacted in Congress the harsh anti-immigrant Alien and Sedition laws.

In the early years of the nineteenth century, the United States harbored immigrants from Latin America who fled from or planned to undertake revolutionary action against Spain. Again in the 1830s and 1840s, the

United States welcomed and supported such leaders as Louis Kossuth from Hungary and others who were working for the overthrow of monarchical regimes in Europe. America was the symbolic republican hope for the insurgents and a real refuge when their revolutions did not succeed, as in 1830 and 1848. Two such refugees who became leaders in the American West were Frederick Munch and Carl Schurz. Schurz became the secretary of the interior in the administration of Rutherford B. Hayes. There also were those in the United States who believed that at least one of these regimes, Austria, supported undermining the republican institutions here through immigrants who adhered to the papacy and traditional conservative European political principles. In these pre–Civil War years, Massachusetts and other states wanted the U.S. government to pressure European countries to stop what they claimed to be a practice of exporting paupers and other undesirable persons to the United States.

In 1868 the United States signed the Burlingame Treaty with China, which agreed to open immigration between the two countries, to provide good treatment for the Chinese who were here, and to foster Sino-American friendship. In 1880 anti-immigration interests in the United States, particularly on the West Coast, persuaded the American government to take advantage of China's weakness and force through a new treaty that would allow Congress to prohibit Chinese immigration to the United States. The federal exclusion act against Chinese workers was passed in 1882. China protested but was too weak to effectuate any change in American policy.

In 1866 Irish Fenians, including immigrants, made unsuccessful raids into Canada from the United States as part of the Irish effort to free Ireland from English rule. Cuban immigrants in the United States cooperated in plans to liberate Cuba from Spain and encouraged and supported the U.S. cause in the Spanish American War. At the turn of the century, Italian immigrants in the United States worked for the overthrow of the monarchy in Italy, and one of them, an anarchist residing in Paterson, New Jersey, returned to that country and assassinated the Italian king. Earlier the Italian government had been alarmed when a New Orleans mob lynched eleven Italian immigrants in 1891.

In the latter part of the nineteenth century, the United States played a key role in persuading Japan to open its doors to trade and relations with other nations. Americans in Hawaii encouraged Japanese laborers to come to the islands to engage in agricultural work. However, when some of the Japanese began to settle in the West Coast states, strong prejudice arose against them as it had earlier against the Chinese. Japan was a nation becoming powerful through Western industrialization, and it insisted that its people be respected abroad; consequently, the U.S. government wanted to avoid insulting them through racist exclusionary legislation. In 1907 President Theodore Roosevelt worked out a "Gentlemen's Agreement" by which there would be no restrictive American legislation and Japan itself would limit the number of Japanese allowed to emigrate to the United States.

Nevertheless, forces, particularly in California, continued to push for exclusionary legislation. Some voices tried to stem the strong fears and virulent racism. The Reverend Sidney Gulick, an advocate of friendship with Japan, in *The American Japanese Problem* published in 1914, maintained that there already was a limitation on Japanese immigration to the United States and that an exclusionary statute would be "humiliating to Japan" and would hurt trade relations with Asia.[2] World War I focused attention on the conflict and quieted for a time the anti-Japanese forces within the United States.

By the early 1920s the exclusionists had regrouped and pushed forward amidst a general postwar surge of anti-immigrant sentiment. In 1924 Congress was ready to pass a law prohibiting the admission of all Japanese to the United States, despite the fact that, as Constantine Panunzio, professor of social economics at Whittier College, wrote in *Immigration Crossroads*, "Japan seems to have done all that was humanly possible faithfully to observe the 'gentlemen's agreement.' "[3] Spokesmen from California urged exclusionary legislation, stating that for twenty years they had been waging "the fight of the Nation against the incoming of alien races whose peaceful penetration must in time with absolute certainly drive the white race to the wall."[4]

U.S. Secretary of State Charles Evans Hughes opposed the proposed law: "[T]he Japanese are a sensitive people, and unquestionably would regard such a legislative enactment as fixing a stigma upon them. . . . I believe such legislative action would largely undo the work of the Washington Conference on Limitation of Armament, which so greatly improved our relations with Japan."[5] Despite this plea and petitions from the Japanese ambassador, Congress unilaterally abrogated the "Gentlemen's Agreement" by passing a law that excluded all Japanese immigration to the United States. This unnecessary, vindictive legislation, which announced to the world that the United States found the Japanese to be an inferior people, caused a deep resentment among them. Panunzio declared, "It is perhaps difficult to realize how deep a wound the exclusion clause inflicted upon the soul of Japan and the entire East." July 1, 1924, designated as "Humiliation Day" in Japan, drew thousands of protestors. "Japan is wondering . . . whether race shall stand against race and color against color."[6]

A different relation of immigration and foreign policy centered on Europe and came to a critical point during and after World War I. Before the United States entered the war, some immigrant and ethnic German Americans opposed the country's foreign policy that was moving toward an Anglo-American rapprochement with England. This alignment with

Great Britain also was opposed by some immigrant and ethnic Irish Americans who despised all things English and supported an Irish rebellion for freedom from England during the war. After the conflict, a number of different immigrant and ethnic groups within the United States lobbied to influence the country's support in the peace negotiations at Versailles for a variety of groups which were seeking self-determination and independence. These activities tended to increase divisions among American ethnic groups, and there were those who criticized these efforts made by immigrants to influence America's foreign policy, including former President Theodore Roosevelt and future President Warren G. Harding.

Immigration policy also intersected with foreign policy along the U.S. southern border with Mexico. This border generally had been unguarded and was open to a free flow of people from both countries. Some American businesses looked to Mexico for a source of cheap labor. The Great Depression of the 1930s, however, brought a major change in border policy and the attitude toward recruiting Mexican workers. The severe economic downturn caused some communities in the Southwest to encourage the government to lighten relief needs by large-scale deportation of Mexican immigrants. The resulting expulsion of several hundred thousand Mexicans stirred resentment and foreign policy friction with the Mexican government. When the United States experienced a labor shortage during World War II, the U.S. government had to repair relations with Mexico in order to arrange for an official importation of Mexicans as contract workers, under the Bracero program. This program ended in 1964, and the United States increased its efforts to tighten control over the undocumented entry of Mexicans at the border and within the country, once again straining relations with the Mexican government.

In the succeeding years, the U.S. government has worked to gain cooperation from Mexico to regulate the flow of migrants across the border and to halt drug traffic. The Mexican government has exerted pressure for a more lenient immigration policy, a continued flow of remittances from immigrants, and good treatment by the United States of those Mexicans who have settled in this country. The president of Mexico, Vicente Fox, has called for greater cooperation between Mexico and the United States and has urged its northern neighbor to be more open to the use of Mexican workers. In fact, Fox proposed transforming the North American Free Trade Agreement (NAFTA) (among the United States, Canada, and Mexico) into a common market, like the European Union, "in which citizens of any one country can work in any other member nation, and passport controls have also largely been abolished."[7]

During World War II, foreign policy considerations encouraged Congress to begin changing, however slightly, immigration laws concerning Asians. When it was learned that Japanese propaganda aimed at China, an American ally, was focusing on the racist exclusionary immigration policy of the United States in regard to their country, Congress agreed in 1943 to give China a quota of 101 persons annually, and, for the first time in the nation's history, to permit Chinese immigrants to become naturalized citizens. A similar quota was extended in 1946 to another ally, India, and to a former American territory, the Philippines, now an independent country. In 1952, as postwar relations were improving with Japan and Korea, they too received a small quota, and immigrants from those countries were then eligible for citizenship.

In the years following World War II, American relations with wartime ally Soviet Russia turned into a Cold War, as a fear of Communist expansion worldwide and at home dominated much American thinking and foreign policy decisions. In the battle for global leadership, each country took actions to appear enlightened and to make the other country appear hostile in order to win continued cooperation from allies and new cooperation from unaligned, emerging nations. Thus, in the late 1940s, for humanitarian and foreign policy reasons, the United States agreed to admit a considerable number of displaced persons, many of whom had fled from the Soviet advance into Eastern Europe. When the Communists achieved victory in China, the United States granted asylum to those Chinese who were studying, working, or visiting in America and who did not want to return to the totalitarian Communist regime in their country. As the Cold War progressed, the American refugee policy became increasingly focused on persons fleeing from Communist-controlled nations. The United States made special provisions for persons fleeing the unsuccessful Hungarian resistance to the Soviets in 1956; to persons fleeing Cuba after the Castro takeover in 1959; to persons fleeing Vietnam and other parts of Southeast Asia after the Communist successes there; to disadvantaged Jewish persons who were able to leave the Soviet Union; to Polish, Yugoslavian, and others leaving Communist regimes in Eastern Europe; and to refugees from the left-wing regimes in Nicaragua and Afghanistan.

In particular, the United States's ready reception of approximately one million persons fleeing from Cuba, after the establishment of Castro's Communist rule there, has been an important component of America's foreign policy strategy and ideology. It was seen, in part, as a signification to the world of the shortcomings of this Soviet ally and of the preference of so many of its people for American democracy. In addition, the U.S. government supported the utilization of Cuban exiles in efforts to overthrow the Castro regime from the Bay of Pigs fiasco of April 1961 to covert operations through the 1970s. In the United States, the Cuban concentration in vote-rich Florida gave them undue influence politically. The Cuban community developed a very influential lobby which has insisted on continued hostility to Castro and has made it difficult for

Congress and the State Department to develop flexibility in its relations with Cuba.

Immigration considerations also have played a role in America's foreign relations with the Dominican Republic in the decades after World War II. Fears that increasing population pressures were aiding a threatened left-wing takeover of a government favored by the United States led this country to admit more immigrants from the Dominican Republic in an effort to alleviate the population problem and relieve pressure on the existing regime.

One aspect of the global rivalry with the Soviet Union that put the United States at a propaganda disadvantage was the American immigration quota system. Although the absolute exclusion of immigrants from Asian countries was terminated during and after World War II, the very marked quota preferences for the countries of Northern and Western Europe over Southern and Eastern Europe and even more over the rest of the Eastern Hemisphere were attacked by the Communists as an example of America's racism which regarded most of the people of the Third World, and even in First World Asia, as inferior. Cold War exigencies forced a reconsideration of U.S. immigration policy. In 1952 President Harry S. Truman, in a veto message of an immigration bill, called unsuccessfully for the end of the discriminatory quota system by insisting that "our immigration policy is . . . important to the conduct of our foreign relations and to our responsibilities of moral leadership in the struggle for world peace."[8] Eleven years later, in 1963, President John F. Kennedy echoed Truman's concern about the quota system in the Cold War: "[I]n an age of interdependence among nations, such a system is an anachronism, for it discriminates among applicants for admission into the United States on the basis of accident of birth. . . . Many problems of fairness and foreign policy are involved in replacing a system so long entrenched."[9]

Thus, for foreign policy and other reasons, growing criticism of the quota system resulted in its elimination in the 1965 immigration law. In its place, Congress enacted an equal annual maximum admission of 20,000 immigrants from any one country to the United States for all countries in the Eastern Hemisphere with an annual ceiling of 170,000, and in 1967, 20,000 for all countries of the Western Hemisphere with an annual limit of an additional 120,000.

In the last third of the twentieth century, refugee and immigration controversies arose between humanitarian and foreign policy concerns in relations with Central America. As revolution swept several of the countries in this region in the 1980s, the U.S. government, in supporting the right-wing regimes in El Salvador and Guatemala, resisted accepting refugees fleeing from those governments, but, opposing the left-wing regime in Nicaragua, the United States was more willing to accept persons seeking asylum from that country. One result was that a considerable number of Americans, many of them clergy, developed an underground "sanctuary movement" that gave help and protection to Salvadoran and other refugees who were able to enter the United States without legal documentation. The U.S. government sought to deport undocumented refugees from El Salvador; however, in 1987, when the Duarte government in El Salvador claimed that returning refugees added to unemployment and threatened to destabilize the country, deportations were suspended.

Likewise, there has been much criticism, by civil rights, humanitarian, and African American groups, of the U.S. government's resistance to give refugee status to Haitians who wanted to come to the United States to escape persecution at the hands of right-wing dictators who were on friendly terms with this country. The critics alleged that a contributing reason was that the Haitian refugees were black. They contrasted the government's policy toward the Haitians with the open welcome to the, at first, mostly white refugees from the Communist regime in Cuba. As the succeeding outflow from Cuba became more mulatto and black, particularly in the large exodus in 1980, there seemed to be less of a welcome from the United States. U.S. government officials have claimed that most of the persons coming from Haiti and more recently from Cuba have left their countries not primarily because of persecution but for economic reasons and thus do not qualify as refugees. The governments of the states in which the refugees were concentrated also put pressure on the federal government to stop the flow of immigrants.

As a result of American efforts to control Communist expansion in Vietnam and the unsuccessful war there, many Vietnamese and other Southeast Asians who cooperated with the United States were admitted to this country as refugees in the 1970s. Succeeding waves of "boat people" and other persons fleeing Vietnam created foreign policy tensions between the United States and Southeast Asian and other nations and brought more refugees to the United States.

Throughout the history of the United States, immigration policies have had an impact on the nation's relations with other countries. At times America's openness to immigrants and refugees has been viewed favorably by other countries in relieving them of excess or undesired peoples and in providing financial remittances from former nationals who became residents in the United States. At other times this openness has been a source of friction when other countries experience America's immigration policies as a brain drain or as an unfriendly, politically motivated encouragement of an exodus of people a nation does not want to lose. On the other hand, America's immigration restrictions and exclusions have at times resulted from agreements with other countries, but more often have been regarded as a humiliation to certain peoples and nations—for example, Japan and China—or as a refusal to alleviate adequately refugee or overpopulation problems, as in the case of El Salvador, Haiti, and Mexico.

By the end of the twentieth century, some of America's immigration and foreign policy related issues have been lessened by the passage of the more globally egalitarian 1965 immigration law, by the end of the Cold War, and by economic improvements in much of Europe and Japan. Still many controversial concerns remain. The United States continues to be a magnet, in part encouraged by American businesses, and even government immigration preferences, for well-educated, skilled persons, particularly from less developed countries. Political as well as humanitarian pressures continue to be put on the U.S. government by the Catholic Church and other religious organizations, as well as by some ethnic groups, to accept as refugees a larger portion of the many millions of persons throughout the world displaced by war, famine, and natural disasters. The greatest challenge comes from neighboring countries. Growing populations, poverty, and political instability make immigration a major issue in the relations of the United States and Mexico, as well as countries in the Caribbean and Central America. Despite some agreements through NAFTA and other negotiations, the needs of Mexicans for employment and of American businesses for less expensive labor continue to make immigration a major concern as the United States and Mexico work to improve their foreign and neighborly relations.

NOTES

1. Paul Wiers, "International Implications of American Immigration Policy," in *Reappraising Our Immigration Policy*, ed. Thorsten Sellin, *Annals*, APSS, 1949, 39–40.

2. Sidney Gulick, *The American Japanese Problem* (New York: Charles Scribner's Sons, 1914), 190–95.

3. Constantine Panunzio, *Immigration Crossroads* (New York: Macmillan, 1927), 168.

4. Ibid., 172.

5. Ibid., 171.

6. Ibid., 181–83.

7. Ginger Thompson, "Fox Urges Opening of U.S.-Mexican Border to Build New Partnership," *New York Times*, August 14, 2000, A8.

8. Harry S. Truman, "To The House of Representatives," H. Doc. 520, *Congressional Record*, 82nd Cong., 2nd sess., 1952, 98: 8082–83.

9. John F. Kennedy, *A Nation of Immigrants* (New York: Harper and Row, 1964), 103.

DOCUMENTS

9.1. No Law Is Needed to Exclude Japanese Immigrants Owing to 1907 Gentlemen's Agreement

While at one time or another some Americans have opposed immigration from almost every country, the opposition to Asians, first to Chinese and then to Japanese, was particularly intense in the nineteenth and early twentieth century. Consequently, exclusion laws were passed against the Chinese, beginning in 1882, at a time when their home government was relatively weak. Then agitation began for the exclusion of the Japanese. Since their home government was westernizing and growing in power, the U.S. government was reluctant to insult them through prohibitory legislation. Instead, President Theodore Roosevelt, in 1907, negotiated a Gentlemen's Agreement by which the Japanese government agreed not to issue passports for laborers to come to the United States. Anti-Japanese advocates, particularly in California, continued, however, to push for federal exclusion laws. In 1914 the Reverend Sidney Gulick, a Congregational missionary dedicated to amicable relations between the United States and Asia and secretary of the National Committee for Constructive Immigration Legislation, wrote The American Japanese Problem, *in which he pointed out the negative impact that exclusionary legislation would have on Japanese-American foreign relations.*

The writer heartily agrees with the fundamental postulate of California's general oriental policy. An immigration from Asia swamping the white man, overturning the democratic institutions of the Pacific coast, and bringing wide economic disaster to Caucasian laborers and farmers is not for a moment to be tolerated. The writer advocates nothing of the kind. Nor does Japan ask for rights of unlimited immigration. Her statesmen see very well that large influx of Japanese and Chinese laborers into the United States would soon produce intolerable conditions and inevitably lead to serious race conflict. All are agreed in regard to this point. I have talked with many Japanese gentlemen on this matter and not one have I found who dissents. . . .

For sixty years the treaties between Japan and the United States have emphasized the friendship of the two peoples. Not the Japanese Government alone but the people also have taken these assurances seriously and have acted, for decades, in harmony with them. Hundreds of Japanese attending our colleges and universities have received ideal treatment from our people and on going back to their land have reported their experiences to their astonished kindred and acquaintances and to public audiences. These reports have contributed to that amazing change of the Japanese national attitude to the white man which has been characteristic of Japan during the past forty years.

Japan on her side has effected changes in her national life, laws, and political organization, unheard of till modern times, granting protection and large opportunity to foreigners in her midst.

Responding to the solicitation of planters in the nineties, many thousand Japanese laborers went to the Hawaiian Islands for work on the sugar plantations, and thus began Japan's first experience of emigration. To facilitate this enterprise there sprang up and flourished in Japan a number of emigration societies. Not until the annexation of Hawaii, in 1899, however, did any considerable emigration arise of Japanese laborers to California. At first they were generally welcomed, but as soon as they came in numbers large enough to form local groups and to assert race distinction then difficulties began to arise. The first conspicuous instance of anti-Japanese feeling was the so-called school question when the School Board of San Francisco adopted the principle of race segregation. This the Japanese resented as contrary to the treaty, invidious, and humiliating. Shortly thereafter came the "gentlemen's agreement," which from 1908 put a complete stop to Japanese labor immigration, the Japanese Government preferring the prevention of immigration undesired by us to the enactment of legislation humiliating to her. In carrying out this arrangement the emigration companies were abolished, causing much hardship. . . .

In connection with the anti-Japanese agitation many things have been said highly insulting to the Japanese and intended to be so. But the Japanese should not take these utterances too much to heart, for they do not represent, I feel confident, the thought of the real majority, even of Californians.

Months of study of this question in California have convinced the writer that the popular approval of the anti-Japanese agitation and legislation does not concern the details of the proposed bills nor the insulting language used by a few, but rests entirely on the conviction that there should be no swamping immigration from Japan. Their universal and unqualified approval of this position, which is fundamental, has led the good people to keep silence in regard to details which they consider are but incidental.

The objectionable features, however, of this anti-Japanese legislation are many and serious.

It is needless; for under the effective operation of the "gentlemen's agreement" Japanese immigration has ceased, and the number of Japanese in America is diminishing. There is, therefore, no danger whatever of a swamping Japanese invasion nor of any considerable purchase by Japanese of agricultural or other land. The number of acres bought by Japanese during the two years preceding the passage of the law was less than two thousand.

It is misleading; for it implies an issue which does not in fact exist.

The policy is *humiliating to Japan*; for it misrepresents her attitude and conduct, treats her as though she could not be trusted, and ignores her friendship, which, however, has been consistently maintained for sixty years.

It disgraces the United States by presenting us in a wrong attitude to a friendly nation and also by making it appear that we cannot distinguish between solid facts and palpable illusions. We seem to be ruled by hallucinations.

This agitation is *positively injurious*; for it antagonizes Japanese landowners and thus interferes with the process of their assimilation. It thus tends to keep them as a permanently alien element in the midst of our people, helping to create the very difficulty it fears.

It is *based on ignorance* of the Japanese. It exaggerates their defects and overlooks their virtues.

The whole agitation is *unscientific*. It does not seek accurate and verified facts; being highly suspicious, it accepts as true every maligning story. Moreover, it defends and justifies itself by discredited theories of race psychology and sociology. It confuses biological and sociological assimilation, regarding the two as inseparable.

It is *unjust and unkind*. The spirit which prompted the fifty-one bills in the last two sessions of the legislature is not one that seeks to deal justly or kindly with the stranger in our land. We criticise the Japanese for lack of the spirit of fair play and for failure to keep an open door for us in Manchuria. Are Americans in California carrying out the spirit of fair play and an open door?

It ignores the new Orient. . . . The world has irrevocably entered on a new era of human development. All the nations of the Orient are awakening to a new life and a new self-consciousness; they are increasingly sensitive to their plight, their needs, and their rights. They are also developing military power. All this is ignored. It is willing to create international difficulty and promote increasing alienation of Asiatic good-will. It pays no attention to the Yellow Peril which it is evoking. As Mr. Rowell well says, "ninety-nine percent of the whole Japanese question is National and International." It ignores the large relations and seeks to settle the problem exclusively from the standpoint of local interests.

It is *short-sighted*. Even from the standpoint of selfish interests, it is calculated to bring disaster. Our international commerce depends in no small degree on the good-will of the purchasing nations. The Chinese boycott of 1905–6 shows what possibilities lie in that direction. Germany and England are competing in the Orient for commercial supremacy. Should wide-spread and strong anti-American feeling in Japan and China be put into the commercial scales, who can foretell the results to our commerce?

Source: Sidney Gulick, *The American Japanese Problem* (New York: Charles Scribner's Sons, 1914), 184–86, 190–96.

9.2. Exclusion Law of 1924 Humiliates Japan and Negatively Impacts Japanese American Relations

Constantine Panunzio, a professor of social economics at Whittier College in California, in his 1927 Immigration Crossroads, *detailed how, in the midst of a general post–World War I wave of anti-immigrant sentiment in the United States, those particularly opposed to the foreign-born from Japan persuaded Congress in 1924 to pass an unnecessary, vindictive law excluding Japanese immigrants from admission to the United States. This action was taken against the advice of U.S. Secretary of State Charles Evans Hughes and others, who, like Panunzio, foretold that this humiliation of Japan would have strong negative consequences for relations between the United States and Japan.*

Japan seems to have done all that was humanly possible faithfully to observe the "gentlemen's agreement", to satisfy the wishes of the American people, and even to comply with the excessive demands of those portions of California's population who were pronouncedly anti-Japanese. Cyrus E. Woods, ex-Ambassador to Japan, in a letter addressed to the Federal Council of Churches in quadrennial session in December 1924, said: "Japan accepted the principle of exclusion in 1908. Since that date the Japanese Government has been loyally coöperating with the Government of the United States in carrying out that policy."

Japan, moreover has at no time thought it expedient that large groups of her people should settle in the United States. Oscar T. Crosby, former Assistant Secretary of the Treasury, in *International War: Its Causes and Cure*, states that "American public opinion on this particular point has been erroneously formed. The idea that the Japanese in California are the forerunners of an overwhelming swarm of Orientals has been widely fostered. Yet from any fairly intelligent study of the situation it is found that public opinion in Japan takes quite a contrary view. The rulers of that country do not believe that a vast movement of their people to our shores is either necessary or desirable, but they do believe that no invidious distinctions should be made against their nationals by the laws of the United States, or of any land."

That this is the spirit which has animated Japan is evident from a number of steps the Japanese Government and people took. In 1913 Japan naturally protested against the California land law on the grounds that the act of that year involved racial discrimination. But in 1920, in order to prevent further misunderstandings, the Japanese Government voluntarily abolished the "picture brides" system (Japanese women who became wives by proxy) even though the "gentlemen's agreement" entitled them to come.

In June 1923 the Japanese-American Relations Committee of Tokyo, realizing that the anti-Japanese movement might endanger international relations, suggested that a joint high commission be established to study the question of Japanese immigration to the United States. The leaders of the anti-Japanese crusade in California objected and as a substitute they agreed to cooperate in an American survey which was being conducted under the leadership of Professor R. E. Park of the University of Chicago for the Institute of Social and Religous Research of New York City, which though contributing to broader understanding actually affected no solution of the immediate problem.

Even as late as February 1924 Japan expressed her readiness to do all in her power to meet America's will in every possible way. Foreign Minister K. Matsui stated officially that Japan was "particularly anxious for American good-will" and that she was "ready to discuss the matter of restriction or exclusion anew, which should be arranged by mutual consideration and consent in agreement, as is customary, instead of through a needlessly arbitrary *ex parte* action." (*New York Times*, Feb. 8, 1924, p. 5.)

In fact, all available official and unofficial information seems to confirm the judgment of E. Alexander Powell that Japan was and is "genuinely, almost pathetically, anxious for American confidence and good will, and, in order to obtain them, she is prepared to make almost every concession that her self-respect will permit and that a fair-minded American can demand." (*Atlantic Monthly*, November 1921.)

The anti-Japanese movement however had gained too great a momentum to be checked. The successes of the general restriction-of-immigration agitation since the World War added determination to the anti-Japanese elements that their goal should be reached. Early in 1924 Representative Albert Johnson of Washington reported his bill containing provisions for the exclusion of Japanese.

On February 8, Secretary to State Hughes addressed a communication to Mr. Johnson as Chairman of the House Committee on Immigration and Naturalization: "the question presented is one of policy. . . . The practical effect of Section 12 (b) is to single out Japanese immigrants for exclusion. The Japanese are a sensitive people, and unquestionably would regard such a legislative enactment as fixing a stigma upon them. . . . I believe such legislative action would largely undo the work of the Washington Conference on Limitation of Armament, which so greatly improved our relations with Japan." . . .

Meanwhile a small group of persons who for years had conducted the anti-Japanese agitation traveled from the Golden Gate to Capitol Hill. Even those who were watching every move in immigration matters in Washington were not aware of their arrival. For the greater part of four days, March 11–15, 1924, they remained with the Senate Immigration Committee. As individuals, as representatives of various Californian organizations and on behalf of the State Government, they pleaded for the exclusion of the Japanese. "For twenty years," said their chief spokesman, we have been waging "the fight of the Nation against the incoming of alien races whose peaceful penetration must in time with absolute certainty drive the white race to the wall." (Senate Committee on Immigration, *Hearings*, 68th Cong., 1st Sess., p. 34.). . . .

[The exclusion bill was enacted.]

It is perhaps difficult to realize how deep a wound the exclusion clause inflicted upon the soul of Japan and the entire East; it is always difficult for those inflicting an injury to realize its effects. On July 1, 1924, designated as "Humiliation Day", popular meetings of protest were held in many cities throughout Japan; in Tokio alone there were twelve such meetings, the largest beginning at 2 P.M. and lasting without a break until 10 P.M., the audience ranging from 5,000 to 12,000. In the weeks immediately following occurred the self-immolation of a Japanese, the demonstration made by some 10,000 Japanese former service men at the national military shrine, the boycotting of American goods, particularly films, the protests of Japanese Christians and their demand for severance of connection with American churches and the disturbances caused by the "rorin". Official Japan, however, has maintained a spirit of utmost dignity although of firmness. . . .

On the return of "Humiliation Day," July 1, 1926, an editorial in the *Mainichi*, a daily morning paper published in Osaka, having a circulation of 1,250,000, declared: "We assert that the pain is becoming more and more acute. . . . Japan and her people will never forgive nor forget the insult and injustice to which they have been subjected. . . . The mental wounds which we sustained cannot be healed. The immigration question is not a problem of statistics. The honor and prestige of this Empire are involved. . . . International democracy . . . will not permit her to be humiliated by disgraceful discrimination. . . . It is our firm conviction that justice will be victorious finally. We are confident that Americans will be aroused to international justice and will correct their mistakes."

Americans who know Japan at first hand understand how deeply the matter goes. William Axling, a leading missionary and author of note, who was in Japan at the time the exclusion law was passed, wrote: "Japan's reaction to America's exclusion move is not so much resentment as it is the dire disappointment and poignant grief that a friend feels when a friend has failed to play fair. And Japan is not thinking of herself alone. She is looking out and considering the whole future of the Pacific. Japan is wondering whether brotherhood is going to be broadcast across this world of ours, or whether race shall stand against race and color against color."

Source: Constantine Panunzio, *Immigration Crossroads* (New York: Macmillan, 1927), 168–72, 181–83.

9.3. President Truman States that 1920s Immigration Quotas Have a Negative Effect on National Foreign Relations

President Harry S. Truman spoke forcefully about the impact of American immigration policy on the nation's foreign policy during the Cold War. Truman believed that the negative effect on the relations of the United States with much of the world was caused by America's prejudicial immigration quota system, enacted in the 1920s, and he called for its repeal. When, in 1952, Congress sent him an extensive immigration bill that retained the quota system and included additional harsh exclusionary provisions, the president attacked it as harmful to American foreign policy interests and vetoed it. This bill, nevertheless, was passed over Truman's veto. Truman's veto message made a case for ending discriminatory quotas as a way to demonstrate American democracy to emerging nations.

I return herewith, without my approval, H. R. 5678, the proposed Immigration and Nationality Act.

In outlining my objections to this bill, I want to make it clear that it contains certain provisions that meet with my approval. This is a long and complex piece of legislation. . . .

A general revision and modernization of these laws unquestionably is needed and long overdue, particularly with respect to immigration. But this bill would not provide us with an immigration policy adequate for the present world situation. . . .

In recent years our immigration policy has become a matter of major national concern. Long dormant questions about the effect of our immigration laws now assume first-rate importance. What we do in the field of immigration and naturalization is vital to the continued growth and internal development of the United States—to the economic and social strength of our country—which is the core of the defense of the free world.

Our immigration policy is equally, if not more, important to the conduct of our foreign relations and to our responsibilities of moral leadership in the struggle for world peace.

In one respect this bill recognizes the great international significance of our immigration and naturalization policy, and takes a step to improve existing laws. All racial bars to naturalization would be removed, and at least some minimum immigration quota would be afforded to each of the free nations of Asia. . . .

But now this most desirable provision comes before me embedded in a mass of legislation which would perpetuate injustices of long standing against many other nations of the world, hamper the efforts we are making to rally the men of East and West alike to the cause of freedom, and intensify the repressive and inhumane aspects of our immigration procedures. The price is too high, and in good conscience I cannot agree to pay it.

I want all our residents of Japanese ancestry, and all our friends throughout the Far East, to understand this point clearly. I cannot take the step I would like to take, and strike down the bars that prejudice has erected against them, without, at the same time, establishing new discriminations against the peoples of Asia and approving harsh and repressive measures directed at all who seek a new life within our boundaries.

I am sure that with a little more time and a little more discussion in this country the public conscience and the good sense of the American people will assert themselves, and we shall be in a position to enact an immigration and naturalization policy that will be fair to all. . . .

The bill would continue, practically without change, the national origins quota system, which was enacted into law in 1924, and put into effect in 1929. This quota system—always based upon assumptions at variance with our American ideals—is long since out of date and more than ever unrealistic in the face of present world conditions.

This system hinders us in dealing with current immigration problems, and is a constant handicap in the conduct of our foreign relations. . . .

The inadequacy of the present quota system has been demonstrated since the end of the war, when we were compelled to resort to emergency legislation to admit displaced persons. If the quota system remains unchanged, we shall be compelled to resort to similar emergency legislation again, in order to admit any substantial portion of the refugees from communism or the victims of overcrowding in Europe.

With the idea of quotas in general there is no quarrel. Some numerical limitation must be set, so that immigration will be within our capacity to absorb. But the over-all limitation of numbers imposed by the national origins quota system is too small for our needs today, and the country-by-country limitations create a pattern that is insulting to large numbers of our finest citizens, irritating to our Allies abroad and foreign to our purposes and ideals. . . .

The greatest vice of the present quota system, however, is that it discriminates, deliberately and intentionally, against many of the peoples of the world. The purpose behind it was to cut down and virtually eliminate immigration to this country from Southern and Eastern Europe. . . .

The idea behind this discriminatory policy was, to put it baldly, that Americans with English or Irish names were better people and better citizens than Americans with Italian or Greek or Polish names. It was thought that people of West European origin made better citizens than Rumanians or Yugoslavs or Ukrainians or Balts or Austrians.

Such a concept is utterly unworthy of our traditions and our ideals. It violates the great political doctrine of the Declaration of Independence that "all men are created equal." It denied the humanitarian creed inscribed beneath the Statue of Liberty proclaiming to all nations:

"Give me your tired, your poor, your huddled masses yearning to breathe free."

It repudiates our basic religious concepts, our belief in the brotherhood of man, and in the words of St. Paul that "there is neither Jew nor Greek, there is neither bond nor free . . . for ye are all one in Christ Jesus."

The basis of this quota system was false and unworthy in 1924. It is even worse now. At the present time this quota system keeps out the very people we want to bring in. It is incredible to me that, in this year of 1952, we should again be enacting into law such a slur on the patriotism, the capacity and the decency of a large part of our citizenry.

Today we have entered into an alliance, the North Atlantic Treaty, with Italy, Greece and Turkey against one of the most terrible threats mankind has ever faced. We are asking them to join with us in protecting the peace of the world. We are helping them to build their defenses, and train their men, in the common cause. But through this bill we say to these people:

You are less worthy to come to this country than Englishmen or Irishmen; you Italians, who need to find homes abroad in the hundreds of thousands—you shall have a quota of 5,645; you Greeks, struggling to assist the helpless victims of a Communist civil war—you shall have a quota of 308; and you Turks, you are brave defenders of the Eastern flank, but you shall have a quota of only 225!

Today, we are "protecting" ourselves, as we were in 1924, against being flooded by immigrants from Eastern Europe. This is fantastic. The countries of Eastern Europe have fallen under the Communist yoke—they are silenced, fenced off by barbed wire and mine fields—no one passes their borders but at the risk of his life.

We do not need to be protected against immigrants from these countries—on the contrary we want to stretch out a helping hand, to save those who have managed to flee into Western Europe, to succor those who are brave enough to escape from barbarism, to welcome and restore them against the day when their countries will, as we hope, be free again.

But this we cannot do, as we would like to do, because the quota for Poland is only 6,500, as against the 138,000 exiled Poles, all over Europe, who are asking to come to these shores; because the quota for the now subjugated Baltic countries is little more than 700—against the 23,000 Baltic refugees imploring us to admit them to a new life here; because the quota for Rumania is only 289, and some 30,000 Rumanians, who have managed to escape the labor camps and the mass deportations of their Soviet masters, have asked our help. These are only a few examples of the absurdity, the cruelty of carrying over into this year of 1952 the isolationist limitations of our 1924 law.

In no other realm of our national life are we so hampered and stultified by the dead hand of the past as we are in this field of immigration. We do not limit our cities to their 1920 boundaries—we do not hold our corporations to their 1920 capitalizations—*we welcome progress and change to meet changing conditions in every sphere of life, except in the field of immigration.*

The time to shake off this dead weight of past mistakes is now. The time to develop a decent policy of immigration—a fitting instrument for our foreign policy and a true reflection of the ideals we stand for, at home and abroad—is now.

Source: Harry S. Truman, "To The House of Representatives," H. Doc. 520, *Congressional Record*, 82nd Cong., 2nd sess., 1952, 98: 8082–83.

9.4. President Kennedy Advocates a More Globally Egalitarian Immigration Policy

When John F. Kennedy became president of the United States in 1961, he renewed President Truman's condemnation of America's national origin immigration system. He, too, regarded it as anachronistic, unfair, and detrimental to American foreign policy, now ten years further into the Cold War. Kennedy pro-

posed a more globally equalitarian immigrant admissions policy for the United States—one that would allow greater flexibility for the reception of refugees. Much of Kennedy's proposal was enacted, after his assassination, in the 1965 immigration law legislated during the administration of his successor, President Lyndon B. Johnson.

Present legislation establishes a system of annual quotas to govern immigration from each country. Under this system, 156,700 quota immigrants are permitted to enter the United States each year. The system is based upon the national origins of the population of the United States in 1920. The use of the year 1920 is arbitrary. It rests upon the fact that this system was introduced in 1924 and the last prior census was in 1920. The use of a national origins system is without basis in either logic or reason. It neither satisfies a national need nor accomplishes an international purpose. In an age of interdependence among nations, such a system is an anachronism, for it discriminates among applicants for admission into the United States on the basis of accident of birth.

Because of the composition of our population in 1920, the system is heavily weighted in favor of immigration from northern Europe and severely limits immigration from southern and eastern Europe and from other parts of the world. An American citizen with a Greek father or mother must wait at least eighteen months to bring his parents here to join him. A citizen whose married son or daughter, or brother or sister, is Italian cannot obtain a quota number for an even longer time. Meanwhile, many thousands of quota numbers are wasted because they are not wanted or needed by nationals of the countries to which they are assigned.

I recommend that there be substituted for the national origins system a formula governing immigration to the United States which takes into account (1) the skills of the immigrant and their relationship to our need; (2) the family relationship between immigrants and persons already here, so that the reuniting of families is encouraged and (3) the priority of registration. Present law grants a preference to immigrants with special skills, education or training. It also grants a preference to various relatives of United States citizens and lawfully resident aliens. But it does so only within a national origins quota. It should be modified so that those with the greatest ability to add to the national welfare, no matter where they were born, are granted the highest priority. The next priority should go to those who seek to be reunited with their relatives. As between applicants with equal claims the earliest registrant should be the first admitted.

Many problems of fairness and foreign policy are involved in replacing a system so long entrenched. The national origins system has produced large backlogs of applications in some countries, and too rapid a change might, in a system of limited immigration, so drastically curtail immigration in some countries the only effect might be to shift the unfairness from one group of nations to another. A reasonable time to adjust to any new system must be provided if individual hardships upon persons who were relying on the present system are to be avoided. In addition, any new system must have sufficient flexibility to allow adjustments to be made when it appears that immigrants from nations closely allied to the United States will be unduly restricted in their freedom to furnish the new seed population that has so long been a source of strength to our nation.

PROPOSAL IN DETAIL

Accordingly, I recommend:

First, that existing quotas be reduced gradually, at the rate of 20 percent a year. The quota numbers released each year would be placed in a quota reserve pool, to be distributed on the new basis.

Second, that natives of no one country receive over 10 percent of the total quota numbers authorized in any one year. This will insure that the pattern of immigration is not distorted by excessive demand from any one country.

Third, that the President be authorized, after receiving recommendations from a seven-man Immigration Board, to reserve up to 50 percent of the unallocated quota numbers for issuance to persons disadvantaged by the change in the quota system, and up to 20 percent to refugees whose sudden dislocation requires special treatment. . . .

As I have already indicated the measures I have outlined will not solve all the problems of immigration. Many of them will require additional legislation; some cannot be solved by any one country. But the legislation I am submitting will insure that progress will continue to be made toward our ideals and toward the realization of humanitarian objectives. The measures I have recommended will help eliminate discrimination between peoples and nations on a basis that is unrelated to any contribution that immigrants can make and is inconsistent with our traditions of welcome. Our investment in new citizens has always been a valuable source of our strength.

Source: John F. Kennedy, *A Nation of Immigrants* (New York: Harper and Row, 1964), 102–7.

9.5. Immigration Is a Key Factor in Relations between Mexico and the United States

---

Paul Taylor, an expert on U.S.–Mexican relations, detailed, in a 1978 essay on "The Future of Mexican Immigration," the past and continuing reciprocal determinants that have made immigration a key factor in dealings between these two neighboring countries. When the U.S. Congress considered legislation in the late 1970s to tighten control of the country's border with Mexico, Taylor called for a balance between security and humanitarian concerns. He foretold that, regardless of the efforts of the United States to strengthen border vigilance, both American and Mexican interests would be such that a high level of Mexican migration would continue and would be a national issue for years to come.

More than ever Mexico's people are close to the United States. The two countries are, in fact, intimately, if not organically, linked by rails, roads, airlines, footpaths, and a common border population. Unlike the 1920s several million underemployed people crowd against the American border, and over the years migratory settlement has continuously oozed over the line so that in the areas, like the lower Rio Grande Valley of Texas, it is essentially one folk culture on both sides. Technology, meanwhile, has never ceased to annihilate distances between the population centers of the two countries. Mexico City is now only a matter of a few hours from Chicago or Milwaukee. Given such obvious facts, one can assume that the United States will go on serving as a natural escape valve for Mexico's surplus population.

Furthermore, the Mexican government long ago recognized that Mexican migratory labor was an exportable resource that could contribute to national income. This was not only true of the 1920s, and of the bracero era, 1942–1964, but it seems even truer today. Perhaps as many as 2 or 3 million expatriate workers in the United States (most of them undocumented) are presently sending money and gifts in various ways to the mother country. Given continued economic underdevelopment, gross disparities in income distribution, balance of payment needs, and population pressures, one can expect, all rhetoric to the contrary, that the Mexican government will continue to favor, *sub rosa*, surplus labor emigration to the United States, and to countenance, however reluctantly, the migration of American industries to Mexico under specified conditions.

American interest in Mexican labor has not really diminished over the years. In the past American employers and the federal government have often regarded Mexico as a labor reserve to be dipped into whenever the need arose. We saw this in World War I; we saw it in the booming 1920s; we saw it during World War II, and during the Korean War; and we see it now in several forms, as when American industries move over the border to take advantage of lowest labor and special tariff exemptions in Mexico's so-called Free Zone, or when American food-processing companies move into Mexico's interior to cut labor costs and produce a variety of foods for both the American and the Mexican markets. And on this side of the border American employers as always use large contingents of legal and illegal Mexican workers, including commuters, immigrant workers, and wetbacks. As for a possible expanded use of Mexican labor—with official approval—who would doubt that if the United States were to mobilize for another major war, or were to face a serious labor shortage of any kind, that the federal government, under employer prodding, would immediately look to Mexico, and that a new version of the bracero program and a relaxed immigration policy would be forthcoming?

Through the years we have seen many turnovers in interest groups, yet a coalition of interests in one shape or another has consistently maintained pressure on the federal government so that special exemptions might be extended to Mexican workers and their families. Agribusiness, railroads, and other corporate groups are not at the moment pressing hard for an open border or a contract-labor program. Mechanization, union protests (including the Huelga movement), the diminishing influence of the farm bloc in Congress, and access by giant agribusiness and certain industrial groups to cheap labor in Mexico itself are some factors that explain the current relaxing of pressure. But new interest groups have emerged that favor large-scale Mexican migration. For example, Mexican-American groups formerly were aggressively in favor of border control, as in the 1950s when illegal laborers and contract braceros threatened jobs and undermined wages and unionization efforts. Now many of these jobs are unwanted by domestic workers, and, in the meantime, a Chicano ethnic movement has arisen that tends to regard immigration control on the Mexican border and deportation of Mexican illegals as a form of ethnic discrimination. Militants push for special exemptions for Mexican immigration largely on the ground that Mexico once owned the Southwest.

Those who favor special exemptions for Mexican migration find themselves in company with the familiar immigrant-aid societies (now reinforced by the minority-rights movement), certain liberal congressmen. Pan American idealists, philanthropic organizations, evangelical ministers, and a variety of employers running businesses, farms, and ranches—many of them marginal in nature—that depend on the availability of low-cost migratory labor. All of the aforementioned groups, as Carey McWilliams once pointed out, hastily adopted the "poor Mexican" when quota laws cut off the supply of huddled masses from Europe and the Orient. Also, the Mexican consuls have not ceased to defend Mexican residents in the United States regardless of their immigration status.

New legislation pending in Congress raises hopes that at last the federal government is moving toward a confrontation with the illegal alien problem that, as far as Mexico is concerned, goes back to World War I. Various bills to amend the Immigration and Nationality Act, sponsored by Congressmen Rodino, Eilberg, and others, would penalize employers who knowingly hire illegal aliens, authorize the confiscation of smugglers' vehicles, and provide for more cooperation from HEW [Federal Department of Health, Education and Welfare] agencies in locating illegal aliens who use social security cards, or receive benefits under social assistance programs. Citizens who for years have been concerned about loopholes and inequities in immigration law and procedures naturally welcome the passage of such proposals.

But the voice of experience might here offer us a word of caution. Hitherto there have been high expectations that new legislation and budgetary increases would serve to place land-border migration under strict control, as, for example, in 1917 when the general immigration law established qualifications of health, literacy, self-support, and a head tax; in 1924 when the visa control system was inaugurated under consular auspices; in 1925 when the Border Patrol was launched; in 1929 when illegal entry by individuals was made a penal offense and visa controls were tightened; during the Great Depression when laws were passed against aliens on relief and on federal job rolls, and when it was believed by many that an era of dependence on foreign labor had come to an end; in the 1940s when so many safeguards and controls were written into the bi-national bracero accords; in 1952 when recruiting, concealing, or harboring illegal aliens was made a penal offense; in 1954 when massive drives against wetbacks, together with immigration service reforms, seemed to have promised effective border control for the first time, and so on. . . .

Appropriate response is neither clear nor simple. On the one hand, we have humanely motivated amnesty measures or larger immigrant quotas for selected countries. On the other, we find proposals to tighten American controls over admission standards and employment of aliens. These are not mutually exclusive, and a search for a balance between them is natural. In fact, the issue is truly international and appropriate for serious consideration in the Organization of the American States and the United Nations, where responsibilities for solutions can be shared.

Given the present socioeconomic and ideological factors at work on both sides of the border, the future holds a promise that an exceptionally high level of Mexican migration in varying forms, legal, illegal, temporary, or permanent, will continue. Thus we conclude that the control and legitimation of this migration, which became a national issue in the 1920s, will remain a national issue for many years to come.

Source: Paul Taylor, "The Future of Mexican Immigration," in *Immigrants—and Immigrants: Perspectives on Mexican Labor Migration to the United States*, ed. Arthur Corwin (Westport, Conn.: Greenwood Press, 1978), 348–52.

9.6. Cuban Americans Pressure United States to Retain Sanctions Against Castro Government

After Fidel Castro established his revolutionary Communist regime in Cuba in the late 1950s, the United States welcomed emigrés fleeing from that neighboring island nation. More than a million Cubans have come over the past four decades. Efforts were made to settle these refugees throughout the United States, but a major concentration developed in south Florida and another in New Jersey, where Cubans have developed considerable political power. They have exerted pressure on the U.S. government to overthrow the Castro government. Even after more than forty years, as exemplified in the October 2000 newspaper advertisement below, Cuban American groups continue to urge the American public and politicians to continue to oppose the Cuban dictator.

The Truth Behind the Face

Castro has not changed in 41 years.

We cannot forget that when the Soviet Union existed, Havana received around seven billion dollars annually in exchange for assisting the Kremlin on its imperialist wars in Angola, Grenada, Nicaragua and other countries in Central and South America. Over twenty thousand young Cubans have died from these actions.

For over forty-one years, Castro has relentlessly opposed and tried to undermine the United States and the democracy of this great nation and the rest of the continent. Shouldn't the Cuban people have the right to choose their own government and leaders in a democratic election?

The totalitarian Cuban Communist regime has not held democratic elections in over four decades. This is the main cause for the social and economic disaster that is stifling Cuba. Meanwhile, nine U.S. presidents have held office, some of them even for two terms and the political environment of Cuba lingers unchanged.

Now, the Cuban dictator wants the American people to indemnify him without giving any democratic concessions, claiming that his communist regime is not responsible for the disastrous effect it has had in Cuba

The reasons why Cuban-Americans vehemently oppose this outrage are self-evident. Fidel Castro is the same dictator who has ruled Cuba for 41 years, violating every human rights law imaginable: oppressing the freedom of speech and press available in any democratic society, declaring his government "atheist" thus subjugating the nation to the same; and even going as far as executing and imprisoning thousands of Cuban citizens for daring to think differently, and for demanding democracy in Cuba.

Cuban Patriotic Forum
2960 Coral Way, Miami, FL 33145

This message has been brought to you by the following Cuban American exile organizations:

- Veteran's Association of the Bay of Pigs (Brigade 2506)
- Cuban Medical Association in Exile
- Democratic Independent Cuban (C.I.D)
- Cuban American National Foundation
- World Federation of Cuban Former Political Prisoners
- Mothers and Women Against Repression (M.A.R)
- Cuban Municipalities in Exile
- Protagonist Party of the People
- Cuban Unity

Source: "The Truth Behind the Face: Castro Has Not Changed in 41 Years," an advertisement (Miami, Fla.: Cuban Patriotic Forum, October 2000).

ANNOTATED SELECTED BIBLIOGRAPHY

Corwin, Arthur, ed. *Immigrants and Immigrants: Perspectives on Mexican Labor Migration to the United States*. Westport, Conn.: Greenwood Press, 1978. Reports on the often conflicting interests between Mexico and the United States in relation to the movement of Mexican citizens into the United States seeking work or responding to job opportunities presented by American employers.

Dunn, Timothy. *The Militarization of the U.S.-Mexican Border, 1978–1992: Low Intensity Conflict Doctrine Comes Home*. Austin: University of Texas Press, 1996. Discusses American efforts to enforce its immigration laws along the extended United States–Mexican border and the impact on the relations between the two countries.

Gerson, Louis. *The Hyphenate in Recent American Politics and Diplomacy*. Lawrence: University Press of Kansas, 1964. The influence of immigrants and ethnics on American foreign policy from the 1920s to the post–World War II years.

Gulick, Sidney. *The American Japanese Problem*. New York: Charles Scribner's Sons, 1914. Calls for Americans to be more open to Japanese immigrants and warns of the negative impact of advocated Japanese exclusion laws on United States-Japanese foreign relations.

Kennedy, John F. *A Nation of Immigrants*. New York: Harper and Row, 1964. Warns that the U.S. immigration quota system, enacted in the 1920s and retained in the 1952 Immigration Law, will harm America's relations with many foreign countries in the post–World War II era.

Levine, Barry, ed. *The Caribbean Exodus*. New York: Praeger, 1987. Discusses immigration from Caribbean and Central American countries and its impact on U.S. immigration policy and foreign policy.

Mitchell, Christopher, ed. *Western Hemisphere Immigration and United States Foreign Policy*. University Park: Pennsylvania State University Press, 1992. Details the relation of U.S. immigration policy decisions to foreign policy considerations, in regard to Cuba, Haiti, Central American, and other Western Hemisphere countries primarily in the last half of the twentieth century.

Panunzio, Constantine. *Immigration Crossroads*. New York: Macmillan, 1927. Includes information on the impact of the Oriental Exclusion Act of 1924 and the immigration quota laws on the relations of the United States with Japan and other countries.

Papademetriou, Demetrios, and Mark Miller, eds. *The Unavoidable Issue: U.S. Immigration Policy in the 1980s*. Philadelphia: Institute for the Study of Human Issues, 1983. Includes essays on immigration and foreign policy and the international setting of American refugee policy in the latter part of the twentieth century.

Sutter, Valerie. *The Indochinese Refugee Dilemma*. Baton Rouge: Louisiana State University Press, 1990. Examines foreign policy issues for the United States in relation to decisions about refugees from Southeast Asia.

Tucker, Robert, Charles Keely, and Linda Wrigley, eds. *Immigration and U.S. Foreign Policy*. Boulder, Colo.: Westview Press, 1990. Considers foreign policy implications for the United States in relation to its immigration and refugee practices since World War I.

10

Are Undocumented Immigrants Helpful or Harmful to the United States?

The issue of undocumented or illegal immigrants in the United States is of recent vintage. It hardly entered public thinking during the first hundred years in the history of immigration in the United States, because no federal laws restricted immigration. In the 1870s, when the United States began to enact statutes that listed categories of people that would not be permitted to enter the country as immigrants, the issue of documents and the rights of newcomers began to surface. The first federal prohibitions in 1875 were against convicts and prostitutes. Then in 1882 Congress added to the list of exclusions lunatics, idiots, persons likely to become public charges, and Chinese laborers. In 1885 contract laborers were banned, and in 1891 the United States added persons suffering from a contagious or loathsome disease and polygamists to the list of those deemed unfit to enter the country. Few Americans objected to such restrictions, although enforcement became an issue.

The federal government, after it passed the initial prohibitions on immigration, did not establish any means for enforcing them before 1891; instead, the federal government relied on state officials. Beginning in the 1850s New York State had an immigrant receiving station, Castle Garden, but there were only very limited facilities in other port cities. Thus, it was not difficult for immigrants, who wished to do so, to evade the early federal exclusion laws, as well as state-imposed quarantines on persons "likely" to carry particular diseases. The congressional Ford Committee in 1889 reported on the situation in New York. It stated that "it was almost impossible to properly inspect the large number of persons who arrive daily during the immigrant season," and therefore "large numbers of persons not lawfully entitled to land in the United States are annually received at this port."[1]

Given the inadequacies of state facilities and the beginning of a new major wave of immigration, the national government in 1891 assumed control of enforcement. It established federal immigrant stations, most notably Ellis Island in New York and Angel Island in San Francisco in 1892. Immigrants who came in steerage were examined at these stations to prevent those who did not meet federal regulations from entering the country. Those who came first or second class were allowed into the country without an examination on the assumption that, if they could afford this type of accommodation and if they were cleared for embarkation by the shipping company, they would not become public charges in the United States.

In the two decades after 1890, additional groups were added to the exclusion list, including epileptics, anarchists and other radicals, those suffering from tuberculosis, and children under the age of sixteen unaccompanied by adults. In 1917 federal legislation required an immigrant to be literate in at least one language. In the 1920s Congress put an annual limit on the number of immigrants to be admitted to the United States, gave varied quotas to different European countries, and excluded most Asians.

Despite federal enforcement efforts made after 1892, at least some immigrants entered the United States without being inspected. Frank Warne, a critic of the large influx of the foreign-born after the turn of the century, in his *The Tide of Immigration* in 1916, expressed the concern of many anti-immigrationists in warning the public about illegal immigrants: "These enter at the recognized ports of entry, at points along the northern and southern borders of the United States, by lakes and rivers, and at unguarded landings on both the Atlantic and Pacific coasts."[2]

In the decades after World War II undocumented immigration markedly increased, became more widely observed, and emerged as a major public concern. The increase in numbers had multiple causes: a marked improvement in transportation, particularly in the use of the airplane; large numbers of displaced and refugee people worldwide owing to war, persecution, ethnic cleansing, and totalitarianism; widespread severe poverty in many parts of the world, including countries located close to the United States; the continuing affluence of the United States sold internationally through the dissemination of American films and television programs; and, efforts, at various times, on the part of the U.S. government, businesses, and service providers to attract and recruit needed persons from abroad.

Most undocumented immigrants, and thus a particular focus of the American concern, have come from neighboring Mexico. The United

States–Mexican border had long been an "open" frontier, and American agriculture, mining, transportation, and factories have utilized Mexican labor for many decades. A major cause of a continuing pattern of reciprocal dependency between workers and employers across the border was the establishment of the Bracero program, which was initiated by the U.S. government and agreed to by the Mexican government during World War II. The war had resulted in a severe American labor shortage at a time when there was a sharp increase in demand for all types of production. To meet this need, at least in part, the United States contracted with tens of thousands of primarily Mexican laborers to engage in mostly agricultural work in California and other Southwestern states. The program, which lasted in various forms until 1964, created a situation in which workers with few or no job opportunities in Mexico came to depend on employment in the United States and in which American agriculturalists came to depend on the Mexicans as a source of reliable, hardworking, cheap labor. Such circumstances, and the long Mexican–United States border, gave every incentive for workers and employers to continue an accustomed pattern, even after it became illegal.

In addition, when Mexico experienced a particularly difficult economic downturn and American unemployment decreased in the 1990s, the Mexicans responded to U.S. employers across the nation who were willing to hire them for work in construction, manufacturing, restaurants, the service sector, and as day laborers. It has always been difficult to calculate with precision the number of illegal Mexicans in this country at any given time. For one thing, a large portion of them are male "sojourners," a mobile population following work opportunities in agriculture and services. Many visit their families in Mexico with some regularity, and most plan eventually to settle back in their homeland. However, a considerable number of the undocumented sojourners do eventually establish homes with families in the United States, as was the case with Italians and others in the earlier waves of immigration. When an amnesty for illegal aliens was legislated in 1986, some 1.2 million Mexicans declared that they had settled in the United States, and they accepted the opportunity to become legalized immigrants.

The pattern of undocumented entry into the United States—work, return, and then settling here—has also been true for many immigrants from the Caribbean, in particular the Dominican Republic and Haiti; from Central America; and, to some extent, from almost all South American countries. A considerable number of Asians also have entered the United States without documentation. Some, particularly Chinese, have been smuggled into the United States, usually in freighters. Once here, they need to work for many years to pay off the debt incurred to those who arranged their transportation.

Undocumented Europeans usually come by plane and then overstay their visas. In New York, in the early 1990s, the Irish were the second largest undocumented ethnic group (the Dominicans were the largest) in that city. They left a 1980s economic downturn in Ireland, obtained jobs here with relatives and friends, and expected to return home when work became available there. Many did return when the Irish economy markedly improved in the 1990s, but a sizeable number also planted roots in the United States and became American citizens, some with the help of special congressional legislation sponsored by Senator Edward Kennedy.

In the last decades of the twentieth century, colleges and universities in the United States have recruited and received tens of thousands of international students each year. Many return to their home country, some get jobs and marry in the United States and become legal immigrants, and some just overstay their student visas and become undocumented aliens.

Because of the issue of legality, it is not possible to make an accurate count of the number of persons residing in the United States without documentation. The consensus seems to put the totals at somewhere between 3,000,000 and 6,000,000 during the last decades of the twentieth century. Such figures would mean that the undocumented constitute about 2 percent of the U.S. population. Most of the undocumented are located in agricultural regions and in large cities. Estimates of the number of undocumented aliens and their children run as high as nearly a million people in the Los Angeles metropolitan area.

According to public opinion polls, most Americans have taken a negative attitude toward undocumented immigrants. A major critique is that they have broken the law in coming into the United States. Lawrence Fuchs, an immigration historian, focused on this issue in a 1984 article on the impact of illegal aliens and reported on native-born Americans' disquiet over illegal immigration: "Failure to enforce our immigration law undermines another principle that holds this nation of diverse peoples together. It is the principle of the rule of law. The presence of large numbers of illegal aliens violates the sense of fairness of most Americans."[3]

Others see this approach as too legalistic and point out that in socioeconomic terms the undocumented, rather than the documented, at the end of the twentieth century are more like the immigrants who came to the United States during much of its history. The supporters of the undocumented talk about their poverty and in some cases their escape from persecution, and they argue that they deserve acceptance from an affluent United States.

The major area of dispute has centered on the economic impact of the presence of immigrants without documentation in the United States. American workers and others declare that these newcomers drive down wages and reduce job opportunities for citizens, particularly those with fewer skills. According to Governor Pete Wilson of California, illegal immigrants were "taking jobs from legal residents—many of them minorities—and killing the American dreams for those who suffer wage and job losses in California and every other state on our southern border."[4]

Others countered, for example, in a 1984 *Business Week* report, that for the most part undocumented immigrants did work that Americans found too physically demanding, too low paying and of low social status, or that they have been doing work in technology firms that cannot find enough citizens to fill all their needed positions, and, without them, would be less globally competitive. In most of these circumstances, they argue that the undocumented tend to push American-born workers up the job scale. Sectors of the American economy have utilized, favored, and at times recruited illegal laborers from abroad, including large agricultural companies, factory owners, local contractors and landscape firms, restaurants, and service providers.[5] Many employers find the undocumented aliens to be hardworking and reliable, and they become very dependent upon them. In addition, American consumers support the lower prices of food and other products made possible by the labor of undocumented workers.

Disagreement also exists about the cost of services for undocumented immigrants. Some of those who want to clamp down on illegal immigration believe that these newcomers work heavily in an underground cash economy and thus avoid paying income tax and social security tax, but they use public health services, send their children to public schools, and, through fraudulent documents, get on welfare roles. Such critics add that, when illegal immigrants take jobs away from citizens, they contribute to their going on welfare. These concerns proved politically volatile in the 1980s and 1990s, particularly in California, with its large undocumented population, and the easy access to the state by additional aliens. Californians could hardly ignore the issue, especially when the cost of "services" rose in the 1980s and taxpayers revolted against supporting the wide array of public benefits the state promised. Governor Wilson expressed the concerns of immigration opponents in his political rise in the late 1980s, and in 1994 he charged, "Our health care facilities are being swamped, but two-thirds of all babies born in Los Angeles Public Hospitals are born to parents who have illegally entered the United States. . . . I've urged Congress to repeal the federal mandates that require states to provide health care, education, and other benefits to illegal immigrants."[6] Such attitudes enabled Wilson and his supporters to push through Proposition 187, which limits undocumented aliens' access to public services.

On the other side are those who have maintained that the undocumented pay sales taxes, through rent contribute to property taxes, and some, who use false documents, find that they are required to pay income and social security taxes. They further argue that these persons pay more taxes than the cost of services for them, since the undocumented tend to avoid government agencies, few are on welfare, and most do not have children living here. A spokesperson for this position, Edwin Reubens, a researcher, wrote in 1978, "There is now some evidence that illegals make proportionately small use of public services, and already make substantial payments toward them. . . . For one thing, most illegals are young, single adults with little need for hospital services or public schools, or even welfare (since most of them find jobs)."[7] Two publicists on behalf of the undocumented, Raul Hinojosa and Peter Schey, argued in 1997 that "undocumented immigrants contribute a significant amount in taxes once federal, state and local taxes are added together."[8]

Additionally, anti-illegal immigrant critics say that the low educational level of many of the undocumented, their limited pay, the uncertainty of their jobs, the lack of adequate health care, and the fact that many do not know English will result in the development of an underclass that will be detrimental to the country and especially to its cities. Others hold that the evidence—from those who have studied the undocumented in general and those who received amnesty in the late 1980s—indicates that the undocumented who have settled here with families have increased their knowledge of English, have sent their children to school, have begun acculturating into American life, and have experienced upward job mobility.

At the dawn of the twenty-first century, the undocumented issue shows every indication of continuing to be a major unresolved immigration concern for the United States. Pressure from people desiring to come to the United States, beyond the equally allotted numbers of the 1965 immigration law, particularly from less affluent countries and more particularly from those poor nations that are America's neighbors, no doubt will continue and even likely grow. Concurrently important agricultural and business interests in the United States will continue to find economic advantages in encouraging and employing the undocumented. Critics of illegal immigration stress the importance in terms of public order of controlling America's borders and of upholding laws relating to aliens; the danger of flooding the labor market with unneeded unskilled workers and of unfair competition for less well-trained citizen laborers, especially among the country's minorities; the friction and division brought by these newcomers in terms of class, cultural, and linguistic differences; and the added cost to the taxpayer for public services used by undocumented immigrants. Americans who speak in behalf of the undocumented stress their contributions to productivity and national economic growth and to lowering costs for businesses and for consumers; the reality of international mobility of labor and capital; the benefits to good relations with other, particularly neighboring, countries; and humanitarian considerations. Thus, while there will continue to be pressure on the federal government to exert more control over undocumented immigration, there also will be pressure to overlook legalities, at least to some extent, in behalf of other interests and values.

NOTES

1. Select Committee to Inquire into the Importation of Contract Laborers, Convicts, Paupers, etc. (Ford Committee), *Report*, 50th Cong., 2d sess. January 1889, H. Rept. 3792.
2. Frank Warne, *The Tide of Immigration* (New York: D. Appleton, 1916), 108–10.
3. Lawrence Fuchs, "Cultural Pluralism and the Future of American Unity: The Impact of Illegal Aliens," *International Migration Review* 18, no. 3 (Fall 1984): 813.
4. Pete Wilson, "Don't Give Me Your Tired, Your Poor . . . ," *San Diego Union-Tribune*, January 9, 1994.
5. "Illegal Immigrants: The U.S. May Gain More Than It Loses," *Business Week*, May 14, 1984, 126–29.
6. Wilson, "Don't Give Me Your Tired."
7. Edwin Reubens, "Aliens, Jobs and Immigration Policy," *Public Interest* 51 (Spring 1978): 121.
8. Raul Hinojosa and Peter Schey, "The Faulty Logic of the Anti-Immigration Rhetoric," *NACLA Report on the Americas* 29, no. 3 (1997): 20.

DOCUMENTS

10.1. Conflicting Issues on the Question of Illegal Immigration in the 1980s

Lawrence Fuchs, a historian of immigration and an influential public policy planner, was the executive director of the Congressional Select Commission on Immigration and Refugee Policy from 1979 to 1981. This commission studied the impact of the changes brought about by the important 1965 immigration law. Included in the study was the increasing number of undocumented immigrants who had been entering the United States since 1965. Fuchs's essay "The Search for a Sound Immigration Policy: A Personal View" was written in 1985 as Congress was considering the Simpson-Mazzoli bill, which included some of the recommendations of the commission, such as curbs on undocumented immigration. In this essay Fuchs presents some of his own, some of the commission's, and some other perspectives on the issue of undocumented immigration and how to bring it under control.

The number of immigrants admitted lawfully to the United States for purposes of work through the third and sixth preference may be no more than 54,000 a year (close to 40,000 one admitted) including children and spouses, who make up about one half of the total. The real labor recruitment immigration policy comes through illegal immigration, a condition that satisfies a great many interests: their employers; some ethnic group mobilization leaders and service providers; the governments of Mexico and other sending countries; and even American consumers. It is no wonder that it is so difficult to achieve a fundamental reform that might deter the flow of illegal or undocumented workers. Those interests are rationalized in terms of six basic perspectives, which would lead one to conclude that since nothing is broken there is nothing to fix. Despite the appeal of several of them, it is an argument I find unpersuasive.

The first perspective is the romantic immigration perspective. It holds that since most of us came from immigrant stock we ought to welcome those who seek opportunity, even if they come illegally. The second perspective focuses particularly on our relationships with Mexico. It holds that we cannot afford to turn off the safety valve of illegal migration from Mexico, even though it may constitute only about half of all illegal migration, because the future stability of that country will be adversely affected if we do. Third is the human rights perspective, holding that since there is a universal right to emigrate there must also be a human right to immigrate. This perspective involves a religious and/or humanistic view which puts the human needs of migrants above the sovereign authority of nations to limit immigration. A fourth outlook is the economic growth perspective, which holds that since undocumented labor actually increases the quality as well as the size of labor in the U.S. and in the aggregate contributes to economic growth, it would be biting off our nose to spite our face to attempt to defeat it.

There are two other more narrowly based perspectives. The first is the employers' perspective, held by those who benefit most directly from the availability of inexpensive labor (although many consumers also have an interest in the lowered cost of items produced by undocumented workers). There also is the perspective of Mexican American leaders, which stems in part from their desire for more constituents to lead and also from brotherly and sisterly feelings toward those who share ancestral culture and language, and who, like their own forebears, seek opportunity in the United States. That perspective is also shaped by some apprehension that new measures to curtail the flow of undocumented aliens will be harmful to Mexican Americans.

There are four other perspectives on illegal migration that would lead one to conclude that strong measures should be taken to prevent it. The xenophobic perspective applies to immigrants generally. The labor standards and labor displacement perspective emphasizes that docile workers lower standards and wages and even cause displacement. The environmental perspective maintains that unbridled illegal immigration will lead to a voracious consumption of resources in this country. The perspective of law and order and national sovereignty emphasizes that our borders are out of control and that the U.S. cannot exercise a basic right of sovereignty unless it regains control of them.

This last view shaped some of the deliberations of the Select Commission, although it seems to me that still other perspectives are the most compelling: fairness and national unity. The fairness perspective holds that it is unfair to have an immigration law that establishes limits and preferences in which a great many people find themselves waiting in line while others abuse their visas or cross the borders without valid documents. The national unity perspective holds that the growth of an underclass identified by ethnicity will undermine the civic culture, which holds American society together, by leading to rigid ethnic stratification, vitiating equal opportunity and protection of the laws.

Out of this melange of perspectives comes [*sic*] six basic approaches to the problem: leave it alone; regularize the flow through a guest-worker program; step up conventional enforcement, mainly at the border and through the enforcement of labor standards; pass an employer sanctions law combined with a secure system of employee eligibility and a legalization program for a substantial portion of the undocumented aliens already here; focus on the economic development of the sending countries; and develop a North American common market.

The last four approaches are not incompatible, and the Select Commission emphasized the third, fourth, and fifth. Its main legislative recommendations—employer sanctions and legalization—were adopted by the Reagan administration and made the centerpieces of the Simpson-Mazzoli bill. But important modifications were made in the recommendations of the commission during debate in Congress. The most important was the weakening of employer sanctions, largely at the behest of the Chamber of Commerce and the growers of perishable fruits and vegetables. Although Mexican American leaders were most noticeable in their opposition to employer sanctions, it was the pressure of the growers and business interests that succeeded in imposing changes intended to weaken and/or postpone employer sanctions. Thus Simpson-Mazzoli included: a transitional program for employers of illegal aliens to keep them for up to three years; a prohibition for the INS on making raids in open fields without a search warrant; and most important of all, a postponement on the development of a secure (counterfeit- and transfer-resistant) system of employee eligibility.

Much was made in the debate over Simpson-Mazzoli about the potential dangers of discrimination against foreign-sounding or foreign-looking persons as a result of employer sanctions. Opponents of the bill often charged that employers would choose not to hire such persons as a way of protecting themselves against potential prosecution. The same opponents usually decried the introduction of a national identification card as a part of the employee eligibility system. Actually, such a card is specifically repudiated in Simpson-Mazzoli, as it was by the commission. Of course, the identifier would have to be universal for the system to be secure and to protect aliens and others against discrimination, a point somehow obscured in much of the debate, but it would be a work-eligibility identifier to be used only when applying for a new job, and not a national ID that had to be carried everywhere or that could be requested by police and other authorities.

Also ignored by the opponents of employer sanctions is the fact that a tremendous amount of discrimination already exists, but mainly against young native-born Americans, particularly young unskilled blacks, and also against lawful resident aliens. The commission heard from many such persons, including one from Oakland, California:

> I knew of many instances where my two younger brothers and other blacks would apply for jobs at the local factories only to be turned away. The pattern soon became very obvious to them. The majority of the workers in unskilled labor positions were Mexicans . . . the Mexican workers were cheaper and easier to have around. Many of the employers saw blacks as asking for too many things, such as equal wages, benefits, improved safety conditions, and unions.

The fear that a system of employer sanctions would lead to discrimination is understandable, given the history of discrimination against Mexicans and Asians, particularly in the West and Southwest. It is a valid fear to the extent that the system is insecure and employers bear a burden of responsibility for deciding who is illegal and who is not. Under Simpson-Mazzoli, the system would have been unreliable for at least three years, but having seen and noted the identification requested, the employer would have a complete legal defense against sanctions, inhibiting an increase in discrimination. Since the appetite of employers for efficient, hardworking, and uncomplaining laborers is enormous, and since illegal aliens would be able to produce documentation providing presumption of legality when they apply for jobs (given the criterion of identification established in Simpson-Mazzoli), the problem would not be an increase in discrimination as much as a fundamental weakness in enforcement. My own view is that both the Congress and the commission failed by not specifying a reliable system of employee eligibility.

It was easy for the commission to agree on the principles that should underlie such a system of employee eligibility—reliability, uniformity and nondiscriminatory application, minimal disruption of existing employer practices, protection of civil liberties, and cost effectiveness—but only eight of the commissioners favored the development of a more secure method of identification beyond existing forms. Most commissioners—including some who voted for an existing form of identification—preferred an updated, counterfeit- and transfer-resistant Social Security card. In my opinion, the Congress should move toward strengthening the reliability of the Social Security card and use it as the identifier in the employee eligibility system under a new employer sanctions law. That is the best way to prevent discrimination and enhance enforcement.

Source: Lawrence Fuchs, "The Search for a Sound Immigration Policy: A Personal View," in *Clamor at the Gates: The New American Immigration*, ed. Nathan Glazer (San Francisco: ICS Press, 1985), 26–30.

10.2. Illegal Immigration Provides a Net Gain for the National Economy

Business Week *is one of America's most widely read publications dealing with business and economic issues. In 1984* Business Week *assigned staff to do a special report on the growing debate about the increasing number of undocumented immigrants in the United States. The writers reported that undocumented immigrants lowered costs for business and downplayed social costs. They concluded that this immigration provided a net gain for the national economy.*

Deep down in their hearts, Americans may believe that the nation's doors should be open to anyone who wants to come here and work. After all, most U.S. citizens are descended from immigrants. But a flood of illegal aliens, especially from Mexico, has ignited fears that more and more Americans will lose their jobs or at the very least see their wages depressed as a result of immigration. Congress is considering a bill, sponsored by Senator Alan K. Simpson (R-Wyo.) and Representative Romano Mazzoli (D-Ky.), that would legalize the status of illegals already here while clamping down on future illegal entry. The bill has a good chance of passing.

Unquestionably, there are social and economic costs to illegal immigration. But new economic evidence suggests that, on balance, the nation benefits more from the increased economic growth and lower inflation stemming from illegal immigration than it loses in jobs, lower wages, and welfare costs.

Hard data on illegals are, of course, difficult to come by. Based on the recent surge in arrests of aliens, however, their numbers are growing. The Census Bureau estimates that there are now 5 million to 7.5 million illegal residents, who may be holding between 4 million and 6 million jobs.

While this seems like a huge number, many are jobs for which Americans do not compete. Some illegals are employed in agriculture, picking strawberries and tomatoes in 100° heat. Others hold such urban jobs as dishwashers, busboys, maids, and sewing-machine operators—unattractive to many Americans and therefore difficult for employers to fill. Michael J. Piore of the Massachusetts Institute of Technology argues that there is in effect a "two-tier" labor market in which low-skilled immigrants take unwanted jobs so that little displacement of American workers occurs.

Most experts, however, agree that illegals compete for some jobs that Americans want. The Immigration & Naturalization Service has found illegal aliens working in the garment and food-processing industries in California, casinos in Atlantic City, and electronics companies in Silicon Valley. Indeed, a 1979 government study estimated that one in five jobs held by an alien—in total, as many as 1.2 million jobs—could be filled by unemployed Americans. Those who are especially hurt by competition from illegals are low-skilled workers, primarily minorities and young people.

However, even 1.2 million jobs represents less than 1% of the total number in the economy. Moreover, that figure is calculated by looking only at the kinds of jobs where immigrants and Americans are most likely to compete. It fails to consider the spur to economic growth that immigration has generated over a long period of time. Illegal immigration, say most economists, has added to the nation's output. This increase in goods and services has created other jobs that have in good part offset the job loss to Americans from direct competition with illegals.

Indeed, many economists view immigration as they do international trade. While the nation as a whole benefits from free trade, uncompetitive industries and their employees can be hurt. Similarly, says Morgan O. Reynolds of Texas A&M University, "open immigration provides net gains for the economy by expanding output and lowering prices, but some people lose."

At the current pace of illegal immigration, which the Census Bureau estimates adds 500,000 people per year, the impact on future unemployment is likely to be quite small. Even if all of those are workers, Data Resources Inc. calculates that it would add only one-tenth of a percentage point to the unemployment rate. The impact on specific regions, such as the Southwest and Florida, would also be modest, says senior economist Elisabeth Allison. The DRI regional models show that higher immigration in these regions will drive up the unemployment rate, but only briefly. Allison explains that people in other states respond to increased immigration by deciding not to move there. This limits the labor force and curbs unemployment.

Such findings do not refute the contention that illegal immigrants drive down wages. Many illegals, for example, are paid less than the minimum: Sheldon L. Maram of California State University found that 21.8% of the illegal restaurant workers he studied were paid less than the minimum wage, compared with 8.4% of the legal workers. Since employers can threaten to report illegals to the authorities, illegals are more likely than others to work for less than the legal minimum wage and put up with sweatshop conditions.

Yet a study by Barton A. Smith of the University of Houston and Robert Newman of the University of British Columbia shows that the effect of lower wages paid to illegals may not be as severe as it seems at first, at least in certain areas. Smith and Newman compared the wages in towns in Texas near the Mexican border, where many illegals live, with towns farther from the border. The average wages in the border cities were 30% to 40% lower than in the more distant areas. But Smith and Newman found that real wages—wages adjusted for the cost of living in each area—were at most only 8% lower. Says Smith: "From the worker's point of view, what he's concerned about is the real wage." Smith believes that lower wages explain part, but not all, of the lower cost of living in the border areas.

Lower wage costs can have other beneficial effects. For one thing, they tend to keep overall prices low. Lower-paid illegal aliens in agriculture help hold down the prices of fresh fruits and vegetables. More important, low wages allow industries facing severe foreign competition to survive. Without lower wages, some industries—such as the garment industry and consumer electronics—would have to go overseas to compete. Says Yale economist Jennifer Roback: "As long as we have international trade, American industry will compete with low-wage workers. It may be better to employ them here than overseas." Despite the benefits of lower prices and the bolstering of otherwise endangered domestic industries, lower wages may lower U.S. productivity. Dale W. Jorgenson of Harvard believes that low-wage labor slows down the growth of capital spending and thus dampens productivity growth. More cheap labor from Latin America "could undermine to a certain extent the capital spending boom we anticipate in the 1980s," he says. Jorgenson points to a similar slowdown in productivity in the 1970s, which he attributes in part to the swollen labor force that reflected the baby boom and new female workers. Indeed, former Labor Secretary Ray Marshall notes that when child labor was abolished in the late 19th century, the garment industry invested in labor-saving equipment. This ultimately increased productivity in the industry and lowered prices. And Philip L. Martin of the University of California at Davis contends that the use of aliens in agriculture is holding back important mechanization.

To some extent, however, the substitution of cheap labor for capital will also be moderated by an expanding economy. Michael L. Wachter of the University of Pennsylvania notes that low-skilled workers may be substitutes for capital, but the increased output they produce also spurs capital investment.

Source: "Illegal Immigrants: The U.S. May Gain More Than It Loses," *Business Week*, May 14, 1984, 126–29.

10.3. Contributions of Undocumented Immigrants to the Economic Growth of Los Angeles: 1970 to 1990

Thomas Muller and Thomas Espenshade, immigrant researchers for the Urban Institute, in a 1985 book, The Fourth Wave: California's Newest Immigrants, *reported on the favorable economic impact of undocumented immigrants in California and particularly in Los Angeles. They attributed much of the economic growth of that city in the 1970s and early 1980s to the availability of undocumented labor. Muller and Espenshade gave statistics showing that such workers will be needed for future economic growth in California.*

[T]he majority of undocumented workers—particularly Mexicans—tend to take jobs that other workers find undesirable because of poor pay, unsatisfactory working conditions, or low social status. During the 1970s Mexican workers frequently held "residual" jobs, and this pattern is expected to continue into the 1980s. For this reason, our method of estimating the demand for undocumented workers is to project what jobs are unlikely to be taken by other groups at current wages, working conditions, and social status, and then to allocate these jobs to undocumented workers on the assumption that sufficient numbers of Hispanics, Asians, and others will enter California illegally to fill the jobs that remain.

The figures discussed so far indicate significant shortfalls in all categories except for professional/managerial jobs. Projections of the available labor supply from legal sources indicate shortages of 216,000 unskilled and semiskilled service and blue-collar workers, 92,000 additional skilled blue collar workers, and 79,000 clerical and sales employees. These shortfalls, combined with the shortfall of 3,000 for professional/managerial jobs, yield a total unmet demand of 390,000 workers.

One reason for believing that many and possibly all of these jobs will be taken by undocumented workers is that employers benefit by their presence. The increase in low-wage blue-collar and service jobs in Los Angeles during the 1970s and early 1980s was almost entirely attributable to undocumented immigrants. Non-Hispanic whites, some blacks, and even some Hispanic Americans have been leaving machine operator and laborer jobs—a trend likely to continue, particularly if the California economy is robust in the 1984–1990 period.

Mexicans and other Hispanics from Central America are expected to take the bulk of non-white-collar jobs filled by undocumented workers. Undoubtedly, most available lower-wage white-collar jobs will be taken by persons having at least some knowledge of English. As with legal immigrants, this group includes many persons from India and the Philippines. Other Asians, particularly from Indochina, can also be expected to take some of the skilled and semi-skilled blue-collar and service jobs.

Source: Thomas Muller and Thomas Espenshade, *The Fourth Wave: California's Newest Immigrants* (Washington, D.C.: Urban Institute, 1985), 172–73.

10.4. Undocumented Immigrants Lower Wages for American Workers and Deter Technological Advances

In 1988 Philip Martin a professor of agricultural economics, at the University of California at Davis and a staff member of the Congressional Select Commission on Immigration and Refugee Policy, reported on the negative impact of undocumented immigration on the American economy. According to Martin, unskilled immigrant labor is no longer needed in the United States and its presence tends to deter technological advances. Undocumented immigrants also lower wages for many American workers.

By conservative estimates the American economy has absorbed three to six million illegal alien workers over the past ten years. Economic theory suggests that the presence of additional workers—be they teenagers, married women or immigrants—tends to depress wages, hold down consumer prices and increase business profits. These profits can then underwrite business investment that results in new firms and factories, new jobs, higher wages and productivity and a growing economy.

This scenario of extra people-lower wages, lower prices-higher profits-faster economic growth rests on two critical assumptions: 1) the availability of idle resources such as land and capital (including technology), and 2) economies-of-scale in production. The "idle resources" argument was true for the first 150 years of American history—the United States had unexploited land and mineral resources that were developed with immigrant workers and both European and American capital. Today the U.S. economy does not have resources that are idle because there is not enough unskilled labor. Solving the challenges on technology's frontiers might be expedited with the help of additional scientists and engineers, but no one seriously argues that a shortage of unskilled labor is slowing down technological progress.

The economic justification for more immigrant workers often rests on the presumed advantages of economies-of-scale. Immigration, it is argued, provides both more workers and more consumers. The additional workers make possible larger industries with greater output at lower unit cost; the increased volume of low-cost products is then consumed and made profitable in a market expanded by immigration.

Dissenting economists argue that economies-of-scale can be obtained with even greater efficiency through international trade and investment. Large-scale, low-cost production can better be achieved by taking the workplace to the labor rather than by bringing the labor to the workplace. Similarly, consumers of an American product can be spread throughout the world and still contribute to the ability of the U.S. consumers to buy that product at lower cost.

A second objection to the proposition that "immigrants don't cost—they pay" is that the lower wages-higher profits claimed are not necessarily translated into business investment that leads to more economic efficiency and lower consumer prices. It is one thing to have profits to invest—it is another to have an incentive to invest. The history of development of industrialized countries shows that rising wages were an incentive for both technological advances and for entrepreneurs to invest in the labor-saving machinery they made possible. These changes increased worker productivity and lowered consumer prices. Higher profits enable businesses to make productivity-increasing investments. The availability of low-wage labor deprives entrepreneurs of incentives to make such investments. As Ray Marshall noted in his dissent to the Final Report of the Select Commission on Immigration and Refugee Policy, "Additional supplies of low-skilled alien workers with third-world wage and employment expectations can not only lead employers to prefer such workers, it can also lead to outmoded labor-intensive production processes, to the detriment of U.S. productivity."

Lower wages and higher profits can become a double-edged sword affecting economic growth. Higher profits enable firms to invest more, but lower wages can discourage firms from buying costly equipment when cheap labor is readily available. Low wages, uncertain economic prospects and high interest rates can discourage productivity-increasing investment despite high profits: as the *Wall Street Journal* notes. "Labor is a relatively cheap and flexible expenditure for companies to make, especially when you compare it with the price of capital and energy." Low wages, uncertainty and high interest rates encourage many firms to hire easily laid-off workers instead of committing themselves to buy equipment which must be paid for whether it operates or not, helping to explain why parts of the American economy remain more labor-intensive in the 1980s. Like other forms of subsidy, illegal immigration has distorted the optimum allocation of resources in developing the economy.

Even though wages have been rising slowly in the 1980s, some U.S. businesses have been investing in labor-saving production methods because their managers believe that over the long haul the United States cannot compete with foreign producers on wages. A rubber company president is quoted as asserting that "We'll never have labor rates [in the U.S.] comparable to developing countries . . . we've got to out-innovate or out-automate the world if we're to have a chance of competing." Even with wages rising slowly, the prospect of rising real wages can be an incentive for businesses to invest in labor-saving innovations. Businesses whose owners depend on immigrant workers and who believe that "cheap labor" will always be available, often fail to plan for higher cost labor in the future. They then echo agriculture's traditional lament that proposed immigration reforms will "put us out of business."

The U.S. economy must first absorb American minorities, teenagers and women—they are already here, and the country has already made a commitment to provide jobs for all Americans who want to work. Controlling the level of immigration is one of the few policy choices universally recognized as a sovereign right of nation-states. As Vernon Briggs emphasizes, immigration affects the number of workers in the United States, the operation of U.S. labor markets and business planning, so the U.S. government can and should regulate the number and kind of immigrants it admits in a way that maximizes the well-being of American workers already here.

The unskilled illegal immigrants who entered the United States labor market over the past decade lowered overall wages, and have had marked effects on wages in particular labor markets. American teenagers and women are spread throughout the country, and their varying levels of education and skill prevent locally concentrated impacts. Immigrants, however, are concentrated in particular industries, areas and occupations, and once they gain a foothold, ethnic network recruitment fills job vacancies and excludes unemployed Americans.

Source: Philip Martin, "Network Recruitment and Labor Displacement," in *U.S. Immigration in the 1980s: Reappraisal and Reform*, ed. David Simcox (Boulder, Colo.: Westview Press, 1988), 82–84.

10.5. Illegal Immigration Contributes to Crowding, Job Competition, and Rising Cost of Public Services in California.

Because of its active economy and its location, California has attracted large numbers of legal and undocumented immigrants.

Crowding, competition for jobs, and the rising cost of public services in the 1980s spurred much opposition to undocumented immigrants. Pete Wilson, a Republican politician who was elected mayor of San Diego and later to the U.S. Senate, supported the anti-immigration discontent in his successful campaign for the governorship of the state in 1990 and for reelection in 1994. In an article published in 1994, Wilson gave his view of the burdens of the undocumented for California and called for federal government action to tighten the borders, help pay California's undocumented immigrant expenses, and amend the Constitution. Wilson's ideas bespoke the anti-immigration movement that thrived in California and threatened to spread to other "sun belt" states in the 1990s.

This year [1994], California faces yet another enormous budget crisis, badly exacerbated by both the policies and the inaction of the federal government.

Defense cuts, environmental decisions, and tax hikes coming from Washington are all hurting California's economy. But nothing is more devastating than Washington's irrational immigration policy that fails to control the border.

During just the past four years, enough people to fill a city the size of Oakland [California] have illegally crossed the border into California. In Los Angeles alone, undocumented aliens and their children total nearly a million people. That's a city of illegal immigrants almost the size of San Diego.

I don't fault people trying to find a better life in our nation. In fact, it's hard not to admire their courage and determination. America is a nation of immigrants—three of my own grandparents were immigrants to America. They came for the same reason anyone comes—to build a better future. They brought their hopes and dreams, and the nation benefited from them and millions like them. But there's a limit to how quickly and how many immigrants we can assimilate at once.

If we ignore this flood of illegal immigration, we'll erode the quality of life for all those who live here legally.

Our classrooms are already bursting, but by federal law they're open to anyone who can clandestinely slip across America's 2,000-mile border. Our public health care facilities are being swamped, but two-thirds of all babies born in Los Angeles public hospitals are born to parents who have illegally entered the United States. And the budgets for our parks, beaches, libraries, and public safety will continue to suffer while California spends billions to incarcerate enough illegal aliens to fill eight state prisons.

The proposals we've heard in recent months—strengthening the Border Patrol, imposing a toll on those who cross the border, deporting more undocumented felons from our prisons—all acknowledge the need for action.

But none of them deals with the incentives by which federal law and immigration policy encourage illegal immigration, and indeed reward those who succeed in violating U.S. law by entering the United States illegally.

We need wholesale reform. We need to strike at the root of the problem. And the root of the problem lies not on our border, but in policies devised 3,000 miles to the east in our nation's capital.

The law is clear that the federal government alone has responsibility—for devising and implementing immigration law and policy. The immigration crisis facing America is the result of a failure of will in Washington.

Federal failure to deal with the problem is taking jobs from legal residents—many of them minorities—and killing the American dreams for those who suffer wage and job losses in California and every other state on our southern border.

That's why we must return reason and fairness to America's immigration laws.

The federal government has failed miserably at controlling the border. Crossing America's southern border is easier than crossing Prospect Street in La Jolla [California]. Millions have done it, and millions more will if we don't take action.

I've already urged President Clinton to seek assistance from the Mexican government to help stop the flood of illegal immigrants on the Mexican side of our border. But controlling the border isn't enough. In fact, there's little point in even having a Border Patrol if we're going to continue to reward those who successfully violate U.S. law and enter our country illegally.

Today, the federal government forces the states to give health care, education and other benefits to individuals who are in our country illegally. These mandated services to illegal immigrants and their children are costing California taxpayers $3.6 billion a year.

Because Washington forces us to fund these services for illegal immigrants, it means we have to cut $3.6 billion worth of health care, education and other services that are needed by, and would otherwise be available for, legal residents of California.

California has initiated an innovative program of preventive services for children in health care, mental health care and preschool, but funding for these programs is being siphoned off to programs for illegal immigrants mandated by the feds.

We're forced to cut aid for the needy elderly, blind and disabled who legally reside in California, because Washington mandates that we spend more than three-quarters of a billion dollars a year on emergency medical services for illegal aliens and more than a billion dollars a year to educate illegal aliens in our schools.

Saving just the $1.7 billion we spend educating illegal immigrants in California schools would allow us to put a new computer on every fifth grader's school desk; provide pre-school services to tens of thousands of four-year-olds; expand Healthy Start Centers [facilities that provide health and social services to predominately low-income students] to hundreds of new sites, *and* provide more than 12 million hours of tutorial and mentoring services to at-risk youth.

Depriving legal California residents of these services is wrong. So I've urged Congress to repeal the federal mandates that require states to provide health care, education, and other benefits to illegal immigrants.

If the members of Congress had as much guts as most illegal immigrants—the guts to tell the truth—they'd admit that they are not only welching on their obligation but insisting that California and other states provide benefits to illegal immigrants even when it means denial of needed services to our legal residents.

The president and Congress should pay for these mandates as long as they require the states to provide them. And we're going to demand that they do meet that obligation and pay California the money they owe us.

Congress should then create a tamper-proof legal resident eligibility card and require it of everyone seeking government benefits.

Finally, we must fundamentally rethink the very foundation of our immigration laws. The Constitution has been interpreted as granting citizenship to every child born in the United States, even the children of illegal aliens. Some illegals come to our country simply to have a child born on U.S. soil who can then gain American citizenship. That, of course, renders the child eligible for a host of public benefits. Just since 1988, the number of children of illegal aliens on our state's welfare rolls has grown more than four-fold.

It's time to amend the Constitution so that citizenship belongs only to the children of legal residents of the United States.

President Clinton did not create the grave problem of illegal immigration, he inherited it. But this exclusively federal responsibility now belongs to him and to Congress.

They must move without delay to enact these critical reforms to our nation's immigration laws. There is no time to waste, because the problem grows every day, swelled by the thousands of illegal aliens who slip across the border every night.

It's endangering the jobs we need to rebuild California's economy and the safety of too many California neighborhoods. And those most endangered in both ways are ironically the legal residents of the same ethnic groups.

We need immigration reform and we need it now.

Source: Pete Wilson, "Don't Give Me Your Tired, Your Poor . . ." *San Diego Union-Tribune*, January 9, 1994.

ANNOTATED SELECTED BIBLIOGRAPHY

Ashabranner, Brent. *Our Beckoning Borders: Illegal Immigration to America*. New York: Cobblehill, 1996. Reports on the history and extent of illegal immigration and includes interviews with undocumented immigrants and with U.S. Border Patrol officers.

Barbour, William, ed. *Illegal Immigration*. San Diego, Calif.: Greenhaven Press, 1994. Includes debates on the seriousness of illegal immigration and the inadequacy of immigration laws in the United States.

Edmonston, Barry, and Jeffrey Passel. *Undocumented Migration to the United States*. Washington, D.C.: Urban Institute Press, 1990. Analyzes the extent and impact of undocumented immigration in the United States.

Gibney, Mark, ed. *Open Borders? Closed Societies? The Ethical and Political Issues*. Westport, Conn.: Greenwood Press, 1988. Considers the issue of the admission of illegal immigrants from a variety of points of view.

Herr, David. *Undocumented Mexicans in the United States*. New York: Cambridge University Press, 1990. A sociological study of the lives of undocumented Mexicans who have crossed the border into the United States.

"Illegal Immigrants: The U.S. May Gain More Than It Loses." *Business Week*, May 14, 1984, 126–29. Special section on illegal immigrants focuses on their economic value to the United States.

James, Daniel. *Illegal Immigration: An Unfolding Crisis*. Lanham, Md.: University Press of America, 1991. Presents the negative aspects of undocumented immigration.

Muller, Thomas, and Thomas Espenshade. *The Fourth Wave: California's Newest Immigrants*. Washington, D.C.: Urban Institute Press, 1985. Discusses benefits of undocumented immigrants to the California economy as well as some of the problems presented by these newcomers.

Papademetriou, Demetrios, and Mark Miller, eds. *The Unavoidable Issue: U.S. Immigration Policy in the 1980s*. Philadelphia: Institute for the Study of Human Issues, 1983. Includes a consideration of the issue of illegal immigration.

Peres, Ramon. *Diary of an Undocumented Immigrant*. Houston, Texas: Arte Publico Press, 1991. A personal account of illegally crossing the border from Mexico, being apprehended by the U.S. Border Patrol, reentering the United States, and life and work in Texas, California, and Washington.

Schuck, Peter H., and Roger M. Smith. *Citizenship without Consent: Illegal Aliens in the American Policy*. New Haven, Conn.: Yale University Press, 1985. Analyzes factors that influence American policies on illegal aliens and presents some of the consequences of these policies.

Siems, Larry, ed. *Between the Lines: Letters between Undocumented Mexican and Central American Immigrants and Their Families and Friends*. Tucson: University of Arizona Press, 1995. Description of travels, entrance into the United States, and life as undocumented persons in the United States.

Simcox, David, ed. *U.S. Immigration in the 1980s: Reappraisal and Reform*. Boulder,

Colo.: Westview Press, 1988. Includes material on the negative impact of illegal immigration in the United States.

Smith, Paul, ed. *Human Smuggling: Chinese Migrant Trafficking and the Challenge to America's Immigration Tradition*. Washington, D.C.: Center for Strategic and International Studies, 1997. Treats the extent and methods of smuggling Chinese aliens into the United States and the challenge that this situation presents to American law enforcement officials and policy makers.

ORGANIZATIONS AND WEB SITES

American Immigration Control Foundation: www.cfw.com

Federation for American Immigration Reform: www.fairus.org

Latino Issues Forum: www.lif.org

League of United Latin American Citizens: www.lulac.org

National Council of La Raza: www.nclr.org

National Network for Immigration and Refugee Rights: www.nnirr.org

Social Contract: www.thesocialcontract.com

U.S. Border Control: www.usbc.org

11

How Vigorously Should the Government Enforce Laws Regulating Undocumented Immigrants?

Although there has been an ongoing debate about the value of undocumented immigrants to the American economy and society, the fact that they are "illegal" means that they pose a concern for and thereby are an aspect of public order. Enforcement of immigration laws has been primarily the responsibility of the federal government, although the government entered upon this task, after decades of reluctance, only in the late nineteenth century.

Earlier, the states where immigrants entered and lived bore the principal burden of screening and controlling newcomers from abroad. Their enforcement of federal statutes was not vigorous. Indeed, a member of a congressional committee who was inspecting the state immigration reception station in New York City in 1889, during its busy season, reported that "the local administration of affairs at Castle Garden, by the method and system now followed, was a perfect farce."[1] This and other reports about irregular, indifferent, and erratic state enforcement of immigration laws, combined with growing public concern about "undesirable" immigrants coming into the country, forced the federal government in 1891 to assume the principal enforcement function.

In the following year, the government established immigrant inspection stations at major ports of entry, mostly notably on Ellis Island in New York and Angel Island in San Francisco. At these stations, immigrants who came by third or steerage class were examined (first- and second-class passengers were not examined). Law enforcement officials at these stations questioned the incoming immigrants and checked their records and their mental and physical health to see if they belonged in any of the legally excluded categories. Some 10,000 a year, at the turn of the century, were refused admission at Ellis Island. Steamship lines, by agreement with the government, were required to return rejected persons back to the port from which they had left for America. The passage back was at no charge; however, many of those who had to return had used all their resources for passage over and would land in a port far from their original home. Ellis Island became known to some as the Isle of Tears, although the number rejected was less than 2 percent of those who were examined there each year.

Despite considerable vigilance at the immigrant stations, some persons in the excluded categories were not detected, particularly on days when the inspectors were faced with many newcomers. Frank Warne, a vigorous anti-immigrant spokesperson, complained in 1916 that persons who had health and other issues that would exclude them from legal entrance into the country "are made acquainted with the fact that in March and April, when large numbers of immigrants are coming to the United States, the examination must necessarily be conducted in a lax manner."[2] Jeremiah Jenks and W. Lauck of the U.S. Immigration Commission (1907–1911) contended that some criminals avoided detection and entered the country.

> It is, of course, impossible for an immigration inspector to tell from the appearance of a man whether or not he has been a criminal. In many cases criminals, especially those who have committed certain classes of serious crimes, such as forgery or even burglary, may be well-dressed, intelligent persons, traveling in first cabin.[3]

Resourceful immigrants, fearful of being rejected or after rejection at a federal immigration station, devised various strategies to avoid examination. They came into smaller ports that had no immigrant stations, they entered by way of Canada, or they crossed the large and mostly unpatrolled southern border with Mexico.

Questions about enforcing immigration restrictions abated as immigration slowed in the 1920s and the 1930s, but after World War II, and particularly after 1965, both legal and undocumented immigration to the United States increased markedly. This inflow brought media attention and public discussion. With it, too, came a growth of anti immigration organizations and strong pressure on the government for heightened vigilance against illegal aliens at the borders and along the coasts and for increased apprehension of those who had managed to settle illegally inside the country.

Enforcement efforts have steadily increased but have never been fully effective. In order to lessen the need for deportation, the federal government shifted much of the screening to the points of embarkation to the United States. Examinations of persons seeking to enter the United States legally for permanent settlement now are conducted at American embassies and consulates in countries worldwide. Again, while there has been much vigilance, the examinations and determination of those who are permitted to come has not always been flawless, owing to mistakes and false documentation.

A greater problem has been the considerable number of persons who receive visitor or student visas for a designated period of time and then overstay the limit. Coming from a wide range of countries, they arrive in the United States, usually by plane, stay with friends or relatives, find work, get jobs after dropping out or graduating from colleges, sometimes enter temporary marriages, and then meld into the general population. Some also come by way of Puerto Rico. Additionally, some arrive and ask for amnesty. Usually these petitioners are interviewed by the Immigration and Naturalization Service (INS) and are released pending legal proceedings, which, due to large backlogs and inadequate judicial personnel, may be delayed many months or years. Many of these people also find their way into the overall American society.

Prospective immigrants in many countries face long waits, sometimes ten or more years, for a visa. Rather than delay, they seek out intermediaries who can get them past the legal barriers to admission to the United States. In 1985 Edwin Harwood, a scholar who has studied illegal immigration at the Hoover Institution in Stanford, California, noted that in many countries "travel agencies and street vendors can be found close by U.S. consulates offering 'shortcuts' to entry in the form of photo-substituted passports and forged visas."[4] Jeffrey Passel, the director of the Program for Research Policy at the Urban Institute in Washington, D.C., wrote in 1996, "About 40–50% of the annual increase or some 120,000 to 150,000 illegal aliens a year, are 'visa abusers'—that is, persons who enter the United States with legal entry visas but stay beyond their expiration date." He adds that this amounts to less than 1 percent of the more than 22,000,000 visitors who came to the United States in a given year—1994.[5]

Another means of entry into the United States for undocumented persons has been by sea in all types of vessels. Since the 1960s many have attempted to reach the Florida shore in small, frequently makeshift boats from such places as Cuba and Haiti. They sometimes land undetected and meld into the population, most often among fellow countrymen. If they are caught, they usually apply for amnesty. The U.S. Coast Guard has succeeded in stopping some such vessels before reaching American waters. If the apprehended people are Haitian, they are returned to their home country; if they are Cuban, they are taken to the American base at Guantanamo Bay where their amnesty application is examined by a U.S. government official.

Other undocumented aliens, a considerable number of whom have been Chinese, have been smuggled into the United States amid the cargo in large freighters. According to the February 2000 issue of *Migration News*,

> migrants have begun to show up in shipping containers at West Coast ports. . . . Smugglers require migrants sent in cargo containers to pay $750 to $1,500 up front and another $25,000 to $30,000 after arrival in the US. In many cases, the migrants become indentured servants in the US, promising future wages to repay the smuggling debt.[6]

Some migrants have died of suffocation in the containers.

A major means of entrance into the United States for the undocumented has been across the country's land borders. Some enter from Canada, but many more come from Mexico. The INS has apprehended large numbers of those attempting to cross the nation's southern border. Many of these undocumented migrants, although caught more than once, keep trying until they succeed. In 1985, in its *Annual Report*, the INS stated that its Border Patrol apprehended 1,265,000 aliens seeking to enter the United States without documentation.[7] Yet the undocumented flow has continued.

Many undocumented Latino immigrants get help from "coyotes" and other middle persons who, for a sizeable fee, help undocumented persons cross the Mexican-American border undetected and then provide transportation and safe houses on the American side of the border until the immigrants reach their destination in the Southwest or beyond. In an interview in 1998 for the U.S. Border Control organization, Gustavo De La Vina, the assistant commissioner for the Border Patrol stated;

> The professionalization of smuggling of illegal aliens is absolutely a huge problem for us. As we become more successful on the border, we're seeing illegal aliens utilizing the "coyotes" and the professional smuggler. . . . We're seeing routes established that had not been there before. . . . It's a lucrative business. . . . In San Diego, where the trip used to be $150, it's gone as high as $700 per person.[8]

According to *Migration News* for February 2000, "More migrants also are being caught presenting counterfeit identification, or that of another person, bought or rented for $50 to $200. . . . An INS raid on January 21, 2000 resulted in the seizure of over one million fake documents, including Social Security cards and driver's licenses."[9]

To counter the coyotes and smugglers, the Border Patrol has received increased funding and added manpower, and it has applied more advanced technology to deter movements across the border. In addition, the federal government has used more advanced fencing in certain areas where the greatest amounts of illegal crossing have occurred. According to *Migration News* for February 2000, "There are about 300 Border Patrol and 1,200 US custom agents on the 4,000-mile US-Canadian border and 7,400 Border Patrol and 2,000 US customs agents on the 2,000-mile US-Mexican border."[10]

The effectiveness of such stepped-up enforcement measures remains debatable. The Border Patrol insists it is making inroads into organized schemes to transport illegal aliens into the United States. Others demur. Passel, for example, reported that, while southern border enforcement efforts have doubled in the 1990s,

> There is little evidence . . . that border interdiction at current or historic levels has deterred potential immigrants from setting forth to enter the United States. . . . Even multiple apprehensions . . . seem to have little deterrent effect because the penalty for getting caught is merely a return trip to Mexico—right across the border—and the chance to try again the next day.[11]

Many Americans want border control to be further enlarged and empowered; some even advocate militarizing the border and guarding it with the army. There is, though, strong opposition to a militarized border on the grounds of its large cost. Moreover, warn detractors, such a move would damage United States–Mexican relations and retard efforts to integrate and improve economic life on both sides of the border. Doubts about its effectiveness further discourage such a radical policy.

Meanwhile, the Immigration Law Enforcement Monitoring Project in Houston, Texas, reported in a 1997 *Fact Sheet*, "Ultimately, dependence of many U.S. industries on undocumented labor encourages contempt for the law, fosters contraband in human beings and the widespread falsification of identity documents."[12] This reality led to a long national and congressional debate on enforcement, through the late 1970s into the 1980s, which resulted in legislation, in 1986, focused on employer sanctions as a major factor in deterring undocumented immigration. This law requires employers to review documentation for every new employee and to fill out a government form. It prohibits employing, knowingly, any person who is not authorized to work. This law penalizes employers up to $10,000 for deliberately hiring an undocumented alien.

Those who have favored these sanctions have argued that, since most of the undocumented come for employment purposes, the threat of penalties would cause employers to stop hiring them. Thus, the undocumented would stop coming or at least come in much smaller numbers. The INS particularly endorsed the policy. Its commissioner, Gene McNary, stated, in a 1992 article, that "employer sanctions are critical to the U.S.'s effort to maintain a viable immigration system."[13]

Opponents of this measure argued that some employers, in their effort to avoid being caught and fined, would not only stop hiring the undocumented, but would cut back on hiring people legally in the United States, including citizens, who looked like illegals, most often Hispanics. Stephen Legomsky, a spokesperson for the opponents, wrote, "Employer sanctions have come at a price. . . . The costs have included the expenses of running the system, the administrative burdens on the employers, and the resulting 'widespread discrimination' against job applicants who look or sound foreign."[14]

While the INS has made raids on workplaces suspected of employing undocumented persons, apprehended some of them, and levied some fines against employers, the efforts of the agency have been spotty and not well sustained. After the passage of the sanctions law in 1986, illegal border crossings decreased for a time, but with increased availability of fraudulent documents and coyotes, the flow of undocumented immigrants became higher than in the past. In addition, many employers who find the undocumented to be compliant, hard workers continue to hire them, feigning ignorance and depending on the lack of INS manpower to make frequent, effective inspections. Susan Martin, executive director of the Congressional Commission on Immigration Reform, stated flatly in 1995 that the employer sanction law "does not do what it was supposed to do, namely deter the employment of illegal aliens."[15]

After supporting employer sanctions, the AFL-CIO, has, according to the February 18, 2000, issue of the *Los Angeles Times*, decided to "call for amnesty for 6 million illegal immigrants and repeal of the federal sanctions against employers who hire them." This move was motivated by the union's hope of organizing these workers and increasing its membership. The new labor stance led Texas Republican Congressman Lamar Smith to complain, "The union bosses have betrayed American workers."[16] In Texas and California, where large numbers of illegal immigrants work, the issue of enforcing employer sanctions and other restrictions regularly informs public debate and even defines political categories.

Many who still support employer sanctions argue that they can be effective, if the nation institutes a national identification system with an electronic data base. According to Susan Martin, the Congressional Commission on Immigration Reform "concluded that the most promising option for secure, nondiscriminatory verification is a computerized registry based on the social security number."[17] David Simcox, the director of the Center for Immigration Studies, reported on two Gallup polls, one in

1983 in which 66 percent favored such an identification for everyone and one in 1993 in which 57 percent favored it.[18]

Opponents to a national ID system fear that it would give the federal government added surveillance power over individuals and erode personal freedom. Some, like the American Civil Liberties Union, regard such a system as a serious threat to Americans' civil rights. John Miller and Stephen Moore, writing in 1995 for the pro-immigration Cato Institute, asserted that

> the worker registry system . . . has no redeeming feature: it would be an invasion of basic civil liberties; it would put in place a technology that could be easily expanded for other purposes; it would increase discrimination against Latino and Asian populations; it would carry a price tag in the billions of dollars; it would be fraught with errors and fraud; and, most important, it would not deter illegal immigration.[19]

A national ID system remains a contentious issue to this day.

The INS has also made efforts to locate undocumented immigrants who have entered the country and have settled here. In addition to workplaces, the INS has checked for the undocumented in ethnic neighborhoods, organizations, eating establishments, and places of recreation, even the residences of supposed marriages. The INS has made some apprehensions and effected some deportations, often with publicity to warn other undocumented immigrants to return home lest they be caught too. Most observers, however, regard the INS efforts as paltry and ineffective. While the funding for the INS and the number of agents have increased, neither has ever been near the level needed to investigate and pursue effectively any sizeable portion of the undocumented immigrants in the country.

An additional problem faced by the INS is the fact that some local law enforcement agencies have refused to cooperate in the apprehension of the undocumented. Political leaders in cities and districts, where there are a large number of legal immigrants who can vote, know that to remain in office they need to be very careful to avoid saying and doing things that might be judged to be anti-immigrant. In addition, there is a realization that, if the undocumented are afraid to talk to the police or use health services, they could be a danger to the whole city. Thus, in 1997, New York Mayor Rudolph Giuliani explained that, under an executive order for New York City issued by Mayor Edward Koch in 1989, which he continued to support, "When an undocumented immigrant reports a crime to the police, seeks medical care or enrolls a child in public school, city employees are barred from turning him over to the federal Immigration and Naturalization Service." He maintained that, if undocumented immigrants failed to utilize these services out of fear of being reported, this would endanger "the health and safety of all Americans." Giuliani also stated that increased reporting would not lead to more deportations. "The federal government seldom deports undocumented immigrants even when the INS has established their identities. In New York City, which has an estimated 400,000 undocumented immigrants, only about 1,500 are deported each year."[20]

Thus, while, according to the U.S. Border Control in 1998, "over the last five years, the budget of the Immigration and Naturalization Service ... has swollen to $3.8 Billion," it seemed to be making fewer, rather than more efforts to find and apprehend the average undocumented immigrant in the country.[21] Instead, the growing fears of international terrorism, drug trafficking, money laundering, and other major crimes have increased pressure on the INS to pursue aliens suspected of being involved in those activities, rather than invest its resources in tracking down illegal alien workers in the United States. During the tight budget days of the early 1990s, funding for the INS did not increase sufficiently to allow the agency to do all demanded of it. Priorities shifted so that a large portion of its resources and manpower were of necessity concentrated on preventing major crimes. This focus has left the great majority of otherwise law-abiding undocumented immigrants undetected and undeterred in their work and lives in the United States. In fact, in some local communities, the police departments claim that the INS does not act on information about the undocumented unless they have committed a major crime. Local police forces often work with the undocumented to ensure peaceful conditions in their communities. They will designate special places, which do not disturb businesses, traffic, or citizens, where undocumented day workers can gather and be picked up by employers who need and want their labor.

An additional policy advocated by some has been for the U.S. government to help improve conditions in countries from which immigrants, particularly undocumented ones, tend to come. It is argued that more foreign aid would improve economic development in such countries, increasing job opportunities there and decreasing incentives for people to emigrate. However, this approach would involve a large increase in the expenditure of federal government funds, a fact that has engendered much opposition in the past and likely will continue to do so in the future. This policy was tried in Haiti. One of the stated reasons for the 1990s intervention of the United States in Haiti was to protect the population from a repressive totalitarian regime that had caused many people to flee the country in terror. This action did not improve the economic situation very much, but it did limit violence, and the flow of people from Haiti to the United States decreased at the same time.

The federal responsibility for the enforcement of immigration laws began in 1891. The establishment of immigrant inspection stations in major port cities worked quite effectively, although some newcomers in the excluded categories did pass undetected at these stations and still others entered through the largely unguarded extensive land borders and through smaller port cities. When undocumented immigration assumed larger proportions in the decades after World War II, the federal INS increased its enforcement endeavors and funding. There has been ongoing controversy as to the most effective ways to deter the undocumented from entering and settling in the United States. Congress has legislated and the INS has attempted to halt the undocumented by increasing the number of agents and technology along, particularly, the nation's southern border; by increasing efforts to search out those already inside the country, especially those known to have a criminal record or who are involved in criminal activity; and by implementing employer sanctions. An important factor in these endeavors is the cost—and how much the public and Congress are willing to spend on them. Given the limits of financing, the question is what should be the INS's priorities in its enforcement activities. An effort to focus on criminals among the undocumented has meant that the otherwise law-abiding illegal immigrants have gone largely undetected, and efforts to increase surveillance at heavily used border crossings has still left many others areas ineffectively patrolled.

Complicating enforcement even further is the fact that many agricultural and business interests in the United States continue to encourage and utilize undocumented workers for profit. This fact, together with limited resources for enforcement, has undermined congressionally mandated employer sanctions. Additionally, a marked increase in middlemen assisting the undocumented over the border for profit and an explosion of fraudulent documents challenge the INS's resources and resolve. How to enforce, even whether to enforce, laws restricting the immigrant flow remains a contentious issue with no likely public consensus as to its resolution in the near future.

NOTES

1. Select Committee to Inquire into the Importation of Contract Laborers, Convicts, Paupers, etc. (Ford Committee), *Report*, 50th Cong. 2d sess., January 1889, H. Rept. 3792.

2. Frank Warne, *The Tide of Immigration* (New York: D. Appleton, 1916), 108–10.

3. Jeremiah Jenks and W. Jett Lauck, "Social Problems of Recent Immigration," in *Immigration and Americanization: Selected Readings*, ed. Philip Davis (Boston: Ginn, 1920), 286.

4. Edwin Harwood, "How Should We Enforce Immigration Law?" in *Clamor*

at the Gates: The New American Immigration, ed. Nathan Glazer (San Francisco: ICS Press, 1985), 75.

5. Jeffrey Passel, "Undocumented Immigration," in *The Debate in the United States over Immigration*, ed. Peter Duignan and L. H. Gann (Stanford, Calif:. Hoover Institution Press, 1998), 194–95.

6. "INS: Border, Smuggling," *Migration News: North America* 7, no. 2 (February 2000): 2–3.

7. *Annual Report of the Attorney General of the United States* (Washington, D.C: Government Printing Office 1986), 197–99.

8. "Exclusive Interview with the New Assistant Commissioner for the Border Patrol, Gustavo 'Gus' De La Vina at His Headquarters in Laguna Niguel, California," *U.S. Border Control*, February 10, 1998, 2–3.

9. "INS: Border, Smuggling," 1, 4.

10. Ibid., 2.

11. Passel, "Undocumented Immigration," 196.

12. Maria Jimenez, "Enforcement: A Tool to Control the Flow of Labor at the U.S. Mexico Border," *Fact Sheets*, Spring 1997. (http://www.nnirr.org/Fact_sheets/1997/spring97/enforcement-labor.html)

13. Gene McNary, "Curbing Illegal Immigration: Employers Must Help," *USA Today Magazine*, September 1992, 22–23.

14. Stephen Legomsky, "Employer Sanctions, Past and Future," in *The Debate in the United States over Immigration*, Peter Duignan and Lewis Gann ed. (Stanford, Calif.: Hoover Institution Press, 1997), 190.

15. Susan Martin, *Testimony*, Subcommittee on Immigration and Claims, Judiciary Committee, U.S. Senate, March 14, 1995.

16. Art Pine, "Union's Immigration Stance Leaves GOP Congress Cold on Labor," *Los Angeles Times*, February 18, 2000, A15.

17. Martin, *Testimony*.

18. David Simcox, "Public Opinion Supports National I.D., *Social Contract*, Winter 1998, 1. (www.thesocialcontract.com)

19. John Miller and Stephen Moore, "A National ID System: Big Brother's Solution to Illegal Immigration," *Cato Policy Analysis*, No. 237, September 7, 1995. (www.cato.org)

20. Rudolph Giuliani, "Keep America's Door Open," *Wall Street Journal*, January 9, 1997, A12.

21. "Exclusive Interview," 1.

DOCUMENTS

11.1. State Enforcement of Federal Immigration Laws Is Inadequate in the 1880s

Although the federal government began to legislate immigration restrictions in the 1870s, by 1889 Congress had yet to enact any national government enforcement capabilities. Instead, the federal government, through the Treasury Department, contracted the task to the states having major ports. Complaints of enforcement inadequacies led to the appointment by Congress of the Ford Committee to inspect state enforcement practices. The committee examined the portal through which more immigrants passed than almost all others combined—New York's Castle Garden immigrant inspection station—and found the enforcement procedures to be very unsatisfactory. Two years later, Congress legislated federal control of immigration law enforcement.

The great majority of immigrants landing in the United States are received at the port of New York; therefore the investigation of the committee was more extended in that city than at any other place. The local affairs of immigration at New York are in charge of the commissioners of immigration of the State of New York, by virtue of a contract entered into with the Secretary of the Treasury on the 27th day of September, 1883. During the fiscal year 1888 the number of immigrants landing at the different seaports of the United States was 546,889. Of this number, 418,423 (or about 76 per cent) came via the port of New York, and the greater portion of them arrived between the months of April and September; and during this period the daily arrival of immigrants is exceedingly large, sometimes amounting to as many as 9,000.

When the vessel containing them has been moored to her dock, the immigrants are transferred to barges, which are towed to Castle Garden. There they disembark, and are required to pass in single file through narrow passage-ways, separated from each other by wooden railings. In about the center of each of these passage-ways there is a desk at which sits a registry clerk, who interrogates the immigrant as to his nationality, occupation, destination, etc.—questions calculated to elicit whether or not he is disqualified by law from landing.

Owing to the large number of immigrants received each day during the spring and summer months these questions must be asked rapidly, and the inspection is necessarily done in a very hurried manner, in order that there may be no undue delay in landing them.

The committee visited Castle Garden on several occasions and witnessed the arrival and inspection of immigrants, and it was very obvious to them that it was almost impossible to properly inspect the large number of persons who arrive daily during the immigrant season with the facilities afforded; and the testimony taken puts it beyond question that large numbers of persons not lawfully entitled to land in the United States are annually received at this port. In fact, one of the commissioners of immigration himself testified that the local administration of affairs at Castle Garden, by the method and system now followed, was a perfect farce.

Upon this subject the committee invite attention to the testimony of Dr. Hoyt, for twenty years connected with the board of charities and corrections, who testified that every charitable institution in the State of New York is now not only filled with occupants, but overflowing, and that the State annually expends in taking care of paupers, insane persons, etc., $20,000,000, and that this condition of affairs is largely due to improper immigration.

Source: Select Committee to Inquire into the Importation of Contract Laborers, Convicts, Paupers, etc. (Ford Committee), *Report*, 50th Cong., 2d sess., January 1889, Vol. 20, H. Rep. 3792.

11.2. Federal Enforcement of Immigration Laws Not Fully Effective in Early Twentieth Century

In 1891 the federal government took responsibility for the enforcement of the nation's immigration laws. The government established immigrant inspection stations and procedures in America's major port cities. In 1916, during the nation's second major wave of immigration, Frank Warne, an opponent of "open immigration" who spoke for many nativists of the day, warned about political radicals, troublemakers, and "unassimilable" new immigrants flooding the country. He also reported that some number of legally excluded immigrants were passing through the immigration stations without being detected and that others were entering the country through unguarded borders and ports. Such complaints about inadequate law enforcement and porous borders contributed to congressional efforts to tighten immigration controls after World War I.

It is plain that all the debris, all the human derelicts washed to our shores by the flow of the immigration tide are not debarred at the tide gates but that some gain access to the tide basin within. These enter at the recognized ports of entry, at points along the northern and southern borders of the United States, by lakes and rivers, and at unguarded landings on both the Atlantic and Pacific coasts.

"Enforcement of the exclusion laws along the borders and even the coast lines and along the lakes and rivers near our boundaries has always been and still is a difficult undertaking," says the Commissioner-General of Immigration. "With the best methods that can be devised and the best force that can be selected it will so continue as long as the Government has to deal with men who make a profession of smuggling and also with people so desirous of entering the country without inspection that to attain their object they will readily assume any risk and pay high prices for the services rendered them, no matter how trivial."

This branch of the immigration service has to its credit since its inauguration "the institution of proceedings against seventy-five persons found engaged in illegal importation of contraband Chinese, sixty-three of whom were arrested—thirty-two have been convicted, thirty are awaiting trial, one had been discharged—and the rest are fugitives from justice. During this period, as a result directly or indirectly of its operations, over four hundred alleged contraband aliens have been apprehended. It should be emphasized that the new system is not complete or extensive enough to cope with the organized efforts on the part of those who engage in the business of bringing aliens into this country contrary to law. This contraband traffic and illegal entry of aliens can only be broken up by a general and complete organization of border patrol and by active measures calculated to seek out, arrest, and deport all who are in the United States in violation of law, treaties, and agreements. More officers and better equipment are absolutely necessary both for land and sea service, so as to equal if not surpass at all times the means employed by the violators of our law."

With a northern border along Canada of nearly four thousand miles in length; with a southern boundary line along Mexico not quite so extensive; with innumerable points advantageous for smugglers to ply their vocation and also for aliens, even unaided by guides, to gain access to the country; with few inspectors to guard these frontiers, coasts, lakes, and rivers—under such conditions the situation is met by the United States Government only in a limited degree.

All this is substantiated by the findings of the Immigration Commission. The report of that Federal investigating body says: "Many undeniably undesirable persons are admitted every year. The Commission's inquiries concerning defective and delinquent classes show this fact very clearly and in a way which, it is believed, will be thoroughly understood and appreciated. In theory, the law debars criminals, but in fact many enter; the law debars persons likely to become public charges, but data secured by the Commission show that too many immigrants become such within a short time after landing. The same is true of other classes nominally, at least, debarred by the law. In short, the law in theory, so far as its exclusion provisions are concerned, is exceptionally strong, but in effect it is, in some respects, weak and ineffectual."

Source: Frank Warne, *The Tide of Immigration* (New York: D. Appleton, 1916), 108–10.

11.3. INS Efforts to Enforce Immigration Laws in the 1980s

The Immigration and Naturalization Service was established as the federal agency responsible for enforcing immigration laws. In its annual reports, the INS, first in 1891 and then in 1933, gives its account of the range and some details of its enforcement work. Excerpts from this agency's 1985 report provide information on the various aspects of INS enforcement efforts and what portion of its resources have been allocated to various facets of its activities.

The immigration and naturalization service (INS) oversees the implementation of the immigration, naturalization, refugee, and asylum laws of the United States, through a broad network of regional and district offices located throughout the country, and in some foreign nations, that function in 2 operational and 2 support areas:

—Examinations, concerning activities related to the admission of people to the United States;

—Enforcement, concerning activities to prevent illegal entries and to apprehend and remove those who enter illegally; and

—Information systems and management support, which provide the support services necessary to conduct the Service's basic missions. . . .

Enforcement Division

The Enforcement Division is responsible for the development and evaluation of programs to guard against illegal entry into the United States and to investigate, apprehend, and remove aliens who are in this country in violation of the law. The functional programs under Enforcement are Border Patrol, Investigations, Anti-Smuggling, Detention and Deportation, and Intelligence.

Border Patrol

The Border Patrol is the mobile, uniformed enforcement arm of the INS, and is charged with detecting and preventing the illegal entry and smuggling of aliens into the United States. Patrol agents operate along 8,000 miles of international boundary and the Gulf Coast using sophisticated technology such as sensors, infrared detection devices, low-light level television, and virtually every kind of conveyance from horses to helicopters. Fiscal Year 1985 records show that more than 1,265,000 aliens were apprehended, which is 11 percent more than the previous year. The Border Patrol seized $118,000,000 worth of narcotics for an increase over the previous year of 180 percent.

In a continuing effort to control border crime and apprehend illegal border crossers, a unique Foot Patrol, consisting of El Paso police officers and Border Patrol agents walking specific "beats" together, made 19,738 apprehensions in Fiscal Year 1985. A similar program using Border Patrol agents and San Diego police officers to patrol the canyons and brushy areas near the border in Southern California to reduce violence by border bandits against illegal border crossers has proven highly successful.

Implementation of the single largest enhancement package in Border Patrol history was accomplished by the addition of 768 new officer positions. Twenty-four basic training classes were commenced at the Border Patrol Academy during Fiscal Year 1985.

Investigations

The Investigations Division identifies violations of the Immigration and Nationality Act and related Federal statutes and presents violators for prosecution. It also gathers information to support administrative proceedings under the Act and to remove aliens who are unlawfully residing in the United States.

In Fiscal Year 1985, Investigations' principal objectives were to concentrate four-fifths of its resources on fraud and high impact level cases. Additionally, investigative task force operations were initiated against major fraud facilitators, document vendors, and employers of illegal aliens to address the problem of displacement of U.S. citizens and legal permanent residents in the national workforce.

These task force investigations with other Federal and State agencies uncovered large-scale document counterfeiting operations, schemes to fraudulently obtain entitlement benefits and loans, and conspiracies to help aliens enter or remain unlawfully in the United States. Task force investigations and other fraud cases have resulted in the successful arrest and prosecution or denial of benefits in 2,442 cases involving marriage fraud, labor certification fraud, and visa fraud facilitators.

The Systematic Alien Verification for Entitlement program, and the INS-conducted entitlement fraud investigations yielded a savings in excess of $120 million in fraudulent claims for entitlement benefits made by ineligible aliens.

Successful employer investigations resulted in the cessation of hiring of illegal aliens by more than 1,100 employers, thereby reducing the 'pull' that potential employment exercises as a motive for illegal entry or stay in the United States.

Anti-Smuggling

The Office of Anti-Smuggling Activities focuses on the detection, apprehension, and prosecution of organized conspiracies engaged in smuggling and transporting illegal aliens into this country. Using sophisticated investigative techniques to identify and infiltrate major violators, this program has successfully terminated criminal operations not only engaged in high volume alien smuggling, but also in extortion, murder, kidnapping, peonage, terrorism, and international document fraud.

Major investigations involving interagency and interregional task forces in 1985 resulted in the successful prosecution of a large-scale alien smuggling and narcotics ring operating out of a truck stop in the El Paso, Texas, area. Another similar operation in the San Diego, California, area resulted in felony smuggling and conspiracy indictments against the head of a smuggling ring and 40 co-conspirators who had brought an estimated 100 aliens into this country daily using commercial and recreational vehicles and even a horse trailer to evade checkpoint inspection.

In Fiscal Year 1985, INS officers apprehended 18,600 alien smugglers and seized 11,000 conveyances used in smuggling operations valued at $25 million.

Detention and Deportation Division

The Detention and Deportation program is responsible for the detention and expulsion of aliens who are in the United States in violation of the law. A major priority of the Service in Fiscal Year 1985 was to provide adequate detention space and services consistent with apprehension needs. Toward that end, the combined rated capacity of the 7 Service Processing centers was expanded to 2,239. Additionally, INS continued to work with the Bureau of Prisons on the design and construction of the 1,000-bed Oakdale, Louisiana, Alien Detention Center which will become operational early in Fiscal Year 1986.

Beginning in December 1984 the INS, the Department of State, and the Bureau of Prisons worked together on the Cuban Repatriation Program. The negotiated list contained the names of 2,746 Mariel Cubans whose return Cuba had agreed to accept. Prior to suspension of the agreement on May 20, 1985, 5 flights into Cuba were conducted which resulted in about 200 criminal Mariel Cubans being repatriated.

The Detention and Deportation Division worked with the Office of Justice Assistance, Research and Statistics on the implementation of Public Law 98–411. That law provided $5 million to be distributed on a one-time basis as a reimbursement to States which had incarcerated Mariel Cubans. A total of 1,869 names were submitted by various State governments and, of those, INS verified, 1,716 as Mariel Cubans.

Intelligence Office

The Intelligence Office provides strategic and tactical intelligence support and technical assistance to INS policy-makers and field personnel to help deter:

(1) Entry into the United States by illegal aliens;

(2) International terrorism;

(3) Narcotics trafficking;

(4) Alien smuggling; and

(5) Fraudulent schemes to gain Federal entitlement benefits. This office works with various Federal law enforcement and intelligence-gathering agencies, both civil and military.

Toward achieving one of the (INS) Commissioner's 1985 priorities, deterrence at overseas locations of illegal entry to the U.S., the Intelligence Office expanded its joint effort with the Department of State by offering training seminars to foreign airline and immigration officials in Haiti, the Dominican Republic, Curacao, the Bahamas, Panama, Mexico, El Salvador, and Guatemala. The seminars focused on more effective detection and fraudulent documents.

Forensic Document Library

The Forensic Document Library (FDL) provides scientific analysis of questioned documents and subsequent testimony in resultant criminal cases. In addition, the Laboratory does research in the field of document fraud, provides technical assistance to field personnel, and assists in developing counterfeit-resistant identification documents. In a complex inter-agency project, the FDL provided critical expert analyses in the highly complex case of the former Nazi "Angel of Death," Josef Mengele.

El Paso Intelligence Center

The El Paso Intelligence Center operation is a multi-Federal law enforcement agency in which INS personnel play a major role by maintaining several data bases, including Mexican Border Smuggling and Fraudulent Document Indexes, in the Integrated Combined Systems. In addition to participating in an around-the-clock watch, INS staff also provide tactical and analytical intelligence support to INS operational field staff and other requestors.

Source: *Annual Report of the Attorney General of the United States* (Washington: U.S. Government Printing Office, 1986), 197–99.

11.4. Employer Sanctions Used to Reduce Number of Undocumented Immigrants in the 1990s

Gene McNary was the commissioner of the INS from 1989 to 1993, after the passage of the 1986 Immigration Reform and Control Act which established sanctions against employers who hired undocumented immigrants and at the time of the Immigration Act of 1990 which authorized an increase in the admission of skilled immigrants. In 1992 McNary explained the INS's procedures and difficulties in implementing employer sanctions, opposition to this law, and his conviction that it could succeed in reducing the number of undocumented immigrants in the United States.

When President Bush signed the Immigration Act of 1990, he endorsed a sweeping reform that opened this nation's doors to many more people from foreign lands—with substantial increases in categories based on skills needed in the U.S. economy. This measure authorizing additional workers from other nations in no way has reduced America's commitment to strong enforcement of the employer sanctions provisions of the Immigration Reform and Control Act (IRCA) of 1986. Rather than a conflict of purposes, this different treatment of legal and illegal immigration profoundly reflects the responsibility to administer laws fairly and from the largest possible perspective. Employer sanctions are critical to the U.S.'s efforts to maintain a viable immigration system.

Immigration laws balance a series of national interests. IRCA did much more than impose sanctions on employers who hire or continue to employ aliens whom they know are not authorized legally to work in the U.S. It provided a generous amnesty that enabled nearly 3,000,000 people to legalize their status—with the eventual possibility of becoming citizens. IRCA also reflected a national commitment to reduce the flow of aliens who enter the country illegally through more effective enforcement of America's land borders.

Within IRCA's provisions authorizing employer sanctions, Congress combined several social objectives, as it simultaneously prohibited illegal employment, guarded against excessive paperwork, and barred discrimination. Employer sanctions, then, must be viewed as a complex balance of national policies addressing ways of protecting all people under law.

American immigration regulations treat generously those who enter legally. To the extent that illegal employment enables some people to gain access to the U.S. market faster than those who follow proper procedures, it jeopardizes the principle of equal treatment for all applicants.

Accordingly, the Immigration and Naturalization Service (INS) has maintained a delicate balance of policy objectives in implementing employer sanctions. Initially, the INS devoted a great deal of attention to educating companies about their responsibilities under the law. It sought to minimize the paperwork necessary to document the employment eligibility of people who are hired, and the General Accounting Office (GAO) concluded that such sanctions did not result in unnecessary paperwork for employers.

All employers (even those with only a single employee) are required by law to verify that the people they hire (whether citizens or aliens with proper employment authorization) are eligible to work in the U.S. At the time of hiring, every employer must request that each employee demonstrate both identity and authorization to work. Employers can satisfy these requirements by reviewing a variety of documents, but can not make different document requests of people who look or sound foreign. The law expects good faith compliance with these verification requirements for all persons hired, since this is essential to ensure that people authorized to work in the U.S. are not deprived of employment because unauthorized individuals are hired.

Too many observers—among them some free-market proponents—dismiss the details of immigration enforcement. Such critics believe that the jobs illegal aliens take are often those that most legally authorized employees would not want. Moreover, they assert, even at sub-minimum U.S. wages, illegal aliens earn much more than they would in their native lands. Despite the recession, this nation has a much stronger economy than nearly all others around the globe—a reality that is dramatized by the efforts of those attempting to enter the U.S. from the many less successful nations. Per capita annual earnings in Mexico are approximately $1,900, compared to nearly 10 times that level in the U.S. Since 1986, the exchange rate for Mexican pesos has shifted from 637 pesos to the dollar to more than 2,880. Other economies are even less prosperous than Mexico's, and some are plummeting even lower than their current low bases.

Employer sanctions also have been attacked by observers asserting that they have resulted in discrimination against people who lawfully are entitled to work in the U.S., especially citizens who look or sound foreign. These critics are supported by a 1990 GAO report maintaining that employer sanctions had resulted in discrimination against some authorized workers, attributing much of it to confusion over document requirements and other procedures associated with this complex legislation. Some of the confusion undoubtedly derives from INS policy allowing employees to present a variety of proofs to establish both identification and work authorization. This policy was adopted to minimize the burden of compliance on people providing documentation to verify their employment status.

Regardless of any source of confusion, the INS fully is committed to the principle that all discrimination is intolerable. It also believes that any discriminatory side effects of the law can be alleviated without jeopardizing its proper purposes—reducing any incentives toward illegal immigration provided by prospects of U.S. employment.

Some members of Congress have advocated repeal of these employer sanctions provisions. Although the alleged discriminatory effects are the most public argument proponents of repeal use, they are joined by a faction opposed to the documentation requirements on free market grounds. As in any case wherein strange political bedfellows apparently desire a common goal for widely varied reasons, by attempting to unravel the complex social fabric of our immigration laws, both sides could learn that they are jeopardizing the public good achieved through that legislation. . . .

The INS consistently has emphasized that voluntary compliance with the law is our first goal in implementing employer sanctions. In a report to the Congress signed by President George Bush on July 11, 1991, the Administration confirmed that we have gained cooperation from an estimated 81% of the nation's employers. Improvements in that rate are essential to sustain appropriate respect for this nation's immigration laws, so we are intensifying enforcement activities directed at violators.

On April 5, 1991, I initiated a pilot program to strengthen INS's employer sanctions enforcement program. Each of our district offices was directed to devote 30% of its investigative time to such cases and another 30% to fraud involved in support of illegal employment schemes. We are intensifying our efforts in the sanctions program while maintaining a concerted program to address the challenges presented to immigration enforcement by criminal aliens.

Our balanced enforcement effort includes investigations of employers selected at random to ensure that no sector of the economy feels isolated from its responsibilities under the law. We will give appropriate publicity where we discover violations, both to maintain public awareness that the law is being enforced, and so that any employers who might be tempted to violate it are deterred. We have instituted a new set of fine guidelines to ensure systematic treatment of those who violate the law, as well as stiff penalties for repeated or aggravated offenders.

Experience in Europe indicates that employer sanctions programs can take as long as 10 years to achieve their desired effects. The goals are not merely punitive, but include better controls on immigration so that decisions about who enters the U.S. and when are consistent with law and national policies. These, in turn, require effective enforcement and compliance as essential elements.

Source: Gene McNary, "Curbing Illegal Immigration: Employers Must Help," *USA Today Magazine*, September 1992, 22–23.

11.5. New York City Mayor Tells Police and Other Officials Not to Report Undocumented Immigrants to the INS

Rudolph Giuliani, Republican mayor of New York City, whose population includes large numbers of foreign-born, in 1997 wrote about his own political party's congressional efforts to increase enforcement of laws against undocumented immigrants. Giuliani organized opposition against these laws, challenged some of their provisions in the courts, and directed the police and other New York City officials not to report the undocumented with whom they came into contact to the INS. Giuliani praised immigrants as contributing significantly to New York City's successes and affluence.

Today on Ellis Island, the golden door through which millions of immigrants passed on their way to a new life in a new land, I will gather with a cross-section of Americans to inaugurate the Immigration Coalition. The group includes business leaders, educators, writers, artists and representatives of virtually every ethnic community in the nation's most diverse city.

The coalition will focus its efforts on educating the public about the vital contributions immigrants make to our nation and on opposing anti-immigrant policies. The contributions of immigrants are especially important to New York, as a report by our Department of City Planning, also being released today, demonstrates.

The coalition's first order of business will be to call on Congress and the president to repeal provisions of the recently enacted welfare and immigration laws that discriminate against immigrants. My administration has already gone to court to challenge some of these measures, which are not only unjust but dangerous to public health and safety.

To discriminate against legal immigrants is simply unfair. The U.S. accepts some 700,000 immigrants a year. We invite them here to create better lives for themselves and their families, and the overwhelming majority of immigrants take great advantage of their new opportunity.

In return for the privileges of American residency, immigrants pay federal, state and local taxes at the same rate as American citizens. But under the new laws, legal immigrants are denied disability benefits and food stamps, and states may also refuse them welfare assistance and nonemergency medical care. Withholding these benefits from immigrants, who are here legally and whose taxes help pay for these very programs, is arguably unconstitutional—and certainly inequitable.

The new federal laws contain another dangerous provision: a stipulation that local governments may not provide a zone of protection for undocumented immigrants. This directly conflicts with a New York City executive order first issued in 1989 by former Mayor Edward I. Koch. Under this order, when an undocumented immigrant reports a crime to the police, seeks medical care or enrolls a child in public school, city employees are barred from turning him over to the federal Immigration and Naturalization Service.

Why shouldn't city employees turn undocumented immigrants over to the INS? Because if immigrants fear being caught and deported, they will avoid the police, hospitals and schools—to the detriment of the entire city. If the federal government fails to fulfill its responsibility to keep undocumented immigrants out of the U.S., then we must afford them certain protections to preserve the health and safety of all Americans.

A criminal who victimizes an undocumented immigrant might attack a legal resident next. Discouraging the reporting of crimes would make it more difficult for the police to track criminal activity. New York now leads the nation in crime reduction, but we cannot catch criminals, prevent crime and protect the public if we don't have accurate information about where and when crimes are occurring.

Immigrants who fail to seek medical care for fear of deportation also pose a substantial danger to the general public.

The misguided new federal law could result in the spread of serious communicable diseases that might easily have been contained if diagnosed and treated early.

And parents who fear deportation might not send their children to public schools. If not in school, some 80,000 children of undocumented immigrants would be on the streets of New York or left alone in apartments. Not only would they suffer irreversible damage, but so many unsupervised children would endanger public safety in the entire city.

What's more, there is no indication that vastly increasing the number of names reported to the INS would even lead to substantially more deportations. The federal government seldom deports undocumented immigrants, even when the INS has established their identities. In New York City, which has an estimated 400,000 undocumented immigrants, only about 1,500 are deported each year. While the recently enacted illegal-immigration law provides new funding for deportation, still less than 1% of the undocumented immigrants already in New York would be deported each year. If the federal government wants to stop illegal immigration, it should work diplomatically with other governments and better secure our national borders, not endanger public safety by recklessly denying critical services to people already here.

And if the federal government wanted to curtail legal immigration—which I believe is neither necessary nor wise—an honest approach would be simply to allow fewer immigrants into the country, not to deny them fair and humane treatment after they are admitted. This, though, would be a mistake. Immigration is good for America. It has been fundamental to the success of our nation for more than 200 years.

New York, more than any other city, has been built by the dedication and dreams of new Americans. The new Department of City Planning report makes clear just how vital immigrants continue to be in our city. More than half of all New Yorkers are foreign-born or have at least one parent who is foreign-born. New York's population grew 4% in the 1980s, a time when cities with few foreign-born residents, like Buffalo, Cleveland, Detroit and St. Louis, were undergoing major population losses. Without immigration, New York's population would have declined by 9% during the '80s.

And immigrants play a crucial role in maintaining our city's housing stock and revitalizing its neighborhoods. Immigrants occupy more than 45% of the city's "accessible" housing units—rental housing that is available for immediate occupancy, without the long waiting lists common in public housing. In some neighborhoods, immigrants occupy more than 80% of all accessible housing. Without immigrants, many of these houses and apartments would go unoccupied and ultimately be abandoned. Neighborhoods would suffer inexorable decay.

New York's immigrant population is an economically diverse group, with substantial numbers in professional, managerial, administrative and blue-collar occupations. Census data show that immigrants in New York work and own businesses in slightly higher percentages than U.S. citizens. They bring new ideas, new energy and an appreciation for American values and ideals. Immigrants challenge us to do better, and we all benefit from their industry and prosperity.

Anti-immigrant sentiment is not new to America. The "Know-Nothings" of the mid-19th century, for example, sought to stop immigration. If they had succeeded, many of us—those whose families are Catholic and Jewish, or whose ancestors came from Southern and Eastern Europe, from Asia, South America and Latin America, as well as from the West Indies and the Caribbean—would not be Americans today.

We are fortunate that leaders with wisdom and foresight, foremost among them Abraham Lincoln, recognized the need for the human renewal and competition immigration inspires. The question today is the same as it was 150 years ago: Are we afraid of competition, or courageous enough to embrace it in all of its dimensions? Do we understand that we need new Americans to keep America vital?

New York is the nation's richest, most successful city, and it's no coincidence that New York is also the nation's greatest city of immigrants. We must lead the way to a deeper national understanding of immigration. By doing so, we will protect our economic interests, the health and safety of the public and the values of strength, optimism, fairness and humanity on which America was founded.

Source: Rudolph Giuliani, "Keep America's Door Open," *Wall Street Journal*, January 9, 1997, A12.

11.6. Rights of Undocumented Workers Must Be Protected as Labor Migrants in an Integrated Global Economic System

Maria Jiménez, writing for the Immigration Law Enforcement Monitoring Project in Houston, Texas, in 1997, wants undocumented workers, particularly Mexicans, to be regarded as international labor migrants in an increasingly integrated global economic system (of which NAFTA is a part). According to Jiménez, INS enforcement efforts, disproportionately aimed at Mexicans, increase the vulnerability and support the exploitation of Mexican workers to the advantage and profit of American employers and businesses. Jiménez calls for a binational immigration policy which will protect the human rights and dignity of Mexican and other international workers in the new world economy.

Immigrants and immigration are buzz words in the U.S. public debate that stir emotions, polarize relations between ethnic and racial groups, and evoke hostility toward anyone foreign-born. Ironically, the process of globalization, economic integration and economic restructuring give rise to an increasing movement of persons across international boundaries. "International labor migrant" is a more precise term to describe those who move in the complex web of a global economic system. Since the 1960s, economic migrants from developing countries to industrialized nations have quadrupled, reaching about 940,000 per year.

Worldwide, immigration policies have made it possible for a small group of people to become more and more mobile by providing the legal flexibility for the exit and entrance of business owners, executives, administrators and support technical labor. However, physical and other barriers to the movement of poor people have proliferated. The inequality of mobility is a part of the maintenance of the larger socio-economic and political inequalities on a national and international scale.

The movement to industrialized countries is not a movement seeking a "transition to prosperity" but rather a response to the politics of economic integration created and imposed by global economic elites. Migration cannot be separated from the policies of debt collection by multi-lateral agencies like the World Bank and International Monetary Fund in acquiescence with domestic elites and national governments. Such policies have caused untold human suffering and widespread environmental destruction, rendering these countries with few resources to invest in economic and human recovery.

Border control is sought as a policy decision not so much to stop unauthorized migration, but to frame the conditions in which international labor participates in economic, social and political spheres. No other border control policies better illustrate this complex facet of global integration and the inequality of the movement of persons than those of the United States with respect to its border with Mexico.

These nations share the most integrated relationship between a rich and poor nation, in terms of debt, trade and migration. Mexico's debt to U.S. banks totals about 150 billion dollars. From 1965 to 1990, some 1.9 million Mexicans were admitted as legal permanent residents. During the same time period, there were more than 36 million undocumented entries from Mexico and more than 31 million departures. The process of social capital formation, human capital accumulation and market integration between the two countries is so far advanced in over 100 years of continuous migratory flows that stopping the flow of migration is impossible.

Increasing the INS budget by 75% to enhance border enforcement reflects more of a rejection of the presence of working poor, Spanish-speaking immigrants than policy decisions based on fact. Traditionally, concern for "borders out of control" has always been about the 2,000 miles of the U.S.-Mexico border and never the 4,000 miles of the U.S.-Canadian border. According to the Urban Institute, only four out of ten individuals who are illegally in the country entered by crossing the southern border; the other six entered with legal visas that later expired. Yet 85% of all the resources of the Immigration and Naturalization Service, including the Border Patrol, are located in southern border communities.

Walls, more agents and military support as tougher border enforcement measures only redirect the flows of undocumented immigrants to other parts of the border, delaying entry and increasing the risks to immigrants as they move toward more dangerous and remote areas of the border. A recent University of Houston study estimated that 190 to 300 persons died annually attempting to cross the Texas border; countless more die crossing the deserts of Arizona and mountains and highways of California.

At the same time, enforcement of immigration laws is selectively applied to persons of Mexican origin and/or descent. Mexican nationals represent 39% of the undocumented immigrants in the U.S., but they are 90 percent of those arrested for illegal entry by the Immigration and Naturalization Service. The Mexican-origin population bears the burden of civil and human rights violations. Deaths, beatings, sexual assaults, illegal arrests and other cases of abuse of authority are often reported by those confronting immigration authorities. In a recent study by the University of Arizona, 18 percent of 200 randomly surveyed persons in South Tucson indicated that they had been mistreated by immigration officials. Of these, 60% were citizens born in the United States.

Violence on the US-Mexico border reinforces temporality and control of Mexican labor on both sides of the border to ensure high profitability in industries on both sides. U.S. immigration policy is an artificial and misdirected effort to intervene in economic transactions between willing sellers of labor and willing buyers by interposing armed force both at the border and at worksites. It is the only aspect of employee and employer relations that is enforced through the use of guns. Ultimately, dependence of many U.S. industries on undocumented labor encourages contempt for the law, fosters contraband in human beings and the widespread falsification of identity documents. The international labor workforce is placed in a position of illegality, vulnerability, exploitation and socio-political marginalization.

In a historical continuum, this is nothing new for Mexican-origin populations in the United States. Racism, exclusion and segregation are all too familiar. The only change currently is that this fervor takes place in the context of the inequalities produced by a global economic system. In the short run, a realistic approach to border control on the U.S.-Mexico border is to recognize the movement of labor as an inevitable consequence of the ongoing processes of the market integration presently occurring and formally recognized by NAFTA. Binational agreements on migratory flows within both countries must move toward developing a flexible legal framework for the movement of labor in both directions, guaranteeing equity and respect for the human rights and dignity of all human beings. In the long run, the construction of immigration control policies must evolve as a product of mutual agreement and acknowledgment between the people of both countries, that together work to construct a world of economic equity, social acceptance and peace.

Source: Maria Jiménez, "Enforcement: A Tool to Control the Flow of Labor at the U.S.-Mexico Border," *Fact Sheets*, National Network for Immigration and Refugee

Rights, Spring 1997, 1–3. (http://www.nnirr.org/Fact_sheets/1997/spring97/enforcement-labor.html)

ANNOTATED BIBLIOGRAPHY

Annual Reports, Immigration and Naturalization Service. Washington, D.C.: U.S. Government Printing Office, 1891–present. Includes description of the Immigration and Naturalization Service's immigration law enforcement strategies.

Duignan, Peter, and Lewis Gann, eds. *The Debate in the United States over Immigration*. Stanford, Calif.: Hoover Institution Press, 1997. Includes chapters on employer sanctions and other enforcement issues.

Dunn, Timothy. *The Militarization of the U.S.-Mexico Border, 1978–1992: Low Intensity Conflict Doctrine Comes Home*. Austin: University of Texas Press, 1996. Discusses American efforts to enforce its immigration laws along the extended United States–Mexican border.

Fix, Michael, ed. *The Paper Curtain: Employer Sanctions: Implementation, Impact and Reform*. Washington, D.C.: Urban Institute Press, 1991. Contains information on the intent of employer sanctions as passed by Congress, problems with the enforcement of the legislation, and the limited effect of this means of curtailing undocumented immigration.

Glazer, Nathan, ed. *Clamor at the Gates: The New American Immigration*. San Francisco: ISC Press, 1985. Contains a number of chapters on various aspects of immigrant law enforcement.

Harwood, Edwin. *In Liberty's Shadow: Illegal Aliens and Immigration Law Enforcement*. Stanford, Calif.: Hoover Institution Press, 1986. Discusses need for and problems related to immigration law enforcement and recommendations for strengthening enforcement efforts.

Moore, Alvin. *Border Patrol*. Santa Fe, N.M.: Sunstone Press, 1988. Reports on the activities of the Border Patrol in attempting to reduce the flow of undocumented immigrants into the United States.

Morris, Milton, and Albert Mayio. *Curbing Illegal Immigration*. Washington, D.C.: Brookings Institution, 1982. Discusses difficulties with preventing undocumented immigration and makes recommendations for improving enforcement methods.

ORGANIZATIONS AND WEB SITES

American Civil Liberties Union: www.aclu.org

American Immigration Control Foundation: www.cfw.com

Federation for American Immigration Reform: www.fairus.org

Latino Issues Forum: www.lif.org

League of United Latin American Citizens: www.lulac.org

Migration News of North America: www.migration.ucdavis.edu

National Council of La Raza: www.nclr.org

National Immigration Law Center: www.nilc.org

National Network for Immigration and Refugee Rights: www.nnirr.org

Numbers USA: www.NumbersUSA.com

Social Contract: www.thesocialcontract.com

U.S. Border Control: www.usbc.org

U.S. Immigration and Naturalization Service: www.usdoj.gov/ins

IV

Human Rights Issues

12

What Rights Should Immigrants Have in the United States?

Once immigrants have entered the United States, whether legally or illegally, many crucial issues related to their rights can arise. Perhaps the most fundamental are the right of the United States as a sovereign nation to deport an immigrant and the newcomer's right to remain in the country. Related are the rights of immigrants who have been detained or are in the process of deportation. Further, there are the questions of the constitutional and human rights of an immigrant who is still an alien to be protected from discriminating state and federal laws, particularly in terms of employment and land ownership. Additionally, differences of opinion persist about the rights of aliens, legal and illegal, to such public services as education, health care, housing, and welfare.

Deportation was an issue as early as the 1790s. The Federalists, then in control of Congress, feared that some immigrants involved with revolutionary France might infect the American state with radical ideas and corrupt American politics and morality. In 1798 a Federalist-controlled Congress enacted the Alien and Sedition Acts, which gave the president the right to deport any alien suspected of advocating ideas considered dangerous to the republican institutions of the country. "It shall be lawful for the President of the United States . . . to order all such aliens as he shall judge dangerous to the peace and safety of the United States . . . to depart out of the territory of the United States." The law permitted an accused alien to appeal his case to the president, but not to a court, thus limiting his or her due process (the right of a person to a legal procedure that accords with established rules and principles).[1]

The Democratic Republicans, the political rivals of the Federalists, strongly objected to the Alien and Sedition Acts, which they insisted were directed at their political friends, threatened to silence dissent, and violated the spirit of the American Revolution. Although no immigrants were ever deported under the law, several politically "radical" and active immigrants left the country during the Federalist reign, and the anti-immigrant policy discouraged political liberals fleeing Europe from entering the United States for a time. When the Democratic Republicans gained control of the government in 1801, they let the Alien and Sedition Acts expire.

The first mass immigration, beginning in the 1840s, and the consequent rise of nativism made deportations an issue at the state level. In the mid-1850s state officials in Massachusetts, against the will of the accused and apparently without legal defense, deported persons accused of being paupers. The *Boston Daily Advertiser*, on May 16, 1855, for example, complained about the deportation of a poor Irish woman and her infant child accused of being a pauper. Included was a report on a Massachusetts statute "which authorizes any Justice of the Peace upon complaint . . . to cause any pauper to be removed out of state, to any place beyond the sea where he belongs." The article also stated that "a practice has arisen by which the Commissioner of Alien Passengers undertakes, even without the warrant of a Justice of Peace, to send back paupers in cases in which he sees fit." According to the article, "the piteous cries of this poor woman with her child were such as to attract the attention of the bystanders as she was led on board the vessel."[2] Massachusetts was not alone in trying to clear its poor rolls of immigrants by deporting them. A New York "Reports of County Superintendents of the Poor," in 1856, called for legislation in that state that would provide for the deportation of alien paupers and criminals in order to relieve the local governments of added expenses.[3]

Beginning in the 1870s, the federal government enacted a series of laws excluding various categories of immigrants and providing for deportation if an excluded person was found to have entered the country illegally. One federal law, passed in 1882, prohibited the admission of Chinese laborers, and another, passed in 1888, prohibited reentry of such workers who had already been residents of the United States. When deportation actions taken against Chinese residents seeking to reenter the country after travel abroad were legally challenged, a number of cases reached the Supreme Court. The decision of the majority in these cases held that the sovereignty of the United States implied full control over immigrants and that since this matter involved foreign relations, the control was to be exercised by Congress and was not subject to judicial review. In *Fong Yue Ting v. United States*, the Supreme Court in 1893 held "the right to exclude or to expel all aliens, or any class of aliens . . . being an inherent and inalienable right of every sovereign and independent nation, essential to its safety, its independence and its welfare . . . [is] absolute and unqualified."[4]

Through the 1890s into the 1920s, during America's second major wave of immigration, now heavily from Eastern and Southern Europe, and with growing pressure from anti-immigrant forces, Congress increased the prohibitions on the admission of newcomers and consequently increased the grounds for deportation. An 1891 law held that any immigrant who became a pauper and a public charge within one year of arriving in the United States could be deported. In a 1903 case involving a Japanese immigrant, the Supreme Court, while maintaining that Congress had full power to deport, ruled that the immigrant had the right to due process in the deportation proceedings. The Court, though, decided that a hearing need not be a judicial one but could be conducted by an immigration official who would render the decision.

Additionally, in 1903, Congress enacted a law prohibiting immigrants who were anarchists from legally entering the country and subjecting those who did settle here to deportation. For the first time, immigrants could be deported for ideological or political beliefs. However, shortly thereafter, American Secretary of State Elihu Root, in 1910, supported an "international minimum standard" in regard to aliens. He stated that the justice due to aliens should be measured "by the justice which it accords to its own citizens."[5] American policy, at that time, fell short of this standard, but over the years it gradually moved in that direction.

In a 1915 case regarding deportation, *Whitfield, Immigrant Inspector, et al. v. Hanges et al.*, the Supreme Court held that

> an alien, as well as a citizen, is protected by the prohibition of deprivation of life, liberty, or property without due process and the equal protection of the laws. This principle is universal. It applies to all persons within the territorial jurisdiction of the United States without regard to any differences of race, or color or of nationality.

The Court further ruled that a hearing by an immigration inspector constituted due process, but that such a hearing had to have "an absence of all abuse of discretion and arbitrary action by the inspector."[6] This ruling was ignored when, in the aftermath of World War I, Red Scare hysteria, fanned by U.S. Attorney General A. Mitchell Palmer, swept the nation. A considerable number of foreign-born persons accused of belonging to radical labor organizations, the Communist Party, and other "radical" groups were detained, and several hundred were deported.

Still the judiciary persisted. In 1920 a federal circuit court, in *Colyer v. Skeffington*, held that "Aliens have constitutional rights. The Fourth, Fifth, Sixth, and Fourteenth Amendments are not limited in their application to citizens. They apply generally to all persons within the jurisdiction of the United States."[7]

Despite these proclamations and rulings, a much more extensive and serious abrogation of immigrant rights occurred during the Great Depression when government action resulted in the forceful deportation of more than 400,000 Mexican immigrants, including some citizens, out of the American Southwest without regard for due process or other civil rights. This was followed a few years later at the outset of World War II when, by federal order, some 110,000 Japanese immigrants and Japanese American citizens, without any due process, were taken from their homes in West Coast states, forced to sell most of their property on very short notice, and placed in distant detention centers. The Supreme Court upheld this latter action as a wartime necessity, but after the war the U.S. government publicly apologized for this gross usurpation of civil rights and awarded modest remuneration to the victims.

Following World War II, the fear of communism's invading and corrupting U.S. institutions, including schools, popular entertainment, and government, led to new restrictions on aliens. Fueled by the rantings of politically ambitious Senator Joseph McCarthy and his supporters, a hysteria, somewhat similar to the Red Scare after World War I, raged in the United States for several years. Given evidence of spying on American atomic and military installations for foreign governments, Congress, in 1950, passed the Internal Security Act, and in 1952, over the veto of President Harry Truman, the McCarran-Walter Immigration Act, which broadened the grounds for deportation of immigrants from those who were actively involved with Communists to those who at any time had belonged to a Communist or other subversive organization. Despite protests, a number of persons were deported.

After the Communist scare subsided and concern about civil rights increased, due process for immigrants improved, although complaints have been raised about the treatment of undocumented Mexicans and others who crossed the border into the United States and of some Haitians, Salvadorans, and Cubans who entered the country, particularly in the 1980s. The heightened fear of international terrorism in the 1990s revived hard-line attitudes toward aliens. This alarm, together with anti-immigrant pressures, led to the passage of an Anti-Terrorism Act and the Illegal Immigration Reform Act in 1996. Since the passage of these laws, the Immigration and Naturalization Service (INS) increased the detentions of aliens from 8,500 in 1996 to 16,000 in 1998. Some of these have involved mandatory detention, some for offenses that do not carry a prison sentence; others have involved indefinite detention for detainees seeking asylum while awaiting hearings on their status. In the latter cases the process may take years, and in some instances, because their country of origin will not allow them to return, some aliens could be detained for life. The American Civil Liberties Union (ACLU) has objected to such practices, arguing that "mandatory detention of non-citizens pending their immigration proceedings violates the right of due process and is inefficient and costly." The ACLU has called for a release of detainees "if the non-citizen is not a danger to the community." The ACLU points out that "several federal district courts have recently ruled that indefinite detention with no realistic prospect of removal is unconstitutional."[8] Nicholas Kristof, who witnessed Chinese prison injustice and who has been a translator for Chinese women in American prisons who are awaiting the outcomes of their asylum applications, wrote in the *New York Times*, on January 16, 2000, about their harsh treatment, which is "denying them the dignity and safeguards Americans demand when they are jailed overseas."[9]

The antiterrorism law also allows the government to deport aliens based on classified evidence that defendants, lawyers, and judges cannot fully review. The law has drawn fire as a threat to basic civil liberties. Gregory Nojeim, an ACLU legislative counsel, stated, "The use of secret evidence is a feature of totalitarian governments. It goes against everything our country stands for. People here have the right to know the evidence against them and to be given an opportunity to rebut it."[10] Susan Sachs concluded a *New York Times* report on this issue in December 1999: "When terrorism is the issue, many people argue that America's security outweighs strict due process for aliens."[11] This dilemma is somewhat similar to that faced by the country during World War II in regard to the detention of Japanese immigrants and Japanese American citizens.

A variety of state regulations on immigrants have also raised questions about rights. From the mid-nineteenth century on, many states have enacted statutes prohibiting immigrants from engaging in various types of employment and in some cases of owning property. By the 1860s, California and other Western states had passed a series of laws detrimental to foreigners, particularly Chinese and Mexicans immigrants, taxing them more heavily than citizens and excluding them from many lines of work. Such actions, at times, led to federal intervention. In 1880 the Supreme Court overruled a San Francisco ordinance that discriminated against Chinese in the licensing of laundries. The Court held that the Fourteenth Amendment of the Constitution requires states to grant equal protection of the laws to all persons regardless of nationality. In *Truax v. Reich* the Supreme Court, in 1915, invalidated an Arizona law restricting employment of aliens, ruling that, under equal protection, an alien could not be denied employment in ordinary occupations without the state demonstrating a "special public interest."[12] Justice Charles Evans Hughes asserted,

> The authority to control immigration—to admit or exclude aliens—is vested solely in the federal government. . . . The assertion of an authority to deny to aliens the opportunity of earning a livelihood when lawfully admitted to the state would be tantamount to the assertion of the right to deny them entrance and abode, for in ordinary cases they cannot live where they cannot work.[13]

The courts were slow in applying the Truax decision to most state restrictions on immigrant employment until after World War II. Then, with the postwar increase in concern about the civil rights of minorities, the Supreme Court, in the *Takahashi v. Fish and Game Commission* case in 1948, effectively ended state restrictions on immigrant employment aimed prejudicially at only certain groups, in this instance, the Japanese.[14] In the same year, in *Oyama v. California*, the Court struck down a California law forbidding land ownership by aliens ineligible for citizenship. Justices Frank Murphy and Wiley Rutledge wrote that this statute was "nothing more than an outright racial discrimination."[15]

In the years since 1948, the Supreme Court has both recognized and tried to check the states' use of the "public interest" doctrine in regard to statutes limiting the employment of immigrants within their jurisdiction. In the early 1970s, the Court nullified a New York law that allowed only citizens to fill civil service positions and a Connecticut measure that prohibited noncitizens from practicing law. In 1978 the Court upheld a New York statute that disallowed noncitizens from being state troopers.

Recently, the right of immigrants, particularly undocumented aliens, to publicly provided services and benefits—including education, health, and welfare—has occasioned much debate and effort to limit the scope of public responsibility for undocumented aliens. The concerns derive from a mixture of anti-immigrant feeling, a negative reaction to persons illegally present in the country, and the growing costs of public services. Such concerns have led to a variety of state laws that withhold welfare and services to those who are not citizens or to those who are not legal residents. Especially evident in such cases is public resentment toward the federal government, which makes immigration policy and is responsible for enforcement or lack of enforcement, but leaves it to the states to bear many of the costs related to the presence of immigrants.

In the early 1970s, in the wake of the civil rights movement, the Supreme Court, holding that the Fourteenth Amendment gave equal protection of the law to all persons in the United States, struck down Arizona and Pennsylvania statues that discriminated against noncitizens in terms of welfare benefits. In *Graham v. Richardson* in 1971, the Court ruled that a state could have no "special public interest" in limiting to citizens the expenditure of tax revenues to which aliens have contributed. The Court declared that "classifications based on alienage, like those based on nationality or race, are inherently suspect and subject to close judicial scrutiny. Aliens as a class are a prime example of a 'discrete and insular' minority . . . for which much heightened judicial solicitude is appropriate." It was noted that this was particularly the case since aliens can neither vote nor hold public office, and they are consequently unable to rely on the political process to protect their interests.[16]

One case that has drawn much attention is *Plyler v. Doe*, in which the Supreme Court, in 1982, declared unconstitutional a Texas law that directed school districts to prohibit the attendance of children of undocumented immigrants or to charge them tuition. Justice William Brennan, writing for the majority, maintained that these children were entitled to equal protection under the Constitution, stressed the pivotal importance of education, and cited the need to avoid the creation of a subclass of illiterates, potentially costly to society in terms of unemployment, welfare, and crime. Justice Warren Burger dissented not because he disagreed with the reasoning of the majority, but on the grounds that it is not the role of the Court, but of the "political branches," to remedy social problems in the nation.[17] In 1986, in the *Lewis v. Gross* case, the Federal District Court of New York held that undocumented immigrants were entitled to Medicaid because the federal Medicaid statute did not explicitly exclude them.

While most states follow the dictums of the federal courts in regard to undocumented immigrants, many Americans disagree with these judicial decisions. Opponents have been particularly strong in California because this state has received a larger portion of the nation's legal and illegal immigrants than any other part of the country. In addition, the people of this state, in the early 1990s, faced rising costs of public services and an economic downturn. Thus, an anti-immigrant coalition succeeded in 1994 in having Proposition 187 put on the California ballot. This proposition declared that illegal aliens were not eligible for public education and for most types of public health services: "[A]ny public entity . . . to whom a person has applied for public social services determines or reasonably suspects, based upon the information provided to it, that the person is an alien in the United States in violation of federal law . . . shall not provide the person with benefits or services."[18]

Proposition 187 was supported by Republican Governor Pete Wilson who, at the time, was running for reelection. Both Wilson and the proposition were successful. Proposition 187 passed by 59 percent to 41 percent with wide Caucasian backing. The new statute, in conflict with Plyler and other federal court cases, became the subject of judicial challenge. A federal judge enjoined it from being put into law, and when this action was repeated in 1998, Proposition 187 was virtually dead.

For immigrant residents in the United States, there have been and there continue to be controversies concerning their internationally recognized human rights and their American constitutional rights on the one hand and the rights of the U.S. government to control aliens within the country on the other hand. Contentions are ongoing in respect to immigrant deportation, the rights of deportees to due process, rights of employment, and rights to public state and federal benefits and services.

NOTES

1. *Alien Act of 1798*, U.S. Statutes, 5th Cong., 2d sess., vol. 1, 570–71.
2. *Boston Daily Advertiser*, May 16, 1855.
3. "Reports of County Superintendents of the Poor, *New York State Assembly Documents*, no. 214, 1856, 8–10.
4. *Fong Yue Ting v. United States*, 149 U.S. 698, 743 (1893).
5. Elihu Root, "The Basis of Protection of Citizens Abroad," *American Journal of International Law* 4 (1910): 521–22.
6. *Whitfield, Immigrant Inspector, et al. v. Hanges et al.*, 222 Federal Reporter 745 (1915).
7. *Colyer v. Skeffington*, 265 Federal Reporter 20 (1920).
8. "Support Fair Detention Policies," *In Congress*, American Civil Liberties Union, 1999, 1–3. (www.aclu.org/congress/1081899a.html)
9. Nicholas Kristof, "Seeking Asylum, Some Immigrants Find a Fate Worse Than Criminal," *New York Times*, January 16, 2000, D7.
10. "Stop the Use of Secret Evidence," *Immigrant Rights*, American Civil Liberties Union, January 19, 2000, 1. (www.aclu.org/issues/immigrant/hmir.html)
11. Susan Sachs, "Due Process, but How Much Is Due?" *New York Times*, December 5, 1999, D4.
12. *Truax v. Reich*, 239 U.S. 33 (1915).
13. Ibid.
14. *Takahashi v. Fish and Game Commission*, 334 U.S. 410 (1948).
15. *Oyama v. California*, 332 U.S. 633 (1948).
16. *Graham v. Richardson*, 403 U.S. 365 (1971).
17. *Plyler v. Doe*, 457 U.S. 202 (1982).
18. Quoted in Juan Perea, ed., *Immigrants Out! The New Nativism and the Anti-Immigrant Impulse in the United States* (New York: New York University Press, 1997), 265.

DOCUMENTS

12.1. Alien and Sedition Law Enables President to Deport Aliens without a Trial

The Federalist majority in the U.S. Congress in the 1790s became fearful that French emigrés in America, following the revolution in their own country, might plant radical ideas in the United States. In 1798 Congress passed the Alien and Sedition laws which gave the president the power to deport aliens without a trial. This arbitrary denial of due process was criticized by the Jeffersonian Democratic Republicans, and the law was not renewed when they came to power in 1801.

An Act Concerning Aliens.

Section 1. *Be it enacted by the Senate and House of Representatives of the United States of America in Congress assembled,* That it shall be lawful for the President of the United States at any time during the continuance of this act, to *order* all such *aliens* as he shall judge dangerous to the peace and safety of the United States, or shall have reasonable grounds to suspect are concerned in any treasonable or secret machinations against the government thereof, to depart out of the territory of the United States, within such time as shall be expressed in such order, which order shall be served on such alien by delivering him a copy thereof, or leaving the same at his usual abode, and returned to the office of the Secretary of State, by the marshal or other person to whom the same shall be directed. And in case any alien, so ordered to depart, shall be found at large within the United States after the time limited in such order for his departure, and not having obtained a *license* from the President to reside therein, or having obtained such *license* shall not have conformed thereto, every such alien shall, on conviction thereof, be imprisoned for a term not exceeding three years, and shall never after be admitted to become a citizen of the United States. *Provided always, and be it further enacted,* that if any alien so ordered to depart shall prove to the satisfaction of the President, by evidence to be taken before such person or persons as the President shall direct, who are for that purpose hereby authorized to administer oaths, that no injury or danger to the United States will arise from suffering such alien to reside therein, the President may grant a *license* to such alien to remain within the United States for such time as he shall judge proper, and at such place as he may designate.

* * *

Sec. 2. *And be it further enacted*, That it shall be lawful for the President of the United States, whenever he may deem it necessary for the public safety, to order to be removed out of the territory thereof, any alien who may or shall be in prison in pursuance of this act; and to cause to be arrested and sent out of the United States such of those aliens as shall have been ordered to depart therefrom and shall not have obtained a license as aforesaid, in all cases where, in the opinion of the President, the public safety requires a speedy removal. And if any alien so removed or sent out of the United States by the President shall voluntarily return thereto, unless by permission of the President of the United States, such alien on conviction thereof, shall be imprisoned so long as, in the opinion of the President, the public safety may require.

Source: Alien Act of 1798, U.S. Statutes, 5th Cong., 2d sess., vol. 1, 570–71.

12.2. Supreme Court Rules That Aliens Are Entitled to Due Process

A case involving an order by the U.S. Department of Labor for the deportation of four Greek immigrants, Whitfield, Immigrant Inspector, et al. V. Hanges et al., *came before the U.S. Supreme Court in 1915. The Court declared that, while it was not questioning the grounds for deportation, it had the duty of judging the legality of the deportation proceedings. The Court held that an alien, as well as a citizen, could not be deprived of life, liberty, or property without due process and the equal protection of the law. Thus, in the case before them, the justices ruled that, since the defendants did not have a fair hearing, they were granted relief from the order of deportation.*

Whitfield, Immigrant Inspector, et al. v. Hanges et al.

Circuit Judge Sanborn:

George Hanges, Demetrios Lamper, Steve Pantza, and Peter Francas, citizens of Greece, were resident aliens who had been admitted to the United States pursuant to its acts of Congress prior to 1907. Two of them owned and operated the Main Café in Mason City, Iowa, where they had lived for years, and two of them were employed in the café. They were arrested by the immigrant inspector on October 24, 1913, and such proceedings were had that he found them guilty, recommended their deportation, and held them in confinement in the charge of the sheriff when, on their petition, the court below issued a writ of habeas corpus and, after a return thereto, and answer to the petition, and a full hearing, ordered their discharge. The inspector has appealed from this order on the grounds that the hearing of the appellees was full and fair, and that he committed no abuse of discretion or arbitrary action.

The deportation of the appellees was recommended by the inspector, and they were held in confinement under his finding that they were guilty of the charge that they were aliens employed by or in connection with a music or dance hall, or other place of amusement, habitually frequented by prostitutes, or where prostitutes gather, that they were aliens connected with the management of a house of prostitution, and that they were aliens found receiving, sharing or deriving benefit from a part or the whole of the earnings of prostitutes. . . . It is well to call to mind the rules and principles which govern proceedings in cases of this nature.

1. A full and fair hearing on the charges which threaten his deportation and an absence of all abuse of discretion and arbitrary action by the inspector or other executive officer, are indispensable to the lawful deportation of an alien. Where, by the abuse of the discretion or the arbitrary action of the inspector, or other executive officer, or without a full and fair hearing, an alien is deprived of his liberty, or is about to be deported, the power is conferred and the duty is imposed upon the courts of the United States to issue a writ of habeas corpus and relieve him. . . .

2. An alien, as well as a citizen, is protected by the prohibition of deprivation of life, liberty, or property without due process and the equal protection of the law. This principle is universal. It applies "to all persons within the territorial jurisdiction of the United States without regard to any differences of race, or color, or of nationality." . . .

An alien is entitled to a hearing upon and a decision of the charge that he has violated the acts of Congress and is therefore liable to deprivation of his liberty and deportation, according to "the fundamental principles that inhere in due process of law." It is not competent for an inspector, or the Secretary of Labor, or any executive officer. . . . Arbitrarily to cause an alien who has entered this country and has become subject in all respects to its jurisdiction and a part of its population, although alleged to be illegally here, to be taken into custody and deported without giving him an opportunity to be heard upon the questions involved, his right to be and remain in the United States. No such arbitrary power can exist where the principles involved in due process of law are recognized [Japanese Immigrant Case, 189 U.S. 86, 100, 101].

3. Indispensable requisites of a fair hearing according to these fun-

damental principles are that the course of proceeding shall be appropriate to the case and just to the party affected; that the accused shall be notified of the nature of the charge against him in time to meet it; that he shall have such an opportunity to be heard that he may, if he chooses, cross-examine the witnesses against him; that he may have time and opportunity, after all the evidence against him is produced and known to him, to produce evidence and witnesses to refute it; that the decision shall be governed by and based upon the evidence at the hearing, and that only; and that the decision shall not be without substantial evidence taken at the hearing to support it. . . . That is not a fair hearing in which the inspector chooses or controls the witnesses, or prevents the accused from procuring the witnesses or evidence or counsel he desires. . . .

6. That was not a fair hearing in which the inspector after the hearing imported into the case and based his finding and recommendation of deportation on hearsay and rumors of alleged facts which there was no evidence to support, and which the accused had no notice of and no opportunity to refute at the hearing. . . .

And because the inspector arbitrarily prevented the aliens from consulting their counsel and arbitrarily prevented their counsel from being present and participating in the hearing until after the inspector had examined the aliens in secret, while he and the police officers held them in confinement; because there was no substantial evidence at the hearing in support of the charges against them; because the inspector prevented the accused from procuring testimony of important witnesses; because the inspector based his findings and recommendation of deportation on hearsay that was not in evidence at the hearing, and much of which the accused had no notice of and no opportunity to refute at the hearing the conclusion is that the court below fell into no error and committed no mistake in its finding that the hearing of the accused was unfair and unjust and entitled the appellees to the relief of the court.

Source: *Whitfield, Immigrant Inspector, et al. v. Hanges et al.*, 222 Federal Reporter 745 (1915).

12.3. Federal Court Declares Aliens Have Right to Due Process in Deportation Hearings

Following World War I and the success of the Bolshevik Revolution in Russia, a Red Scare hysteria arose in the United States. Driven by Attorney General A. Mitchell Palmer, the federal government on the basis of legislation passed in 1918 ordered the deportation of several thousand immigrants who were alleged to belong to the Communist Party or other radical organizations. Twenty of the aliens ordered deported petitioned the court for habeas corpus (the right of a person to obtain protection against illegal imprisonment). A federal circuit court, in Colyer v. Skeffington, *declared that, while Congress had the right to legislate the grounds for deportation of aliens, it was the courts' duty to rule on due process (the right of a person to a legal procedure that accords with established rules and principles) in the deportation proceedings. The court declared that aliens have constitutional rights and are protected by the Fourth, Fifth, Sixth, and Fourteenth Amendments. While courts and other governmental authorities have not always provided immigrants with these protections, pressure has been increased in their behalf, particularly in the years since the civil rights movement of the 1960s.*

Colyer v. Skeffington

Circuit Judge Anderson:

These are petitions for habeas corpus brought by or in behalf of 20 aliens against the Commissioner of Immigration at Boston. They were heard together; they fall into two classes: William T. Colyer, Amy Colyer, Frank Mack, Lew Bonder, Frank Matchian, Tehon Lanovoy, Trofim Yarmoluk, Anton Harbatuk, Anton Gessewich, Fred Chaika, Koly Honcheroeff, Adam Musky, and Sedar Serachuk have, after appeal to the Secretary of Labor, been ordered by him to be deported. Seven of the aliens were at the time of the filing of the petitions held at Deer Island by the respondent in default of bail, fixed, on recommendation of Assistant Commissioner of Immigration Sullivan, as follows:

Ivan T. Hyrnchuk	$10,000
Theodore Pashukoff...	5,000
William Maches	5,000
William Chriupko	5,000
Joe Sinkus.............	5,000
Wladimir Serachuk....	5,000
Samuel Drakewich	5,000

Near the end of the long hearing, in which it clearly appeared that none of the aliens were in any way involved, by the use of bombs, guns, or other weapons, in plans of injuring persons or property, and that the cases could not for many months be finally disposed of, the writs were ordered issued, and all the petitioners admitted by this court to bail in the sum of $500 each. No such responsibility would have been taken by the court if there had been a scintilla of evidence that any alien thus set at liberty was committed in any way to acts of force or violence against person or property.

At the opening of the trial the cases were said by counsel on both sides to be, in many important aspects, test cases of the legality of an undertaking of the government to deport several thousand aliens' alleged to be proscribed by a portion of section 1 of the Act of October 16, 1918, as follows:

That . . . aliens who are members of or affiliated with any organization that entertains a belief in, teaches, or advocates the overthrow by force or violence of the government of the United States . . . shall be excluded from admission into the United States.

Section 2 (section 4289¼*b* [2]) provides for the deportation of such aliens, irrespective of the time of their entry.

The sole charge against these aliens is membership in the Communist Party or the Communist Labor Party. The proposition of the Department of Justice, adopted by the Commissioner General of Immigration, as hereafter set forth, is that membership in one of these parties is, alone, enough to bring the aliens within the purview of this provision; that both parties are committed to a scheme to overthrow our government by force or violence. In both classes of cases the petitioners attack, on grounds fatal if sustained, the validity of the proceedings, instituted by the government on January 2, 1920, for their deportation. . . .

A preliminary statement of the well-settled and familiar principles of law on which all of these habeas corpus cases involving the exclusion or deportation of aliens depend will bring into clearer perspective the field of facts in which this court must perform its most important duties.

1. It has been repeatedly held that "the right to exclude or to expel all aliens, or any class of aliens, absolutely or upon certain conditions, in war or in peace," is "an inherent and inalienable right of every sovereign and independent nation, essential to its safety, its independence, and its welfare"; that this "power to exclude and to expel aliens, being a power affecting international relations, is vested in the political departments of the government, and is to be regulated by treaty or by act of Congress, and to be executed by the executive authority according to the regulations so established, except so far as the judicial department has been authorized by treaty or by statute, or is required by the paramount law of the Constitution, to intervene."

Otherwise stated, there is no constitutional limit to the power of Congress to exclude or expel aliens. An invitation once extended to the alien to come within our borders may be withdrawn. He has no vested right to remain. This was expressly adjudicated in the Chinese Exclusion Cases, 130 U.S. 581, in which the Supreme Court unanimously held that the fact that a Chinese laborer had legally entered the United States conferred upon him no right of which he could not be deprived by a subsequent act of Congress.

2. It is also familiar and perfectly well-settled law that the courts have no jurisdiction, on habeas corpus proceedings, to interfere with the proceedings in the Department of Labor concerning the exclusion or the expulsion of aliens, unless and until there is some error of law in that department. Unless the proceedings in that department are unfair, thus lacking some of the essential elements of due process of law, or are based upon some misconstruction of the statute or disregard of the rules made pursuant thereto, or on other vitiating error of law, the courts have no jurisdiction. In these habeas corpus cases, therefore, it may be said that the primary function of the court is to try, not the right of the alien to enter or to remain in the United States, but to try the trial of the alien in the Department of Labor; if that trial was fair and legal, even though the result was, in the opinion of the court, erroneous on the facts, the court has no right to interfere; it may not, in habeas corpus proceedings, usurp the function that Congress has delegated by statute to the Department of Labor.

3. But, while the courts have no jurisdiction on habeas corpus to substitute their judgment on pure questions of fact for that of the Secretary of Labor, it is equally well settled that if the proceedings in the Department of Labor are shown to be unfair or otherwise lacking in the essential elements of due process of law, then the courts must review.

4. While deportation proceedings are not criminal proceedings, aliens who are thereby deprived of their liberty may have their legal right to liberty tested on habeas corpus proceedings. . . .

Aliens have constitutional rights. The Fourth, Fifth, Sixth, and Fourteenth Amendments are not limited in their application to citizens. They apply generally to all persons within the jurisdiction of the United States.

Source: *Colyer v. Skeffington*, 265 Federal Reporter 20 (1920).

12.4. Federal Laws Criticized for Detaining Accused Alien Terrorists Without Due Process

The involvement of the United States, since World War II, in conflicts worldwide, and particularly in the Middle East, has resulted in the reality and the fear of terrorist attacks abroad and at home. In 1996, following the bombing of the World Trade Center in New York City, Congress passed the Anti-Terrorism and Effective Death Penalty Act and the Illegal Immigration Reform and Immigrant Responsibility Act. One result of these stat-

utes has been an increase in both mandatory detention and indefinite detention of immigrants. The American Civil Liberties Union has argued that mandatory detention violates due process and that indefinite detention is unconstitutional.

The 1996 Anti-terrorism and Effective Death Penalty Act (AEDPA) and the 1996 Illegal Immigration Reform and Immigrant Responsibility Act (IIRAIRA) have had the combined effect of dramatically increasing the number of immigrants in Immigration and Naturalization Services (INS) detention from 8,500 in 1996 to nearly 16,000 in 1998. While detention-related problems are legion, we focus here on two: mandatory detention of non-citizens awaiting a decision as to whether they are deportable, and indefinite detention of non-citizens ordered removed to countries that will not accept them.

MANDATORY DETENTION

A rational detention policy and the right to due process both demand that INS be given, and that it fairly exercise, discretion to ensure that only those non-citizens who are a danger to the community or a flight risk are detained pending a decision on whether the non-citizen is removable from the United States.

AEDPA required the mandatory detention of non-citizens convicted of a wide range of offenses, including minor drug offenses. IIRIRA further expanded the list of offenses for which mandatory detention was required. Under these amendments, Congress required the detention of non-citizens convicted of *any* two crimes of moral turpitude (regardless of when the crimes were committed or potential sentence they carried), or any one crime of moral turpitude for which a sentence of at least one year was imposed (even if suspended). In other words, even if the person was convicted of a crime for which no time in prison was actually served because the crime was so insignificant, the person might be subjected to mandatory detention on account of that crime while his deportation case was pending. In addition, by expanding the definition of "aggravated felonies" to include even misdemeanors under state law, Congress dramatically increased the categories of crimes for which mandatory detention could be imposed.

Mandatory detention of non-citizens pending their immigration proceedings violates the right to due process and is inefficient and costly. The burden placed on the family of the detainee is substantial. The Attorney General should have the discretion (subject to judicial review) to release non-citizens awaiting resolution of their cases if the non-citizen is not a danger to the community or a flight risk. Mandatory detention also stymies development of alternatives to detention that would address legitimate concerns about insuring the appearance and ultimate removal of deportable aliens.

Mandatory detention violates due process. By depriving individuals of any opportunity to demonstrate their suitability for release, mandatory detention violates a principle fundamental to our legal system—that people cannot be deprived of liberty without due process of law. In other pretrial settings, the courts have found that the Constitution clearly prohibits mandatory detention absent proof of danger or a flight risk. Federal courts in New York, Massachusetts, Illinois, Michigan, Minnesota, Colorado, Oregon and California have come to the same conclusion in the immigration context.

Furthermore, many of those subject to mandatory detention are ultimately found eligible for relief from deportation and are not deported. For example, a lawful permanent resident ("LPR") who is deportable based on a crime that is not deemed an "aggravated felony" remains eligible for naturalization. In addition, a non-LPR with an aggravated felony conviction may be eligible for relief as well, depending on the circumstances. These individuals have an obvious incentive to appear for their immigration proceedings and are unlikely to flee. Yet, they too are subject to mandatory detention, notwithstanding alternative means to insure appearance at hearings, such as bond and reporting requirements. In addition, many of those subject to mandatory detention pose no danger to the community. They have been convicted of relatively minor crimes, or have since demonstrated rehabilitation.

Mandatory detention is irrational and costly. Given INS's limited detention space, it is irrational and inefficient to require unnecessary and costly detention of individuals who pose neither a danger to the community nor a flight risk. The INS recognizes this and has proposed legislation to restore discretion to release such non-citizens. Detention costs the INS on average $58 a day per detainee, and one-half million dollars per day cumulatively, to detain aliens in state and local jails. In addition, many of those detained are longtime residents of the United States with U.S. citizen family members who depend on them for economic and emotional support. Detention interferes with their ability to work and support their families, resulting in additional costs to the government, which must often step in to provide for these families. According to Human Rights Watch, detainees held in prisons and jails are subjected to inhumane living conditions such as inadequate and poor nourishment, lack of clothing, and overcrowding and that correctional officers often lack the language skills necessary to meet special needs of immigrants.

Mandatory detention interferes with the development of detention alternatives. Mandatory detention also hampers INS initiatives to develop alternatives to detention. These initiatives, such as the ambitious 3-year contract INS entered into with the Vera institute for Criminal Justice to test an "Appearance Assistance Project," offer the possibility of developing alternatives to detention that could more efficiently and humanely insure the appearance of non-citizens at their immigration hearings and restore integrity to the removal process. The new detention mandates limit attempts to test the effectiveness of these alternatives to detention.

Non-citizens who do not pose a risk to the community or flight risk should be released pending resolution of their cases.

INDEFINITE DETENTION

The detention mandates described above apply to non-citizens awaiting a determination as to whether they are removable from the United States. Indefinite detention applies to non-citizens ordered removed from the United States whose countries refuse to accept them or who have no country because they are stateless. INS officials often refer to these individuals as "lifers." This reflects the current INS policy of detaining indefinitely non-citizens ordered removed, even if there is virtually no chance they will actually be removed. "Lifers" come from countries such as Laos, Vietnam, Iraq, Cuba, Iran, and the former Soviet Union.

Prior to 1990, there was a six-month limit on how long INS could detain a non-citizen with a final order of deportation. After the six-month period expired, the non-citizen had to be released under supervision unless he or she was obstructing deportation. The law was changed in 1990 when Congress created an exception to the six-month release rule for "aggravated felons." In 1996, IIRAIRA and AEDPA expanded the definition of "aggravated felony." As a direct result, the number of non-citizens subjected to indefinite detention increased dramatically. According to the INS, approximately 3,500 detained non-citizens cannot be removed. They face life-long detention for crimes committed for which they have already served their criminal sentences. The INS asserts the unbridled power to indefinitely detain any non-citizen it has failed to remove from the United States if it decides that person may be dangerous.

Indefinite detention is a feature we expect of repressive regimes, not of our own. The INS's authority to detain a non-citizen ordered removed derives from one purpose: effectuating removal. Once it becomes clear that removal is not possible, the rationale for continued detention evaporates and the non-citizen's liberty rights demand that he or she be released under supervision. It is grossly unfair to detain a person forever, after they have served their time in prison, just because the INS has been unable to remove them.

The courts are beginning to agree. Several federal district courts have recently ruled that indefinite detention with no realistic prospect of removal is unconstitutional. On July 9, a panel of five district court judges in Seattle reached the same conclusion in five cases that should have nation-wide implications.

It is time for Congress to agree as well. Legislation will likely be introduced in September to reign-in the power of the INS to continue to detain non-citizens ordered removed after it becomes clear that they are clearly not-removable. Under the legislation, such persons would be released under conditions of supervision designed to ensure their ultimate removal should removal become possible in the future.

Source: "Support Fair Detention Policies," *In Congress*, American Civil Liberties Union, August 18, 1999, 1–4. (http://www.aclu.org/congress/1081899a.html)

12.5. Supreme Court Declares Right of Undocumented Children to Attend Public Schools

Since World War II, particularly after the civil rights movement of the 1960s, the Supreme Court increasingly has demanded that the equal protection of the law and due process be accorded immigrants in cases related to statutes enacted by individual states. In 1982, in Plyler v. Doe, *the Court ruled against a Texas statute that forbade its public schools to accept children of undocumented immigrants. Justice William Brennan of the majority argued that an alien, even if undocumented, was still a person within the jurisdiction of the United States and as such was entitled to constitutional due process and equal protection. Chief Justice Warren Burger, of the minority, argued that court decisions to remedy social problems are examples of unwarranted judicial action.*

Opinion of the Court, Mr. Justice Brennan.

The Fourteenth Amendment provides that "[n]o State shall . . . deprive any person of life, liberty, or property, without due process of law; nor deny to *any person within its jurisdiction* the equal protection of the laws." Appellants argue at the outset that undocumented aliens, because of their immigration status, are not "persons within the jurisdiction" of the State of Texas, and that they therefore have no right to the equal protection of Texas law. We reject this argument. Whatever his status under the immigration laws, an alien is surely a "person" in any ordinary sense of that term. Aliens, even aliens whose presence in this country is unlawful, have long been recognized as "persons" guaranteed due process of law by the Fifth and Fourteenth Amendments. Indeed, we have clearly held that the Fifth Amendment protects aliens whose presence in this country is unlawful from invidious discrimination by the Federal Government.

Appellants seek to distinguish our prior cases, emphasizing that the Equal Protection Clause directs a State to afford its protection to persons *within its jurisdiction* while the Due Process Clauses of the Fifth and Fourteenth Amendments contain no such assertedly limiting phrase. In appellants' view, persons who have entered the United States illegally are not "within the jurisdiction" of a State even if they are present within a State's boundaries and subject to its laws. Neither our cases nor the logic of the Fourteenth Amendment supports that constricting construction of the phrase "within its jurisdiction." We have never suggested that the class of persons who might avail themselves of the equal protection guarantee is less than coextensive with that entitled to due process. To the contrary, we have recognized that both provisions were fashioned to protect an identical class of persons, and to reach every exercise of state authority. . . .

There is simply no support for appellants' suggestion that "due process" is somehow of greater stature than "equal protection" and therefore available to a larger class of persons. To the contrary, each aspect of the Fourteenth Amendment reflects an elementary limitation on state power. To permit a State to employ the phrase "within its jurisdiction" in order to identify subclasses of persons whom it would define as beyond its jurisdiction, thereby relieving itself of the obligation to assure that its laws are designed and applied equally to those persons, would undermine the principal purpose for which the Equal Protection Clause was incorporated in the Fourteenth Amendment. The Equal Protection Clause was intended to work nothing less than the abolition of all caste-based and invidious class-based legislation. That objective is fundamentally at odds with the power the State asserts here to classify persons subject to its laws as nonetheless excepted from its protection. . . .

Use of the phrase "within its jurisdiction" thus does not detract from, but rather confirms, the understanding that the protection of the Fourteenth Amendment extends to anyone, citizen or stranger, who *is* subject to the laws of a State, and reaches into every corner of a State's territory. That a person's initial entry into a State, or into the United States, was unlawful, and that he may for that reason be expelled, cannot negate the simple fact of his presence within the State's territorial perimeter. Given such presence, he is subject to the full range of obligations imposed by the State's civil and criminal laws. And until he leaves the jurisdiction—either voluntarily, or involuntarily in accordance with the Constitution and laws of the United States—he is entitled to the equal protection of the laws that a State may choose to establish.

Our conclusion that the illegal aliens who are plaintiffs in these cases may claim the benefit of the Fourteenth Amendment's guarantee of equal protection only begins the inquiry. The more difficult question is whether the Equal Protection Clause has been violated by the refusal of the State of Texas to reimburse local school boards for the education of children who cannot demonstrate that their presence within the United States is lawful, or by the imposition by those school boards of the burden of tuition on those children. It is to this question that we now turn. . . .

Sheer incapability or lax enforcement of the laws barring-entry into this country coupled with the failure to establish an effective bar to the employment of undocumented aliens, has resulted in the creation of a substantial "shadow population" of illegal migrants—numbering in the millions—within our borders. This situation raises the specter of a permanent caste of undocumented resident aliens, encouraged by some to remain here as a source of cheap labor, but nevertheless denied the benefits that our society makes available to citizens and lawful residents. The existence of such an underclass presents most difficult problems for a Nation that prides itself on adherence to principles of equality under law.

The children who are plaintiffs in these cases are special members of this underclass. Persuasive arguments support the view that a State may withhold its beneficence from those whose very presence within the United States is the product of their own unlawful conduct. These arguments do not apply with the same force to classifications imposing disabilities on the minor *children* of such illegal entrants. At the least, those who elect to enter our territory by stealth and in violation of our law should be prepared to bear the consequences, including, but not limited to, deportation. But the children of those illegal entrants are not comparably situated. Their "parents have the ability to conform their conduct to societal norms," and presumably the ability to remove them selves from the State's jurisdiction; but the children who are plaintiffs in these cases "can affect neither their parents' conduct nor their own status." . . .

Of course, undocumented status is not irrelevant to any proper legislative goal. Nor is undocumented status an absolutely immutable characteristic since it is the product of conscious, indeed unlawful, action. But § 21.031 is directed against children, and imposes its discriminatory burden on the basis of a legal characteristic over which children can have little control. It is thus difficult to conceive of a rational justification for penalizing these children for their presence within the United States. Yet that appears to be precisely the effect of § 21.031.

Public education is not a "right" granted to individuals by the Constitution. But neither is it merely some governmental "benefit" indistinguishable from other forms of social welfare legislation. Both the importance of education in maintaining our basic institutions, and the lasting impact of its deprivation on the life of the child, mark the distinction. The "American people have always regarded education and

[the] acquisition of knowledge as matters of supreme importance." We have recognized "the public schools as a most vital civic institution for the preservation of a democratic system of government," and as the primary vehicle for transmitting "the values on which our society rests." "[A]s . . . pointed out early in our history, . . . some degree of education is necessary to prepare citizens to participate effectively and intelligently in our open political system if we are to preserve freedom and independence." In addition, education provides the basic tools by which individuals might lead economically productive lives to the benefit of us all. In sum, education has a fundamental role in maintaining the fabric of our society. We cannot ignore the significant social costs borne by our Nation when select groups are denied the means to absorb the values and skills upon which our social order rests.

In addition to the pivotal role of education in sustaining our political and cultural heritage, denial of education to some isolated group of children poses an affront to one of the goals of the Equal Protection Clause: the abolition of governmental barriers presenting unreasonable obstacles to advancement on the basis of individual merit. Paradoxically, by depriving the children of any disfavored group of an education, we foreclose the means by which that group might raise the level of esteem in which it is held by the majority. But more directly, "education prepares individuals to be self-reliant and self-sufficient participants in society." Illiteracy is an enduring disability. The inability to read and write will handicap the individual deprived of a basic education each and every day of his life. The inestimable toll of that deprivation on the social, economic, intellectual, and psychological well-being of the individual, and the obstacle it poses to individual achievement, make it most difficult to reconcile the cost or the principle of a status-based denial of basic education with the framework of equality embodied in the Equal Protection Clause.

Dissenting Opinion, Chief Justice Burger.

Were it our business to set the Nation's social policy, I would agree without hesitation that it is senseless for an enlightened society to deprive any children—including illegal aliens—of an elementary education. I fully agree that it would be folly—and wrong—to tolerate creation of a segment of society made up of illiterate persons, many having a limited or no command of our language. However, the Constitution does not constitute us as "Platonic Guardians" nor does it vest in this Court the authority to strike down laws because they do not meet our standards of desirable social policy, "wisdom," or "common sense." We trespass on the assigned function of the political branches under our structure of limited and separated powers when we assume a policy-making role as the Court does today.

The Court makes no attempt to disguise that it is acting to make up for Congress's lack of "effective leadership" in dealing with the serious national problems caused by the influx of uncountable millions of illegal aliens across our borders. The failure of enforcement of the immigration laws over more than a decade and the inherent difficulty and expense of sealing our vast borders have combined to create a grave socio-economic dilemma. It is a dilemma that has not yet even been fully assessed, let alone addressed. However, it is not the function of the judiciary to provide "effective leadership" simply because the political branches of government fail to do so.

The Court's holding today manifests the justly criticized judicial tendency to attempt speedy and wholesale formulation of "remedies" for the failures—or simply the laggard pace—of the political processes of our system of government. The Court employs, and in my view abuses, the Fourteenth Amendment in an effort to become an omnipotent and omniscient problem solver. That the motives for doing so are noble and compassionate does not alter the fact that the Court distorts our constitutional function to make amends for the defaults of others. . . .

The dispositive issue in these cases, simply put, is whether, for purposes of allocating its finite resources, a state has a legitimate reason to differentiate between persons who are lawfully within the state and those who are unlawfully there. The distinction the State of Texas has drawn—based not only upon its own legitimate interests but on classifications established by the Federal Government in its immigration laws and policies—is not unconstitutional.

The Court acknowledges that, except in those cases when state classifications disadvantage a "suspect class" or impinge upon a "fundamental right," the Equal Protection Clause permits a state "substantial latitude" in distinguishing between different groups of persons. Moreover, the Court expressly—and correctly—rejects any suggestion that illegal aliens are a suspect class, or that education is a fundamental right. Yet by patching together bits and pieces of what might be termed quasi-suspect class and quasi-fundamental-rights analysis, the Court spins out a theory custom-tailored to the facts of these cases.

In the end, we are told little more than that the level of scrutiny employed to strike down the Texas law applies only when illegal alien children are deprived of a public education. If ever a court was guilty of an unabashedly result-oriented approach, this case is a prime example.

The Court first suggests that these illegal alien children, although not a suspect class, are entitled to special solicitude under the Equal Protection Clause because they lack "control" over or "responsibility" for their unlawful entry into this country. Similarly, the Court appears to take the position that § 21.031 is presumptively "irrational" because it has the effect of imposing "penalties" on "innocent" children. However, the Equal Protection Clause does not preclude legislators from classifying among persons on the basis of factors and characteristics over which individuals may be said to lack "control." Indeed, in some circumstances persons generally, and children in particular, may have little control over or responsibility for such things as their ill health, need for public assistance, or place of residence. Yet a state legislature is not barred from considering, for example, relevant differences between the mentally healthy and the mentally ill, or between the residents of different counties, simply because these may be factors unrelated to individual choice or to any "wrongdoing." The Equal Protection Clause protects against arbitrary and irrational classifications, and against invidious discrimination stemming from prejudice and hostility; it is not an all-encompassing "equalizer" designed to eradicate every distinction for which persons are not "responsible."

The Court does not presume to suggest that appellees' purported lack of culpability for their illegal status prevents them from being deported or otherwise "penalized" under federal law. Yet would deportation be any less a "penalty" than denial of privileges provided to legal residents? Illegality of presence in the United States does not—and need not—depend on some amorphous concept of "guilt" or "innocence" concerning an alien's entry. Similarly, a state's use of federal immigration status as a basis for legislative classification is not necessarily rendered suspect for its failure to take such factors into account. . . .

[T]he Court's analysis rests on the premise that, although public education is not a constitutionally guaranteed right, "neither is it merely some governmental 'benefit' indistinguishable from other forms of social welfare legislation." Whatever meaning or relevance this opaque observation might have in some other context, it simply has no bearing on the issues at hand. Indeed, it is never made clear what the Court's opinion means on this score.

The importance of education is beyond dispute. Yet we have held repeatedly that the importance of a governmental service does not elevate it to the status of a "fundamental right" for purposes of equal protection analysis. Moreover, the Court points to no meaningful way to distinguish between education and other governmental benefits in this context. Is the Court suggesting that education is more "fundamental" than food, shelter, or medical care? . . .

Denying a free education to illegal alien children is not a choice I would make were I a legislator. Apart from compassionate considerations, the long-range costs of excluding any children from the public schools may well outweigh the costs of educating them. But that is not the issue: the fact that there are sound *policy* arguments against the Texas Legislature's choice does not render that choice an unconstitutional one.

The Constitution does not provide a cure for every social ill, nor does it vest judges with a mandate to try to remedy every social problem.

Moreover, when this Court rushes in to remedy what it perceives to be the failings of the political processes, it deprives those processes of an opportunity to function. When the political institutions are not forced to exercise constitutionally allocated powers and responsibilities, those powers, like muscles not used, tend to atrophy. Today's cases, I regret to say, present yet another example of unwarranted judicial action which in the long run tends to contribute to the weakening of our political processes.

Source: *Plyler v. Doe*, 457 U.S. 202 (1982).

12.6. The Supreme Court Ruling in the *Plyler* Case Has Been Criticized by Some and Supported by Others in the Years Since 1982

The Plyler decision of the Supreme Court (See Document 12.5), requiring states to provide regular public education for the children of undocumented immigrants, drew much support from pro-immigrant Americans, vigorous opposition from anti-immigrant groups, and interest and concern in legal circles. Professor Peter Schuck of the Yale Law School, a major authority on American immigrant law, warned about the potential impact of this decision in an article published in the January 1984 Columbia Law Review. *According to Schuck, the courts' efforts to protect the rights to education for innocent children of undocumented immigrants undermines state and federal government efforts, and thus the sovereign rights of the nation, to thwart illegal immigration. While the courts have been slow to build on the precedents established in the Plyler case, the principles involved therein were instrumental in the court's nullification of California's Proposition 187, which denied undocumented immigrants access to a number of public services.*

The Supreme Court's recent decision in *Plyler v. Doe*, compelling a state to provide the children of undocumented aliens with a free public education, may ultimately come to have the same epochal significance for that group that *Brown v. Board of Education* has had for black Americans. In one sense, of course, *Plyler* may be read narrowly as nothing more than an equal protection case in which the state failed to adduce a "substantial purpose" for treating the children of undocumented aliens differently than it treated their documented alien or citizen peers. In this view, the question of how the national community ought to be defined was not even at issue: *Plyler*, after all, invalidated a state law, not a federal one, and only the latter can prescribe the contours of that community. But in another, broader sense, the decision may mark a fundamental break with classical immigration law's concept of national community and of the scope of congressional power to decide who is entitled to the benefits of membership.

Plyler effects this change on three different levels. First, it inducts into the national community a new group of uncertain size and composition. These uncertainties do not simply reflect our ignorance about which aliens are here illegally and how numerous they are, for even the defining characteristic of the new group remains opaque. Previous expansions of the national community, most notably the fourteenth amendment's extension of citizenship to the freed slaves and the nineteenth amendment's extension of suffrage to women, admitted well-defined, undifferentiated categories of individuals; within those categories, membership was universal. But neither *Plyler*'s holding about public benefits nor its more general spirit necessarily embraces undocumented aliens as an undifferentiated group. To be sure, the Court reaffirmed a principle that had been clearly established for a century—that all aliens "within" the United States, whatever their legal status, are entitled to some constitutional protection. But it was the "innocent" children, not their "guilty" parents, to whom Texas denied equal protection; although it is children, not parents, who attend public school, the unconstitutionality of the state law involved more than the withholding of educational benefits from aliens in general. Had Texas adopted an analogous system of free public *adult* education or job training, for example, the Court apparently would not have upheld an equal protection claim by the *parents*. The enduring importance of education benefits for *children*, moreover, accounted both for the level of scrutiny selected and the extent of the right created.

These narrowing distinctions—between undocumented alien parents and their children, and between education and other services—raise a number of significant problems with the Court's reasoning, and suggest that those distinctions may be difficult to sustain in future cases. For example, the Court failed to explain why denying educational benefits to an innocent child differs from the denial of other governmental benefits to her undocumented parent, upon whose income and well-being the child's welfare ultimately depends. If Texas may not harm innocent children by depriving them of access to public education, why may it harm these same innocents—who may actually be United States *citizens*—even more grievously by denying their parents access to welfare benefits or public or private employment, which provides their essential economic support? Does *Plyler* mean that a state may not exclude from public housing a family in which an adult has committed a crime? Can the Court's "innocent children" rationale be harmonized with its willingness to allow the routine deportation of children who are not only innocent of their parents' wrongdoing but are United States citizens? Are not these deprivations as directly a result of parental status or wrongdoing as the deprivation that the Court refused to countenance in *Plyler*? Because the Court addressed none of these questions, the potential scope of *Plyler* remains an open question.

Second, *Plyler* not only enlarged the national community to uncertain dimensions and on the basis of uncertain principles, but did so in the face of a congressional policy to exclude undocumented aliens from the country *altogether*. Some have doubted that such a policy can even be said to exist, given the historical ambivalence of Southern States toward the entry of low-cost agricultural labor. In *Plyler*, the Court went so far as to deny that the Texas statute "corresponds to any identifiable congressional policy," or "operate[s] harmoniously within the federal program."

This proposition is demonstrably false, at least under current conditions. Unauthorized entry, after all, is a federal crime. In recent years, considerable law enforcement effort has been devoted to preventing it. Congress has excluded undocumented aliens from numerous federal benefit programs. Indeed, the Court only six years earlier in *De Canas v. Bica* had deemed Congress's policy against illegal aliens to be strong enough to sustain a state statute barring their employment; it was enough for the Court that the statute was consistent with federal law. The *Plyler* majority's effort to distinguish *De Canas* is utterly unpersuasive. Its other arguments—that because some undocumented aliens might ultimately escape deportation and because denial of benefits did not stem the influx of illegal aliens, Texas's approach was thereby rendered irrational—stand on no firmer ground. If substantial effectiveness were the criterion, most regulatory statutes would probably be doomed. Certainly, there are few areas in which the public policy options are as problematic as in the control of illegal immigration. What is disturbing about *Plyler* is not that it makes the policymaker's task more difficult—any judicial invalidation of a statute does that. *Plyler*'s peculiar vice is that it uses the inherent difficulty of a problem as a justification for making it even more intractable.

Third, *Plyler* could perhaps be understood and even defended as a case of federal preemption that merely reaffirms the exclusive, plenary power of Congress to regulate immigration. This view, however, is undercut by the Court's previous decision in *De Canas*. That case announced a broad tolerance for state legislation that discourages immigration in areas traditionally of local concern, such as labor markets and public education, in ways that are generally consistent with federal policy. Unless this aspect of *De Canas* has been overruled sub silentio, *Plyler* must be seen as the germination of a new and quite different principle. This principle seems to be that a state may not seek to discourage illegal entry by means of disincentives that may harm the children of those who, because the disincentives are ineffective, decide to enter anyway. This principle, of course, would have dictated a different result in *De Canas,* since it would have invalidated the statute in that case. Even more important, the principle would seem to require that result even if *Congress,* rather than a state, enacted the statute.

If that is the meaning of *Plyler,* it constitutes a conceptual watershed in immigration law, the most powerful rejection to date of classical immigration law's notion of plenary national sovereignty over our borders. If those to whom we have refused entry are entitled by their mere presence—together with the presence of their children—to claim not only constitutional procedural protections, but also the significant substantive entitlements that legislatures grant to lawful residents, then immigration law's ideal of national community has also been transformed. In the classical view, the political branches of government defined the boundaries of that community and the consequences of exclusion. That definition, responsive to the political values, local interests and policy concerns that animate Congress, has tended to exclude those whose entry was believed to threaten these interests. The most important meaning of *Plyler* may be that the courts are beginning to assert a coordinate, if not supervisory, role in defining the dimensions and meaning of national community in the immigration context. Courts are expositors of a constitutional tradition that increasingly emphasizes not the parochial and the situational, but the universal, transcendant values of equality and fairness imminent in the due process and equal protection principles. In that capacity, they have also asserted a larger role in the creation and distribution of opportunities and status in the administrative state. In *Plyler,* the Supreme Court moved boldly on both fronts. In doing so, the Court seems to have begun to redefine the community to include all those whose destinies have somehow, even in violation of our law, become linked with ours.

Source: Peter Schuck, "The Transformation of Immigration Law," *Columbia Law Review* 84, no. 1 (January 1984): 54–58.

ANNOTATED SELECTED BIBLIOGRAPHY

Balderrama, Francisco, and Raymond Rodriguez. *Decade of Betrayal: Mexican Repatriation in the 1930s*. Albuquerque: University of New Mexico Press, 1995. Reports on the unlawful search and seizure of Mexican Americans during the 1930s Great Depression and their wholesale deportation, including some persons who were American citizens.

Carliner, David, et al. *The Right of Aliens and Refugees: The Basic ACLU Guide to Alien and Refugee Rights*, 2d ed. Carbondale: Southern Illinois University Press, 1990. A compilation of the rights of aliens as of 1990 including rights to work, own property, receive government benefits, remain in the United States, and rights during deportation proceedings.

Chang, Robert. *Dis-Oriented: Asian Americans, Law, and the Nation-State*. New York: New York University Press, 1996. Discusses legal restraints, including the deprivation of rights, placed on Asian Americans across the decades of U.S. history.

Claghorn, Kate. *The Immigrant's Day in Court*. New York: Harper and Brothers, 1923. Includes information on immigrant laws and court cases during the second wave of immigration and deportation actions in 1919 and 1920.

Daniel, Roger. *Prisoners without Trial: Japanese Americans in World War II*. New York: Hill and Wang, 1993. Discusses the how and why of Japanese American incarceration during World War II.

Guerin-Gonzales, Camille. *Mexican Workers and American Dreams: Immigration, Repatriation and California Labor 1900–1939*. New Brunswick, N.J.: Rutgers University Press, 1994. Treats the early twentieth-century flow of Mexicans into California in search of work, their usefulness for employers, and the abrogation of their rights in their expulsion during the Great Depression.

Hofstetter, Richard R., ed. *U.S. Immigration Policy*. Durham, N.C.: Duke University Press, 1984. Analyzes the place of rights in terms of other forces that have helped to shape American immigration policy in the post–World War II era.

Hull, Elizabeth. *Without Justice for All: The Constitutional Rights of Aliens*. Westport, Conn.: Greenwood Press, 1985. Discusses the extent to which constitutional rights are extended and not extended to aliens in the United States.

Maki, Mitchell, et al. *Achieving the Impossible Dream: How Japanese Americans Obtained Redress*. Urbana: University of Illinois Press, 1999. Describes how Japanese Americans continued to fight for their rights after World War II.

Murray, Robert. *Red Scare: A Study in National Hysteria, 1919–1920*. Minneapolis: University of Minnesota Press, 1955. Discusses the suppression of rights and the deportation of aliens accused of radical affiliations in the years immediately following World War I.

Panunzio, Constantine. *The Deportation Cases of 1919–1920*. New York: Commission on the Church and Social Service, Federal Council of the Churches of Christ in America. Reprint, New York: Da Capo Press, 1970. Details the abrogation of rights of aliens in the anti-red hysteria deportation cases against foreign-born persons accused of being radicals following World War I.

Pozzetta, George, ed. *Law, Crime, Justice: Naturalization and Citizenship*. Vol. 17, *American Immigration and Ethnicity*. New York: Garland Publishing, 1991. Contains articles on laws and court cases relating to the rights of immigrants who have settled in the United States.

Smith, James Morton. *Freedom's Fetters: The Alien and Sedition Law and American Civil Liberties*. Ithaca, N.Y.: Cornell University Press, 1956. Gives an account of the Alien and Sedition laws passed in the 1790s and how they ran counter to the rights of Americans.

U.S. Commission on Civil Rights. *The Tarnished Golden Door: Civil Rights Issues in Immigration*. Washington, D.C.: U.S. Government Printing Office, 1980. In the wake of the civil rights movement, this government report describes the multiple ways in which rights were being denied to immigrants in the United States.

ORGANIZATIONS AND WEB SITES

American Civil Liberties Union: www.aclu.org

American Immigration Control Foundation: www.cfw.com

American Immigration Lawyers Association: www.aila.org

Americas Watch: www.hrw.org

Center for Human Rights and Constitutional Law: www.centerforhumanrights.org

Federation for American Immigration Reform: www.fairus.org

Latino Issues Forum: www.lif.org

League of United Latin American Citizens: www.lulac.org

National Immigration Law Center: www.nilc.org

National Network for Immigration and Refugee Rights: www.nnirr.org

Social Contract: www.thesocialcontract.com

U.S. Border Control: www.usbc.org

Appendix 1: Immigration to the United States by Country for the Decades from 1820 to 1995

Figures are approximate because of different counting methods.

Notes: From 1820–1867, figures represent alien passengers arrived; from 1868–1891 and 1895–1897, immigrant aliens arrived; from 1892–1894 and 1898 to the present time, immigrant aliens admitted. Data for the years prior to 1906 relate to country whence alien came; data from 1906–1979 and 1984 are for country of last permanent residence; and data for 1980–1983 refer to country of birth. Because of changes in boundaries and changes in lists of countries, data for certain countries are not comparable throughout.

The periods covered are as follows: from 1820–1831 and 1843–1849, the fiscal years ended on September 30 of the respective year—fiscal year 1843 covers 9 months. From 1832–1842 and 1850–1867, fiscal years ended on December 31 of the respective year—fiscal years 1832 and 1850 cover 15 months. For 1868, the period ended on June 30 and covers 6 months. Fiscal years 1868–1976 ended on June 30 of the respective year. The transition quarter (TQ) for 1976 covers the 3-month period, July–September 1976.

Source: Leonard Dinnerstein and David M. Reimers, *Ethnic Americans: A History of Immigration* 4th ed. (New York: Columbia University Press, 1999), 218–21.

Table A.1 Immigration to the United States by Country for Decades 1820–1995

Country	*1820*	*1821–1830*	*1831–1840*	*1841–1850*	*1851–1860*	*1861–1870*
All countries	8,385	143,439	599,125	1,713,251	2,598,214	2,314,824
Europe	7,690	98,797	495,681	1,597,442	2,452,577	2,065,141
Austria-Hungary	—	—	—	—	—	7,800
Austria	NA	NA	NA	453,649	32,868	3,563
Hungary	NA	NA	NA	442,693	30,680	7,861
Belgium	1	27	22	5,074	4,738	6,734
Denmark	20	169	1,063	539	3,749	17,094
France	371	8,497	45,575	77,262	76,358	35,986
Germany	968	6,761	152,454	434,626	951,667	787,468
Great Britain (former UK)	2,410	25,079	75,810	267,044	423,974	606,896
England	1,782	14,055	7,611	32,092	247,125	222,277
Scotland	268	2,912	2,667	3,712	38,331	38,769
Wales	—	170	185	1,261	6,319	4,313
Northern Ireland	NA	NA	NA	NA	NA	NA
Not specified	360	7,942	65,347	229,979	132,199	341,537
Greece	—	20	49	16	31	72
Ireland	3,614	50,724	207,381	780,719	914,119	435,778
Italy	30	409	2,253	1,870	9,231	11,725
Netherlands	49	1,078	1,412	8,251	10,789	9,102
Norway–Sweden	3	91	1,201	13,903	20,931	109,298
Norway	NA	NA	NA	NA	NA	71,631
Sweden	NA	NA	NA	NA	NA	37,667
Poland	5	16	369	105	1,164	2,027
Portugal	35	145	829	550	1,055	2,658
Romania	—	—	—	—	—	—
Spain	139	2,477	2,125	2,209	9,298	6,697
Switzerland	31	3,226	4,821	4,644	25,011	23,286
U.S.S.R.	14	75	277	551	457	2,512
Yugoslavia	—	—	—	—	—	—
Other Europe	—	3	40	79	5	8
Asia	6	30	55	141	41,538	64,759
China	1	2	8	35	41,397	64,301
India	1	8	39	36	43	69
Israel	—	—	—	—	—	—
Japan	—	—	—	—	—	186
Turkey	1	20	7	59	83	131
Other Asia	3	—	1	11	15	72
America	387	11,564	33,424	62,469	74,720	166,607
Canada & Newfoundland	209	2,277	13,624	41,723	59,309	153,878
Mexico	1	4,817	6,599	3,271	3,078	2,191
Caribbean	164	3,834	12,301	13,528	10,660	9,046
Central America	2	105	44	368	449	95
South America	11	531	856	3,579	1,224	1,397
Other America	—	—	—	—	—	—
Africa	1	16	54	55	210	312
Australia & New Zealand	—	—	—	—	—	36
Pacific Islands (U.S. adm.)	—	—	—	—	—	—
Other	301	33,032	69,911	53,144	29,169	17,969

FIGURES ARE APPROXIMATE BECAUSE OF DIFFERENT COUNTING METHODS.

Notes: From 1820–1867, figures represent alien passengers arrived; from 1868–1891 and 1895–1897, immigrant aliens arrived; from 1892–1894 and 1898 to the present time, immigrant aliens admitted. Data for the years prior to 1906 relate to country whence alien came; data from 1906–1979 and 1984 are for country of last permanent residence; and data for 1980–1983 refer to country of birth. Because of changes in boundaries and changes in lists of countries, data for certain countries are not comparable throughout.

The periods covered are as follows: from 1820–1831 and 1843–1849, the fiscal years ended on September 30 of the respective year—fiscal year 1843 covers 9 months. From 1832–1842 and 1850–1867, fiscal years ended on December 31 of the respective year—fiscal years 1832 and 1850 cover 15 months. For 1868, the period ended on June 30 and covers 6 months. Fiscal years 1868–1976 ended on June 30 of the respective year. The transition quarter (TQ) for 1976 covers the 3-month period, July–September 1976.

SOURCE: U.S. IMMIGRATION AND NATURALIZATION SERVICE.

1871–1880	1881–1890	1891–1900	1901–1910	1911–1920	1921–1930	1931–1940
2,812,191	5,246,613	3,687,564	8,795,386	5,735,811	4,107,209	528,431
2,271,925	4,735,484	3,555,352	8,056,040	4,321,887	2,463,194	347,552
72,969	353,719	592,707	2,145,266	896,342	63,548	11,424
24,860	67,106	20,621	9,478	18,340	3,511	2,895
3,469	36,637	5,401	6,550	6,545	944	1,039
7,221	20,177	18,167	41,635	33,746	15,846	4,817
31,771	88,132	50,231	65,285	41,983	32,430	2,559
72,206	50,464	30,770	73,379	61,897	49,610	12,623
718,182	1,452,970	505,152	341,498	143,945	412,202	114,058
548,043	807,357	271,538	525,950	341,408	340,780	31,572
437,706	644,680	216,726	388,017	249,944	157,420	21,756
87,564	149,869	44,188	120,469	78,357	159,781	6,887
6,631	12,640	10,557	17,464	13,107	13,012	735
NA	NA	NA	NA	NA	10,567	2,194
16,142	168	67	—	—	—	—
210	2,308	15,979	167,519	184,201	51,084	9,119
436,871	655,482	388,416	339,065	146,181	210,024	10,973
55,759	307,309	651,893	2,045,877	1,109,524	455,315	68,028
16,541	53,701	26,758	48,262	43,718	26,948	7,150
211,245	568,362	321,281	440,039	161,469	165,780	8,700
95,323	391,776	226,266	249,534	95,074	97,249	3,960
115,922	176,586	95,015	190,505	66,395	68,531	4,740
12,970	51,806	96,720	—	4,813	227,734	17,026
14,082	16,978	27,508	69,149	89,732	29,994	3,329
11	6,348	12,750	53,008	13,311	67,646	3,871
5,266	4,419	8,731	27,935	68,611	28,958	3,258
28,293	81,988	31,179	34,922	23,091	29,676	5,512
39,284	213,282	505,290	1,597,306	921,201	61,742	1,356
—	—	—	—	1,888	49,064	5,835
1,001	682	122	665	8,111	22,983	2,361
124,180	69,942	74,862	323,543	247,236	112,059	16,081
123,201	61,711	14,799	20,605	21,278	29,907	4,928
163	269	68	4,713	2,082	1,886	496
—	—	—	—	—	—	—
149	2,270	25,942	129,797	83,837	33,462	1,948
404	3,782	30,425	157,369	134,066	33,824	1,065
243	1,910	3,628	11,059	5,973	12,980	7,644
404,044	426,967	38,972	361,888	1,143,671	1,516,716	160,037
383,640	393,304	3,311	179,226	742,185	924,515	108,527
5,162	1,913	971	49,642	219,004	459,287	22,319
13,957	29,042	33,066	107,548	123,424	74,899	15,502
157	404	549	8,192	17,159	15,769	5,861
1,128	2,304	1,075	17,280	41,899	42,215	7,803
—	—	—	—	—	31	25
358	857	350	7,368	8,443	6,286	1,750
9,886	7,017	2,740	11,975	12,348	8,299	2,231
1,028	5,557	1,225	1,049	1,079	427	780
790	789	14,063	33,523	1,147	228	—

Table A.1 Immigration to the United States by Country for Decades 1820–1995 (continued)

Country	1941–1950	1951–1960	1961–1970	1971–1980	1981–90
All countries	1,035,039	2,515,479	3,321,677	4,493,314	7,338,062
Europe	621,124	1,325,727	1,123,492	800,368	761,550
Austria-Hungary	28,329	103,743	26,022	16,028	24,885
Austria	1,880	1,314	1,340	641,425	
Hungary	1,034	809	850	544,512	
Belgium	12,189	18,575	9,192	5,329	7,066
Denmark	5,393	10,984	9,201	4,439	5,370
France	38,809	51,121	45,237	25,069	32,353
Germany	226,578	477,765	190,796	74,414	91,961
Great Britain (former UK)	139,306	204,468	214,518	137,374	14,667
England	112,252	156,171	174,452	NA	NA
Scotland	16,131	32,854	29,849	NA	NA
Wales	3,209	2,589	2,052	NA	NA
Northern Ireland	7,714	8,970	7,469	NA	NA
Not specified	—	3,884	696	NA	NA
Greece	8,973	47,608	85,969	92,369	38,377
Ireland	19,789	48,362	32,966	11,490	31,969
Italy	57,661	185,491	214,111	129,368	67,254
Netherlands	14,860	52,277	30,606	10,492	12,238
Norway–Sweden	20,765	44,632	32,600	10,472	15,182
Norway	10,665	22,935	15,484	3,941	4,164
Sweden	10,100	21,697	17,116	6,531	11,018
Poland	7,571	9,985	53,539	37,234	83,252
Portugal	7,423	19,588	76,065	101,710	40,431
Romania	1,076	1,039	2,531	12,393	30,857
Spain	2,898	7,894	44,659	39,141	8,849
Switzerland	10,547	17,675	18,453	8,235	57,677
U.S.S.R.	548	671	2,465	38,961	20,433
Yugoslavia	1,576	8,225	20,381	30,540	18,762
Other Europe	3,447	14,706	10,908	9,287	15,532
Asia	32,360	153,249	427,642	1,588,178	2,738,157
China	16,709	9,657	34,764	124,326	346,747
India	1,761	1,973	27,189	164,134	250,786
Israel	—	25,476	29,602	37,713	44,273
Japan	1,555	46,250	39,988	49,775	47,085
Turkey	798	3,519	10,142	13,399	23,233
Other Asia	11,537	66,374	285,957	1,198,831	2,026,033
America	354,804	996,944	1,716,374	1,982,529	3,615,225
Canada & Newfoundland	171,718	377,952	413,310	169,939	156,938
Mexico	60,589	299,811	453,937	640,294	1,655,843
Caribbean	49,725	123,091	470,213	741,126	872,057
Central America	21,665	44,751	101,330	134,640	468,088
South America	21,831	91,628	257,954	295,741	461,847
Other America	29,276	59,711	19,630	789	458
Africa	7,367	14,092	28,954	80,779	176,893
Australia & New Zealand	13,805	11,506	19,562	23,788	20,169
Pacific Islands (U.S. adm.)	5,437	1,470	1,769	1,806	21,041
Other	142	12,491	3,884	15,866	1,032

1991	*1992*	*1993*	*1994*	*1995*	*TOTAL*
1,827,167	973,977	904,292	804,416	720,461	62,224,327
146,671	153,260	165,711	166,279	132,914	37,865,858
4,455	3,934	2,914	2,123	2,190	4,358,398
701	957	776	621	694	214,305
629	769	762	639	588	373,799
3,978	4,492	3,959	3,592	3,178	806,786
10,887	12,875	9,965	8,940	7,896	7,134,028
16,768	21,924	20,422	17,666	14,207	5,069,181
NA	NA	NA	NA	NA	3,084,066
NA	NA	NA	NA	NA	812,608
NA	NA	NA	NA	NA	94,244
NA	NA	NA	NA	NA	36,914
NA	NA	NA	NA	NA	798,321
2,929	2,168	2,460	2,539	2,404	716,404
4,608	12,035	13,396	16,525	4,851	4,775,338
30,316	11,962	3,899	2,664	2,594	5,424,543
1,303	1,687	1,542	1,359	1,284	381,407
1,796	2,296	2,253	1,804	1,607	2,155,710
554	790	713	515	465	1,291,039
1,242	1,506	1,540	1,289	1,142	828,812
17,106	24,491	27,288	27,597	13,570	716,388
4,576	2,774	2,075	2,163	2,611	515,480
6,786	4,907	4,517	2,932	4,565	228,548
2,663	2,041	1,791	1,756	1,664	283,479
1,003	1,303	1,263	1,183	1,119	414,138
31,557	37,069	59,949	64,502	54,133	3,653,635
2,802	2,741	2,781	3,183	7,828	155,606
1,183	1,961	2,907	3,732	4,874	201,589
342,157	344,802	345,425	282,449	259,984	7,588,835
23,995	29,554	57,775	58,867	41,112	1,125,679
42,707	34,841	38,653	33,173	33,060	638,150
5,116	5,938	5,216	3,982	3,188	160,504
5,600	11,735	7,673	6,974	5,556	499,782
3,466	3,203	3,487	3,880	4,806	431,169
261,273	259,531	232,621	175,573	172,262	4,733,531
1,297,580	445,194	361,476	325,173	282,270	15,779,035
19,931	21,541	23,898	22,243	18,117	4,401,315
947,923	214,128	126,642	111,415	90,045	5,378,882
138,591	95,945	98,185	103,750	96,021	3,235,669
110,820	57,849	58,666	40,256	32,020	1,119,239
80,308	55,725	54,077	47,505	46,063	1,533,981
7	6	8	4	4	109,949
33,542	24,707	25,532	24,864	39,818	482,608
—	—	—	—	—	143,362
—	—	—	—	—	42,668
7,217	6,014	6,148	5,651	5,475	317,986

Appendix 2: Chronological Listing of Documents by Major Periods of Immigration

In this appendix, documents favorable to immigration are indicated by the letter f in parentheses at the end of the entry; documents critical of immigration are indicated by the letter c in parentheses at the end of the entry.

FIRST YEARS OF THE NATION—RELATIVELY LIGHT IMMIGRATION: 1790–1840

J. Hector St. John de Crèvecoeur, *Letters from an American Farmer* (London: Thomas Davies, 1782; reprint, New York: E. P. Dutton, 1957), 39–40. Mixing of people creates a new American. (f), CH. 5, 5.1.

Mathew Carey, "Thoughts on the Policy of Encouraging Migration," in *Miscellaneous Trifles in Prose* (Philadelphia, 1796), 110–24. Immigrants were being assimilated well into the new United States. (f), CH. 7, 7.1.

Alien Act of 1798, U.S. Statutes, 5th Cong., 2d sess., vol. 1, 570–71. Limits rights of immigrants in deportation cases. (c), CH. 12, 12.1.

Alexander Hamilton, "Examination of Jefferson's Message to Congress of December 7th, 1801," in *Works of Alexander Hamilton*, ed. Henry Cabot Lodge (New York: G. P. Putnam's Sons, 1885–86), vol. 8, 284–88. Immigrants threaten American republican institutions. (c), CH. 5, 5.2.

"Too Many Immigrants," *Niles' Weekly Register* 17, September 18, 1819, 36. At a time of a business downturn immigrants judged to be more than economy could support. (c), CH. 4, 4.1.

Baltimore American, October 3, 1835. Calls for deportation of immigrant paupers. (c), CH. 2, 2.1.

An American (Samuel Finley Breese Morse), *Imminent Dangers to the Free Institutions of the United States through Foreign Immigration, and the Present State of the Naturalization Laws* (1835; in new edition, New York, 1854), 23–29. Sees Catholics as a threat to nation's security. (c), CH. 8, 8.1.

FIRST MAJOR WAVE OF IMMIGRATION: 1840–1880

Samuel Griswold Goodrich, *Ireland and the Irish* (Boston, 1841), 111–17. Advocates empathy and benevolence toward immigrants. (f), CH. 2, 2.2.

Thomas L. Nichols, *Lecture on Immigration and Right of Naturalization* (New York: 1845), 3–4, 21, 24–32. Immigration diversity strengthens America. (f), CH. 3, 3.2.

Address of the Delegates of the Native American National Convention, Assembled at Philadelphia, July 4, 1845, to the Citizens of the United States (Philadelphia, 1845), 2–9. Immigrants endanger America's political institutions. (c), CH. 5, 5.3

Garrett Davis, *Speech of Hon. Garrett Davis upon His Proposal to Impose Further Restrictions upon Foreign Immigration: Delivered in the Convention to Revise the Constitution of Kentucky, December 15, 1849* (Frankfort, Ky.: 1855), 7–11, 30–32. Immigrants are too heterogeneous and cause discord and dissension. (c), CH. 3, 3.1.

Edward Everett Hale, *Letters on Irish Emigration* (Boston, 1852), 47–58. Irish are a benefit to the nation and are in process of being acculturated into American society. (f), CH. 7, 7.2.

Edward Everett, "Discovery of America," June 1, 1853, *Orations and Speeches*, vol. 3 (Boston: Little, Brown, 1892), 213–16, 220–23. Rejects nativism and calls for benevolence for immigrants. (f), CH. 2, 2.3.

A Foreigner, *Emigration, Emigrants, and Know Nothings* (Philadelphia, 1854), 30–36. Immigrants harmful to America and American workers. (c), CH. 1, 1.1.

W. A. Lord, *A Tract for the Times: National Hospitality* (Montpelier, Vt.: 1855), 21–44. Immigrants too culturally and ethnically different to deserve humanitarian concern. (c), CH. 2, 2.4.

Parke Goodwin, "Secret Societies—The Know-Nothings," *Putnam's Monthly* 5, January 1855, 95–97. Calls nativist un-American; immigrants adhere to the "American Idea." (f), CH. 5, 5.4.

Martin Spalding, *Miscellanea: Comprising Reviews, Lectures, and Essays, on Historical, Theological and Miscellaneous Subjects* (Louisville: 1855), xlviii, lii–lviii. Defends the loyalty of Catholics to America. (f), CH. 5, 5.6, CH. 8, 8.2.

A. Woodbury, "The Moral of Statistics," *New Englander*, vol. 13 (1855), 189–91. United States has extensive space for more immigrants. (f), CH. 4, 4.2.

New York Mirror, in *The Wide-Awake Gift: A Know-Nothing Token for 1855*, ed. "One of 'Em" (New York: 1855), 40–43. Immigrants are a threat to American political and religious institutions. (c), CH. 5, 5.5.

Rollo Ogden, ed., *Life and Letters of Edwin Lawrence Godkin* (New York: Macmillian, 1907), vol. 1, 181–84. In an 1859 letter Godkin expressed the fear that the Irish would not be acculturated into American civic culture. (c), CH. 7, 7.3.

U.S. Senate, *Report from the Committee on Agriculture . . . on the Enactment of Suitable Laws for the Encouragement and Protection of Foreign Immigrants Arriving within Jurisdiction of the United States*, 38th Cong., 1st sess., February 18, 1864, S. Rep. 15. During the Civil War, the Union government praises contributions of immigrants and wants more of them recruited to meet wartime labor shortage. (f), CH. 1, 1.2.

SECOND MAJOR WAVE OF IMMIGRATION: 1880–1930

Emma Lazarus, "The New Colossus," 1883. In Morris Schoppes, *Emma Lazarus, Selections from Her Poetry and Prose* (New York: Cooperative Book League, 1944), 40–41. Inscribed at the base of the Statue of Liberty. Sees America as refuge for the poor and displaced from abroad. (f), CH. 2, 2.5.

Select Committee to Inquire into the Importation of Contract Laborers, Convicts, Paupers, etc. (Ford Committee), *Report*, 50th Cong., 2d sess., January 1889, H. Rep. 3792. Congressional committee reports on inadequacy of state enforcement of federal immigration laws. (c), CH. 11, 11.1.

U.S. Congress, House of Representatives, 52nd Cong., 1st sess., vol. 23, H. Rep. 255, February 10, 1892. Chinese are distinct race and a source of danger to the United States. (c), CH. 3, 3.3.

Senator Henry Cabot Lodge, *Congressional Record*, 54th Cong., 1st sess., 1896, 28: 2817–20. Advocates a literacy test as a means of immigration restriction. (c), CH. 6, 6.2.

President Grover Cleveland, "Veto Message" (1897) *Congressional Record*, 54th Congress, 2nd Session, Senate Document 185. Praises immigrants and calls the literacy test bill contrary to American immigration tradition. (f), CH. 6, 6.4.

Francis A. Walker, *Economics and Statistics*, vol. 2 (New York: Henry Holt, 1899), 437–50. Immigrants a danger to culture and unity of the United States; rejects humanitarian concern for immigrants. (c), CH. 2, 2.6.

Halvor Steenerson, *Congressional Record*, 59th Cong., 1st sess., 1906, 40: Appendix, 110–11. There is no relation between a requirement for literacy and an immigrant's good moral character. (f), CH. 6, 6.3.

E. A. Goldenweiser, "Immigrants in Cities," *Survey*, January 1, 1911, 596–602. New immigrants were being absorbed well into the American melting pot. (f), CH. 7, 7.5.

The Editor, "The Selection of Immigrants," *Survey*, February 4, 1911, 715–716. Immigration must be restricted to protect American working standards. (c), CH. 1, 1.3.

New York Evening Sun, March 28, 1912. New immigrants lower the intelligence of the electorate. (c), CH. 5, 5.7.

Henry Fairchild, *Immigration* (New York, Macmillian, 1913) 302–304. Immigrants lower the wages and working standards of American laborers. (c), CH. 1, 1.4.

William Howard Taft. "Veto Message" (1913) *Congressional Record*, 62nd Cong., 2nd sess., Senate Document 1087, 1–4. Maintains the literacy test bill is contrary to good immigration policy. (f), CH. 6, 6.4.

Sidney Gulick, *The American Japanese Problem* (New York: Charles Scribner's Sons, 1914), 184–86, 190–96. Warns about the harmful impact on the foreign relations of the United States with Japan from proposed legislation to exclude Japanese immigrants. (c), CH. 9, 9.1.

Edward A. Ross, *The Old World in the New* (New York: Century, 1914), 239–40. New immigrants harmful to the United States because of their inferiority and their contributions to urban crowding. (c), CH. 4, 4.3.

Louis D. Brandeis, "True Americanism," *Boston City Record*, July 10, 1915. American ideals support and welcome immigrants. (f), CH. 5, 5.8.

Lillian Wald, *House on Henry Street* (New York: Henry Holt, 1915), 306–7. Immigrants bring new life and blood to America. (f), CH. 3, 3.6.

Whitfield, Immigrant Inspector, et al. v. Hanges et al., 222 Federal Reporter 745 (1915). In deportation cases, aliens, like citizens, cannot be deprived of life, liberty, and property without due process and equal protection of the law. (f), CH. 12, 12.2.

Woodrow Wilson, "Veto Message" (1915) *Congressional Record*, 63rd Cong., 3rd sess., 52: 2481–82 and House Document 1527, 3–4. The literacy test bill is contrary to the mission and spirit of the United States in its relations to the people of the world. (f), CH. 6, 6.4.

Theodore Roosevelt, "Americanism," Address before the Knights of Colombus, Carnegie Hall, New York, October 12, 1915. Favorable to immigrants, but only those who fully assimilate; opposed to hyphenated Americans. (f and c), CH. 7, 7.6.

Frank Warne, *The Tide of Immigration* (New York: D. Appleton, 1916), 108–110. Enforcement of immigration laws fails to detect some illegal immigrants at immigration stations and at unguarded ports and borders. (c), CH. 11, 11.2.

Randolph Bourne, "Trans-National America," *Atlantic Monthly*, 118 (July 1916): 92–97. America is a cosmopolitan federation of national enclaves. (f), CH. 7, 7.7.

W. L. Harding, "Proclamation about Language," Des Moines, Iowa, May 23, 1918. Banned use of German in Iowa during World War I. (c), CH. 6, 6.1.

Colyer v. Skeffington, 265 Federal Reporter 20 (1920). Aliens have constitutional rights and are protected by the Fourth, Fifth, Sixth, and Fourteenth Amendments. (f), CH. 12, 12.3.

Julius Drachsler, *Democracy and Assimilation* (New York: Macmillan, 1920), 20–22, 40–45. Describes reports that maintain that the new immigrants are racially and culturally inferior to already established Americans. (c), CH. 3, 3.5, CH. 8, 8.3.

Warren G. Harding, *Our Common Country* (Indianapolis: Bobbs-Merrill, 1921), 161–65. Advocacy by American ethnic groups, in behalf of the interests of their former homelands, is divisive and a threat to the security of the United States. (c), CH. 8, 8.4

John Palmer Gavit, *Survey* 42 (February 25, 1922). Diversity is a basic characteristic of the American identity. (f), CH. 3, 3.4.

Henry Pratt Fairchild, *The Melting-Pot Mistake* (Boston: Little, Brown, 1926), 208–20. New Immigrants form foreign colonies and are not melting into American society. (c), CH. 7, 7.4.

Constantine Panunzio, *Immigration Crossroads* (New York: Macmillan, 1927), 168–72, 181–83. The 1924 Oriental Exclusion Act had a very negative impact on Japanese American foreign relations. (c), CH. 9, 9.2.

THIRD MAJOR WAVE OF IMMIGRATION: 1946–2000

William Bernard, ed., *American Immigration Policy, A Reappraisal* (New York: Harper and Brothers, 1950), 56–63, 66, 148–53. Immigrants have contributed significantly to American productivity and security. (f), CH. 1, 1.5, CH. 8, 8.5.

Harry S. Truman, "To The House of Representatives," H. Doc. 520, *Congressional Record*, June 25, 1952, 82nd Cong., 2nd sess. 98: 8082–83. Vetoes 1952 immigration bill for being harshly exclusionary and harmful to American foreign policy; calls for the repeal of the National Origins Act. (f), CH. 9, 9.3.

John F. Kennedy, *A Nation of Immigrants* (New York: Harper and Row, 1964), 77–83, 102–107. Praises immigrant diversity and contributions to America and calls for a repeal of the National Origins Act. (f), CH. 3, 3.7, CH. 9, 9.4.

Edward Kennedy, U.S. Senate, *Congressional Record*, 89th Cong., 1st sess., 1965, 111: 24, 228. New immigrants of past forty years are acculturating well into American society. (f), CH. 7, 7.8.

Lyndon B. Johnson, "Remarks on Immigration Law," *Congressional Quarterly* 23, October 1965, 2063–64. Celebrates immigration diversity and the passage of the 1965 immigration law. (f), CH. 5, 5.9.

Paul Taylor, "The Future of Mexican Immigration," in *Immigrants—and Immigrants: Perspectives on Mexican Labor Migration to the United States*, Arthur Corwin, ed. (Westport, Conn.: Greenwood Press, 1978), 348–52. Calls for humanitarianism in American policy toward Mexicans seeking to enter the United States. (f), CH. 9, 9.5.

Douglas Massey, "Dimensions of the New Immigration to the United States and the Prospects for Assimilation," *Annual Review of Sociology* 7 (1981): 70–74. Acculturation of new Asian and Latin Americans indicated by high degree of intermarriage. (f), CH. 7, 7.10.

Plyler v. Doe, 457 U.S. 202 (1982). Children of undocumented immigrants have a right to attend American public schools. (f), CH. 12, 12.5.

Peter Schuck, "The Transformation of Immigration Law," *Columbia Law Review* 84, no. 1 (January 1984): 54–58. Causes of changes in immigration law in the second half of the twentieth century. (c and f), CH. 12, 12.6.

"Illegal Immigrants: The U.S. May Gain More Than It Loses," *Business Week*, May 14, 1984, 126–29. Undocumented immigrants represent a net gain for America's national economy. (f), CH. 10, 10.2.

Richard D. Lamm and Gary Imhoff, *The Immigration Time Bomb: The Fragmenting of America* (New York: E. P. Dutton, 1985), 76–79, 99–124. Immigrants increase population and thus endanger American quality of life; they are a threat to American culture and identity; their lack of knowledge of English is divisive. (f), CH. 5, 5.10, CH. 6, 6.5.

Thomas Muller and Thomas Espenshade, *The Fourth Wave: California's Newest Immigrants* (Washington, D.C.: Urban Institute, 1985), 172–73. Economic growth of Los Angeles in the 1970s and 1980s is in part attributed to the work of undocumented immigrants. (f), CH. 10, 10.3.

Lawrence Fuchs, "The Search for a Sound Immigration Policy: A Personal View," in *Clamor at the Gates: The New American Immigration*, ed. Nathan Glazer (San Francisco: ISC Press, 1985), 26–30. Arguments for and against the presence of undocumented immigrants in the United States. (c and f), CH. 10, 10.1.

Annual Report of the Attorney General of the United States, (Washington, D.C.: U.S. Government Printing Office, 1986) 197–99. The Immigration and Naturalization Service's enforcement strategies. (c), CH. 11, 11.3.

Philip Martin, "Network Recruitment and Labor Displacement," in *U.S. Immigration in the 1980s: Reappraisal and Reform*, ed. David Simcox (Boulder, Colo.: Westview Press, 1988), 82–84. Undocumented immigrants have a negative impact on American economy because they lower wages and deter technological advances. (c), CH. 10, 10.4.

Lindsey Grant, "How Many Americans?," in *U.S. Immigration in the 1980s: Reappraisal and Reform*, ed. David Simcox (Boulder, Colo.: Westview Press, 1988), 279–80. American immigration policy is overly humanitarian and is harmful to the country. (c), CH. 2, 2.8.

Andrew E. Schacknove, "American Duties to Refugees: Their Scope and Limits," in *Open Borders? Closed Societies? The Ethical and Political Issues*, ed. Mark Gibney (Westport, Conn.: Greenwood Press, 1988), 131, 136–38. Calls for a more open American policy toward international refugees. (f), CH. 2, 2.7.

Arturo Madrid, "Official English: A False Policy Issue," *Annals*, AAPSS, March 1990, 62–65. Attacks the official English movement as anti-immigrant and as divisive for the country. (f), CH. 6, 6.6.

Peggy Noonan, "Why the World Comes Here," *Readers Digest*, July 1991, 39–42. Immigrants have chosen America and her identifying ideals of liberty and opportunity. (f), CH. 5, 5.11.

Gene McNary, "Curbing Illegal Immigration: Employers Must Help," *USA Today Magazine*, September 1992, 22–23. Urges employers to cooperate in making employer sanctions law effective against undocumented immigrants. (c), CH. 11, 11.4.

Wayne Lutton, "Welfare Cost for Immigrants," *Social Contract*, Fall 1992, 1–3. (www.thesocialcontract.com). Immigrants hurt American economy by increasing costs of public services. (c), CH. 1, 1.6.

Pete Wilson, "Don't Give Me Your Tired, Your Poor . . . ," *San Diego Union-Tribune*, January 9, 1994. Undocumented and legal immigrants cause crowding, competition for jobs, and the rising cost of public services. (c), CH. 10, 10.5.

"Religion and Immigration," *Migration News, North America* 3, no. 12 (December 1996): 1–3 (www.migration.ucdavis.edu). Religious groups in the United States are aided by immigration. (f), CH. 3, 3.9.

Rudolph Giuliani, "Keep America's Door Open," *Wall Street Journal*, January 9, 1997. New York City government will not cooperate with the INS in apprehending undocumented immigrants. (f), CH. 11, 11.5.

Maria Jimenez, "Enforcement: A Tool to Control the Flow of Labor at the U.S.-Mexico Border," *Fact Sheets*, National Network for Immigration and Refugee Rights, Spring 1997. (http://www.nnirr.org/Fact_sheets/1997/spring97/enforcement-labor.html). INS enforcement policy helps in the exploitation of Mexican workers; she advocates for the protection of human rights of all international laborers. (f and c), CH. 11, 11.6.

Mark Krikorian, "Will Americanization Work in America?" *Freedom Review*, Fall 1997. (http://www.cis.org/articles/1997/freedom_review.html). New immigrants are not assimilating well and are contributing to divisiveness in the United States. (c), CH. 7, 7.9.

Rosalie Pedalino Porter, "The Case against Bilingual Education," *Atlantic Monthly* 281, no. 5 (May 1998): 28–39. Arguments for and against bilingual education. (f and c), CH. 6, 6.7.

"Criminal Aliens," *Issue Brief*, FAIR, December 1998, 1–3. (http://fairus.org/html/04110608.htm). Immigrants who are criminals are a threat to public safety and national security (c), CH. 8, 8.6.

Paul Craig Roberts, "The Ethnic Cleansing of European-Americans," *Washington Times National Weekly*, June 21–27, 1999. (www.usbc.org). Too much diversity threatens cultural homogeneity in the United States. (c), CH. 3, 3.8.

"Skilled Immigrants and Silicon Valley," *Immigration Policy Reports*, American Immigration Law Foundation (July 1999): 1–3. (www.ailf.org). Skilled immigrant entrepreneurs contribute significantly to the economic development of Silicon Valley and the United States. (f), CH. 1, 1.7.

"Support Fair Detention Policies," *In Congress* American Civil Liberties Union (August 18, 1999), 1–4. (http://www.aclu.org/congress/1081899a.html). Criticizes mandatory detention and indefinite detention of immigrants. (f), CH. 12, 12.4.

"Newcomers Help Massachusetts Economy," *Immigration Policy Reports*, American Immigration Law Foundation (January 2000), 1–3. (www.ailf.org). Immigrants contribute to manufacturing, service, and professional sectors of the Massachusetts economy. (f), CH. 1, 1.8.

"The Truth behind the Face: Castro Has Not Changed in 41 Years," an advertisement, Miami, Fla.: Cuban Patriotic Forum, October 2000. Cuban Americans put continuing pressure on the U.S. government to overthrow Fidel Castro and his Communist regime in Cuba. (f and c), CH. 9, 9.6.

"Why Environmentalists Support Immigration Reform," *Issue Brief*, FAIR, November 2000. (www.fairus.org). Immigration contributes to environmental degradation in the United States. (c), CH. 4, 4.4.

"Immigration: The Demographic and Economic Facts, Effects on Natural Resources and the Environment," Cato Institute and the National Immigration Forum, November 17, 2000, 1–3. (www.cato.org). Increased population, including more immigrants, stimulates technological advances that lead to an improvement in the environment. (f), CH. 4, 4.5.

Select Bibliography

Abbot, Edith. *Immigration: Select Documents and Case Records*. Chicago: University of Chicago Press, 1924. Reprint, New York: Arno Press, 1969.

———. *Historical Aspects of the Immigration Problem: Selected Documents*. Chicago: University of Chicago Press, 1926. Reprint, New York: Arno Press, 1969.

Ashabranner, Brent, *Our Beckoning Borders: Illegal Immigration to America*. New York: Cobblehill, 1996.

Barbour, William, ed. *Illegal Immigration*. San Diego, Calif.: Greenhaven Press, 1994.

Beck, Roy H. *The Case against Immigration: The Moral, Economic, Social, and Environmental Reasons for Reducing U.S. Immigration Back to Traditional Levels*. New York: W. W. Norton, 1996.

Billington, Ray. *The Protestant Crusade, 1800–1860: A Study of the Origins of American Nativism*. New York: Macmillan, 1938.

———. *The Origins of Nativism in the United States, 1800–1844*. New York: Arno Press, 1974.

Binder, Frederick, and David Reimers. *All the Nations under Heaven: An Ethnic and Racial History of New York City*. New York: Columbia University Press, 1995.

Bouvier, Leon, and Lindsey Grant. *How Many Americans? Population, Immigration, and the Environment*. San Francisco: Sierra Club Books, 1994.

Briggs, Vernon M. *Mass Immigration and the National Interest*. Armonk, N.Y.: M. E. Sharpe, 1992.

Brimelow, Peter. *Alien Nation: Common Sense about America's Immigration Disaster*. New York: Random House, 1995.

Bryce-Laporte, R. S. *Sourcebook on the New Immigration: Implications for the United*

States and the International Community. New Brunswick, N.J.: Transaction Books, 1980.

Carliner, David, et al. *The Rights of Aliens and Refugees: The Basic ACLU Guide to Alien and Refugee Rights*. 2d ed. Carbondale: Southern Illinois University Press, 1990.

Chiswick, Barry, ed. *The Gateway: U.S. Immigration Issues and Policies*. Washington, D.C.: American Enterprise Institute, 1982.

Craig, Richard B. *The Bracero Program: Interest Groups and Foreign Policy*. Austin: University of Texas Press, 1971.

Crewdson, John. *The Tarnished Door: The New Immigrants and the Transformation of America*. New York: Times Books, 1983.

Davis, Philip, ed. *Immigration and Americanization: Selected Readings*. Boston: Ginn and Company, 1920.

Dinnerstein, Leonard, and David Reimers. *Ethnic Americans: A History of Immigration*. 4th ed. New York: Columbia University Press, 1999.

Duignan, Peter, and L. H. Gann, eds. *The Debate in the United States over Immigration*. Stanford, Calif.: Hoover Institution Press, 1998.

Dunn, Timothy. *The Militarization of the U.S.-Mexico Border, 1978–1992: Low Intensity Conflict Doctrine Comes Home*. Austin: University of Texas Press, 1996.

Feingold, Henry L. *The Politics of Rescue: The Roosevelt Administration and the Holocaust, 1938–1945*. New Brunswick, N.J.: Rutgers University Press, 1970.

Fuchs, Lawrence. *The American Kaleidoscope: Race, Ethnicity and the Civic Culture*. Hanover, N.H.: Wesleyan University Press, 1990.

Glazer, Nathan, and Daniel Moynihan. *Beyond the Melting Pot: The Negroes, Puerto Ricans, Jews, Italians, and Irish of New York City*. Cambridge, Mass.: Harvard University Press, 1973.

Grant, Madison. *The Passing of the Great Race*. New York: Charles Scribner's Sons, 1916.

Greeley, Andrew. *Why Can't They Be Like Us?* New York: Dutton, 1972.

Handlin, Oscar, ed. *Immigration as a Factor in American History*. Englewood Cliffs, N.J.: Prentice-Hall, 1959.

———. *The Uprooted*. 2d ed. Boston: Little, Brown, 1973.

Harwood, Edwin. *In Liberty's Shadow: Illegal Aliens and Immigration Law Enforcement*. Stanford, Calif.: Hoover Institution Press, 1986.

Higham, John. *Strangers in the Land: Patterns of American Nativism, 1860–1925*. New Brunswick, N.J.: Rutgers University Press, 1955.

Hoffman, Abraham. *Unwanted Mexican Americans in the Great Depression: Repatriation Pressures, 1929–1939*. Tuscon: University of Arizona Press, 1974.

Howe, Irving. *World of Our Fathers*. New York: Simon and Schuster, 1976.

Hutchinson, Edward P. *Legislative History of American Immigration Policy, 1798–1965*. New Brunswick, N.J.: Rutgers University Press, 1970.

Isbister, John. *The Immigration Debate*. West Hartford, Conn.: Kumarian Press, 1996.

James, Daniel. *Illegal Immigration: An Unfolding Crisis*. Lanham, Md.: University Press of America, 1991.

Jasso, Guillermina, and Mark Rosenzweig. *The New Chosen People: Immigrants in the United States*. New York: Russell Sage, 1990.

Kallen, Horace. *Culture and Democracy in the United States*. New York: Boni and Liveright, 1924.
Knobel, Dale, *"America for the Americans": The Nativist Movement in the United States*. New York: Twayne, 1996.
Konvitz, Milton R. *Civil Rights in Immigration*. Ithaca, N.Y.: Cornell University Press, 1953.
Kraut, Alan. *The Huddled Masses: The Immigrant in America Society, 1880–1921*. Arlington Heights, Ill.: Harlan Davidson, 1982.
———. *Silent Travelers: Germs, Genes, and the "Immigrant Menace."* New York: Basic Books, 1994.
Kritz, Mary M. *Immigration and Refugee Policy: Global and Domestic Issues*. Lexington, Mass.: Lexington Books, 1983.
Lamphere, Louise, et al. *Newcomers in the Workplace: Immigrants and the Restructuring of the U.S. Economy*. Philadelphia: Temple University Press, 1994.
Levine, Barry, ed. *The Caribbean Exodus*. New York: Praeger, 1987.
Lieberson, Stanley, and Mary Waters. *From Many Strands: Ethnic and Racial Groups in Contemporary America*. New York: Russell Sage, 1988.
Lutton, Wayne, and John Tanton. *The Immigration Invasion*. Petoskey, Mich.: Social Contract Press, 1994.
Mangiafico, Luciano. *Contemporary American Immigrants: Patterns of Filipino, Korean, and Chinese Settlement in the United States*. New York: Praeger, 1988.
Masud-Piloto, Felex. *With Open Arms: Cuban Migration in the United States*. Totowa, N.J.: Rowman and Littlefield, 1987.
McClellan, Grant S., ed. *Immigrants, Refugees, and U.S. Policy*. New York: H. W. Wilson, 1981.
Miller, Jake. *The Plight of Haitian Refugees*. New York: Praeger, 1984.
Miller, Randall M., and Thomas D. Marzik, eds. *Immigrants and Religion in Urban America*. Philadelphia: Temple University Press, 1977.
Millman, Joel. *The Other Americans: How Immigrants Renew Our Country, Our Economy and Our Values*. New York: Viking Press, 1997.
Mills, Nicolaus, ed. *Arguing Immigration: The Debate over the Changing Face of America*. New York: Simon and Schuster, 1994.
Moore, Joan, and Harry Pachon. *Hispanics in the United States*. Englewood Cliffs, N.J.: Prentice-Hall, 1985.
Novak, Michael. *The Rise of the Unmeltable Ethnics*. New York: Macmillan, 1972.
Novatny, Ann. *Strangers at the Door*. Toronto, Ont.: Bantam, 1974.
Parrillo, Vincent. *Strangers to These Shores*. Boston: Houghton Mifflin, 1980.
Pedraza, Silvia, and Ruben Rumbaut, eds. *Origins and Destinies: Immigration, Race and Ethnicity in America*. Belmont, Calif.: Wadsworth, 1996.
Perea, Juan, ed. *Immigrants Out! The New Nativism and the Anti-Immigrant Impulse in the United States*. New York: New York University Press, 1997.
Portes, Alejandro, and Ruben Rumbaut. *Immigrant America: A Portrait*. Berkeley: University of California Press, 1990.
Pozzetta, George, ed. *American Immigration and Ethnicity*. 20 vols. New York: Garland Publishing, 1991.
Preston, William. *Aliens and Dissenters, Federal Suppression of Radicals, 1903–1933*. Cambridge, Mass.: Harvard University Press, 1933.

Reimers, David. *Still the Golden Door: The Third World Comes to America*. 2nd ed. New York: Columbia University Press, 1992.

———. *Unwelcome Strangers: American Identity and the Turn against Immigration*. New York: Columbia University Press, 1998.

Rischin, Moses, ed. *Immigration and the American Tradition*. Indianapolis: Bobbs-Merrill, 1976.

Salins, Peter. *Assimilation, American Style*. New York: Basic Books, 1997.

Salyer, Lucy. *Laws Harsh as Tigers: Chinese Immigrants and the Shaping of Modern Immigration Law*. Chapel Hill: University of North Carolina Press, 1995.

Schuck, Peter, H. and Roger M. Smith. *Citizenship without Consent: Illegal Aliens in the American Polity*. New Haven, Conn.: Yale University Press, 1985.

Select Commission on Immigration and Refugee Policy. *U.S. Immigration Policy and the National Interest*. Washington, D.C.: U.S. Government Printing Office, 1981.

Seller, Maxine. *To Seek America: A History of Ethnic Life in the United States*. Englewood Cliffs, N.J.: J. S. Ozer, 1977.

Seller, Maxine, ed. *Immigrant Women*. Philadelphia: Temple University Press, 1981.

Smith, James Morton. *Freedom's Fetters: The Alien and Sedition Law and American Civil Liberties*. Ithaca, N.Y.: Cornell University Press, 1956.

Thernstrom, Stephen, et al., eds. *Harvard Encyclopedia of American Ethnic Groups*. Cambridge, Mass.: Harvard University Press, 1980.

Unger, Sanford. *Fresh Blood: The New American Immigrants*. New York: Simon and Schuster, 1995.

Wattenberg, Ben J. *The First Universal Nation*. New York: Maxwell Macmillan International, 1991.

Weinberg, Sydney. *The World of Our Mothers: The Lives of Jewish Immigrant Women*. Chapel Hill: University of North Carolina Press, 1988.

Weissbrodt, David. *Immigration Law and Procedure*. St. Paul, Minn.: West Publishing, 1984.

Williamson, Chilton. *The Immigration Mystique: America's False Conscience*. New York: Basic Books, 1996.

Zucker, Norman, and Naomi Zucker. *Desperate Crossing: Seeking Refuge in America*. Armonk, N.Y.: M. E. Sharpe, 1996.

Index

About the Author

HENRY BISCHOFF is Professor Emeritus in the School of Social Sciences and Human Services at Ramapo College. He has written books and articles on immigration and local history. He was the director of the Garden State Immigration History Consortium and the recipient of the New Jersey Historical Commission Award of Recognition.